A Guide to

The Norton Reader

A Guide to
The Norton Reader

Fourteenth Edition

Melissa A. Goldthwaite
Saint Joseph's University

Joseph Bizup
Boston University

John C. Brereton
University of Massachusetts, Boston

Anne E. Fernald
Fordham University

Linda H. Peterson
Late of Yale University

Charles Hood
Antelope Valley College

W·W·NORTON & COMPANY
NEW YORK · LONDON

W. W. Norton & Company has been independent since its founding in 1923, when William Warder Norton and Mary D. Herter Norton first published lectures delivered at the People's Institute, the adult education division of New York City's Cooper Union. The firm soon expanded its program beyond the Institute, publishing books by celebrated academics from America and abroad. By midcentury, the two major pillars of Norton's publishing program—trade books and college texts—were firmly established. In the 1950s, the Norton family transferred control of the company to its employees, and today—with a staff of four hundred and a comparable number of trade, college, and professional titles published each year—W. W. Norton & Company stands as the largest and oldest publishing house owned wholly by its employees.

Editor: Marilyn Moller
Associate Editor: Ariella Foss
Project Editors: Shuli Traub, Katie Callahan
Assistant Editor: Claire Wallace
Copy Editor: Katharine Ings
Senior Production Supervisor: Ashley Horna
Managing Editor, College: Marian Johnson
Marketing Manager: Megan Zwilling
Composition: Westchester Book Group
Manufacturing: Maple Press

ISBN 978-0-393-26583-5 (pbk.)

W. W. Norton & Company, Inc., 500 Fifth Avenue, New York, NY 10110
wwnorton.com

W. W. Norton & Company Ltd., Castle House,
75/76 Wells Street, London W1T 3QT

1 2 3 4 5 6 7 8 9 0

Contents

PART II: THE READINGS   57

PERSONAL ACCOUNTS

SEE ALSO

PROFILES

*Indicates selections included in the Shorter Edition.

*Indicates selections included in the Shorter Edition.

FOOD

*Indicates selections included in the Shorter Edition.

SPORTS

SEE ALSO

OP-EDS

SEE ALSO

EDUCATION

*Indicates selections included in the Shorter Edition.

*Indicates selections included in the Shorter Edition.

NATURE AND THE ENVIRONMENT

SEE ALSO

MEDIA AND TECHNOLOGY

SEE ALSO

*Indicates selections included in the Shorter Edition.

ETHICS

SEE ALSO

HISTORY AND POLITICS

SEE ALSO

*Indicates selections included in the Shorter Edition.

*Indicates selections included in the Shorter Edition.

A Guide to

The Norton Reader

PART I

TEACHING WITH
THE NORTON READER

To Teachers Using The Norton Reader

We have put together this expanded edition of *A Guide to The Norton Reader* with many different instructors and courses in mind. We hope that you will find ideas here to inspire you, whether you are a new teacher or a veteran. First-year writing courses are designed along many models, but whether your course is organized around great ideas in the liberal arts, genres of nonfiction prose, issues in contemporary culture, or a series of themes, *The Norton Reader* provides a rich range of essays for you to choose from. New to this edition is an expanded table of contents that cross-lists readings and the new chapters "Food," "Sports," and "Media and Technology." We have also completely revised the chapter "Science" and expanded the scope of "Gender and Human Nature." On the website nortonreader.com, you can browse the readings in the book and sort and search for them by theme, genre, rhetorical mode, and more.

For all the ways that print culture and technologies of reading have changed, students still need our help reading college-level texts. We have selected the essays for *The Norton Reader* and written this *Guide* to help you draw students into the world of reading and writing with great prose from across the history of the English language. In choosing which essays to include, the editors and nominees have sought all kinds of topics, all kinds of representation, but we have continued our uncompromising quest for great writing that will inspire students to read and to produce their best writing. This anthology is designed to show students the power and flexibility of the written language.

One of the great challenges for students moving into college-level discourse at any age is finding an intellectual space between an elementary Manichaeism on the one hand (this is right and that is wrong) and a fuzzy relativism on the other (everyone has a right to his or her opinion). Again and again, these essays offer models for more nuanced thinking. In "The Case for Single-Child Families," for example, Bill McKibben positions himself between those who are childless by choice, many of whom he finds selfish even as he shares their professional aspirations, and those who choose not to practice birth control, whose faith he admires but whose failure to consider the implications of overpopulation he finds reckless. McKibben is hardly splitting the difference. He argues for a new position. Jo-Ann Pilardi's editorial, "Immigration Problem Is about Us, Not Them," offers another kind of complex response: entering the conversation about immigration not so much by taking a side as by shifting the focus of the national debate. That need to forge a new position is the subject of Marion Nestle's "Utopian Dream: A New Farm Bill," which critiques the farm bill and offers guidelines for new legislation. In fact, students are familiar with weighing choices in other parts of their lives all the time. Economic choices, for example, almost always have greater complexity than a simple up-or-down vote and usually come with a range of preferences and consequences. Similarly, the decision about which presidential candidate to support is often complex even when the vote itself is very clear: the most partisan of students likely can list points of disagreement with his or her candidate of choice. Once students see the sophistication of their thinking in these arenas and read the variety of opinions in the *Reader*, they can begin to become the writers we hope them to be.

Sometimes it seems daunting to ask students to reach beyond the five-paragraph essay when they have barely mastered it. Still, reading a stack of essays, each beginning with an introduction that announces its three examples, passing on to three examples in turn, and concluding with a paragraph reviewing the three examples as they relate to the stated theme, can be a mind-numbing experience for the instructor. There is a pragmatic middle ground to be found and it can work to the benefit of students and teachers alike. Each of the essays in "Op-Eds" accomplishes much in a brief space; yet none is a five-paragraph essay. Molly Ivins's "Get a Knife, Get a Dog, but Get Rid of Guns," for example, uses humor and a close reading of the Second Amendment to make an argument for stricter gun control. And Jane McGonigal, in "Be a Gamer, Save the World," uses clear topic sentences and supporting evidence to advance her claim that gaming can help solve real-world problems. Many of the entries within the *Guide* offer suggestions for teaching your students to see the structure of such arguments so they can learn and adapt such strategies in their own essays.

True enough, most essays begin with an introduction of some kind, though there is not always a thesis statement; additionally, this section may continue beyond a single paragraph. In the middle, many essays present a range of evidence—be it narrative, scientific, or something in between. Most essays end with some kind of shift outward, from a presentation of evidence to some kind of larger gesture. Students need to learn which pieces of the model are fixed, which are portable, which are necessary to the essay they are writing, and which are optional. Then they can learn why it often makes sense to put the topic sentence first. At the same time, they can experiment with putting it in other places. They will see that, in their own reading, articles with traditional topic sentences are often more immediately accessible, especially when they cover a complex or abstract topic. They will also come to see the power of occasionally withholding a topic sentence.

As you work through the readings with your students, you can help them identify elements of the essay: topic sentences, motivating questions, examples, narrative explanations, and moments of meta-discourse. As you discuss the readings with your students, you can help them think through the logic of an author's choices. Then it becomes easier to discuss alternate ways for them to consider ordering their own arguments, thinking about the elements of their own paper—the sentences, quotations, and paragraphs—building to a gradually unfolding and *developing* whole.

One of the most important skills we can teach our students is the ability to analyze evidence with care. For this reason, it makes sense to revisit the basic process of analyzing a quotation over and over again in your class. Even when students choose quotations well, most will believe that the quotation speaks for itself, following it with "This shows . . ." as if the implications of the quotation were self-evident. The *Reader* illustrates how to effectively analyze the words of others to strengthen your own argument. In "'Idiot,' 'Yahoo,' 'Original Gorilla': How Lincoln Was Dissed in His Day," Mark Bowden quotes many politicians and writers from the era of Abraham Lincoln's presidency to support his argument that although Lincoln is remembered for his successes as president, he was severely critiqued by his contemporaries. And Bill McKibben considers the first commandment, quoting it, meditating on it, and considering the extent to which we are still bound by it and the other nine.

Wherever you are in your teaching career, there is always a lot to think about and juggle as the term begins. We have endeavored to anticipate many of these issues in this new edition of the *Guide*. Just as we hope the readings in the *Reader* inspire your students to produce their best work, we hope this *Guide* helps inspire your teaching. Our aims are also pragmatic. To that end, in Part I you will find tips on planning your course, creating syllabi, and classroom techniques. In Part II: The Readings, you will find entries for each essay, consisting of three or four parts:

1. An introduction to the essay and the author, which may be supplemented with the biographical sketches in the "Author Biographies" section of the *Reader*.

2. Questions reprinted from the *Reader*.

3. "Teaching Suggestions," which take up matters of form and content, rhetoric and style. These questions are meant to help you plan your syllabus and to spark class discussion. They take students more deeply into the text than most will have delved on their own.

4. "Suggested Writing Assignments," which supplement assignments in the *Reader* itself and draw on key concepts from the work, other readings related in theme or style, and topics that touch on students' lives—all with the aim of giving students provocative, wide-ranging possibilities for writing.

A NOTE FOR WRITING PROGRAM ADMINISTRATORS

If you are a program or course administrator, you will find much here to help you orient new instructors to the text. The entries for each individual essay are designed to offer information that might help an instructor choose a new essay: some summary, a discussion of major themes, and connections to other texts in *The Norton Reader*. Additionally, there is a short biographical entry on each essayist at the back of the *Reader* itself. This *Guide* includes a chapter on designing a syllabus as well as sample syllabi, meant for you to use, adapt, and recommend to your colleagues and faculty. Thus, whether you are designing a syllabus for your faculty or allowing them more flexibility within a general rubric, this guide and the anthology itself are designed to support you.

The essays in the *Reader* are grouped roughly by type of essay or discipline of origin. In addition to this grouping, we have provided rhetorical modes, generic, thematic, and chronological indices. These should help you quickly find, for example, an argument (rhetorical mode and genre) about food (theme), such as Michael Pollan's "An Animal's Place," or a graphic memoir (genre) about home and family (theme) that uses narrative (rhetorical mode), such as Alison Bechdel's selection from *Fun Home*. Thus, by checking to see how essays are cross-listed, you or your faculty can choose the right readings for each part of the semester.

Melissa A. Goldthwaite's chapter, "Planning Your Course" (p. 11), emphasizes the many options the *Reader* provides for designing a course; it also helps you chart a path for your program. However much guidance you give your instructors in syllabus design, you and your faculty will be aided by reading her encouraging advice on course planning. Sample syllabi, too, are here for you and your faculty to adopt and adapt.

Charles Hood's chapter on ten- and thirty-minute things to do with the *Reader* in class is full of ideas that can work at any moment in the term, in any writing class. They are meant to help instructors when a lesson plan somehow does not fill up the class period. Please direct your faculty's attention here: familiarity with these ideas early in the term will make it easy to implement them on the fly.

A Note for Teachers at Community Colleges and Teachers of Developmental Writing

Whatever the skill and preparation level of your students, it is wise to ask them to read aloud early in the term. While not a perfect gauge, hearing where your students stumble orally will give you important indicators as to their silent reading skills, their vocabulary, and their overall comprehension. Students forced to pronounce an unfamiliar word are usually willing to ask for its definition—something they might otherwise forget to do. Reading aloud can continue to be a valuable part of class throughout the semester. Hearing language in the air helps focus students, and helps train their ears to the rhythms of prose; students who are not confident readers may have better comprehension when they hear part of an essay in class. Listening to and analyzing speeches early in the term can bring the room alive and provide important early practice with rhetorical analysis. Many other selections lend themselves well to such treatment, too: some of the profiles, the passionate and personal arguments by Molly Ivins and Lynda Barry, as well as the excerpts from Martin Luther King Jr.'s "Letter from Birmingham Jail," are all good candidates for reading aloud.

Reading, including reading aloud, is one of the surest ways to help writers make the transition from oral expression—where many are confident and eloquent—to the kind of written expression that does justice to their intellect and their ideas. Our job as instructors is to introduce students to the nuances of language, to help them see that qualifications that strike them as frustrating and confusing are actually useful and intelligent distinctions, distinctions necessary for college-level thought. Students in developmental writing or college preparatory classes need extra practice reading as they work to master writing at the college level. Since reading is often difficult for these students, it is particularly important to design a syllabus comprised of readings that help them build their confidence and skills. Thus, rather than covering many, many types of essays, it is often smarter and more effective to have students read several essays of the same type and write a couple of similar responses to them before moving on.

Medical students learning a new procedure are taught to watch one, do one, teach one. We regularly ask the same of our composition students: they read a model (watch one), write a version of that model (do one), and then critique a peer's effort at the same project (teach one). However, community college students and basic writers everywhere can benefit greatly from even more practice, so it often makes sense to assign two versions of each type of paper. For example, the first two essays in the *Reader*, by Joan Didion and Chang-rae Lee, explore the concept of home; Toni Morrison, James Baldwin, and Brent Staples all look at the idea of being—or seeing—a "stranger"; and David Foster Wallace and Malcolm Gladwell both do extended analyses on often overlooked edibles (lobster and coffee). Many Teaching Suggestions and Suggested Writing Assignments within the *Guide* are designed to lead you to other resonant pairings. Once you start thinking in pairs, you will see them proliferate throughout the *Reader*, and you will find your students grateful for the reinforcement that a pair of essays provides.

It is especially important to think about sequence and practice when teaching college preparatory classes, developmental writing, or writing at a community college. Where more advanced writers can discern the use of a model essay off the topic of their own writing, developmental writers tend to get frustrated at being asked to read anything that is not doing double duty: serving as a model for the type of paper they are writing and providing evidence for that paper.

Most students immediately warm to the personal essays with which this book begins and, for that reason, you may want to start there. Other chapters of the *Reader* lend themselves particularly well to teaching community college students. The "Op-Eds" chapter consists of short pieces written for a wide audience and can give students important early practice in understanding and responding to an opinion. Speeches and journals, too, help students bridge the gap between oral and written, casual and formal prose. Speeches show them, for example, how the repetitive cadences of politicians and preachers are made up of parallel structures, while journals help them see the point of the kind of preparatory writing we ask of them: if Joan Didion finds merit in taking notes, they may, too. The "Education" and "Language and Communication" chapters also work very well with community college students. Essays by Joey Franklin, Mike Rose, and Gerald Graff powerfully address issues of class, education, and ambition. When people are making great sacrifices to attend college, they often take courage in reading about the struggles of others. Frederick Douglass's account of his passionate quest to learn to read while still a slave is a particularly harrowing and moving example. After reading his story, few students will complain about having homework.

A NOTE FOR NEW TEACHERS

If this is your first semester teaching, the project of designing a syllabus can be daunting. Speak to your program administrator to learn how flexibly you can plan your course and about the model of first-year writing she or he recommends. *The Norton Reader* has a thematic index as well as indices of genres, rhetorical modes, and chronology, so however your curriculum is organized, you will be able to find readings that will serve as models and springboards for student writing. The next chapter offers strategies for designing a syllabus as well as sample syllabi, and we urge you to borrow liberally from them. It may feel like "copying" to borrow a whole syllabus—especially in a composition classroom where you are teaching students to avoid plagiarism. But someone else's syllabus is more analogous to a musical score than an essay. Like any conductor, your originality, your work, and your innovations will lie in how you interpret the syllabus. And again, like any conductor, your interpretation will be enhanced, limited, and transformed by the performance of your orchestra— the specific group of students you have in your classroom.

Remember that you are teaching a writing class, not a class in literary interpretation. However much these skills overlap, however intrinsically linked these skills may be, in a writing class, writing should be your first emphasis. So, with each reading you select, ask yourself how it connects to the writing you are asking your students to do in that unit and on that particular day. This principle may mean that you have to omit a favorite text that does not fit into your course goals. It may, on the other hand, inspire you to create a new assignment. In designing your syllabi, work backward from your writing goal for each particular unit to the steps necessary to get students there, from the time students need to spend preparing each paper (including workshops and preparatory writing exercises) to the reading that will inform the writing.[1]

Which essays you choose will of course depend on the kind of class you are teaching. Your program administrator and the next chapter can help you design

---

1. For specific advice about building a composition course with student writing at its heart but with reading still a key component, see Joseph Harris, *Rewriting* (Logan, UT: Utah State UP, 2006).

your syllabus, but you will still have readings to choose from. Remember that in a single class session of fifty to seventy-five minutes, it is difficult to talk about more than two essays in any detail. (Of course, later in a longer unit, you can fruitfully build on prior discussions.) Then, choose essays and texts by writers you admire or on topics that matter to you. It is always easier to manage the other details of a class—attendance, coming up with good discussion questions, linking reading and writing, encouraging participation—when you are comfortable with and excited about the readings.

Once you have chosen some pieces that matter to you, check your choices for balance of all kinds. In the end, if you want the best chance of reaching the most students, you will have chosen a wide range of readings, not just readings in your own taste. So ask yourself if you have a mix of easy and difficult readings, of new and of old, of texts by men and women, of texts by writers from many cultural and racial backgrounds, of texts representing a range of political perspectives, and of texts representing numerous styles.

Experienced teachers know that students for whom reading is difficult or for whom college is new often feel reassured and welcomed by reading personal accounts: this is why so many anthologies begin with these essays. Even if you do not ask your students to write their own personal essay (and there are good reasons to invite, avoid, and carefully manage expressive writing in college composition), these essays can be good initial reading for textual analysis.

Any teacher learns quickly the value of being flexible. If you find that the readings on your syllabus are too numerous or too difficult, consider making some of them optional or substituting shorter, simpler texts. Nonetheless, every syllabus should include challenges. The bewildering and disorienting experience of being asked to read something hard will be a familiar one, but you can make good use of class time by teaching students strategies to tame the unruly, difficult reading, to learn its meaning and make it their own. After all, students are sure to encounter difficult readings in other courses. If you can provide them with strategies for taking notes, asking questions, and decoding difficult reading, you will have equipped them with one of the most important skills they will need as they move forward in their education. As the term goes on, you may find days when you are at a loss for what to do. For those days, you may want to turn to the mini-lessons in Charles Hood's chapter (p. 44): he has collected a range of ten- and thirty-minute activities for you to use. Familiarize yourself with these now: they are designed to fit in almost anywhere and to rescue a faltering class session with integrity and verve.

As you look at the course as a whole, you will want to think about a logical sequence of assignments. Students can take on greater and greater challenges as the semester progresses. It makes sense to ask them to compare two texts after you have given them the chance to analyze one. Still, such sequences are not set in stone. While experienced writers benefit from being restricted to a very tight word limit, beginning writers, who often struggle to get to the point, can need a page or two just to warm up. Similarly, while it is traditional to make the final paper a research paper, it sometimes works better to make this the second-to-last, rather than final, assignment. Students are less exhausted and overwhelmed and thus may be less likely to plagiarize. Furthermore, the research paper itself, while teaching important skills, is not as intellectually demanding as more reflective pieces of writing. Asking students to synthesize several readings within a larger framework can be much more challenging for them than a traditional research paper.

Once again, we hope you find this *Guide* useful. Our suggestions represent the collective wisdom of former authors of the *Guide*; the editors emeriti, most notably Joan Hartman; our editors at Norton, Ariella Foss and Marilyn Moller; and our colleagues at our home institutions and in the profession at large.

> Melissa A. Goldthwaite, Saint Joseph's University
> Joseph Bizup, Boston University
> John Brereton, University of Massachusetts, Boston
> Anne Fernald, Fordham University
> Linda Peterson, Late of Yale University
> Charles Hood, Antelope Valley College

Planning Your Course
Melissa A. Goldthwaite

The Norton Reader provides options. It includes a large number of essays on a range of topics; it demonstrates the protean nature of the essay genre; and because of its multiplicity, it invites various approaches to teaching its content. In this chapter on planning your course, we provide guiding questions and suggestions to help you sort through the possibilities, find your focus, and create a syllabus that will aid you and your students in achieving your course's goals. Please also visit *The Norton Reader* website at nortonreader.com, where you can sort and search for readings by theme, rhetorical mode, genre, and more, and select essays for building your syllabus.

The organization of a syllabus, like the organization of an essay, depends on purpose and audience, as well as selection, ordering, and pacing. As you begin writing your syllabus, you will need to consider a series of questions: What do I (or my department, college, or university) want students to learn from this class? Which readings and assignments will help us work toward these goals? What is the reading and writing level of the students who will take this class? How many readings and assignments can we realistically cover? How many drafts of each major assignment should students write? What additional activities (workshops, peer review, student/teacher conferences, group or individual presentations) will I structure into the course? Will I use a rhetoric or handbook in addition to this anthology? These are some but not all of the questions that you will need to ask yourself.

PURPOSE

Teachers of composition share many goals: to help students become attentive, thoughtful, and critical readers as well as rhetorically aware writers. The paths to achieving such goals, however, often differ significantly. For that reason, we provide several sample syllabi and encourage you to borrow ideas and perhaps even structures as you create the syllabus that will best help you and your students work toward your objectives. We understand, too, that individual teachers do not always have autonomy in choosing the exact shape and focus of their courses. Some departments and writing programs, for example, require the teaching of modes of discourse, while others require instead a focus on particular topics; still others recognize the complexity of various methods of rhetorical development and ask students to identify and analyze complexity in a professional writer's work—and to bring that sophistication into their own work as well. The range of genres in *The Norton Reader*—and the varied examples this

Guide offers—should provide the flexibility to help you work toward your own goals even as you work within the goals set by your institution.

If you want students to learn various rhetorical methods of development— how they can use those methods discretely and in combination for specific purposes—you can use the index of rhetorical modes to help choose readings. You can also find examples in many of the sample syllabi of assignments that call for different modes of rhetorical development. The sample syllabus on "Persuasion and Argument," for example, also considers exposition and narrative as kinds of evidence in persuasive arguments. Likewise, "The Genres of the Essay" sample syllabus demonstrates an overlap among essay genres.

Or perhaps you want students to explore significant questions related to human experience, to gain foundational knowledge of how writers and thinkers have answered such questions over the centuries, to consider how the answers to such questions change over time, and to explore their own responses and answers through writing. If so, the "Great Ideas and Enduring Questions" sample syllabus offers a start.

A related, though more specific, approach would be to narrow the scope of the course to several overlapping aspects of human experience, as does the sample syllabus on "Race, Class, and Gender." A topical course, such as one on "Food, Sports, and Media and Technology," provides opportunity for various kinds of writing and for seeing the overlap between different modes of rhetorical development (for example, attention to the ways writers use narratives of personal experience in making arguments). This course also provides a sequence of and options for assignments, helping students analyze and develop writing that includes visual and audio components. It also gives students the opportunity to present their work to the class.

You might want students to practice writing to learn, no matter their major or area of academic interest. Or your goal might be to introduce students to the rhetorical conventions of academic discourse in various fields. In either case, the "Writing across the Curriculum" sample syllabus offers options for how you might organize your course. This model provides another example of ways to link discussions of rhetorical choices (especially as they are related to particular fields of study) with topics of interest and ideas worth writing about and discussing.

AUDIENCE

How you use *The Norton Reader* will depend not only on purpose but also on audience—the level of your class; the range of ages, backgrounds, and experiences of students; and other factors such as whether all students are native speakers of English or whether yours is their first college-level writing class. Such issues will affect not only the number and length of readings you choose, but also the balance you achieve between discussion of student writing and discussion of the texts—and how they relate.

This balance can also be affected by the supplementary texts you select. Rhetorics, for example, usually offer an overview of the writing process—from invention exercises to strategies for revision and documenting sources—as well as guidance on style, punctuation, and mechanics. They provide an introduction to basic elements of the rhetorical situation, including attention to the speaker or writer, audience, purpose, genre, and context. Increasingly, rhetorics also provide information on electronic research and on creating multimodal texts and presentations. Incorporating a rhetoric into your syllabus can help you tailor your course to the needs of your students—whether they need additional help with grammar and punctuation, with the conventions of academic discourse, or with learning a new style of documentation. Most rhetorics also include a section for students for whom English is not a first language. You can use a rhetoric successfully in a writing class of any level, but it can be especially valuable for students taking their first college writing class, whether that class is traditional first-year composition or a developmental writing class.

If you are using *The Norton Reader* in a developmental writing class, you might wish to assign fewer readings for each class period (one or two instead of three or four) and begin the term with shorter essays, ones that allow you to make clear links between the readings and student writing (in terms of topic, purpose, genre, style, or some mix of these elements). Limiting the number and length of readings will provide more time for attention to students' writing processes. That is, you can use more class time for unpacking the writing assignments you give, doing invention exercises, and working on revision through workshops and peer review. You can include longer or otherwise more challenging readings later in the semester, once students are more aware of your expectations and of their own writing processes.

Another way of using *The Norton Reader* in a developmental writing class would be to use the essays as explicit models for student writing. If students are having difficulty with introductions, for instance, you could pick three or four essays that have especially strong introductions and—as a class—analyze why those introductions are effective (how they draw readers in and gesture to purpose—sometimes through an implied thesis). Building on the foundation provided by examples, you can encourage students to choose a similar strategy for the introduction to their current writing assignment. The same approach can be taken in teaching other elements of writing: varied sentence structure, memorable conclusions, or incorporations of research.

If you are teaching an honors course, you will likely use *The Norton Reader* in a different way, perhaps as a means of foregrounding issues and arguments on which students will conduct their own research. For honors students, not only can you choose longer or more complex readings, but you can also devote more class time to discussing historical context for selected readings (especially those grouped in the "History and Politics" chapter), and you can ask students to do outside research.

Rhetorical and formal considerations, too, are appropriate topics for discussion in honors classes, but such considerations can go beyond the rudimen-
tary concerns to a close study of the nuances of writing that casual readers
overlook—from the power of schemes of repetition (such as anaphora and
epistrophe) to a writer's use of schemes of omission (such as ellipsis, asyn-
deton, or polysyndeton).

Most likely, you will have a range and mix of students—some who need
help with basic elements of academic writing, such as thesis statements; others
skilled enough to write and support elegant, multi-part, implied theses; some
who are confined by familiar patterns of organization, such as the five-
paragraph essay; others who link organization to purpose; some who grow frustrated with challenging texts; and others who trace each allusion and look up
the meanings of unfamiliar words and concepts. Because classes are rarely
homogenous, it can be difficult to anticipate the needs of students while you
are planning your course. You can, however, build flexibility into the syllabus
by choosing required readings of different lengths and levels of difficulty, providing recommended readings, and reserving time each week for attention to
student concerns.

SELECTING AND ORDERING

A strong syllabus makes clear connections for students, helping them understand various important links between readings, between readings and student writing, and between each of the assignments you ask students to do.

Sequencing Readings

The organization of *The Norton Reader* makes some connections for instructors and students, linking some readings topically, other readings by the prose
genre exhibited. As you create your syllabus, however, you will likely pick and
choose from already established groupings, perhaps linking readings not only
on the basis of topic or form but also by some other principle: the time period
in which it was written or some specific rhetorical strategy. The sample syllabi
and table of contents with cross-listed readings provide additional options for
grouping selections.

No matter what groupings you choose, you should have a rationale for the
sequence of readings—from day to day and over the course of the term. Even
if part of your rationale for selection is to provide topical and formal variety,
thoughtfully ordering those selections will create both cohesion and coherence in your course.

Readings and Writing Assignments

One method for linking readings and writings is to consider the ways in which
the essays serve as models or prompts for student thinking and writing. For
most writing assignments, you should be able to point to assigned readings that
in length and scope do what you want the students to do in their writing.
Depending on the focus of your course, you might not be able to make formal

connections between student writing and every essay you discuss, but for each major assignment, you should be able to provide a couple of fitting examples, perhaps pointing to an author's effective use of tone and diction, development of ideas (organization), or use of concrete examples.

If the authors make choices different from the ones you wish students to make, be prepared to discuss those differences too. Many times, the conventions of writing for a popular audience differ from conventions of academic writing—especially in terms of methods of citation and whether an explicit thesis statement is included. For example, Michael Pollan's "An Animal's Place" first appeared in the *New York Times Magazine* rather than an academic journal or book. Pollan makes and supports an argument against the treatment of animals in American factory farms, but he doesn't foreground an explicit thesis statement. He quotes sources appropriate to his topic but doesn't include a bibliography or works cited page. In teaching this essay, you might comment positively on how Pollan introduces and contextualizes sources, and encourage students to do the same in their arguments, but also be sure to remind students if you require a particular format, such as MLA, for citations. Finding both similarities and differences between the genres you ask students to write and the readings you select will help make your expectations clear and will provide fitting examples for students to follow.

Another method for linking reading and writing assignments is to use in-class writings and longer assignments as forums in which students can take a position on some issue suggested by the reading. We have included sample prompts for making such connections in the "Suggested Writing Assignments" sections of this *Guide*.

Sequencing Writing Assignments

In making links between earlier assignments and later assignments, you want your students to build on their knowledge and on previously practiced skills. Many instructors start with short assignments that require a response based on past experiences and then move to longer, more nuanced arguments that require external and carefully documented research. Other instructors begin by teaching analysis of a particular genre and then ask students to write an example of the genre they have analyzed. Still others move from very structured assignments in which students are given little choice (for example, reading responses that answer specific questions about an assigned reading) to open-ended assignments that give students freedom to choose not only their topic but also the genre they will write (for example, a term project that engages some element of the course). Each of these ways of sequencing makes assumptions about how students learn and about which tasks are more demanding. Some teachers move from personal writing to argument, assuming that writing about oneself is less cognitively demanding than more abstract forms of reasoning; others recognize the complex literary conventions significant to the genre of the personal essay and teach those conventions throughout the term, ending by having students write their own personal essays. The sequence you choose, again, will depend on your purpose and audience.

Pacing

Whether your course meets for ten weeks, sixteen weeks, or an entire year, it is unlikely you will assign more than a fraction of the readings included in *The Norton Reader*. Even after you limit the scope of your course, you will need to pay close attention to pacing.

If your class meets three times a week for fifty-minute increments, you will most likely be able to discuss two readings each class period. If you meet twice a week for seventy-five minutes, three readings will probably be your limit, especially if you are asking students to do in-class writings or small-group work. Another important consideration when you are designing your syllabus is the amount of class time you will spend working directly on student writing. Be sure to leave plenty of time to introduce new assignments, to do invention exercises, and to answer questions. Workshopping and peer review also take significant time commitments.

Successfully incorporating workshops on student writing into a class takes time commitment, both in and out of class. Students learn more from examples than from being told what to do in abstract terms. That is, injunctions to "write a clear thesis" or "use fitting details and examples" will mean little unless you teach students to do what you are asking. Workshops allow you to teach through example, to point out what is working well in students' writing—and what needs more work.

Early in the term, it is useful to set aside an entire class period to model appropriate and useful ways of responding to student writing. The first time you do a whole-class workshop, you can ask for two student volunteers and work on both papers as a class. Provide each student with copies of both papers as well as a handout that directs their attention to the qualities most important to the assignment you have given. Read each paper aloud in class, give students some time to write a response, and then spend twenty to thirty minutes discussing each paper. For the first workshop, you will probably be doing much of the talking (or directing the conversation at the very least), but with time and experience, students will gain confidence and do most of the talking.

Whole-class workshops provide a foundation for the kind of work students then can do in their peer-review groups. If they lack extensive experience doing peer review, it is worth the time to meet with each peer review group outside of class, to again model helpful ways of responding to student texts in a group setting. After the experience of a whole-class workshop and meeting in small groups with you, peer response groups should be prepared to work together in class, with you taking a less active role—just walking around to answer questions. Some peer review groups are responsible enough to meet outside class on their own time, but many students work better in the structured classroom setting.

As you consider the amount of time you will reserve for workshopping and peer review, you will need to decide how many drafts students will write and what kinds of responses they will get to each draft. How many drafts will you respond to—and in what forum? (Will you do individual conferences? Will you write responses and hand them back in class? Will you respond to drafts online or through email?) Your answers to such questions will help determine how you structure time in class.

The following sample syllabi can be expanded or contracted, depending on the varied considerations that help determine pacing: the length of your term, the number of days per week that you meet, the level of your course, the number of writing assignments you give, and many other considerations. The introductions to the syllabi will also help you determine ways you can modify these syllabi to suit your own objectives and student populations, or you can use them simply as springboards for your own ideas.

Sample Syllabi

GREAT IDEAS AND ENDURING QUESTIONS: SAMPLE SYLLABUS

Each of the six units below introduces a question central to human experience that has provoked response from writers and thinkers over many centuries. Each unit is designed to last two weeks. The first week concentrates on readings that can serve to sharpen critical thinking skills through discussion and response. The second week allows time for conducting workshops on the students' essays and discussing additional essays that further reflect on the central question of the unit. To supplement the content of any unit, instructors can invite students to bring in newspaper or magazine articles or other readings that put the central question in a contemporary light.

Identity: What Does It Mean to Be Human?

FIRST WEEK: *Readings and draft of an essay. The readings might focus on the concept of identity within a special group, in terms of ethnicity, gender, or sexual orientation, or they might take up general questions of human life and death.*

SECOND WEEK: *Additional readings on the concept of identity, plus writing workshops and/or peer-review sessions.*

Essays on gender and sexuality:

Amy Cunningham, "Why Women Smile"

Paul Theroux, "Being a Man"

*Anna Quindlen, "Between the Sexes, a Great Divide"

*Sojourner Truth, "Ain't I a Woman?"

*Roxane Gay, "A Tale of Three Coming Out Stories"

Gwendolyn Ann Smith, "We're All Someone's Freak"

Essays on race and ethnicity:

James Baldwin, "Stranger in the Village"

*Henry Louis Gates Jr., "In the Kitchen"

Zora Neale Hurston, "How It Feels to Be Colored Me"

*Essays in the Shorter Edition of *The Norton Reader*

*Brent Staples, "Black Men and Public Space"
Gloria Naylor, "Mommy, What Does 'Nigger' Mean?"

Essays on life and death:

*Henry Petroski, "Falling Down Is Part of Growing Up"
*Elisabeth Kübler-Ross, "On the Fear of Death"
David James Duncan, "The Mickey Mantle Koan"
*Virginia Woolf, "The Death of the Moth"

Writing Assignment: Draft and revision of an essay, as suggested in the "Suggested Writing Assignments" in the *Guide*.

Learning and Language: What Is the Purpose of Education?

First week: *Readings on literacy and education and draft of an essay.*

Second week: *Writing workshops and peer review, plus additional assignments on education, if desired.*

Essays on literacy:

*Gerald Graff, "Hidden Intellectualism"
*Frederick Douglass, "Learning to Read"
Eudora Welty, "Clamorous to Learn"

Essays on education:

*Lynda Barry, "The Sanctuary of School"
*Jonathan Kozol, "Fremont High School"
*Richard Rodriguez, "Aria"
*Maxine Hong Kingston, "Tongue-Tied"

Writing Assignment: Draft and revision of an essay as suggested in the *Guide*. A personal literacy narrative could be especially appropriate for this unit.

Memory, Imagination, and Expression: Why and How Do We Interpret Experience?

First week: *Readings on interpretation and draft of a writing assignment.*

Second week: *Writing workshops and peer review, plus additional readings. Instructors may wish to consider both verbal and nonverbal ways of interpreting experience or to use essays, like Scott McCloud's "Understanding Comics," Nora Ephron's "The Boston Photographs," or Alison Bechdel's "Fun Home" that combine verbal and visual elements.*

*Essays in the Shorter Edition of *The Norton Reader*

Essays on interpreting personal experience:

N. Scott Momaday, "The Way to Rainy Mountain"

*George Orwell, "Shooting an Elephant"

*E. B. White, "Once More to the Lake"

*Maya Angelou, "Graduation"

David Sedaris, "Loggerheads"

(Many other personal essays will work equally well.)

Essays on interpretation in literature, music, art, and film:

Northrop Frye, "The Motive for Metaphor" (literature)

Nora Ephron, "The Boston Photographs" (ethics)

Aaron Copland, "How We Listen" (music)

*Michael Chabon, "Kids' Stuff" (comics)

*Scott McCloud, from "Understanding Comics" (comics)

Susan Sontag, "A Century of Cinema" (film)

Philip Kennicott, "How to View Art: Be Dead Serious about It, but Don't Expect Too Much" (art)

*Michael Hamad, "Song Schematics" (music)

Writing Assignment: Draft and revision of a writing assignment suggested in the *Guide*.

Nature and Technology: How Should We Live in Our Environment?

FIRST WEEK: *Readings from "Nature and the Environment" and other chapters, plus draft of an essay.*

SECOND WEEK: *Writing workshops, peer review, and additional readings.*

Essays on living in or with nature:

*Brian Doyle, "Joyas Voladoras"

*John McPhee, "Under the Snow"

*Henry David Thoreau, "Where I Lived, and What I Lived For"

Edward Abbey, "The Great American Desert"

William Cronon, "The Trouble with Wilderness"

*Chief Seattle, "Letter to President Pierce, 1855"

Sandra Steingraber, "Tune of the Tuna Fish"

*Essays in the Shorter Edition of *The Norton Reader*

*Terry Tempest Williams, "The Clan of One-Breasted Women"
Michelle Nijhuis, "Which Species Will Live?"

Writing Assignment: Write a personal essay that describes an ideal or appropriate relation between human beings and the environment. Alternatives might include keeping a nature journal, writing about an environmental issue of local importance, or choosing one of the "Suggested Writing Assignments" in the *Guide*.

Freedom, Power, and Justice: What Is the Individual's Relationship to Government?

FIRST WEEK: *Readings and draft of a writing assignment.*

SECOND WEEK: *Writing workshops, plus additional readings. One topic for group discussion might be the politics of revision in the two versions of "The Declaration of Independence."*

Classic essays and speeches on government:

*Niccolò Machiavelli, "The Morals of the Prince"

*Abraham Lincoln, "Second Inaugural Address"

*John F. Kennedy, "Inaugural Address"

*Thomas Jefferson and Others, "The Declaration of Independence," Original Draft

*Thomas Jefferson and Others, "The Declaration of Independence," Final Draft

*Elizabeth Cady Stanton, "Declaration of Sentiments and Resolutions"

Essays that reflect on or challenge existing forms of government:

*George Orwell, "Shooting an Elephant"

Martin Luther King Jr., "Letter from Birmingham Jail"

Edwidge Danticat, "Another Country"

Jeffrey Owen Jones, "The Man Who Wrote the Pledge of Allegiance"

Writing Assignment: Draft and revision of a writing assignment suggested in the *Guide*.

Truth and Belief: How Do We Know Right from Wrong?

FIRST WEEK: *Readings on ethical issues and draft of a writing assignment.*

SECOND WEEK: *Writing workshops, plus additional readings on myth, parable, and fable as means of conveying moral or ethical teachings.*

*Essays in the Shorter Edition of *The Norton Reader*

Essays on ethics:

*Mark Twain, "Advice to Youth"

*Peter Singer, "What Should a Billionaire Give—and What Should You?"

*Atul Gawande, "When Doctors Make Mistakes"

Tom Regan, "The Case for Animal Rights"

*Michael Pollan, "An Animal's Place"

David Foster Wallace, "Consider the Lobster"

*Sallie Tisdale, "We Do Abortions Here: A Nurse's Story"

Nora Ephron, "The Boston Photographs"

Paul Fussell, "Thank God for the Atom Bomb"

*David Eagleman, "The Brain on Trial"

Parables included in "Philosophy and Religion":

*Plato, "The Allegory of the Cave"

*Zen Parables, "Muddy Road, A Parable, Learning to Be Silent"

*Jesus, "Parables of the Kingdom"

Writing Assignment: Draft and revision of a writing assignment suggested in the *Guide*. An alternative or additional assignment might be to write (or rewrite) a parable that conveys a modern-day moral lesson.

Writing across the Curriculum: Sample Syllabus

The second half of *The Norton Reader* is readily adaptable to a writing-across-the-curriculum course, whether one that emphasizes writing to learn or one that focuses on the rhetorical conventions of academic discourse. Instructors might simply choose five or six chapters of the *Reader* and use a sampling of essays to construct a syllabus for such a course. We have outlined six possible units corresponding to chapters of the *Reader*. Within these units, we have integrated selections from other chapters of the *Reader* so that multiple connections will emerge.

The six units below are each designed to last two weeks. If an instructor feels the pace is too fast or wishes to give additional reading or writing assignments, any unit can be expanded to three weeks—and, of course, an instructor might choose to use only four or five units.

The first week concentrates on readings that show conventions of critical thinking and writing in the discipline and that might serve, in some ways, as models for the students' own writing. The second week allows time for conducting workshops on the students' essays and for discussing additional essays

*Essays in the Shorter Edition of *The Norton Reader*

that reflect on the nature and concerns of the discipline. The content of any unit might be supplemented with articles written by professors at one's own college or university, with visits from such professors to discuss their own work, or with newspaper and magazine articles that address similar issues as they are addressed to a general audience.

Education

First week: *Education from the teacher's point of view.*

*Gerald Graff, " Hidden Intellectualism"

*Mike Rose, "Blue-Collar Brilliance"

Adrienne Rich, "Taking Women Students Seriously"

*William Zinsser, "College Pressures"

Assignment: See suggestions in the *Guide* for the essays listed above.

Second week: *Education from the learner's point of view.*

*Lynda Barry, "The Sanctuary of School"

*Frederick Douglass, "Learning to Read"

*Eudora Welty, "One Writer's Beginnings"

*Maya Angelou, "Graduation"

*Maxine Hong Kingston, "Tongue-Tied"

*Richard Rodriguez, "Aria"

*Stephen King, "On Writing"

Assignment: A personal essay about an educational experience or one of the writing assignments suggested in the *Guide*.

Environmental Studies

First week: *Readings in natural history and draft of a writing assignment.*

Edward Abbey, "The Great American Desert" (natural history)

*Chief Seattle, "Letter to President Pierce, 1855" (environmental advocacy)

*Henry David Thoreau, "Where I Lived, and What I Lived For" (classic American statement of the value of nature)

*Brian Doyle, "Joyas Voladoras" (natural history)

*John McPhee, "Under the Snow" (natural history)

Assignment: An essay about something in nature, whether an animal, a plant, or a place, or an argument about an environmental issue, based on suggestions from the *Guide*.

*Essays in the Shorter Edition of *The Norton Reader*

SECOND WEEK: *Writing workshops and readings about contemporary environmental issues.*

*Terry Tempest Williams, "The Clan of One-Breasted Women" (environmental advocacy)

William Cronon, "The Trouble with Wilderness" (reflections on American attitudes)

Sandra Steingraber, "Tune of the Tuna Fish" (environmental advocacy)

Assignment: Writing workshop or peer review, followed by revision of draft. Because this unit is especially rich and diverse in its forms, it could be divided into two units, one on nature writing, another on environmental issues. Students might then try writing one essay of each kind.

Science

FIRST WEEK: *Readings on theories of science and draft of a writing assignment.*

T. H. Huxley, "Goethe: Aphorisms on Nature"

*Alan Lightman, "Our Place in the Universe: Face to Face with the Infinite"

Isaac Asimov, "The Relativity of Wrong"

*Thomas S. Kuhn, "The Route to Normal Science"

*Stephen Hawking and Leonard Mlodinow, "The (Elusive) Theory of Everything"

Assignment: Draft of a writing assignment suggested in the *Guide*.

SECOND WEEK: *Writing workshops, plus readings on scientific practices.*

*Stephen Jay Gould, "Sex, Drugs, Disasters, and the Extinction of Dinosaurs"

Michelle Nijhuis, "Which Species Will Live?"

David H. Freedman, "Lies, Damned Lies, and Medical Science"

*Rebecca Skloot, "The Woman in the Photograph"

Assignment: Writing workshop or peer review, followed by revision of draft.

Philosophy and Religion

FIRST WEEK: *Readings and draft of a writing assignment.*

Philosophy:

*Plato, "The Allegory of the Cave" (philosophical text)

*Henry David Thoreau, "Where I Lived, and What I Lived For" (classic Transcendental philosophy)

*Jesus, "Parables of the Kingdom" (religious text)

*Essays in the Shorter Edition of *The Norton Reader*

*Zen Parables, "Muddy Road, A Parable, Learning to Be Silent" (religious document)

Assignment: Draft of an essay that explores one of the above philosophies in greater depth. See writing assignment suggestions in the *Guide*.

SECOND WEEK: *Writing workshops, plus additional readings. Because the philosophical positions presented above are so complex, instructors may wish to devote additional discussion to each. Alternatively, one might concentrate on ethical questions such as those raised by the following essays from "Ethics":*

Paul Fussell, "Thank God for the Atom Bomb"

*Sallie Tisdale, "We Do Abortions Here: A Nurse's Story"

*David Eagleman, "The Brain on Trial"

Assignment: Writing workshop or peer review, followed by revision of draft. Students who have chosen to write on the same issue might work together in small groups to test and refine their arguments.

Literature and the Arts

FIRST WEEK: *Readings on literature and draft of a writing assignment.*

*Vladimir Nabokov, "Good Readers and Good Writers"

*Eudora Welty, "One Writer's Beginnings"

Northrop Frye, "The Motive for Metaphor"

*Virginia Woolf, "In Search of a Room of One's Own"

Supplementary Reading: A short story by Nabokov, Welty, or Woolf.

Assignment: Draft of an assignment suggested in the *Guide*.

SECOND WEEK: *Writing workshop, plus additional readings in other arts. Instructors may wish to consider a second art form, such as film or music.*

Susan Sontag, "A Century of Cinema" (film)

Nora Ephron, "The Boston Photographs" (photojournalism)

Philip Kennicott, "How to View Art: Be Dead Serious about It, but Don't Expect Too Much" (art)

*Michael Chabon, "Kids' Stuff" (comics)

*Scott McCloud, from "Understanding Comics" (comics/graphic art)

Aaron Copland, "How We Listen" (music)

*Michael Hamad, "Song Schematics" (music)

Assignment: Writing workshop or peer review, followed by revision of draft.

*Essays in the Shorter Edition of *The Norton Reader*

Politics and Government

First week: *Readings and draft of a writing assignment.*
*Niccolò Machiavelli, "The Morals of the Prince" (political treatise)
Martin Luther King Jr., "Letter from Birmingham Jail" (political treatise)
*Jonathan Swift, "A Modest Proposal" (parody of political treatise)
*George Orwell, "Shooting an Elephant" (personal essay on colonialism)

Assignment: A writing assignment suggested in the *Guide.*

Second week: *Writing workshops, plus additional readings on American politics.*
*Thomas Jefferson and Others, "The Declaration of Independence"
*Elizabeth Cady Stanton, "Declaration of Sentiments and Resolutions"
*Abraham Lincoln, "Second Inaugural Address"
*John F. Kennedy, "Inaugural Address"

Assignment: Workshop on assignment from the first week. Alternatively, this unit might focus on "The Declaration of Independence," its original and final drafts, and its influence on later documents such as Stanton's.

Race, Class, and Gender: Sample Syllabus

The fourteenth edition of *The Norton Reader* lends itself particularly well to extended classroom explorations of race, class, and gender. Many essays that directly address these issues are grouped together in separate sections (such as the end of "Cultural Analysis"). But since essays in all parts of the book deal with race, class, and gender, we have outlined five possible two-week units. Instructors can assign any number of these units, since the selections do not overlap. Thus in a one-semester course an instructor may wish to assign the two-week unit "Race, Ethnicity, and Language" and the two-week unit "Gender and Sexuality." A deeper examination of these issues is possible by assigning the additional two-week units on race and on gender.

We present these units as suggestions. If an instructor feels the pace is too fast or wishes to give additional reading or writing assignments, any of the five units could be expanded to three weeks. And the reading selections given in the five units do not exhaust all of *The Norton Reader*'s rich collection of essays touching on race, class, or gender. Instructors can use many additional essays from other parts of the book and may also want to assign other essays and reading selections from current books, newspapers, or periodicals.

*Essays in the Shorter Edition of *The Norton Reader*

In each of the five units, the first week introduces the issue and includes an essay assignment. The second week allows time for workshops, for further drafts of the first week's essay, and for additional reading and writing assignments.

The Struggle for Equality

First week: *Readings and draft of a writing assignment.*

Martin Luther King Jr., "Letter from Birmingham Jail"

*Maya Angelou, "Graduation"

James Baldwin, "Stranger in the Village"

*Brent Staples, "Black Men and Public Space"

Gloria Naylor, "Mommy, What Does 'Nigger' Mean?"

*Roxane Gay, "A Tale of Three Coming Out Stories"

Jaswinder Bolina, "Writing Like a White Guy: On Language, Race, and Poetry"

Assignment: Describe whether you think these writers' dependence on their personal experiences strengthens or weakens their cases for racial equality. What does a writer gain from using his or her own experience? What are the potential losses or limitations?

Second week: *Writing workshops and additional drafts of week one's writing assignment, along with essays that add complexity to the first week's readings.*

Zora Neale Hurston, "How It Feels to Be Colored Me"

*Henry Louis Gates Jr., "In the Kitchen"

Debra Dickerson, "Who Shot Johnny?"

Assignment: Writing workshop or peer review, followed by revision of draft. All three of the second week's essays employ personal experience. It is useful to have students trace the arguments in favor of equality that are implicit in each essay.

Race, Ethnicity, and Language

First week: *Readings and draft of a writing assignment.*

*Gloria Anzaldúa, "How to Tame a Wild Tongue"

*Richard Rodriguez, "Aria"

*Maxine Hong Kingston, "Tongue-Tied"

Assignment: Draft an essay about "language" in American society. Use examples from your own experience, the week's readings, and perspectives of people you know about.

*Essays in the Shorter Edition of *The Norton Reader*

Second week: *Writing workshops and additional drafts of week one's writing assignment, along with essays that add complexity to the first week's readings.*

Patricia Williams, "The Death of the Profane: The Rhetoric of Race and Rights"

Jaswinder Bolina, "Writing Like a White Guy: On Language, Race, and Poetry"

Assignment: Writing workshop or peer review, followed by revision of draft.

Class

First week: *Readings and draft of a writing assignment.*

*Lars Eighner, "On Dumpster Diving" (homelessness)

*Joey Franklin, "Working at Wendy's" (class assumptions)

*George Orwell, "Shooting an Elephant" (colonial rule and subalterns)

*Niccolò Machiavelli, "The Morals of the Prince" (training for aristocrats)

*Mike Rose, "Blue-Collar Brilliance" (class assumptions)

Assignment: Draft an essay on how these authors react to others who aren't of the same standing in society. What is their opinion of people who are higher or lower on the social ladder? How much do they identify with people who are at the same level they are? How do they regard the struggle for power?

Second week: *Writing workshops and additional drafts of week one's writing assignment, along with essays that add complexity to the first week's readings.*

*Jonathan Swift, "A Modest Proposal"

Ngũgĩ wa Thiong'o, "Decolonizing the Mind"

Assignment: Writing workshop or peer review, followed by revision of draft. The second week's readings stand in stark contrast to each other (and to the first week's readings as well). Both Swift and Ngũgĩ offer solutions to the problems of colonized peoples, but Swift uses satire, whereas Ngũgĩ uses "straight" argument. Students need to see that Swift, two centuries ago, rejects the meliorist solutions proposed by moderates and instead reacts with barely suppressed rage. (Some students need to be shown that Swift's "solution" is not merely ghoulishly clever but represents a moment of genuine despair about the possibility that any simple "project" can improve the lot of the poor.)

Gender: Women's and Men's Perspectives

First week: *Readings and draft of a writing assignment.*

*Anna Quindlen, "Between the Sexes, a Great Divide"

Paul Theroux, "Being a Man"

---

*Essays in the Shorter Edition of *The Norton Reader*

*Sojourner Truth, "Ain't I a Woman?"

Amy Cunningham, "Why Women Smile"

Assignment: Draft an essay exploring the degree to which gender differences are inherent in human nature or the product of society. Base your essay on the beliefs of those you know and of these writers.

Second week: *Writing workshops and additional drafts of week one's writing assignment, along with essays on gender and education.*

Adrienne Rich, "Taking Women Students Seriously"

David Brooks, "The Gender Gap at School"

Gender and Sexuality

The readings in this unit help complicate some of the positions in the first unit on gender, showing that gendered experiences and expectations go beyond differences between men's and women's perspectives. These readings on gender and sexuality show how celebrity, childhood experiences, technology, and the expectations of others shape identity and language.

First week: *Readings and draft of a writing assignment.*

*Roxane Gay, "A Tale of Three Coming Out Stories"

Gwendolyn Ann Smith, "We're All Someone's Freak"

*Dennis Baron, "Facebook Multiplies Genders but Offers Users the Same Three Tired Pronouns"

Assignment: Using your own experiences and the works you have read, analyze one of the ways people are socialized to understand and communicate some aspect of gender or sexuality.

Second week: *Writing workshops and additional drafts of week one's writing assignment, along with additional essays.*

David Sedaris, "Loggerheads"

Alison Bechdel, from "Fun Home"

Food, Sports, and Media and Technology: Sample Syllabus

This sample syllabus highlights three new thematic chapters in the fourteenth edition of *The Norton Reader* and provides options for both traditional and multimodal assignments, ones that help students analyze and create projects

*Essays in the Shorter Edition of *The Norton Reader*

that combine visual, audio, and textual components. Students will also practice different genres, drawing on both personal experience and research to create narratives, reflections, profiles, analyses, and arguments.

This syllabus includes three four-week units, one on each theme, and a final unit during which students can prepare and present final projects. Because many students will not be equally interested in every theme, many options for assignments are provided. Instructors can ask students to respond to one assignment per unit and do a final project, or can provide more flexibility, allowing students to focus on the topics and assignments that interest them most. Individual assignments can be graded throughout the term or with a portfolio system, allowing students to refine their ideas and revise their writing throughout the course. Whatever method you choose, be sure to provide specific due dates, including time for drafting, response, and revision.

The last few weeks of class are reserved for research, drafting, conferencing and peer review, and presentations of final projects. Be sure to give students time in class to analyze multimodal texts and presentations—and to get some practice with any specialized software or applications you want them to use. The final project options help students expand on the reflections, analyses, and arguments they have read and written earlier in the course.

The final project asks students to build on skills they have developed in the course—and to share them. They might, for example, choose to collaborate in creating a short film for a larger audience; expand a written profile into a multimedia profile that shows attention to design as well as other visual and audio components; or synthesize the topics they have explored and skills they have developed, perhaps by offering a solution to a particular problem they see related to food, sports, or technology.

Food: home, education, and work

FIRST WEEK:

Chang-rae Lee, "Coming Home Again"

*Lad Tobin, "Here Everything Is Possible"

Teresa Lust, "The Same Old Stuffing"

*M. F. K. Fisher, "Young Hunger"

SECOND WEEK:

Julia Child, "Le Cordon Bleu"

*Chris Wiewiora, "This Is Tossing"

*JJ Goode, "Single-Handed Cooking"

*Essays in the Shorter Edition of *The Norton Reader*

Assignment Options:

• Write a personal essay in which you narrate, describe, and reflect on the place of food in your family. You may describe a family holiday tradition, compare and contrast your own relationship to food to another family member's, or show your relationship to food during a particular time in your life by providing scenes or examples.

• Whether because of level of experience, cultural differences, time constraints, or disability, cooking sometimes represents a challenge. Write an essay in which you describe a challenge you have faced in preparing food.

• Chris Wiewiora uses sensory language to guide readers in the process of tossing pizza dough. Create a photo essay that helps guide readers in the process of making a particular dish.

Food arguments: sustainability, ethics, and legislation

Third week:

Sandra Steingraber, "Tune of the Tuna Fish"

*Annie Leonard, "The Story of Bottled Water: A Footnoted and Annotated Script"

*Dan Barry, "Back When a Chocolate Puck Tasted, Guiltily, Like America"

Fourth week:

*Dan Barber, "What Farm-to-Table Got Wrong"

*Michael Pollan, "An Animal's Place"

David Foster Wallace, "Consider the Lobster"

*Marion Nestle, "Utopian Dream: A New Farm Bill"

Assignment Options:

• Write an op-ed piece in which you argue for or against a particular approach to producing or procuring food. Include at least one image.

• Write an essay exploring the ethics of eating a particular food.

• Write an analysis of a law, policy, or regulation involving food. If you find it lacking, offer an alternative.

Sports: reflections and profiles

First week:

*Roger Angell, "The Interior Stadium"

A. Bartlett Giamatti, "The Green Fields of the Mind"

David James Duncan, "The Mickey Mantle Koan"

*Essays in the Shorter Edition of *The Norton Reader*

Second week:

Joe Posnanski, "Mariano Rivera's a True Yankee"

DeNeen Brown, "Six-Pack Abs at Age 74"

*David Halberstam, "Jordan's Moment"

Assignment Options:

• Write an essay describing and reflecting on one or more related sports events you have witnessed. You may, like Roger Angell, write about several games and reflect on larger issues related to the sport; like A. Bartlett Giamatti, reflect on the meaning of the game to you; or like David Halberstam, use the game to reveal something about a particular player.

• Write a profile for your campus newspaper of an athlete or coach at your school. Include a photo of that person.

• David James Duncan writes about Mickey Mantle; Joe Posnanski writes about Mariano Rivera; David Halberstam writes about Michael Jordan. Choose a sports legend and write an essay describing that person's contribution to the sport, a team, or your own life.

Sports and culture: analyses and arguments

Third week:

*Maya Angelou, "Champion of the World"

*Joyce Carol Oates, "Rape and the Boxing Ring"

Franklin Foer, "How Soccer Explains the American Culture Wars"

Fourth week:

*Michael Lewis, from "The Blind Side"

*David Epstein, "Sports Should Be Child's Play"

*Stephen King, "On Writing"

Assignment Options:

• Using Maya Angelou's, Joyce Carol Oates's, or Franklin Foer's essay as a model, write about a sport or player who represents something larger (whether positive or negative) to a particular group or culture.

• David Epstein argues in his op-ed piece that early specialization in sports is not good for children. Choose a sports-related issue and write an op-ed piece in which you make and support an argument.

• After reading Stephen King's "On Writing," use the advice he provides to write and revise an essay.

*Essays in the Shorter Edition of *The Norton Reader*

Media and Technology: listening and gaming

First week:

Aaron Copland, "How We Listen"

*Michael Hamad, "Song Schematics"

Second week:

*Tom Bissell, "Extra Lives: Why Video Games Matter"

*Jane McGonigal, "Be a Gamer, Save the World"

Assignment Options:

• After reading Aaron Copland's "How We Listen" and Michael Hamad's "Song Schematics," write an analysis of how you listen and include a drawing to illustrate your experience of one song.

• Tom Bissell analyzes his experience of playing a specific game, *Fallout 3*. Pick a specific product or technology (a game, an app, a social media site), and write an essay in which you analyze your experience of using that product or technology.

• Jane McGonigal points to the positive effects of gaming. Research other positions, ones that argue there are negative effects. Then write an essay in which you take your own position on either the negative or positive effects of gaming. Quote other writers either in support of your position or to answer counterarguments.

A closer look at technology: critiques and appreciations

Third week:

Thomas Goetz, "Harnessing the Power of Feedback Loops"

*Nicholas Carr, "Is Google Making Us Stupid?"

*Tasneem Raja, "Is Coding the New Literacy?"

Fourth week:

Fred Vogelstein, "And Then Steve Said, 'Let There Be an iPhone'"

*Judith Newman, "To Siri, with Love: How One Boy with Autism Became BFF with Apple's Siri"

Dennis Baron, "Facebook Multiplies Genders but Offers Users the Same Three Tired Pronouns"

Assignment Options:

• Choose a particular technology or medium of technology and write an essay analyzing its effects. Is it limiting—even potentially dangerous—in some way? Is it empowering? Does it open new possibilities for a particular person or group?

*Essays in the Shorter Edition of *The Norton Reader*

• Judith Newman describes and uses examples to illustrate an unexpected positive effect of a specific technology. Write an essay in which you describe and illustrate a positive effect of technology.

• Thomas Goetz explains the importance of feedback loops for solving specific problems (for example, the problem of people speeding in school zones or the problem of people not taking their medicine). Write an essay in which you identify another problem and show how feedback loops could help solve that problem.

Synthesizing and Sharing

FIRST WEEK: *Draft final projects.*

SECOND WEEK: *Peer review and conferences.*

Final Project Options

• After reading Annie Leonard's footnoted and annotated script "The Story of Bottled Water," watch the short film online at storyofstuff.org/movies/story-of-bottled-water. Work with a small group of classmates to research some other product or process related to food or sports. Together, write a footnoted and annotated script for a short film, which you will make as a group. As you create your film, be attentive to sounds and visuals that will help support your main point or argument.

• After reading the profiles included on the syllabus, analyze some profiles that have been published online. After reading David Halberstam's "Jordan's Moment," check out Michael Jordan's profile on nba.com. After reading David James Duncan's "The Mickey Mantle Koan," look up Mantle's profile on biography.com. Note the design of online profiles and what they include: videos, text, photos, and other features. Create a multimodal profile of someone from your campus or local community. With permission, record interviews with that person and people who know him or her. Photograph and video your subject as well. You might choose a farmer, an athlete, a gamer, a musician—anyone of interest. Then show—through your writing, design, and selection of audio and video—why that person should be of interest to others.

• Choose a problem you identified and wrote about earlier in the course. What practical solution—or way of addressing that problem—can you offer? Is there a way modern technology can help address that problem? Start to address that problem, perhaps by creating a website, a film, or by using existing social media to educate your audience and provide a call for action.

THIRD AND FOURTH WEEKS: *Presentations.*

Assignment: Prepare an eight-minute presentation in which you share your final project with the class. You can introduce and play your group's short film, unveil the online profile you created, or show how you are addressing the problem you identified.

Persuasion and Argument: Sample Syllabus

The Norton Reader lends itself to a course emphasizing persuasion and argument by including many essays that illustrate a range of argumentative strategies and personae. The chapters "Op-Eds," "Ethics," "History and Politics," and "Nature and the Environment" are the most concentrated sources of persuasive and argumentative essays. Appended to this syllabus are the argumentative and persuasive essays in the Full Edition listed by section; those that also appear in the Shorter Edition are asterisked.

At the same time *The Norton Reader* includes other kinds of essays that provide material for persuasive and argumentative essays and suggests assignments using them. Typical assignments for persuasive and argumentative essays, in both the *Reader* and the *Guide*, ask students to take a position and support it by drawing on their experience, observation, and reading.

This syllabus is set up for a fourteen-week semester. It contains five units of two weeks each and a four-week unit on a longer paper with attention to library research and documentation. It assigns students five papers in two drafts: a paper analyzing an essay, a personal account, two persuasive/argumentative essays, and a longer persuasive/argumentative paper using library research. It also assigns them a third draft of one of the persuasive/argumentative essays and, at the end of the course, in first draft only, an analysis of their experience in writing persuasion and argument. Any of these units can be repeated using additional essays; any of them can be dropped.

Class discussion should focus on purpose, evidence, personae, and audience, both in the essays assigned from the *Reader* and in students' own writing. Both editions of the *Reader* offer a rich variety of all these.

First week:

Reading Assignment: *Read the following selections in the "Op-Eds" chapter.*

*Molly Ivins, "Get a Knife, Get a Dog, but Get Rid of Guns"

Brent Staples, "Why Colleges Shower Their Students with A's"

Jo-Ann Pilardi, "Immigration Problem Is about Us, Not Them"

*Dan Barber, "What Farm-to-Table Got Wrong"

In-class: Analyze, for several of these selections, the author's purpose and evidence, the kind of persona the author creates, how, and for what audience. How effective is the author's evidence and persona?

Writing Assignment (Draft): Draft an essay about one of the selections in the "Op-Eds" chapter not discussed in class. Analyze what the author's evidence is, how it is deployed, what kind of persona the author creates, how, and for what

*Essays in the Shorter Edition of *The Norton Reader*

audience. How effective do you find the author's evidence and persona? Append a paragraph in which you consider whether you, as a student, could adopt a similar persona or, if not, what kind of persona would be suitable to the audiences you will be addressing as a writer in college.

SECOND WEEK:
Reading Assignment:

*David Eagleman, "The Brain on Trial" (Ethics)

Michelle Nijhuis, "Which Species Will Live?" (Nature and the Environment)

In-class: Discuss logic, evidence, and persona in the Eagleman and Nijhuis essays.

Writing Assignment (Revision): Divide into groups for peer review of drafts; revised drafts to be handed in at the next class.

THIRD WEEK:
Reading Assignment:

*Scott Russell Sanders, "Under the Influence" (Profiles)

Gwendolyn Ann Smith, "We're All Someone's Freak" (Gender and Human Nature)

Nora Ephron, "The Boston Photographs" (Ethics)

Jaswinder Bolina, "Writing Like a White Guy: On Language, Race, and Poetry" (Language and Communication)

In-class: Discuss several of these essays as narrative or exposition, and consider how they provide material that could be used in arguing a controversial issue.

Writing Assignment (Draft): Draft a personal essay based on an experience or experiences that will provide material to be used in arguing a controversial issue.

FOURTH WEEK:
Reading Assignment:

*Maya Angelou, "Graduation" (Personal Accounts)

*Lars Eighner, "On Dumpster Diving" (Personal Accounts)

*Roxane Gay "A Tale of Three Coming Out Stories" (Gender and Human Nature)

In-class: Discuss how one or more of these essays could be used as evidence in taking a position or in arguing for a social change or changes.

Writing Assignment (Revision): Divide into groups for peer review of drafts; revised drafts to be handed in at the next class.

*Essays in the Shorter Edition of *The Norton Reader*

Fifth week:
Reading Assignment:

*Atul Gawande, "When Doctors Make Mistakes" (Ethics)

Patricia Williams, "The Death of the Profane: The Rhetoric of Race and Rights" (Cultural Analysis)

Martin Luther King Jr., "Letter from Birmingham Jail" (History and Politics)

In-class: Discuss evidence and personae in the Gawande, Williams, and King essays.

Writing Assignment (Draft): Draft a persuasive or argumentative essay that uses as evidence experience, observation, and reading of one of the essays above or any other essay in *The Norton Reader*.

Sixth week:
Reading Assignment:

*Maya Angelou, "Champion of the World" (Sports)

*Joyce Carol Oates, "Rape and the Boxing Ring" (Sports)

In-class: Discuss the principles and values that underlie the differences between Angelou and Oates.

Writing Assignment (Revision): Divide into groups for peer review of drafts; revised drafts to be handed in at the next class.

Seventh week:
Reading Assignment:

*Thomas Jefferson and Others, "The Declaration of Independence" (History and Politics)

*Elizabeth Cady Stanton, "Declaration of Sentiments and Resolutions" (History and Politics)

In-class: Discuss syllogistic argument: a major premise, a minor premise, and a conclusion.

Writing Assignment (Draft): Draft an essay on a controversial topic that highlights the major premises (or principles and values) about which you and your opponents cannot agree.

Eighth week:
Reading Assignment:

*Stephen Jay Gould, "Sex, Drugs, Disasters, and the Extinction of Dinosaurs" (Science)

Michelle Nijhuis, "Which Species Will Live?" (Nature and the Environment)

*Essays in the Shorter Edition of *The Norton Reader*

David H. Freedman, "Lies, Damned Lies, and Medical Science" (Science)

*Rebecca Skloot, "The Woman in the Photograph" (Science)

In-class: Discuss the conventions of writing about science and medical issues for a popular audience. How does this writing—and way of persuading—differ from scientific and medical writing for an audience of specialists?

Writing Assignment (Revision): Divide into groups for peer review of drafts; revised drafts to be handed in at the next class.

NINTH WEEK:
Reading Assignment: *Read through the essays in "Nature and the Environment," "Ethics," "History and Politics," and begin library research in preparation for writing a persuasive or argumentative essay on an issue that appears in one of them.*

In-class: Introduction to print and electronic resources in the library.

Writing Assignment (Draft): Brainstorm, make notes, list, free write—whatever works best to get you started—about what you know and what you need to know, where you are in your research, where you are going, and where you think you will come out.

TENTH WEEK:
Reading Assignment: *Continue library research.*

Writing Assignment (Draft): Divide into groups for peer review of brainstorming, etc. Begin to draft a persuasive or argumentative essay that incorporates library research.

ELEVENTH WEEK:
In-class: Discuss the purposes of bibliography and notes, and review their form.

Writing Assignment (Draft): Divide into groups for peer review of drafts.

TWELFTH WEEK:
Writing Assignment: Divide into groups for peer review of bibliography and notes; final draft of essay that incorporates library research due.

THIRTEENTH WEEK:
Reading Assignment: *Read persuasive and argumentative essays in either "Cultural Analysis" or "Education."*

*Tom Bissell, "Extra Lives: Why Video Games Matter" (Cultural Analysis)

*Annie Leonard, "The Story of Bottled Water: A Footnoted and Annotated Script" (Cultural Analysis)

*Brent Staples, "Black Men and Public Space" (Cultural Analysis)

*Caroline Bird, "College Is a Waste of Time and Money" (Education)

*Essays in the Shorter Edition of *The Norton Reader*

Adrienne Rich, "Taking Women Students Seriously" (Education)

Writing Assignment (Draft): Draft an essay in which you review the papers you wrote this semester and analyze your strengths and difficulties in writing persuasion and argument.

Fourteenth week:
Writing Assignment (Draft): Divide into groups, share drafts, and report to class the issues concerning persuasion and argument that emerged in the groups.

Assignment (Revision): Revise one of your earlier papers from this course and hand it in; append a paragraph in which you describe what you aimed for in your revision.

Essays Exemplifying Persuasion and Argument (by chapter)

Cultural Analysis

*Annie Leonard, "The Story of Bottled Water: A Footnoted and Annotated Script"

*Tom Bissell, "Extra Lives: Why Video Games Matter"

*Bill McKibben, "The Case for Single-Child Families"

*Brent Staples, "Black Men and Public Space"

Op-Eds

*Anna Quindlen, "Stuff Is Not Salvation"

*Tim Kreider, "The 'Busy' Trap"

*Molly Ivins, "Get a Knife, Get a Dog, but Get Rid of Guns"

Jo-Ann Pilardi, "Immigration Problem Is about Us, Not Them"

Brent Staples, "Why Colleges Shower Their Students with A's"

David Brooks, "The Gender Gap at School"

*David Epstein, "Sports Should Be Child's Play"

*Jane McGonigal, "Be a Gamer, Save the World"

*Dan Barber, "What Farm-to-Table Got Wrong"

Education

*Lynda Barry, "The Sanctuary of School"

*Gerald Graff, "Hidden Intellectualism"

*Jonathan Kozol, "Fremont High School"

*Caroline Bird, "College Is a Waste of Time and Money"

Adrienne Rich, "Taking Women Students Seriously"

*Mike Rose, "Blue-Collar Brilliance"

*Essays in the Shorter Edition of *The Norton Reader*

Nature and the Environment

*Chief Seattle, "Letter to President Pierce, 1855"

William Cronon, "The Trouble with Wilderness"

*Terry Tempest Williams, "The Clan of One-Breasted Women"

Ethics

*Peter Singer, "What Should a Billionaire Give—and What Should You?"

*Atul Gawande, "When Doctors Make Mistakes"

Tom Regan, "The Case for Animal Rights"

*Michael Pollan, "An Animal's Place"

*Sallie Tisdale, "We Do Abortions Here: A Nurse's Story"

Nora Ephron, "The Boston Photographs"

Paul Fussell, "Thank God for the Atom Bomb"

*David Eagleman, "The Brain on Trial"

History and Politics

*Jonathan Swift, "A Modest Proposal"

*Thomas Jefferson and Others, "The Declaration of Independence"

Edwidge Danticat, "Another Country"

*Elizabeth Cady Stanton, "Declaration of Sentiments and Resolutions"

*Abraham Lincoln, "Second Inaugural Address"

*John F. Kennedy, "Inaugural Address"

Martin Luther King Jr., "Letter from Birmingham Jail"

Literature and the Arts

Ngũgĩ wa Thiong'o, "Decolonizing the Mind"

*Virginia Woolf, "In Search of a Room of One's Own"

Philosophy and Religion

Leon Wieseltier, "Ring the Bells"

*Henry David Thoreau, "Where I Lived, and What I Lived For"

THE GENRES OF THE ESSAY: SAMPLE SYLLABUS

This syllabus explores essay genres. Each unit asks students to read classic and contemporary examples and then to draw on their personal experience and knowledge to write in the same form. The essay genres are loosely grouped:

*Essays in the Shorter Edition of *The Norton Reader*

the personal experience essay, the biographical profile, the essay about a place, an analysis of a cultural phenomenon or cultural critique, and an op-ed piece that makes a contribution to an issue of public concern. A discussion of these genres can be found in the introduction to *The Norton Reader*.

The emphasis in each unit is on writing the essay—hence the detailed writing assignments. Essays that fit the genre are listed, but many other examples can be found in the *Reader* and in local and national newspapers and journals. (See the essays listed under "Cultural Analysis," "Literacy Narratives," "Memoirs and Personal Essays," "Profile of a Person," and "Profile of a Place" in the Genres Index in the back of the *Reader*.) The readings provide "models" in the sense that they suggest ways that professional writers have explored their personal experience or analyzed a contemporary phenomenon or argued a case in the public realm. But the "models" are plural, multiple, and complex—not simple or singular.

I. Interpreting Personal Experience

Assignment: Write an essay, based on personal experience, in which you both narrate and interpret the significance of a personal experience. In common with the essays read in this unit, focus your essay on a single story or event (although it may include earlier or peripheral incidents if you wish) and aim to make a single, public point. In other words, you should not only tell your story, but you should seek to affect the way your readers will think about the specific problem or issue you raise in telling it.

Readings:

*George Orwell, "Shooting an Elephant"

*Langston Hughes, "Salvation"

*Terry Tempest Williams, "The Clan of One-Breasted Women"

Debra Dickerson, "Who Shot Johnny?"

*Brent Staples, "Black Men and Public Space"

*Joan Didion, "On Going Home"

Chang-rae Lee, "Coming Home Again"

*Alice Walker, "Beauty: When the Other Dancer Is the Self"

*E. B. White, "Once More to the Lake"

David Sedaris, "Loggerheads"

II. Portraying a Person

Assignment: Write an essay that portrays a person in his or her typical context. Whether you write about a person you know well or someone you know only slightly or through the media, gather new, additional information about

*Essays in the Shorter Edition of *The Norton Reader*

that person, whether through interviews or research or both, and incorporate it into your account. If you write about a family member, interview other family members who know (or knew) the person. If you write about someone local, interview your subject and others who know—or work with—him or her. If you write about a public figure, find ways to gather information and interpret it in a new way.

Readings:

Tom Wolfe, "Yeager"

*Annie Dillard, from *An American Childhood*

*Scott Russell Sanders, "Under the Influence"

*Judith Ortiz Cofer, "More Room"

David James Duncan, "The Mickey Mantle Koan"

Virginia Woolf, "Ellen Terry"

Joe Posnanski, "Mariano Rivera's a True Yankee"

DeNeen Brown, "Six-Pack Abs at Age 74"

*David Halberstam, "Jordan's Moment"

III. Understanding a Place

Assignment: Write an essay for a wide audience that describes, creates the essence of, and interprets the meaning of a place. The place may be as small as a room, the size of a campus building, or as large as a town. Choose a place that you can observe as you write this essay or that you know so well you need not observe it anew. Incorporate not only observations from the present or memories from the past, but information about the place that will help you convey its "meaning" to your readers (possibilities: its history; its inhabitants; responses of people who see the place for the first time or who live or work there; information about its founding, its changing fortune, or its demise).

Readings:

N. Scott Momaday, "The Way to Rainy Mountain"

Jhumpa Lahiri, "Rhode Island"

*Ian Frazier, "Take the F"

*E. B. White, "Once More to the Lake"

Edward Abbey, "The Great American Desert"

IV. Cultural Analysis

Assignment: Write an essay that analyzes and comments on a specific feature of modern culture. Your focus should be on a concrete, recognizable object or

*Essays in the Shorter Edition of *The Norton Reader*

phenomenon, not on some broad historical or political trend (even though you may want to use history or politics to analyze your object of choice). Look closely at your object or phenomenon: describe it, describe who uses it, think about why it has become popular, explain the values or beliefs it embeds or conveys.

Readings:

*Dan Barry, "Back When a Chocolate Puck Tasted, Guiltily, Like America"

Teresa Lust, "The Same Old Stuffing"

Leslie Jamison, "Mark My Words. Maybe."

David Foster Wallace, "Consider the Lobster"

*Eula Biss, "Time and Distance Overcome"

*Henry Louis Gates Jr., "In the Kitchen"

*Jessica Mitford, "Behind the Formaldehyde Curtain"

Malcolm Gladwell, "Java Man"

V. Op-Eds

Assignment: Write an op-ed piece (a short persuasive essay or argument) meant to influence a wide audience, following the lines of the opinion pieces and editorials read in the "Op-Eds" chapter. Your op-ed may use any of the types of evidence that appear in the readings, including personal experience, statistical data, authoritative opinion, expert testimony, and so on. Try to make your argument engage some important public issue of current interest, possibly taking a position against some already published essay.

Readings:

*Tim Kreider, "The 'Busy' Trap"

Jo-Ann Pilardi, "Immigration Problem Is about Us, Not Them"

*David Epstein, "Sports Should Be Child's Play"

*Jane McGonigal, "Be a Gamer, Save the World"

*Dan Barber, "What Farm-to-Table Got Wrong"

*Anna Quindlen, "Between the Sexes, a Great Divide"

*Molly Ivins, "Get a Knife, Get a Dog, but Get Rid of Guns"

Brent Staples, "Why Colleges Shower Their Students with A's"

David Brooks, "The Gender Gap at School"

*Anna Quindlen, "Stuff Is Not Salvation"

*Essays in the Shorter Edition of *The Norton Reader*

Classroom Techniques and Tactics

Charles Hood

TEN 10-MINUTE THINGS TO DO IN CLASS WITH *THE NORTON READER*

Let's say, for the sake of argument, that you are a teacher of writing, perhaps new to teaching or perhaps not, and you have an assigned class period of an hour and twenty minutes. Allowing for the usual business at the start and end of most classes, on a particular day you have divided the remaining hour block into two solid lessons of thirty minutes each.

The first lesson goes just as you intended, and (just as planned) fills up about thirty minutes of class time. So far so good. Feeling pleased, you turn now to the second component of the day, a lesson that also should last a good thirty minutes, if not longer.

And that one? Oh dear. That one bombs.

No class discussion, no hands in the air, no happy sparks of learning. For whatever reason, after five minutes the second lesson is completely over, done, finished.

You look at the clock, you look down at your lesson notes, you look back at the clock. The room is silent.

Now what?

It has happened to us all: no matter how carefully planned out, no matter how pedagogically sound, no matter how good on paper a given lesson looks, there comes the day when that same lesson (one which may even have worked perfectly successfully five or six times previously) is delivered to the class and turns out to be so inert it could be bottled up in Mason jars and sold to chemistry labs.

Not to worry. This is when you pull out Plan B, namely a writing lesson that would be useful to cover at some point during a term but whose placement in the sequence is flexible. Such a lesson can come at the start of a period or the end; it can come early in a semester or further along. Either way, it is a foolproof way of reigniting the launch sequence and getting the class ready for orbit once again.

Over time you will develop your own repertoire of surefire backup lessons. Until then, here are a few that the editors of this book have found useful, and that work especially well with *The Norton Reader*. Some require a bit of advance prep (like bringing in postcards); many do not.

These mini-lessons work well in almost any situation. Like a good basic cookie recipe, each is elastic enough to accommodate whichever special flavors work best for you—cranberries instead of raisins, white sugar instead of brown. If you have particularly successful variations on these ideas, do please share them either in a private note to the editors or, even better, in public via the course support website. We all are in this together, and even the most experienced teachers are always ready to learn new ways of making writing happen.

1. READ IT ALOUD/ACT IT OUT

Classic classroom activity to engage the shy ones and try to get the class discussion rolling again if things have gone quiet.

In an essay with a fair amount of human voice present on the page, ask each student to find three or four sentences to read aloud with passion and conviction, whether or not he or she cares about the topic (or even knows what all the words mean). Give the class a few minutes (just long enough to find a passage and rehearse it mentally a few times) and maybe ask for volunteers at first. Run up and down a few rows as well—to have enough random and forced participation so that even quiet students get a chance to speak up. If you have a good rapport, maybe tease a few students over weak readings and have them read again, backed by your coaching. Also productive is to ask them why they picked the sentences they did; with luck, some will have strong and interesting motives for the text snippets they selected. This technique can be expanded or contracted to fill ten minutes up to twenty-five, but it usually fits nicely as a brisk transition between other projects. If it feels labored, give it up and move on.

2. "GEE, I HATE THIS"

Response papers inverted, encouraging dissent.

Often writing classes start with a journal prompt to write about that day's reading, or some kind of summary or response to ideas present in homework. Partway into the term have students write about which essay or essays in *The Norton Reader* they have disliked the most up to that point. Be serious in encouraging some honest hatred with this one, so that they know it is safe to reject those texts dearest to you personally.

With luck, class discussion will do several things afterward. First and most important, students see that good writing often starts out of emotion. Further, this tactic shows how you as an instructor actively discourage currying favor in trade for an authentic sharing of ideas. You may even find yourself saying, "Yeah, I hated that one too—what was I thinking of when I assigned it?" It is okay not to engage with every piece every single time.

Something else, however, can come from this. As students articulate their exclusion from or discomfort with some of the harder pieces, you can champion them a second time, saying in a new or clearer way just why the piece is so good. Part of this can be a claim of consensus, as you speak up on behalf of the academy, making the case for the value (and pleasure) of difficulty, for an unpopular opinion, or for an unexpected and perhaps even unconventional style. You may wish to share an experience you had with a once-foreign (but now beloved) text.

3. PUNCTUATION MAPS

This is a lesson in style and punctuation; it assumes that good writers vary punctuation and that beginning writers too often do not. It serves the function of an X-ray, revealing the hidden structure of external features.

Pick an entry with jazzy writing such as those by Joan Didion, David Foster Wallace, or Tom Wolfe. It does not matter if it was recent homework or not, though that helps. Pick a paragraph from the essay that uses a wide variety of punctuation marks. Have the class turn to it. The students are going to make an individual list of each sentence from that paragraph, either on scratch paper, the board, or in their journals. (This is a solo rather than a group activity.) Do the first sentence or two as demonstration, then have students finish the paragraph(s) on their own.

For every word in the sample sentence, students draw a little underline mark, as a visual place marker to show the number of words in a row. Punctuation, wherever it occurs, is written in as what it is (a comma is a comma), but circled, so that it stands out from the little place marker lines. At the end of the sentence, write down the number of words in the sentence. Sentence two gets listed separately below the first (like an item on a grocery list), and so on, through a paragraph or two. When finished, you have a visual portrayal of short and long sentences, and a vivid example of how many marks of punctuation a good writer typically uses. If you have time, you could then have students map out their (often short, often repetitive) sentences for comparison.

Wallace's "Lobster" essay would look like this if we mapped out his first three sentences:

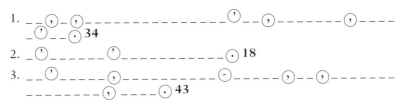

If at some point you start talking about whether a hyphenated word counts as one unit or two or if superscript numbers are punctuation, *great*—now the class is finally looking at language as active writers, not passive readers.

4. STRUCTURE MAPS

This replicates the above idea for paragraphs.

Using a short but varied essay, one whose structure may include intentional space breaks but which definitely has some long paragraphs as well, have students in their journals or scratch pages make a pictorial representation of the number of sentences per paragraph, diagramming a whole essay. Each sentence is a wide line, drawn without words—just one line per sentence. If a paragraph has ten sentences, then on the page there is a horizontal row of ten lines. It may work better if students draw a little cartoon box around each completed paragraph, to show how many there are in the essay and if (and when) short transition paragraphs follow longer, more substantive ones. Again, you can follow this up by asking them to map their own final drafts, which typically have short, mono-length paragraphs. This reminds them to see *The Norton Reader* not only as a repository of ideas but also as a collection of fairly blatant examples of how writing is done.

5. VOCABULARY: MAKING UP NEW MEANINGS

Encouraging responsibility for active reading and yet having fun, this quick, playful exercise gets students talking about context and word origins.

Pick an essay with advanced vocabulary and ask students to make a list of every word on a page (or two pages) whose exact meaning they are not sure of. Good essays to look at are those by Susan Sontag, Vladimir Nabokov, or Thomas Kuhn. This is a penalty-free lesson: no threats, no chastising, we just want students to be honest and engaged, and to list everything they should have looked up but did not. Students then write out definitions for what they think their words *should* mean, guessing and inventing as wildly as they wish. (You may start this with a few extravagant definitions on the board.)

They read their results aloud, with the usual positive feedback from you, but at the end of the discussion, for each new word you see whether anybody knows the true meaning, and also if anybody can find what linguistic or contextual clues would push us toward the correct definition. It is okay to laugh and make this fun since some of the guessed definitions may be way out there, but the final emphasis is on students' need to be responsible, as writers, for actively expanding their control of the language. A fair question to ask is, why *don't* they know these words, and what do they plan to do to make sure that they learn them, sooner rather than later.

6. CANDLES

Warning: this works better if you have tenure.

Many newer teachers are untenured or adjunct so they cannot take many risks. If, however, you feel secure in your job and if you can afford to pick up a box or two of votive candles on sale, and if you teach in rooms with some storage bins somewhere, it can be fun to stash away a box of candles and some matches.

The Norton Reader's texts vary from the clinical to the personal, and some are easier to teach in a class setting than others. The things we love best can be the hardest to share. Especially tricky are the things with the most heart and soul (such as Maya Angelou, N. Scott Momaday, and maybe a supplemental handout on Emily Dickinson). If this has been your experience, one hitch could be the setting. Fluorescent lights ruin many things, but are especially lethal to fashion photography, romantic dinners, and reading moving essays.

Try shutting the blinds, handing out candles, and reading the text (you aloud, them silently) by candlelight. The room has a warmth and a hush many students have never experienced before, at least not in the context of letting language work right, and, so long as nothing catches on fire, you may find that this becomes one of the most memorable lessons of the term. Students enjoy feeling like they are breaking the rules, so doing something like this makes you all collaborators, conspiring to do something ever so slightly illicit. As they bond with you and themselves, they take ownership of the texts in new ways.

7. POSTCARDS

This is about making abstract ideas tangible, and also about claims and evidence.

Postcards are cheap, and almost every art museum has a batch of surplus stock marked down. Collect a class set of at least ten nonrepresentational images, or, if you do not have any cards on hand, before class you can xerox some or scan images from books. Divide the class into small groups and give each group one abstract postcard.

Their task is to find the matching essay in *The Norton Reader* that "is" that card—because of its passion (red), because of its transitions (starts out blue, ends up green), because of its surprise (the more you look, the more is revealed), or whatever. This will not be easy, and by design, it is not supposed to be. A smart aleck may come up with some intentionally off-the-wall reason, parodying, perhaps, pretentious art criticism. If so, so much the better—parodies often have great energy, and if we can let students spoof formal discourse, that is a good discussion point, too. It does not matter what connections they make between the postcard and the essay, so long as they come up with an assertion and have at least some evidence to support it. Process here matters far more than product.

If your campus has an art gallery, maybe precede this lesson (the same day or a day or two prior) with a tour of that space, wherein students write their impressions of whatever is on exhibit and perhaps receive a reasonably informed discussion of a work or two, either from you or a gallery docent.

8. THE OPENING-LINES POEM

Launching essays and creating found texts: two lessons in one.

Great opening lines fill *The Norton Reader*, the kinds of first sentences that may well make you yourself think, "I wish I had written that!"

Alone or in groups, students go through the book, writing down five or ten opening sentences that grab them, whether they know the essay or not. (How many they pick depends on time available. More is better.) Once they have done that, and once a few are shared aloud, they get the next instructions. It is important that they do not know these at first. Using what they have so far, alone or in groups they reorder the sentences into lines, to make a found poem. After a few minutes, they read the results out loud.

Juxtapositions may be profound or silly, but in each instance, new contexts create new meanings, which is always a good lesson to reinforce. More important though is to look at the drama and power of a great introduction—good writing draws us in, while weak writing does not, and which one they create is a choice they unconsciously or consciously make. We ask students to make a poem from opening lines not to learn about poetry (though that can be important), but as a way of staying longer with their original selections, which are powerful models.

9. SIGNAL PHRASES

Paying attention to connectors.

When working with argument, put students into small groups and ask them to highlight all the signal words and transition phrases (e.g., furthermore, next, on the one hand, first) they can find in a specific page. (Maybe give the groups different source pages.) Make a list of all such words and phrases and then discuss how they help readers follow the reading. Discuss which they might adopt in their own writing. You probably will need to do this lesson more than once. This helps students learn the ways writers guide us through their essays without numbers or bullet points.

10. PLANS FOR IMPROVEMENT

Paying attention to suggestions and examples.

Unlike the other suggestions in this section, this activity should come on a specific day, though with some modification, you can do a similar exercise on any day. The purpose of this assignment in either incarnation is to help students slow down, reflect, and make a plan for improving their writing.

Sometimes students are in such a rush that they fail to read and reflect on the comments and suggestions you and their classmates have made on their work. On a day that you hand back drafts you've reviewed or a day when you've reserved time for peer review, ask students to take the last ten minutes of class to look over and think about the comments others have made on their papers and to make a plan for revision. Ten minutes may not be enough time to draft a full plan for revision, but it will help students begin the process, and it ensures that they have at least read the suggestions you or their classmates have made.

Alternatively, here's an exercise for any class period. You can ask students to reflect on their own writing in the context of essays they've read for class (essays in *The Norton Reader* and ones their peers have written). Ask them to brainstorm two lists: one of what they're already doing well in their writing and a second for areas they wish to improve. See if they can link these lists to essays they've read. Perhaps, like E. B. White, a student is good at including sensory details in an essay, but maybe that student wants to work on varying sentence length, which is something E. B. White's "Once More to the Lake" effectively illustrates. You can do this exercise, too, and share your own strengths as a writer—and elements you want to work on—and show how your reading helps make you aware of ways you can improve.

Ten 30-Minute Things to Do in Class with *The Norton Reader*

The previous class projects were meant to be quick, fun, and "doable" without much advance planning. This second list contains suggestions that in a few cases require you to know in advance what day the activity will fall on. Just as the previous list of ten could be expanded outward to last longer than ten minutes, the following ten lessons often can be trimmed down to fifteen or twenty minutes if that is all the period has left, or if your students get the point straightaway.

A note here on conventions. Both sets of offerings assume that your typical core discussions explore the ideas presented in *The Norton Reader* readings, as well as the rhetorical moves used to present those ideas. This section and the previous one build on that method by providing ways to change the pace and tone of class discussions, as well as activities aimed directly at producing better student writing.

As said elsewhere in this guide, let us hear about what works, what does not work, and what you have discovered that does these same moves even better. While we may not live in Dr. Pangloss's best of all possible worlds, we do at least live in a world where writing teachers can help one another out. What is exciting is how often—and how productively—we get to do so. Please let us hear from you.

1. SUMMARY VERSUS ANALYSIS

A way to address a common problem in beginning college writing. Often needs to be done more than once per term.

At the beginning of class, ask students to review the reading they did for that day. For each reading they've done, ask students to divide a notebook page in half vertically. On the left side, they write an objective, noninterpretive summary of each essay. Facing it, on the other side, they provide some kind of analysis or commentary, also one entry per original text. When most of the class has done it, they share them in groups or as a class, with you making clear (multiple times) the necessary distinction between mere summary and productive, intellectually rigorous analysis.

2. MLA WORKSHOP

Hands-on and in-class, this is an easy way to review correct citation format. It especially helps kinesthetic learners.

On a day when students already have read about MLA (or APA) format for homework or had previous session work in citation, bring to class four or five book bags of reference materials, plus some sticky notes. Divide the class into teams. Each team gets a book bag, which has in it a range of hard-copy materials one might cite from: a scholarly journal, a popular magazine, an edited collection, an Internet printout, and so on. (Bags are each similar in their mixes.) As a team they are to come up with an alphabetical, correctly formatted works cited page. If any other textbooks or novels are required in class as well, include those in the project. This is open-book and collaborative.

3. SOUND TRACKS AND THEME SONGS

Music and literature—new ways to revisit the old idea of thesis and audience.

Ask (without musical prompts) students to write about their favorite movies and TV shows, focusing on the kinds of music those programs rely on. This part of the exercise can be linked to a discussion of the music from *The Godfather* or *Star Wars,* for example, and how those audio riffs have become cultural icons. In any case, your own musical tastes should become public, since this is a good chance to humanize the classroom as we all share our likes and dislikes. The working subtitle of this lesson could be, "From punk to polka to Prokofiev."

Next, you take an essay from *The Norton Reader* and explain how you would set it to music if you were scoring the piece's accompanying sound track in relation to meaning and style. Do this in class, with actual music, showing how the theme of an essay can be reinforced, counterpointed, or undercut if accompanied by one kind of musical effect versus another. The class needs to know the basic essay you are illuminating, so stick to assigned readings.

Third, students work alone or in groups to come up with their own sound tracks for other essays in the *Reader.* This can be verbal ("I would use that song by Eminem, how does it go?") or students could be allowed to play a song on *YouTube* or another site. (External speakers with a cord or Bluetooth technology would be good to have on hand for this lesson.) All that matters is (a) that each claim is backed up with a legitimate reason for the music's inclusion, and (b) that students take ownership of the intellectual process of analysis and support. A small note of caution—if your classroom's walls are thin, try not to be so exuberant that you disrupt the midterm next door.

4. DRAWING A RIVER OF ANCESTORS

Personal narratives made better by encouraging detail and image.

While *The Norton Reader* has a lot of variety, the front third in particular allows for personal reflection and provides good models in the sections on personal accounts, profiles, and so on. Still, student responses in their own personal narratives can be tepid, generic, undeveloped. As a way of encouraging metaphor and image in their descriptions, try this.

Students take out a scratch page and on it they have to draw all the members of their family, using whatever definition of "family" (uncle, stepdad, baby sister, whatever) feels right. Stick figures are discouraged, as is much narrative labeling. (A few labels are okay.) Tell them, if your mom is a multitasker, doing a zillion things at once, maybe she can have octopus arms, each with its own wristwatch. Dad the cook of the family? He gets the giant spatula. Is brother a couch potato? Spuds it is then—and so on. They probably will resist, insisting they cannot draw. (Even ones who *can* draw will say this.) Ignore the resistance. This lesson is not about drawing, it is about finding a specific trait to embody as an image. Give them a few minutes to draw their family. When most have finished, put them in groups, have them share. From there, ask the group to nominate a few examples to share with the whole class. As a general rule, people love talking about their families (more than they think they will), and other students are often very interested in hearing family stories. This is a good icebreaker to build up some shared *esprit de corps* early in the term. One follow-up can be some ungraded writing, trying to capture one of the family members vividly in words, now that the pre-visualization exercise has revealed specific character traits. If nothing else, they have a better appreciation of their classmates as people.

5. LONG-LOST COUSINS

Hidden connections from text to text, asserted and defended.

Chug, chug, clunk, clunk: comparison/contrast is a quick default mode for beginning writers, and as a mode, probably has been over-assigned (and under-taught) in your students' earlier writing careers. Even so, there is some mileage left in that rusty beater yet.

Students in this case select and compare two pieces from *The Norton Reader*, explaining how the texts are seemingly disparate yet in actuality are long-lost cousins. Least interesting is to match subject matter; rather, insist on a deeper analysis. For example, David Foster Wallace's "Consider the Lobster" pairs up with Scott McCloud's "Understanding Comics" because both take a fresh look at an overlooked topic. Alternatively, McCloud's subterranean connection is not to any of the pop culture writers like Tom Wolfe but to Gloria Naylor, whose essay on the N-word reveals the horror (and lethality) of caricatures and tag words. Racism is cartoon thinking, but a cartoon with insidious power, power that in turn can be fought in simple, declarative sentences, such as those Thomas Jefferson uses or the ones driving Sallie Tisdale's essay.

Convergence might be based on similarity of style, on parallel rhetorical and structural moves, or even just on a certain buoyancy the piece creates in the reader—as before, what matters is claim and support less than one particular right answer. To ensure that we move beyond the surface connections of similar subject matters ("these two match because they both are about animals"), you might insist that the two paired pieces come from at least fifty pages apart in the book.

6. MAGAZINE COLLAGES

Glue stick time, as ideas are coaxed into manifesting themselves visually.

Unless you are a Blake scholar or a film studies major, your academic training (like that of the rest of us) was probably based on close readings of dense and un-illustrated texts. Our casual reading, however, often is highly charged with visual illustration. Even the *New Yorker* features top drawer photography to accompany its profiles, and most academic journals incorporate visuals—from cover art to pull quotes, from graphs to photographs. This lesson lets public practice and private reading collide.

Warned in advance to do so, students arrive in class with glue sticks, back issues of magazines, scissors, and a journal or blank paper. Some will probably forget, but usually there are enough supplies to go around if people share. It may look and feel like something from grade school. That is fine and even preferred. Their task? To illustrate an essay.

You either can assign all the class the same reading from *The Norton Reader* or let students pick individual choices, but in the style of Sunday insert magazines and book reviews everywhere, they have to craft some combination of word and image into a collage that captures—at a glance—the essence of their assigned reading. Bring samples if you worry this will not be immediately obvious, looking, for example, at all the ways *Outside* magazine tries to enliven its pages (and to position itself as an edgier publication, for instance, than *National Geographic*).

Your job is to circulate with the trash can, provide lavish praise, and to broker trades—"anybody here have a really big picture of bright green lips? Jamie needs them for her collage but has finished with this issue of *Cosmo*, if you want some fashion ads." After half an hour or so, discuss the results, looking especially for interpretations that capture the essay's essence most convincingly.

7 · INTRODUCING A WRITING ASSIGNMENT

Connecting reading and writing.

Ideally, each writing assignment you give should be connected to the reading students do for class—and not just because of the topic. That is, you should be able to point to both connections and disjunctions between the writing professionals do and the writing you expect students to do. When you introduce a new writing assignment, choose at least three essays students have read from *The Norton Reader* that serve—in some ways—as models. Does the essay you've chosen demonstrate an effective use of evidence? Does the author provide and answer counterarguments? Which essays include model thesis statements?

Often, a piece of professional writing does not include all the elements you require from students. For example, essays and articles written for many magazines and most newspapers do not include citations. If you expect students to use citations according to a particular format, such as MLA, mention that. The fourteenth edition makes it even easier to do so now that an MLA citation appears at the end of each reading.

Also note differences in required length. The essays students read may be longer or shorter than the ones you assign. You can use this difference to explain how to expand or contract writing, depending on purpose and audience. A 500-word op-ed piece (roughly two double-spaced word-processed pages) might provide a good model for introducing a topic and making a claim, but a student's 1,000-word argument can include more evidence and support—and a works cited page.

As you compare and contrast what other writers have done to what you expect students to do, you can explain academic conventions and help students see how purpose, audience, context, and constraints shape writing. This exercise is one you can repeat throughout the term. After the first time, you can ask students to do the work of comparing and contrasting.

8. PULL QUOTES AND FOOTNOTES

Finding key moments in good writing by using the tricks of modern layout and design.

Many national magazines contain lurid blurbs on their covers and lay out text inside with overlapping color fields and enlarged phrases from the story, usually called pull quotes. Even academic journals use sidebars and other intra-text insertions. Separate from that trend, textbooks that anthologize identical plays by Shakespeare or poems by T. S. Eliot differ widely in how many allusions or tough diction choices they footnote. Each choice creates a different effect.

In this project, students, alone or in groups, are assigned an essay that they have to re-typeset, deciding which sentences would make great stand-alone quotations, and which words (if any) need additional footnoting. This is hypothetical—they are not cutting apart their books or drawing in the margins. They are, however, trying to find key moments in the text in question where all the argument can be summed up in one logical and fair (if slightly elided) pull quote. That the original author would be horrified to be so reduced is not our concern—just wait until the marketing department has finished working over Henry David Thoreau!—so long as issues of audience, summary, and thesis can be explored and made real. You may need to hold up some examples first to make students' tasks more obvious.

9. CLOSE READING

Good writers need to be good readers, and focusing on craft links both.

Pick a short passage from a particularly densely written essay and ask students to list everything they notice in the passage. Get them to focus on the language of the passage. As you let them brainstorm, you can interrupt, reminding them of categories of things to notice (punctuation, imagery, sentence length and structure, vocabulary). Put a sampling of these observations on the board, again, categorizing their observations as seems useful.

Now, ask them to return to the same passage and brainstorm how it makes them feel. This time, ask them to list their emotional responses to both the experience of reading (I love the description here) and the topic of the passage (the story makes me sad for the narrator). Again, put a sampling of these on the board.

Finally, discuss what choices on the part of the writer helped to create the feelings that students felt. Help students see that all the emotions they had emerged from a collection of black marks on a page. That's the writer's power.

And their power as writers about prose lies in their ability to write "the author's vivid description of the burnt patch on the lawn contributes to the essay's overwhelming sense of sadness."

10. NEW COVERS FOR THE NEXT EDITION

Authors revise work extensively, and even textbooks grow and change. A lesson here on the relationship between form and content, indirectly linked to semiotics.

We end with something that may sound like a concern from an art and design seminar or a class in marketing but actually represents applied analysis. Start the session off with students alone or in teams writing about what they think the cover of *The Norton Reader*, fourteenth edition, "means." If we assume that art—like music or poetry or the graffiti on a bridge—has a theme, and if we assume further that the publishers of a book promote an overall message or thematic concern with their cover art, then what does this edition's cover mean? Do this quickly, maybe five minutes, and if it is not catching on, either do it aloud or move on. After discussing the current cover, next form small groups (or keep the existing pairs) and hand out either a stack of art museum postcards (see previous section) or some old art, photography, or *Photoshop* magazines. With advance warning, students could be asked to bring these in; you just need a mix of jazzy, high-impact artworks in any genre that is not overtly porno-graphic. They then pick out what should go on the next cover, explaining why either verbally or in writing. What does it mean to "read," to be a reader, to collect great work in one place? To them, is this another version of the five-foot-shelf, dusty classics forced on them like a dose of cod liver oil? Or is reading more like a snowboard exploding through waist-deep powder, ideas as fresh and bracing as winter air? From the rhetoric of war to wedding vows to anti-drug campaigns, we live and die by metaphors. What metaphor or symbol best represents the writing in this book?

PART II

THE READINGS

Personal Accounts

Joan Didion

On Going Home

Full Edition, p. 1; Shorter Edition, p. 1

In this short essay (of six paragraphs) Joan Didion describes returning to her family's home to celebrate her daughter's first birthday. Her husband remains in Los Angeles, while she reenters the world of her father, mother, brother, and great-aunts. "On Going Home" proceeds by association: one experience reminds her of another, one question leads to another. What is "home"? Can you go home again? How does memory work to connect past and present, one home with another? Didion's essay links past and present by shifting incessantly back and forth between them. If you also teach Chang-rae Lee's "Coming Home Again" (FE p. 3) and discuss his use of a recursive style, you might also want to outline or construct a flowchart for Didion's essay, and discuss how and why Didion moves from one experience to another.

Questions from *The Norton Reader*

1. Joan Didion speaks of herself at home as "paralyzed by the neurotic lassitude engendered by meeting one's past at every turn" (paragraph 3). What about the essay helps explain these feelings?

2. Consider the metaphors Didion uses to describe the relationship she has with her family (for example, "guerrilla warfare" in paragraph 3), and the body language she uses to describe interactions with family members (for example, "My mother shrugs" in paragraph 4). Based on your analysis of Didion's use of language, how would you characterize her family relationships?

3. In paragraph 6 Didion says she would like to give her daughter "*home* for her birthday, but we live differently now." In an essay, explain whether or not you think parents today can give their children "home." Include examples to support your argument.

Teaching Suggestions

1. How does the "vital although troublesome distinction" (paragraph 1) between home as the place where Didion lives with her husband and baby in Los Angeles and home as the place where her family lives in the Central Valley of California thread through "On Going Home"?

2. Ask students to look closely at "On Going Home" as an essay developed by association and, in particular, at how Didion maintains the illusion of free

association while behaving responsibly toward her readers. She is careful to do two things: to let us know where in time she is, particularly with respect to present and past, and to provide thematic coherence. For the first, you might ask students to look at transitions between paragraphs and then within them; for the second, ask them to elucidate the several concerns that run through the essay.

3. Look at Didion's "On Keeping a Notebook" (FE p. 487) in conjunction with "On Going Home" with respect to their development and rhetorical techniques. How do objects function in them? How do images function?

4. Consider the titles of both essays—"On Keeping a Notebook," "On Going Home." What does "on" followed by a participle serve to suggest about the kind of essay each will be?

SUGGESTED WRITING ASSIGNMENTS

1. Write a personal essay developed by associations radiating out from a return to a place. Give it a title beginning with "On," followed by a participle (a verb ending in "-ing").

2. One technique Didion uses is to organize her associations around objects. Write a personal essay in which you focus on objects. Attend to maintaining the illusion of free association while providing thematic coherence.

3. Read another essay about coming back to one's parents' house as an adult (Chang-rae Lee's "Coming Home Again" [FE p. 3] or N. Scott Momaday's "The Way to Rainy Mountain" [FE p. 136]), and write an essay comparing the attitudes toward home expressed in each essay.

CHANG-RAE LEE
Coming Home Again

Full Edition, p. 3

Korean American novelist Chang-rae Lee graduated from Yale in 1988 and received his MFA in 1995 from the University of Oregon, where he taught writing. His first novel, *Native Speaker* (1995), won the PEN/Faulkner Award; his second novel, *A Gesture Life* (1999), won the Anisfield-Wolf Literary Award and was a finalist for the *New Yorker* Book Award. He currently teaches creative writing at Princeton University, and has recently published *The Surrendered* (2010), a novel about the aftereffects of the Korean War.

In this essay, Lee describes his mother cooking for her family and trading cooking lessons with an American suburban mom: macaroni and cheese for *kimchi*. Lee is accepting of his own and his mother's desire to fit in, and is fond of the woman who was their friend. The center of the essay, however, describes how he cooked Korean dishes for his family when his mother was too ill with cancer to do so, and thus it focuses on the importance of his Korean heritage at a time of crisis. There is a lot to admire and discuss here: a version of multiculturalism that accepts (and embraces) it as fact, a story about the pain of leaving home for boarding school (Exeter), and a son who cooks, thus both satisfying his family's commitment to tradition and disappointing its ambitions for a *son*.

Students will immediately grasp the gentle irony of calling macaroni and cheese "exotic." This can be the springboard for a larger discussion of the symbolic importance of food—a central theme in Lee's essay. Food means one set of things within Lee's family and another when he compares his family to mainstream America (Mrs. Churchill, dorm food at boarding school). You might begin the discussion by asking students to list the meanings of food in each context and compare them. Does food and cooking mean the same thing to each member of Lee's family? What role does it seem to play in his parents' marriage?

QUESTIONS FROM *THE NORTON READER*

1. Because Chang-rae Lee begins his essay at a late stage of his mother's illness, he often flashes back to earlier points in their relationship. Mark the flashbacks in the text and explain the purpose of each.

2. Details of food and cooking appear throughout the essay—for example, in paragraphs 8–9, 11–13, and 32–36. Besides giving us a flavor of Korean food, what function do these details serve?

3. Lee titles his essay "Coming Home Again," whereas Joan Didion titles hers "On Going Home" (FE p. 1, SE p. 1). What different connotations do "coming home" and "going home" suggest? How do these differences emerge in the personal accounts of each writer?

4. Write a personal essay about "coming home" or "going home."

TEACHING SUGGESTIONS

1. In paragraph 8, Lee offers an intensely detailed description of his mother making *kalbi*, Korean short ribs. Analyze and discuss the language here. Could you make the dish based on his description? How is it different from a recipe, and why is it different? What do we learn about Lee and his mother from this description?

2. This essay moves back and forth among many moments in Lee's life. It may help students understand Lee's themes—and discern the overall point—if you make a paragraph outline on the board, listing the topic of each successive paragraph. Show them the way he dances from his boyhood to his departure for boarding school to his return home during his mother's final illness and back. Once they see his timeline and structure on the board, discuss Lee's choices. Why is this recursive style appropriate to an essay called "Coming Home Again"? What does it tell us about his attitude to the revelation that his mother regrets sending him away for high school?

3. Ask students to identify what, for them, is the turning point of the essay. Then ask them to justify their choice in a few sentences. Discussing their different choices and the reasons for them will help them clarify what they see as the essay's core: the mother's death, her regret at sending him off to school,

the lessons in Korean culture she offered through cooking, Lee's successful assimilation, or his reverence for his Korean heritage.

SUGGESTED WRITING ASSIGNMENTS

1. Write a short essay in which you pay tribute to a family member by describing the way she or he cooks. Aim for the kind of precise attention to method and ingredients that Lee exhibits here.

2. Read another essay about coming back to one's parents' house as an adult (Joan Didion's "On Going Home" [FE p. 1, SE p. 1] or N. Scott Momaday's "The Way to Rainy Mountain" [FE p. 136]), and write an essay comparing the attitudes in Didion's or Momaday's essay with Lee's.

ALISON BECHDEL

From *Fun Home*

Full Edition, p. 12

Graphic memoirist Alison Bechdel got her start writing the comic *Dykes to Watch Out For* (1983–2008), a serial strip about young women, many of them lesbians, in a college town, but it was the memoir *Fun Home: A Family Tragicomic* that brought her fame. In it, Bechdel describes growing up in the family funeral home (given the ironic nickname "fun home" by Bechdel and her siblings). Her memoir recounts two generations of coming to terms with sexual orientation: her father's life as a married man who secretly slept with men and Bechdel's own coming out. Additionally, Bechdel writes about her father's death, a probable suicide (he appears to have thrown himself in front of a truck). These events are foreshadowed in this excerpt. In 2015, the stage adaptation of Bechdel's story won five Tony Awards including Best Musical.

While the memoir goes into more detail about sex and sexuality as it progresses, this opening chapter focuses on young Alison's life, especially family secrets and the gap between the appearance of happiness and the reality of a cold, controlling father. Rarely has the tired old theme of appearance versus reality received such a stark, witty treatment and students may enjoy cataloging the many ironies and hypocrisies detailed here. *YouTube* has several video interviews with Bechdel, including some in which she describes her painstaking creative process (see the one on *MindTV35* from 2009). Watching these videos can help students see the care that goes into researching and drawing a strip.

QUESTIONS FROM *THE NORTON READER*

1. Alison Bechdel compares her father to both Daedalus and Icarus from Greek mythology. She also mentions Daedalus's Labyrinth and the Minotaur. Trace the references to the Daedalus and Icarus myths throughout. What is Bechdel trying to get across about her father by making these comparisons?

2. Consider Bechdel's use of foreshadowing. For example, in panel 4, she writes, ". . . it was not me but my father who was to plummet from the sky," and in panel 8 she states that her family was unusual, though she "wouldn't appreciate exactly how unusual until much later." What was her father's secret? Where does she reveal it?

3. In a graphic memoir, the images are as important as the words. What do you learn from Bechdel's images that you might not have picked up from her words?

4. Write a piece about a person or a place (or both). Like Bechdel, use allusions to myth or some other well-known story. If you are comfortable drawing, consider making your text a graphic essay.

Teaching Suggestions

1. Although students are steeped in images, they may have trouble analyzing them. Have students read Scott McCloud's "Understanding Comics" (FE p. 921, SE p. 537) and make a list of ways that images work. From that catalogue, analyze some of Bechdel's frames and pages: how is she using some of the tools that McCloud identifies to tell her story?

2. Bechdel's writing is as precise as her drawing. Help students see how she uses language to distinguish between her childhood and adult selves. In the second panel, for example, little Alison only says "OOF!" but the caption explains, "As he launched me, my full weight would fall on the pivot point between his feet and my stomach."

3. Review the story of Daedalus and Icarus with your students. (You may want to look at the story of the Labyrinth and the Minotaur as well as that of the waxen wings.) Discuss the ways in which it is a good metaphor for Alison's relationship with her father. Tease out the similarities and differences. What does the tragedy of Icarus's fatal fall suggest for Alison, who outlives her father?

Suggested Writing Assignments

1. Choose several panels—separate ones or several that work well together on a page—and write an essay analyzing the way image and word are interdependent.

2. Write an essay in which you use a myth or superhero story to describe an important relationship in your life. Be sure to consider how your story both is and is not like the archetype to which you compare it.

DAVID SEDARIS
Loggerheads

Full Edition, p. 34

Humorist David Sedaris is the author of over seven books and, with his sister Amy Sedaris, several plays. He uses satire to skewer euphemisms and conventional thinking of all kinds. One of his classic pieces, "Santaland Diaries," exposes the rules and regulations involved in working as a Christmas "elf" at Macy's Department Store. His affection for his large family is matched by his mockery for the unreflective traditions and arbitrary rules that govern childhood. Sedaris's personal website (www.davidsedarisbooks.com) has a rich archive of his radio appearances and reviews of his many books.

This essay contains Sedaris's characteristic humor, which often makes abrupt shifts in tone so that even mild profanity carries a shock, such as when Sedaris calls the receipt of a lei upon arriving in Hawaii "an Olympic medal for sitting on your ass" (paragraph 1). Such tonal shifts take finesse and students may enjoy identifying and experimenting with such shifts in their own personal essays, experiments that can become a good occasion to discuss diction, tone, and genre. Academic writing cannot always accommodate some of the play that Sedaris enjoys here. This essay uses humor for other more serious purposes, weaving together themes of childhood, environmentalism, sexual identity, race, class, and literacy. While students will likely take joy in the irreverence, it may be more challenging to get them to pause over the purpose of the humor.

Questions from *The Norton Reader*

1. David Sedaris writes about both childhood and more recent experiences with animals. How do those experiences differ? In what ways has his understanding of animals changed?

2. Sedaris considers both power and fear in this essay. For example, he recalls, "When I saw that he was afraid of me, I felt powerful" (paragraph 27). Look for other places in the essay where the themes of power and fear are present. How does Sedaris portray the relationship between power and fear throughout?

3. Write a personal essay that demonstrates the difference between your childhood and adult understanding of something or someone.

Teaching Suggestions

1. In addition to feeling wonder in the presence of the sea turtle, Sedaris wonders "that she could ever have forgiven me" (paragraph 5). Discuss his use of forgiveness in this context. What responsibility does he bear for his cruelty to the turtles years ago?

2. Deepen the discussion about fear and power by looking at how it operates in the various contexts of the story: Sedaris's feelings of powerlessness as a Scout may seem to contrast with the power he has over the men he encounters in the bathroom, but both situations are marked by his fear about his own sexuality in a homophobic world. Help students tease out this strand and then discuss the ways in which these themes intersect with and complicate the stories of fear, tenderness, and power surrounding animals.

3. Sedaris is a frequent guest on National Public Radio (npr.org), known and immediately recognizable for his distinctive, expressive voice. Listen to him (his pieces on Billie Holiday—"Music Lessons"—or his time working as a

Christmas elf—"Santaland Diaries"—are classics) in class and discuss what hearing his voice adds to his storytelling.

Suggested Writing Assignments

1. Sedaris's essay describes multiple secrets. Write a brief essay analyzing these secrets, using them to make an argument about when secrets are appropriate to keep and when—and with whom—they are important to share.

2. Write an essay that incorporates a series of memories of your childhood encounters with animals—including pets, wild animals, and even stuffed animals.

3. Record a personal essay as a podcast. It can be one of your own or someone else's, but choose one that includes both humorous moments and a larger, serious point. Write a brief reflection on what you were trying to convey in your performance: what parts of the essay were most challenging to get right?

Zora Neale Hurston
How It Feels to Be Colored Me

Full Edition, p. 42

For many years Zora Neale Hurston was regarded by members of the African American literary community as someone whose works could not be taken seriously or even discussed. (And of course during that time she, like the vast majority of African American writers, was completely ignored by most white readers and critics.) In the past two decades Hurston's works have been revived, her biography written, and her status as a major American writer achieved. This essay provides an interesting insight into the ups and downs of Hurston's changing reputation. Perhaps she plays with the stereotypes too much; perhaps she makes "proper" or highly political people in the black community uncomfortable. At the same time, there's a spirit conveyed in the essay, a sense of life that shines as a beacon to writers so that they can feel comfortable in being different, and particularly to those proud of their African American identity. (A major force behind Hurston's revival was the African American writer Alice Walker, who became interested in Hurston's feminism and edited some of Hurston's out-of-print works.)

In paragraph 7 Hurston turns her back on the legacy of slavery—or at least claims to. In paragraph 14 she literally steps into the Harlem Renaissance, that outpouring of poetry, fiction, and music that influenced so much of both black and white America in the 1920s. Hurston is proud and defiant, exulting in the freedom she believes the times have granted her. As a black woman in 1920s America, she feels triumphant. One question for students might be, how much of Hurston's triumph is genuine and how much is bravado, like whistling in a graveyard? It is useful to point out the extent to which Hurston's joy and anticipation are connected with place. She is happiest in Eatonville, the town of her African American family home in Florida, and in Harlem, surrounded by black Americans in a time of prosperity and the building of a genuine community. She feels most uncomfortable at Barnard, where she is overwhelmed by "the thousand white persons" (paragraph 10). (Note that Barnard is just less than a mile from Seventh Avenue and 125th Street, the center of Harlem.) A careful reading reveals that Hurston is fully aware that she can be herself only where other black Americans are free. She is quite aware of discrimination (paragraph 16) even if she says it doesn't bother her.

Questions from *The Norton Reader*

1. From the beginning Zora Neale Hurston startles us: "I remember the very day that I became colored" (paragraph 2). Why does Hurston insist that one *becomes* colored? What happened on that day to make her so?

2. Each section of Hurston's essay explores a different possible identity, some based on skin color, others emphasizing history, culture, or gender. What does Hurston accomplish by such an approach?

3. The final paragraph introduces a key simile: "like a brown bag of miscellany propped against a wall." How does Hurston develop this simile? What does she mean by it?

4. Like Nancy Mairs in "On Being a Cripple" (FE p. 64), Hurston chooses a label, "colored me," to explore questions of personal identity. Compare Hurston's use of "colored" with Mairs's use of "cripple."

Teaching Suggestions

1. In what sense is Hurston's manifesto a product of the optimism that characterized the boom years of the 1920s? (President Hoover promised, for instance, "A chicken in every pot, two cars in every garage.")

2. Try to pin down Hurston's tone. What kind of persona does she convey in this essay? Students will need to know that she was an accomplished novelist and writer who knew very well how to achieve an effect. In other words, she was consciously aiming to present herself in a particular way. The question is, exactly what way is that?

3. How do metaphors help Hurston articulate her sense of self? See, e.g., paragraphs 10, 14, 15, 17.

Suggested Writing Assignments

1. Write an essay that connects Hurston's outlook in the 1920s with Alice Walker's in "Beauty: When the Other Dancer Is the Self" in the 1980s (FE p. 74, SE p. 22) and Henry Louis Gates Jr.'s in "In the Kitchen" in the 1990s (FE p. 245, SE p. 135). In what ways does Hurston's attitude toward race and participation in American society anticipate Walker's and Gates's essays? In what ways does she differ?

2. Walker and Gates are great admirers of Hurston and have been instrumental in reviving her reputation. Write an essay that explains what in Hurston's

work might have made Gates and Walker such admirers, using their own accounts of African American life as evidence.

3. Write a Hurston-like essay, using a personal characteristic that some might view as a liability and treating it as an asset. Suggestions: short or tall, heavy or thin, from the "wrong" part of town (or the "wrong" state), Greek or independent, interested in a particular kind of art or music, or dressing in a way that stands out.

MAYA ANGELOU
Graduation

Full Edition, p. 45; Shorter Edition, p. 4

Maya Angelou's "Graduation," taken from the first volume of her autobiography, *I Know Why the Caged Bird Sings* (1969), focuses on a single, significant event: her graduation from eighth grade in Stamps, Arkansas, in 1940. The essay is organized chronologically. Angelou begins with the town's, her family's, and her own preparation for graduation; describes the excitement and anticipation of the event; and ends with the ceremony itself, particularly the speech of the white politician that deflates the expectations of young blacks in the audience. Chronology is a natural ordering for autobiographical narrative and, in Angelou's hands, an effective one. You might ask students to look at the "real" time and the "fictional" time in "Graduation"; the "real" time of events leading up to the ceremony is compressed in relation to the "real" time of the ceremony itself, or, conversely, the "fictional" time of the ceremony is extended with description, dialogue, and the young Angelou's own responses.

Chronological narrative is a form that students can handle well, provided they see that "real" time is malleable and in their control. This genre also offers students opportunities for significant reflection on their experiences. The events of "Graduation" are told in the narrative voice that belongs to the mature Angelou looking back in 1969 at something that happened almost thirty years earlier. Like Alice Walker in "Beauty: When the Other Dancer Is the Self" (FE p. 74, SE p. 22), Angelou uses adult language but maintains the perspective of a twelve-year-old. Students may need to be reminded of events between 1940 and 1969, notably the Supreme Court's school-desegregation decision of 1954 that abolished "separate but equal" black and white schools in places like Stamps. One argument against segregated education was that it disadvantaged black children. Although the mature Angelou's sense of being disadvantaged undoubtedly differs from that of the young Angelou, in "Graduation" she re-creates the sense of her young self.

QUESTIONS FROM *THE NORTON READER*

1. Presumably, all of Maya Angelou's readers would have witnessed a graduation ceremony and brought their memories to her essay. How does she

fulfill the reader's expectations for what graduation includes? How does she surprise us with details we may not expect?

2. In paragraph 43 Angelou writes that "the ancient tragedy was being replayed." What does she mean? How does her essay help to resist the tragic script?

3. Write a personal essay about an event you anticipated hopefully but that did not fulfill your expectations, incorporating an explanation of your disappointment into your account, as Angelou does.

Teaching Suggestions

1. Ask students to examine the structure of "Graduation" and diagram the relation of "real" to "fictional" time. How can we measure "real" time? How can we measure "fictional" time?

2. Alternatively, ask students to examine the structure of the essay in terms of "anticipation" and "fulfillment" or "reality." How does Angelou build the readers' sense of anticipation? How does she convey the disappointment she and her fellow students felt?

3. What information does "Graduation" offer about the elementary-school education of black students in Stamps? To what extent was it vocational? To what extent were they "tracked"?

4. In paragraphs 33 through 49, Angelou recounts the speech that Edward Donleavy, a white man running for political office in Stamps, gave at her graduation ceremony. How does Angelou convey both the racist assumptions of the speech and her own better-informed sense of black history?

5. How does Angelou use the valedictory address of Henry Reed to rebut Donleavy's speech and to convey her own determination to be "a proud member of the wonderful, beautiful Negro race" (paragraph 61)?

Suggested Writing Assignments

1. Write a retrospective account of an important event that occurred when you were young. Use adult language but maintain the perspective of a child; manipulate "real" and "fictional" time.

2. Using the content of Angelou's narrative to illustrate and support your points, write an argumentative essay against tracking students who are different by virtue of race, gender, ethnicity, or national origin.

Lars Eighner
On Dumpster Diving
Full Editon, p. 55; Shorter Edition, p. 13

Originally written as a separate essay, "On Dumpster Diving" later appeared in Lars Eighner's first book, *Travels with Lizbeth* (1993). It gives an account of the time he spent homeless, getting much of what he needed from what people threw away in Dumpsters. Eighner's essay has five parts: (1) a brief introduction (paragraphs 1 to 6) about words: the derivation of "Dumpster," the appropriateness of scavenging or foraging; (2) the inevitable question, as if posed by an imaginary interlocutor: "What is safe to eat?" (paragraphs 7 to 30); (3) a chronology of his own Dumpster diving, from beginning to scavenge to making the rounds of Dumpsters, with a concluding disquisition on what is wrong with can scroungers (paragraphs 31 to 48); (4) an examination of items found in Dumpsters (paragraphs 49 to 59); and (5) a philosophical conclusion that meditates on a throwaway society (paragraphs 60 to 68). Building on the first question in *The Norton Reader*, you might want to discuss why Eighner begins and ends where he does, and how he moves from description to social analysis.

QUESTIONS FROM *THE NORTON READER*

1. How does Lars Eighner organize his essay? What might such an organization imply?

2. Eighner's simple, understated tone suggests that anyone can adapt to Dumpster diving with a little practice. Why do you think he uses such a tone?

3. Write about someone who, as Eighner criticizes in his closing paragraphs, "invests objects with sentimental value" (paragraph 65). Let your description reveal whether or not you agree with Eighner.

TEACHING SUGGESTIONS

1. It's useful to ask about the idea of recycling. Is Eighner an example of "creative reuse"? Brainstorm a broad list of recycling, upcycling, and creative reuse practices and discuss the ethics and the palatability of each. Some students may have made "finds" of their own, appropriating items of furniture or clothing that have been used before. Ask them to discuss the pros and cons of such a practice. Would they "reuse" a mattress? a pair of shoes? Underwear? a couch? Where would they draw the line?

2. Ask students to speculate on why Eighner doesn't tell what made him homeless or precisely what made him begin raiding Dumpsters. How would mentioning the causes of his scavenging alter the essay?

3. Use this essay as an occasion to talk more broadly about homelessness, poverty, and the challenges of solving those problems. Does Eighner's essay suggest any new ways of addressing these larger social problems?

SUGGESTED WRITING ASSIGNMENTS

1. Invent a name for something you do (as Eighner did for Dumpster diving) and describe its hazards and rewards.

2. Write three to five paragraphs (serious or humorous) defining and discussing the appropriate term for something you do, modeling them on Eighner's discussion of the proper term for his activities.

3. Eighner researched the term "Dumpster." Do your own research on a trade name or the correct term for a well-known product (examples: "boysenberry," "Polaroid Land Camera," "Oldsmobile," "Bostitch stapler," "Birds Eye" frozen foods, "shrapnel"). Explain how you went about your research as well as what you found.

Nancy Mairs
On Being a Cripple
Full Edition, p. 64

Nancy Mairs has written extensively about disability, using her own experience as a starting point. This essay directly confronts her multiple sclerosis, beginning with a comic reflection on the relation of writing and disability. Thinking about writing the essay makes her lose track of her disability, yet forgetting causes an accident that makes her think again about writing. There's a wry message here: writing may make one a more acute observer, but it can make one lose sight of the real situation as well. (There's a story about the Greek astronomer Thales who was so busy looking at the stars that he lost track of his way and fell into a ditch.) You may want to use this essay not only to discuss how people come to terms with disabilities (or fail to) but also how writing helps us understand the predicaments we find ourselves in, the experiences we must live through, and the pasts we carry with us.

Questions from *The Norton Reader*

1. How does Nancy Mairs organize her essay? What connects the different parts to each other?

2. What stereotypes of "disabled" people does Mairs expect us to believe in? How does she set out to counter them?

3. Mairs deliberately chooses to call herself a "cripple." Select a person or group that deliberately chooses its own name or description and explain in an essay the rationale behind the choice.

Teaching Suggestions

1. Why is Mairs so concerned with terminology? Discuss the importance of naming or identifying with a specific term.

2. In the 1990s many people or groups willingly accepted terms that in earlier decades might have incensed them. Mairs calls herself a "cripple"; Henry Louis Gates Jr. titles his book *Colored People* (FE p. 245, SE p. 135); Eighner invents "Dumpster diving" (FE p. 55, SE p. 13). Back in the 1920s Zora Neale Hurston playfully dealt with "Colored Me" (FE p. 42). Gay people and literary critics speak of "queer theory." What do these acts of appropriation suggest? What is gained in taking a term once used in derision and proudly accepting or claiming it?

Suggested Writing Assignments

1. Use a collegiate dictionary to examine the differences among words like "cripple," "handicapped," and "disabled." Then have students ask three or four people what the terms mean to them. Ask students to use the results of their reading and the survey to write an essay about the nuances of such words.

2. Compare Mairs's attitude toward her impairment with JJ Goode's attitude toward his lack of an arm (FE p. 280, SE p. 150) or Eighner's attitude toward Dumpster diving (FE p. 55, SE p. 13). Write an essay in which you discuss the ways their essays and attitudes are alike.

ALICE WALKER
Beauty: When the Other Dancer Is the Self
Full Edition, p. 74; Shorter Edition, p. 22

Alice Walker writes about a wound she received in her eye when she was a child and its effect on her subsequent life. She chooses to write in the present, providing glimpses of separate moments from her life: before the accident, the years spent with a disfiguring white spot on her eye, after the spot was surgically removed. The perspective is extremely close up. We never see Walker's affliction in any way but through her understanding of it. In a sense this approach mimics Walker's actual attitude: she cannot get out of her own feelings, her own "take" on her wound. When her mother tells her that there was no difference in her behavior before or after the accident, she is shocked. For years what Walker thought of as the central event in her life—the "accident"—has made little impression on those closest to her.

The essay exists in a world where readers are expected to know certain words of wisdom: "Beauty is in the eye of the beholder" and "How can we know the dancer from the dance?" Significantly, it ends with Walker's persona dancing to the music of a blind musician, Stevie Wonder, and embracing "another bright-faced dancer"—herself. You might introduce these sayings in the course of discussion and ask students how Walker both illustrates and challenges them.

QUESTIONS FROM *THE NORTON READER*

1. From paragraph 12 onward, Alice Walker refers to the "accident." Why does she put the word in quotation marks? To what extent has Walker made peace with the "accident" and its consequences?

2. Walker writes her essay by selecting particular moments in her life. What are these moments and what do they tell us about Walker's theme?

3. What is the effect of ending the essay by recounting a dream? How does the dream relate to the essay's title?

4. Write an essay comparing and contrasting Walker's essay and Nancy Mairs's "On Being a Cripple" (FE p. 64). Consider especially the two authors' responses and attitudes toward injury or illness.

TEACHING SUGGESTIONS

1. What is the effect of using the present tense throughout?
2. How do the white spaces in Walker's essay help shape our reading of it?

3. This essay is about Walker "making peace" with the accident. To what extent is it also about making peace with other things? Is the accident some kind of metaphor, or by calling it one, do we diminish the impact it had on her life?

Suggested Writing Assignments

1. Take an event that helped shape your life, a "defining moment," and tell about it and its influence as a series of moments narrated in the present tense.

2. Read Annie Dillard's "Sight into Insight" (FE p. 978, SE p. 576) in connection with Walker's essay, and then write an essay of your own that addresses the way these two writers use different meanings of the word "see." You'll probably find yourself expanding on their notions, explaining what they're getting at, or agreeing or disagreeing with them.

Joey Franklin
Working at Wendy's

Full Edition, p. 80; Shorter Edition, p. 29

Joey Franklin's essay appeared in *Twentysomething Essays by Twentysomething Writers*, a collection of pieces by young writers, people largely unpublished. It's a highly personal account of his fairly recent experience at a fast-food restaurant, a position that may be quite familiar to more than a few college students. His neutral attitude toward his job is significant. He could easily have acted superior to the other workers at Wendy's or become embarrassed by his experience there. Instead, he seems to regard the job as perfectly normal, far from unusual, as indeed it has been for many young Americans. Since publishing his essay Franklin has received an M.A. from Ohio University and entered the Ph.D. program at Texas Tech University.

Students can immediately relate to Franklin's experience, and they can use his essay as a useful model for their own writing. Particularly, they can model some of their writing on Franklin's use of vignettes, short descriptions of his fellow workers. Franklin's essay also provides a nice introduction to narrating a story by using the historical present, a technique that most students will not have tried. It's worth discussing what he gains by employing the technique. Question 3 from *The Norton Reader*, below, directs students to a consideration of Franklin's use of the present.

Questions from *The Norton Reader*

1. What is Joey Franklin's attitude toward working at Wendy's? How does he demonstrate it? In answering these questions, look especially at the conclusion of the essay and at the details he chooses about how others respond to him.

2. Franklin uses considerable detail to develop his coworkers as characters (see paragraph 13 for an example). Which details do you find especially effective? Why?

3. Most of this essay is written in the present tense (with past-tense reflections about former jobs held by family members). What is the effect of Franklin's use of this verb tense? How would the essay differ if he wrote the entire essay in past tense?

4. Write an essay about a job you've held. Use dialogue and details to develop characters.

Teaching Suggestions

1. It's useful to ask students to characterize Franklin's personality type and then ask what would be different if Franklin were a different kind of person. It's important for students to understand how accepting Franklin portrays himself, how low-key he appears. (In real life Franklin has been a graduate student of Creative Writing and a Mormon missionary in Japan.)

2. A good class discussion can ensue from asking students what they like and dislike about fast-food restaurants. Some students will become remarkably involved, pointing out very strong likes and dislikes. These strongly held beliefs can easily lead to impassioned pieces of writing, full of rich description.

3. Ask students to list the kinds of details Franklin provides about the Wendy's workers. What's included and, even more important, what's left out? Ask "Is that the way you would have gone about describing people you worked with? Why or why not?"

Suggested Writing Assignments

1. Give one-paragraph descriptions of three or four people you know, omitting physical traits and concentrating on how actions reveal personality. Model your descriptions on Franklin's techniques.

2. The Wendy's job doesn't make use of Franklin's education in the slightest. Describe a job you've held that had a similar mismatch between your own education and the demands of the workplace. How did you respond to that mismatch, if at all?

3. Write an essay attacking or defending fast-food restaurants. Why should people support or avoid them? Think of your essay as an op-ed piece in a local newspaper.

Profiles

SCOTT RUSSELL SANDERS

Under the Influence

Full Edition, p. 87; Shorter Edition, p. 36

Scott Sanders's father was not, by most standards, an exemplary person; he drank too much, and his alcoholism did permanent harm to himself, his wife, and especially his children. Yet Sanders's essay is not a melodramatic account of the dangers of alcoholism or child abuse. It is an honest reminiscence and sensitive analysis of a father and his problem, and it contains thorough, relevant research on alcoholism as a disease and "public scourge" (paragraph 8). Sanders provides an excellent model for treating a difficult biographical subject with fairness and candor.

QUESTIONS FROM *THE NORTON READER*

1. Scott Russell Sanders frequently punctuates his memories of his father with information from other sources—dictionaries, medical encyclopedias, poems and short stories, the Bible. What function do these sources perform? How do they enlarge and enrich Sanders's essay?

2. Why does Sanders conclude his essay with paragraphs 53–55? What effect do they create that would be lost without them?

3. Drawing on your memories of a friend or family member, write an essay about a problem that person had and its effect on your life.

TEACHING SUGGESTIONS

1. Using the responses to question 1 (above), chart the structure of Sanders's essay, especially his placement of external, objective sources and their relation to personal experience and memory.

2. One source that Sanders gives prominence is the New Testament story of the madman possessed by demons and the Gadarene swine. Ask students to read an original version of the story (Matthew 8, Mark 5, or Luke 8) and compare it with Sanders's retelling. What does Sanders emphasize? How does he apply the story? How does he later echo it (paragraph 51)?

3. Why does Greeley Ray Sanders drink? Consider those moments in the essay when Sanders seems ready to give an answer. Does he—or does he resist a final explanation?

4. Ask students what parallels Sanders sees between his own life as a "workaholic" and his father's as an "alcoholic." What are the differences between

74

father and son? Why might Sanders want to draw parallels, even though the differences are significant?

SUGGESTED WRITING ASSIGNMENTS

1. Write a short sketch of a friend or family member who faced a serious problem, whether it was one he or she overcame or succumbed to.

2. Is alcoholism a "public scourge," as Sanders suggests in paragraph 8? Do research on this topic and write an "objective" report on your findings.

3. Is a "workaholic" really like an "alcoholic," as Sanders implies at the end of his essay? Write a brief essay comparing and contrasting the two types and pointing out differences as well as similarities.

ANNIE DILLARD
From *An American Childhood*

Full Edition, p. 98; Shorter Edition, p. 47

Taken from Annie Dillard's 1987 autobiography, this selection might as readily have been titled "My Mother" as anything else, for in it Dillard attempts to characterize her mother—with all her amusing idiosyncrasies and annoying quirks, her remarkable strengths and forgivable weaknesses. Because Dillard depicts a person she knows well, her essay might be compared with Scott Russell Sanders's "Under the Influence" (FE p. 87, SE p. 36) and Judith Ortiz Cofer's "More Room" (FE p. 132, SE p. 56) to raise questions about how a writer conveys a familiar subject to an audience unfamiliar with the person (through anecdotes rather than adjectives, through the subject's favorite phrases as much as the writer's own words). In contrast, you might use Tom Wolfe's "Yeager" (FE p. 114) to ask about the techniques needed to characterize someone famous whom the writer has never met.

QUESTIONS FROM *THE NORTON READER*

1. Annie Dillard piles up examples in this excerpt, barely creating transitions between them. What do the many examples add up to? What is the overall point she wishes to make?

2. When this piece was originally published in Dillard's *An American Childhood*, the chapter had no title. If you could title this piece, what would that title be? Why?

3. Dillard, like Scott Russell Sanders in "Under the Influence" (FE p. 87, SE p. 36), writes about a parent. Compare the two essays. How do they differ? How are they similar?

4. Do some freewriting about one of your parents or someone important in your life when you were a child. Like Dillard, use as many specific examples as possible to communicate that person's character and personality.

Teaching Suggestions

1. You might ask students what anecdotes they remember best about Dillard's mother, why they remember them, and what the anecdotes reveal about the mother's personality.

2. Dillard's mother has many personal qualities her daughter admires. What are those qualities? Does she have qualities about which Dillard is ambivalent? How does Dillard convey her attitude?

3. Dillard's mother lived during a time when the possibilities for women were more limited than they are now, yet Dillard never belabors this point. She simply says, "Mother's energy and intelligence suited her for a greater role in a larger arena—mayor of New York, say—than the one she had" (paragraph 27). Why does Dillard work implicitly rather than explicitly? How does she make her point through examples and anecdotes?

4. This essay is constructed as a series of vignettes, each a page or two long. How does Dillard construct a single vignette? (You might compare the first with the last.) What organization does Dillard give to the series of vignettes—e.g., why does she begin as she does and end where she ends?

Suggested Writing Assignments

1. Write a character sketch about your mother or some other family member, using techniques from Dillard that you found particularly effective.

2. "Torpid conformity was a kind of sin; it was stupidity itself," according to Dillard's mother (paragraph 33). Write an essay in which you illustrate this thesis with examples from your own experience.

3. Take a phrase or common saying from your own family's history. Write a brief essay in which you convey what that phrase or saying means to you and your family.

David James Duncan
The Mickey Mantle Koan

Full Edition, p. 104

David James Duncan is the author of several books, both fiction and nonfiction, including *The River Why* and *The Brothers K*. In them, he strives to combine his love of the Pacific Northwest with his interest in Zen philosophy, as he does here. Although this essay has a famous ballplayer in its title, it is really a tribute to Duncan's brother John, who died as a young man. As such, the essay offers students a way to think about character and the ways a writer can introduce us to an ordinary person whom we will never meet. You might start with Duncan's criticism of the minister who eulogized John without knowing any of his true qualities; Duncan then lists these quirky qualities, ones that help the reader come to know something about John. The essay also includes a symbol: the baseball Mickey Mantle signed. Some background information on Mantle himself may help students grasp John's reverence for him and deepen their understanding of John's growing recognition that he would never achieve what his hero did. Another key contextual idea here is that of the Zen koan. Share a definition and some examples with your students. Duncan offers an explanation of his understanding of the genre in paragraphs 29–34. Discuss the koan as its own genre, its relevance and usefulness to Duncan here, and how this idea helps Duncan use writing as a way to grieve his brother's death.

Questions from *The Norton Reader*

1. David James Duncan includes a list in paragraph 3 to show his and his brother John's preferences. In paragraph 14 he includes other lists describing John. What do these lists tell you about John? How do they reveal his character?

2. The autographed baseball functions as a symbol in this essay. What does it symbolize? In what way did the ball from Mickey Mantle serve another purpose even though John did not see the ball when he was alive?

3. Write an essay about someone you know well. As Duncan does, include lists of specific qualities and preferences that reveal that person's character. Also include anecdotes to provide a greater understanding of that person.

Teaching Suggestions

1. The one-sentence paragraph 34 claims to have solved the koan. Like parables, koans are stories whose wisdom emerges in part from their mystery. They cannot be "solved" as a riddle or even a fable can. Share some traditional koans with your students, and discuss the ways this essay is like a Zen koan.

2. Our heroes tell us a lot about ourselves. Duncan discusses why his brother admired the Yankees and Mickey Mantle in particular. Starting from that example, and the consequences of his admiration, have students discuss the value as well as the possible downside of having a hero. What happens when we cannot live up to the ideal our hero represents? What happens when our heroes disappoint us?

3. Duncan's relationship with his brother deepened through long games of catch (paragraphs 3–8). Examine that passage with your students, and discuss what it reveals about the bond between these brothers. Broaden the discussion to explore how the activities we share in families come to define and build our relationships.

Suggested Writing Assignments

1. Write an essay about a hero and someone who looks up to that person. What qualities do they share? What distinguishes them?

2. Write an essay about a relationship that uses and develops a symbol to characterize the relationship as Duncan does with the autographed baseball.

3. Read several koans and think of a challenging experience in your past from which you have drawn a lesson. Write about it in the form of a koan.

TOM WOLFE

Yeager

Full Edition, p. 114

Tom Wolfe's now-famous description of Chuck Yeager, the pilot who broke the sound barrier and helped teach some of the first American astronauts, comes from chapter 3 of *The Right Stuff* (1979). In vivid, often breathtaking prose, Wolfe gives an account of a popular American hero and an analysis of what makes such a man popular, what charisma or mystique appeals to the public and makes a superman of an ordinary man. As a form of biography, "Yeager" allows students to see how a writer moves from specific details and facts to larger claims about character and historical significance. As a form of history, Wolfe's book depends on the interweaving of the personal, private lives of early test pilots with the larger public history of the American space program. It provides a good model for writing projects that ask students to connect their own or their families' experiences with some aspect of the public history of the United States or Canada.

QUESTIONS FROM *THE NORTON READER*

1. Before recounting Yeager's personal history or the story of breaking the sound barrier, Wolfe begins with the voice of an airline pilot. Why does he begin this way? What connection does the first paragraph have with the rest of the essay?

2. Wolfe interweaves Yeager's personal history with a more public, official history of the space program. Make a flowchart or diagram to show how this interweaving works.

3. Write an essay that interweaves some part of your personal history with some larger, public story.

TEACHING SUGGESTIONS

1. The opening three paragraphs establish interest and significance. Ask students what made them interested in Yeager and what significance Wolfe establishes by showing the influence of Yeager's voice and personal style.

2. Perhaps in small groups, ask students to chart the interweaving of Yeager's personal history and the history of the space program: paragraphs 4 to 7, Yeager; 8 to 14, space program; 15, Pancho's Fly Inn; 16 to 18, space program; 19 to 21, Yeager; 22 to 41, October 14, 1947, the day Yeager broke the sound barrier. What advantages does Wolfe gain by combining personal details with official history?

3. How does Wolfe describe places, planes, and other details unfamiliar to most readers? Ask small groups of students to choose one such detail—whether the landscape at Muroc, Muroc air base, the X-1 plane, Pancho's Fly Inn, or some other detail—and figure out Wolfe's techniques.

4. Compare Wolfe's voice as an author with the voice he creates for Yeager. Ask students how they would describe Wolfe's voice (educated, ironic, intelligent, etc.) and why they think he chooses this voice for himself.

5. How does the ending echo—in style and content—the opening? After finishing the essay, what further significance do readers discover in the opening three paragraphs?

SUGGESTED WRITING ASSIGNMENTS

1. Write an account of another person important to the U.S. space program, using some of Wolfe's techniques for presenting a character.

2. View the movie version of *The Right Stuff* and write an account of how the movie adapts or uses Wolfe's account of Yeager's life and character.

3. Explain how some part of your personal history relates to or is an example of some larger, public story.

VIRGINIA WOOLF
Ellen Terry

Full Edition, p. 124

This essay offers a portrait of an actress through sketches of her at different moments of her career. Students are unlikely to have heard of the actress Ellen Terry (1847–1928) and Virginia Woolf's essay avoids the traditional landmarks of official biography. Nonetheless, this essay offers an innovative method for capturing the many aspects of a person's life. As such, it also affords an occasion to consider what it is we expect of people—perhaps especially women, perhaps especially celebrities. Students may be interested to compare Woolf's treatment of the difference between private and public lives with celebrity profiles today. Like Tom Wolfe in his portrait of Chuck Yeager, Woolf takes the hackneyed form of the celebrity profile and gives it her distinctive spin. In doing so, she teaches us about both her subject and how to refresh a tired writing assignment. Terry was much photographed and painted in her lifetime and this essay affords opportunities to compare Woolf's portrait with both official biographical information as well as with images.

QUESTIONS FROM *THE NORTON READER*

1. In this profile of Ellen Terry, what Virginia Woolf does not include is as interesting as what she does include. She does not include a list of Terry's accomplishments, her honors, or reviews of her acting. How does Woolf persuade readers of Terry's importance? What does she want us to know of Terry beyond her acting?

2. Much of this essay takes the form of descriptions of actual photographs and imagined drawings. What does this technique help Woolf convey about Terry? How is it effective?

3. Write a profile of someone who is famous. As Woolf does, try to give readers a picture of that person's personality—not just his or her professional accomplishments.

Teaching Suggestions

1. Bring in a short biography of Ellen Terry (the *Oxford Dictionary of National Biography* is a terrific resource if your university library subscribes to its database) and ask students to compare the official story to Woolf's version.

2. Ellen Terry was often photographed, including, famously by Woolf's aunt, Julia Margaret Cameron, a pioneering Victorian photographer known for her portraits of celebrities. Share some images of Terry with the class and have students compare the woman in the photograph with one of Woolf's descriptions.

3. Celebrity culture and our hunger to *know* another person have only grown since Woolf wrote this essay. Use a discussion of Woolf's technique as a springboard to talk about our desire to know more about others, especially actors and performers. What can writing about another's life teach us about ourselves and others?

4. One of Woolf's themes is the challenge of capturing a performance in prose. Discuss her strategies and brainstorm other possible ways to use language to capture a fleeting action. Ask students who are athletes and performers to share how they experience differences, performance to performance, game to game, and compare those to what spectators might or might not notice.

Suggested Writing Assignments

1. Research Terry's life, looking for biographical sources as well as images, and write an essay on her in which you use Woolf as one among several sources of information. As you write, reflect on the kind of information that helps you.

2. Gather five or six photographs over time of a famous person whom you admire, and write an essay on the model of Woolf's, using each photograph to represent an age and phase of his or her career.

3. Go to a ball game or a live performance and write an essay describing the event. Strive to capture not simply the facts of the evening, but also some elements that might be lost to time if not for your written account.

Toni Morrison

Strangers

Full Edition, p. 129; Shorter Edition, p. 53

This essay by Toni Morrison serves as an introduction for a book of photographs by Robert Bergman, his first publication. It seems to work by indirection, and students can make some useful comparisons between it and Wolfe's portrait of Yeager (FE p. 114). The two writers take very different approaches: Wolfe describes his subject in minute detail, relating Yeager's personal history to the history of World War II and the rise of the space program; he emphasizes the man within history. Morrison, on the other hand, tells a personal story that illustrates her point about others—one that will be familiar to readers of Morrison's novels and essays. The *other* is always a key issue for her, and it appears here in two forms—the old woman she "meets" at the outset and these portraits, which she saves until the very end of her introduction.

Morrison is totally reticent about the photographs' details and technical qualities, but totally absorbing about what the encounter with them *means* to her. She doesn't write of the encounter with Bergman's people but with a person she may or may not have actually met and what that signifies to her. The images evoke a general mood, not accountable to any specific detail but by the overall presence of the people depicted in them. These are not static works of art demanding close inspection and commentary but images of the *other* that must be met and understood.

QUESTIONS FROM *The Norton Reader*

1. In his book *A Kind of Rapture*, Robert Bergman included photographs of people he encountered on the streets of America. Why does Toni Morrison not dwell on this fact?

2. In paragraphs 1–3 Morrison relates a story about a woman she sees fishing near her property; later in the essay she expresses regret, even guilt, that her story "sentimentalized and appropriated" the woman (paragraphs 6–7). What does Morrison mean by this self-criticism? Do you agree that it may be ethically wrong to create stories about the strangers we see?

3. Write an essay in which you describe and reflect on an encounter you have had with a stranger.

TEACHING SUGGESTIONS

1. What changes in Morrison between the time she first tells the story of the woman and her next-to-last paragraph?

2. How did Morrison's initial reaction to the woman she met fit into Sartre's warning about "love as possession" (paragraph 4)?

SUGGESTED WRITING ASSIGNMENTS

1. In one or two sentences, explain how Bergman's portraits connect with Morrison's notion of strangers.

2. How would you describe common features of these Bergman photographs? What generalizations might you make based on this small sample?

JUDITH ORTIZ COFER
More Room
Full Edition, p. 132; Shorter Edition, p. 56

Born in Hormigueros, Puerto Rico, Judith Ortiz Cofer spent much of her childhood traveling between her Puerto Rican home and Paterson, New Jersey, where she also lived. This essay recalls her grandmother's bedroom: its sights, smells, symbols, and wonders. It also narrates the tale of a Puerto Rican woman who maintained control of her body and personal space. As such, it might be called a feminist parable, yet it is never so didactic that the message (made explicit in the final paragraph) intrudes upon the pleasure of the story. You might want students to use Cofer's essay as a model for their own exemplary tales: narratives and family stories that taught them a lesson about life.

Questions from *The Norton Reader*

1. At the end of the essay, Judith Ortiz Cofer explains in fairly direct terms why her grandmother wanted "more room." Why do you think she uses narration as the primary mode in the rest of the essay? What does she gain by first narrating, then explaining?

2. Cofer uses many similes (comparisons with "like" or "as") and metaphors (comparisons without specific connectors)—for example, in paragraph 1 she says that her grandmother's house was "like a chambered nautilus" and in paragraph 5 that her grandmother's Bible was "her security system." Discuss the use of one or two such comparisons that you find particularly effective.

3. What are the possible meanings of the title?

4. Write about a favorite or mysterious place you remember from childhood.

Teaching Suggestions

1. This is a short essay, only eleven paragraphs, similar in length to many essays students are asked to write. You might ask students to map out the "flow" of the essay: what happens in each paragraph, where Cofer allows herself more space (paragraphs 5 to 6), where she creates suspense and picks up the pace (paragraphs 10 to 11).

2. In preparing question 2, above, students will have identified some of the key similes and metaphors in this essay: "like a chambered nautilus" (paragraph 1), "like a great blue bird" (paragraph 2), "like a wise empress" (paragraph 3), the Bible as "her security system" (paragraph 5), etc. List their findings on the board and discuss the way each metaphor either clarifies or enriches Cofer's description of "la casa de Mamá."

3. Discuss the importance of the final paragraph, which explicitly states the reasons Cofer's grandmother needed her own room. If the students are writing essays similar to Cofer's, ask them to end with a similar explication of their story's meaning.

Suggested Writing Assignments

1. Retell a story often told within your family. Concentrate on a single person or place as Cofer does and suggest, either implicitly or explicitly, why this tale is so important to you or your family.

2. Write about a favorite place you remember from childhood, using details and metaphors as Cofer does to bring it alive.

3. Compare and contrast Cofer's depiction of her grandmother with N. Scott Momaday's of his grandmother in "The Way to Rainy Mountain" (FE p. 136). Where they differ, suggest why their differences might reflect different backgrounds or intentions.

N. Scott Momaday
The Way to Rainy Mountain

Full Edition, p. 136

N. Scott Momaday's description of his grandmother and his return to Rainy Mountain, a place sacred to the Kiowa Indians, employs a structure common to many cultures: the journey as an actual and metaphorical quest. You might ask students about their own journeys and journeys they have read about in literature—whether in Homer's *Odyssey* or Jack Kerouac's *On the Road* or some even more recent book of travel writing. Why do we travel? What do we expect to gain from travel? What did Momaday hope to discover by returning to his grandmother's house and retracing the traditional movements of the Kiowas? Such questions might help students to think about the journey structure as a possible one for their own personal reports or for their descriptions of a place of special interest to them. The journey Momaday describes in "Rainy Mountain" beautifully links realistic descriptions of the West, sacred myths of the Kiowas, and memories of his grandmother and her stories to evoke a sense of the importance of place in his own life.

Questions from *The Norton Reader*

1. Throughout this essay, N. Scott Momaday uses similes (comparisons with "like" or "as") and metaphors (comparisons without specific connectors). Which comparisons were most helpful in aiding your understanding? Which comparison was most surprising?

2. Momaday connects personal and cultural history to a particular place. Find another essay, either in "Profiles" or "Nature and the Environment," that makes similar connections. Write a comparison of the two essays.

3. In paragraph 10, Momaday describes the roles that women played in his grandmother's Kiowa culture. Consider the roles women played in your grandmother's generation and culture; perhaps ask your mother or grandmother about their experiences. To what extent have those roles remained the same or changed in your generation? Write an essay based on your conversations with older family members and your own personal knowledge.

Teaching Suggestions

1. What is the structure of this essay? You might ask students to compare Momaday's actual journey (introduced in paragraph 2 and again in paragraph 5) with the historical journeys of his ancestors, the Kiowas. How are the two journeys linked?

2. Why does Momaday begin and end with descriptions of Rainy Mountain? How and why are the two descriptions different?

3. Where does Momaday include cultural myths, historical events, or his grandmother's stories in this essay? How do these enrich our understanding of the places Momaday revisits?

4. To what extent are "people" essential to our understanding of "place"? Discuss the ways in which Momaday describes his grandmother both as grandmother (i.e., a real person, a family member) and as Kiowa Indian (i.e., a representative of an older culture that no longer exists). Why do we need both views of his grandmother to understand the significance of Momaday's return to his ancestral home?

5. Look closely at sentences in which Momaday chooses words with metaphorical or symbolic significance—for example, in paragraph 1, where he links Rainy Mountain to the place "where Creation was begun," or in paragraph 5, where he refers to his journey as a "pilgrimage," or in paragraph 9, where he refers to the soldiers' stopping of Indian rituals as "deicide." Discuss the connotations of such words and how they enrich the literal journey Momaday takes.

Suggested Writing Assignments

1. Write about a journey you took to an important place in your family's history—whether an ancestral home, the home of a relative, or a home you lived in as a child.

2. Write about a place with historical and cultural significance, combining your own observations with history, legend, and/or myth.

3. Write a descriptive essay about a person and place that seem intertwined. In doing so, think about why the person seems so essential to understanding the place.

Jhumpa Lahiri
Rhode Island

Full Edition, p. 142

This essay is titled "Rhode Island," but it is as much about Jhumpa Lahiri as it is about the place she continues to say she is "from" (paragraph 4). More precisely, it is about her own complex relationship to that place. From her opening sentence—"Rhode Island is not an island"—Lahiri presents the state as a place of tension and paradox. As the essay progresses, Lahiri weaves various levels of history and story—of the state, of her family, of her own life—into a sustained reflection on the tensions the state embodies. In its style and affectionate descriptions, the essay exudes sincere warmth, but it is also marked by a sense of unease, a sense that she and her family "didn't fundamentally belong" (paragraph 5). When discussing this essay with students, you might encourage them to consider Lahiri's complex posture toward the place she says she is "from." Like much of Lahiri's other work, the essay offers a nuanced reflection on the contemporary immigrant experience from different generational perspectives. It offers fine models of economical yet detailed description and exposition, and it might fruitfully be compared with the selection from Annie Dillard's *An American Childhood* (FE p. 98, SE p. 47), Ian Frazier's "Take the F" (FE p. 151, SE p. 59), or Chang-rae Lee's "Coming Home Again" (FE p. 3).

QUESTIONS FROM *THE NORTON READER*

1. One purpose of the collection in which Jhumpa Lahiri's essay appeared is to show the diversity of the fifty American states. How does Lahiri achieve this purpose? What details does she provide that are unique to Rhode Island or New England?

2. Lahiri is a novelist who alludes to other authors and their writing. Choose one allusion to a novel or short story, and explain how this reference enriches Lahiri's narrative.

3. Lahiri gives both her personal history and a brief history of the state in which she grew up. What connections might be drawn between the personal and the regional? Consider both the explicit and implicit connections.

4. Write an account of the region or state in which you grew up, integrating some of its history with your personal experience.

TEACHING SUGGESTIONS

1. Ask students to consider the connections between people and place that Lahiri develops in the essay. What, for example, are the affinities between the geography and architecture of Rolling Acres and the people who live there? Between the cold and colorless Atlantic and the bathers at Scarborough? Between the place and the people Lahiri is "from" (paragraph 4)?

2. In her second paragraph, Lahiri groups the people of Rhode Island into three categories: "those who come only in the warm months," "those full-time residents who never seem to go anywhere else," and "those who pass through without stopping." Apply this framework to the people who populate the essay: the "three graces" who staff the Kingston Free Library (paragraph 8), the students who attend the university, or even Lahiri's parents and Lahiri herself. Do the people in the essay fit neatly into these categories? What does reading the essay through these categories reveal or occlude?

3. Lahiri's relationship to Rhode Island changes, both as she grows from a child to a teenager to a woman with children of her own and over the course of the essay itself. Ask students to reflect on the nature of these changes. What does Lahiri gain and lose with each transition? How does Lahiri handle these transitions stylistically? How does she use them to structure the essay?

4. Lahiri does not view Rhode Island through rose-colored glasses. Ask students to consider some of the fissures or tensions Lahiri notices in her essay, for example, between historic Kingston and the Rolling Acres housing development or between the responses of the Indian community and the community in general to the xenophobic notes given to Lahiri's mother. What kinds of judgments, if any, does she make or imply?

SUGGESTED WRITING ASSIGNMENTS

1. Lahiri describes her family as a "hybrid" (paragraph 5). Write a paper in which you first define this term and then deploy it in an interpretation of Lahiri's essay.

2. Conduct some additional research on one of the historical events or figures Lahiri mentions in the essay—Roger Williams, say, or King Philip's War. Write an essay in which you bring what you learned through your research to bear on the essay itself. How does your new knowledge about Lahiri's references enrich your understanding of her essay?

3. Lahiri explores her perceptions of and relationship to Rhode Island at different points in her life: as a child, as a teenager, as a mature woman who lives away from the place she is from. Write an essay about a place you have known since childhood. How have your perceptions of and relationship to that place changed with time?

IAN FRAZIER
Take the F

Full Edition, p. 151; Shorter Edition, p. 59

This essay, originally published in the *New Yorker* in 1995 and republished in Ian Frazier's book *Gone to New York: Adventures in the City* in 2005, captures in rich detail Frazier's sense of Brooklyn. In many ways, "Take the F" is typical of its genre. For example, it is written in the first person, from the perspective of a more-or-less neutral observer who reports the sights, sounds, tastes, and even smells of the place he is describing. Yet although the essay is told from Frazier's perspective, it reveals few details of Frazier's personal history or relationships. The essay thus provides an occasion for exploring both the construction and the effect of point of view. Also in keeping with its genre, Frazier's essay is deeply concerned with evoking the unique quality of the place about which he writes. "Like many Americans," he comments, "I fear living in a nowhere, in a place that is no-place; in Brooklyn, that doesn't trouble me at all" (paragraph 6). The essay provides opportunities for broaching questions about the nature of place and the contemporary loss of place in general. In its structure and style, as well as for the themes it explores, it might usefully be paired with Jhumpa Lahiri's "Rhode Island" (FE p. 142).

QUESTIONS FROM *THE NORTON READER*

1. According to Ian Frazier, Brooklynites identify themselves by neighborhood and subway line (paragraph 1). In addition to his subway line, how does Frazier describe where he lives? What techniques help him present his Brooklyn neighborhood to readers who are nonresidents?

2. Frazier engages all of the senses—sight, sound, smell, taste, and touch—to portray his Brooklyn home. Choose one example of each that stands out to you. How do these examples create a sense of place?

3. Like Jhumpa Lahiri in "Rhode Island" (FE p. 142), Frazier wishes to establish the uniqueness of his home. What features seem to be unique? What features seem universal? What relation do you see between the unique and the universal?

4. Write an essay about your neighborhood, using techniques identified in questions 1 and 2.

TEACHING SUGGESTIONS

1. Frazier's essay is replete with lists of the various people, things, events, even smells he has seen or experienced in Brooklyn. Ask students to consider Frazier's choice to structure his essay around such lists. What are the effects of this choice? What does it convey about his experience of Brooklyn? How does he handle such lists stylistically?

2. Unlike his daughter, Frazier is not a "city kid" (paragraph 2). Ask students to think about how Frazier's status as a transplant affects his experience of Brooklyn.

3. Brooklyn is home to people of widely varying ethnicities, beliefs, and social classes. How does Frazier represent this diversity in his essay? How does Frazier represent ethnic or class tensions?

4. Movement is a prominent theme in this essay, the bulk of which is devoted to Frazier's cataloguing of people and things he has seen while riding the subway or walking through the city. Why does Frazier choose to organize his essay around his movements? What does that say or capture about the place he is profiling?

SUGGESTED WRITING ASSIGNMENTS

1. Write an analysis of Frazier's representation and handling of ethnic and social tensions in the essay. Focus your analysis on one or more specific scenes or incidents he describes: the conflict over charcoal barbecuing in Prospect Park, perhaps, or the vignette about the man soliciting signatures for a petition to close the homeless shelter. What, in general, is Frazier's view of such conflicts?

2. Frazier has gleaned much of his knowledge of Brooklyn from his long walks in the city. Take a long walk through your own neighborhood or through a neighborhood near your campus. Using Frazier's essay as a model, write an essay describing your walk. Do not limit yourself only to things you saw but write also about what you heard, felt, smelled, and perhaps even tasted.

3. "Like many Americans," Frazier writes, "I fear living in a nowhere, in a place that is no-place; in Brooklyn, that doesn't trouble me at all" (paragraph 6). Write an essay contrasting a "place" you know with a "no-place" you know. What makes a place a place? What makes a no-place a no-place?

E. B. White
Once More to the Lake

Full Edition, p. 158; Shorter Edition, p. 66

"Once More to the Lake" is a classic essay on revisiting the past. With his son, E. B. White revisits the lake where he went as a child, and his account, by shifting between present and past, measures the passage of time. Generations blur: as White sees his younger self in his son, so he sees his father in his present self. The final sentence—"As he [White's son] buckled the swollen belt suddenly my groin felt the chill of death"—may startle readers at first, but on reflection we realize that White prepares us for it. His narrative spans a natural cycle of life passing from one generation to the next; his rendering of natural landscape and pleasurable activity keeps the somber potential meanings of the cycle in the background until, at the very end, he foregrounds them.

In "Once More to the Lake" White combines particular and composite narrative. The particular narrative takes place in the present: White and his son return to the lake on a single occasion. The composite narrative takes place in the past: White recollects repeated episodes from the Augusts he vacationed at the lake. He moves easily but clearly back and forth in time. You might have students notice the shifts in the first paragraph: "One summer, along about 1904," "summer after summer," "A few weeks ago." These references mark transitions fluently, without emphatic breaks. You might ask students to continue to note how White marks them.

Questions from *The Norton Reader*

1. E. B. White includes many details to describe his impressions of the lake when he went there as a child and when he returns as an adult—for example, about the road, the dragonfly, and the boat's motor. What are some other details, and what do they tell us about what has changed or stayed the same?

2. White's last sentence often surprises readers. Go back through the essay and pick out sections, words, or phrases that seem to prepare for the ending.

3. Write about revisiting a place that has special meaning for you, including details of your early memories and reflections on your more recent visit.

Teaching Suggestions

1. How important is White's son to "Once More to the Lake"? How does his presence heighten the passage of time and the theme of mortality? Ask students to imagine the essay without him.

2. Comparison is an important device in this essay, as White again and again balances details from the past against details from the present. Sometimes things change, sometimes they don't. You might ask students which comparisons they remember and then ask them to reread the essay looking for additional ones.

3. Discuss what White reveals about himself (or his "persona," his created self) in "Once More to the Lake." Ask what in the text enables us to construct an image of the author.

Suggested Writing Assignments

1. Write an essay about revisiting a place you cherished as a child. Where does "change" lie? In the place? In yourself? Did the experience lead you to sober reflection on big issues? If so, structure your essay so that you can include reflection as well as narrative and description.

2. Write an essay in which you move retrospectively from the present to the past, drawing specific comparisons between them. Make your thematic emphasis that of loss through the passage of time.

Gender and Human Nature

ANNA QUINDLEN
Between the Sexes, a Great Divide

Full Edition, p. 164; Shorter Edition, p. 72

Anna Quindlen begins this brief essay with a "perhaps"—"Perhaps we all have the same memory of the first boy-girl party we attended"—and expands it into an exploration of gender differences. If students haven't paused over the "perhaps," ask them about it. Is the memory shared, or is it gendered female? Is it gendered uniformly female? What would be a male memory—or male memories—of such a party? How might the entire essay be rewritten from a different memory of a similar event? Instructors may profitably move from this discussion to a discussion of the "great divide" of the waxed floor: how it originates as a real object of somewhat indeterminate meaning and then takes on complex meanings through Quindlen's embedding it within a context. Students like to say "this symbolizes that," as if to symbolize means to equal. This essay illustrates the making of a symbol, the loading of that "great divide" with more meanings that can simply be predicated of it. Quindlen makes much out of little; her essay, which contains approximately one thousand words, appeared as a "Hers" column in the *New York Times*, as did Gloria Naylor's "Mommy, What Does 'Nigger' Mean?" in "Language and Communication" (FE p. 481).

Quindlen joined the *New York Times* in 1977 as a reporter. She became metropolitan editor, columnist, and writer for the Op-Ed page; in line to become an editor in the early 1990s, she resigned to have time to write fiction. As she explains in "Altogether Female," the introduction to a collection of her essays, *Thinking Out Loud: On the Personal, the Political, the Public, and the Private* (1993), she benefited from affirmative action in both her hiring and promotion: six women brought a class-action suit against the *Times* in 1974 that was settled in 1978, and as a result the *Times* began to hire and promote women.

QUESTIONS FROM *THE NORTON READER*

1. Note the places in this essay where Anna Quindlen, after describing "the first boy-girl party we attended" (paragraph 1), returns to it. How does she turn this moment into an observation about the differences between men and women?

2. Quindlen writes about two genders—male and female—but some recent theorists describe multiple genders. Read Gwendolyn Ann Smith's "We're All

Someone's Freak" (FE p. 184) and compare Quindlen's classification to hers. What changes when new categories are added? What problems persist?

3. As Quindlen does with the "boy-girl party" in this essay, describe a memorable event and turn it into a greater observation about an issue important to you.

Teaching Suggestions

1. Ask students to look at the amaryllis in the bathroom (paragraph 8) as another example of Quindlen's symbol-making.

2. "I've always been a feminist," Quindlen writes (paragraph 4). How, in the course of this essay, does she define feminism? Are there other definitions of feminism? Where do they come from? Who uses them? Why is "feminism" a term whose meaning needs to be stipulated when it is used?

3. Does Quindlen lock herself into binary thinking about gender differences?

Suggested Writing Assignments

1. Most people engage in binary thinking about gender differences: as Quindlen points out, they help children "classify the world" (paragraph 10). Catch yourself doing it or hearing someone else doing it until you locate an instance you interpret as damaging, another you interpret as innocuous. Write an essay in which you reflect on what each instance entails and the differences between them.

2. What does Quindlen mean by "linear thinking" (paragraph 9)? What would be its opposite? Write an essay in which you offer one or more examples of each and discuss their advantages and disadvantages. You may also wish to consider whether these two kinds of thinking are necessarily gendered.

3. Read four or five additional essays on gender issues by Quindlen—a number of them can be found in her collection *Thinking Out Loud* (1993)—and write an essay in which you trace several concerns of Quindlen's that run through them.

PAUL THEROUX
Being a Man

Full Edition, p. 166

Paul Theroux is a novelist and essayist known for his writing on travel, particularly by train. "Being a Man" was published in a collection called *Sunrise with Seamonsters* (1985). Theroux takes a calculatedly strong and unqualified line that is both personal—"I have always disliked being a man" (paragraph 2)—and general—"Any objective study would find the quest for manliness essentially right-wing, puritanical, cowardly, neurotic and fueled largely by a fear of women" (paragraph 7). Midway through the essay he discloses an ax to grind, his desire to be a writer when in the United States to write, especially fiction, is considered unmanly. His personal involvement, however, does not lead him to qualify his assertion that the quest for manliness is bad for everybody. It is possible to argue that Theroux's strong line is subverted by his involvement. But is that necessarily the case? Academic writing, which minimizes personal involvement, is usually qualified writing, but it is only one kind of writing, and its rules are the rules of a specialized discourse.

QUESTIONS FROM *THE NORTON READER*

1. In this essay, Paul Theroux makes many negative statements about being a man and being manly. Do you agree with his assessment of what it means to be a man or to be manly? Why or why not?

2. In paragraph 2, Theroux uses similes to describe his feelings about masculinity and femininity: he claims that "masculinity is . . . like having to wear an ill-fitting coat for one's entire life" and imagines "femininity to be an oppressive sense of nakedness." Write two similes, one describing your sense of what it is to be masculine, the other describing your sense of what it is to be feminine. How do your similes supplement, or differ from, Theroux's?

3. In paragraph 6, Theroux says he regards "high school sports as a drug far worse than marijuana." Consider his attitude toward sports throughout the essay. How does his sense of sports compare to yours? Explain the differences and similarities in a brief essay.

TEACHING SUGGESTIONS

1. Ask students to mark Theroux's generalizations and consider how he makes them. You may also ask them to rewrite one or two as qualified generalizations.

2. Call attention to Theroux's examples. Ordinarily he uses one for each point he makes. The exception comes in paragraphs 10 and 11, where he surveys a number of writers. What are the uses of single and multiple examples?

3. Theroux asserts that men, at least in America, aren't expected to be writers; many feminists claim that women aren't expected to be scientists. What kind of thinking lies behind these expectations?

SUGGESTED WRITING ASSIGNMENTS

1. Do library research on one or more of the writers Theroux mentions in paragraphs 10 and 11. Write an essay in which you test his assertion that the quest for manliness is particularly destructive for writers. In qualifying his generalization, be sure to qualify your own.

2. Write an essay called "Being a Student" in which you argue forcefully that being a student constitutes a hardship.

SOJOURNER TRUTH

Ain't I a Woman?

Full Edition, p. 170; Shorter Edition, p. 75

Sojourner Truth was born into slavery in the late 1700s and escaped in 1826. In 1851, she gave an extemporaneous speech—now called "Ain't I a Woman?"—at the Women's Rights Convention in Akron, Ohio. In *The Norton Reader*, we include two versions of this short speech, neither written down by Truth, but both transcribed by people who were present at her speech. Slaves were denied literacy, so we don't have Sojourner Truth's written words. The different versions of the speech are both a legacy of slavery and proof that people's recollections differ—as do their purposes in reporting what someone else allegedly said. It's important to honor both Truth's reputation and historical accuracy. Although the 1863 version with the refrain "Ain't I a Woman?" is more popular, it includes inaccuracies that many historians have noted: Truth was from New York, a native speaker of Dutch, who prided herself on her English, so she probably wouldn't have used the Southern colloquialisms reflected in that version. She also did not have thirteen children (or as many sold into slavery). As you discuss these versions of the speech in class, ask students to consider both the textual features and the historical context of this speech.

QUESTIONS FROM *THE NORTON READER*

1. Sojourner Truth uses both comparison and contrast to develop her speech. How does she compare herself to a man? In what ways does she believe she is not like a man? What do these similarities and differences tell us about how she understands gender?

2. Discuss Truth's use of the Bible to challenge the limitations others try to impose on her. How does her use of biblical allusions support her argument?

3. Compare the two versions of this speech. What similar elements are included in both versions? What significant differences are there? Write an essay about these similarities and differences. Explain why one version is better than the other or why both are equally important.

TEACHING SUGGESTIONS

1. For the first two questions in *The Norton Reader*, you can ask students to focus on one version of the speech or both, understanding that their answers will differ depending on the version they choose. Or you can divide the class in two, asking half to focus on one version in answering the questions, and the other half to focus on the other version.

2. Ask for two volunteers to read the different versions of Truth's speech aloud. What stands out when they are read? How do students perceive the author differently as a result of hearing the two versions?

3. Ask students to do outside research on the historical and biographical context of these two versions of the speech and Truth's life and legacy.

SUGGESTED WRITING ASSIGNMENTS

1. Write a short speech in which you support the rights of an underrepresented or underprivileged group. Imagine a specific audience and include information and sources that will be persuasive to that audience.

2. Research the publication history of different versions of Truth's speech. Where were they published? Who wrote them? Write an essay in which you inform the reader about the different contexts and motives that may have shaped at least two versions of this speech.

3. Anna Quindlen in "Between the Sexes, a Great Divide" (FE p. 164, SE p. 72) and Paul Theroux in "Being a Man" (FE p. 166) both write about gender differences. How might Truth respond to their claims? Write a conversation among these three authors accounting for their different positions and experiences.

AMY CUNNINGHAM
Why Women Smile

Full Edition, p. 172

Amy Cunningham's text is an accessible and effective model of an *exploratory* essay. Her essay is centered not on a thesis she is seeking to support, but rather revolves around a specific yet fecund question she is attempting to answer: "What is it in our culture that keeps [women's] smiles on automatic pilot?" Her essay does not endeavor to present a single, most convincing answer to this question; nor does it argue that one interpretive lens is more productive than others. Rather, it attempts to explore the topic, to offer as many *different* worthwhile answers to the question as it can muster.

The essay is also a useful example of the need for and value of interdisciplinary research when attempting to construct whole and complex answers to questions of human nature. In exploring her question, Cunningham ranges freely across disciplinary boundaries, weaving together information from wildlife biology, literary studies, medicine, developmental psychology, anthropology, feminist studies, anatomy, theology, art history, cultural studies, management science, sociology, and communication studies, among other fields.

Finally, this piece is quite effective in helping students understand the value of analytical thinking, of pursuing "small" topics, of attending to the significances of those things we typically overlook as unworthy of our interest. "Smiles," Cunningham writes, "are not the small and innocuous things they appear to be." In contrast to taking on massive, earth-shattering topics in an effort to manufacture authority and significance in their writing, students realize they can insert their own pet topics into her construction to launch personally meaningful research projects that still speak cogently to a wide audience: "Kisses [billiard balls, running shoes, fireflies, etc.] are not the small and innocuous things they appear to be" (paragraph 3).

1. Have you or people you know ever been urged to smile or to smile more? How was the advice given? What do you think the motive was?

2. Collect some observational data on the way men and women interact with strangers and see if you can confirm any part of Amy Cunningham's essay.

3. Several years after Cunningham wrote "Why Women Smile," she discovered new research on smiling ("All Smiles Now" [FE p. 177], an entry that Cunningham posted in 2006 on her blog *Chattering Minds* at beliefnet.com). This research has made her change her view on women's smiles. Write a brief account of what these changes are and what new evidence they reflect.

4. Do you think that Paul Ekman's research on Buddhist monks fully applies to American women and their smiles? What issues remain? Write about the issues in an essay that draws on your own experience and observation.

Teaching Suggestions

1. Ask students to reread Cunningham's 2006 blog entry on how "a whole chunk" of her article is incorrect (FE p. 177). How much do her conclusions depend on that "chunk," Ekman's research? How does her blog entry alter the opinion of the article?

a. Cunningham's essay ranges freely across a variety of different academic disciplines as she develops her topic. How many different fields of study does she cite research from? Name them.

b. Which of these fields of study did you find offered the most *surprising* explanation as to why women smile? Why? Which one offered the most *compelling* explanation? Why? Which one offered the *weakest* account for the phenomenon?

c. What is the effect on the reader of this kind of interdisciplinary development within an essay? How does it work to construct your sense of the subject matter? How does it work to construct your sense of the author?

d. In sum, do you *like* Cunningham's approach here? Why or why not? In what ways do you find her interdisciplinary roaming and ever-widening lens engaging and effective? In what ways is her refusal to focus on a single analytical perspective or interpretive lens frustrating or disappointing?

2. Have students consider the exploratory nature of the text.

a. Cunningham's text is decidedly unlike most of the short pieces of intellectual nonfiction. Rather than featuring a central claim or assertion that it attempts to support with evidence, her text features a central *question* which it attempts to answer in as many worthwhile ways as possible. What is your personal response to this *exploratory* form? Do you like this approach? Why or why not? Do you find its lack of straightforwardness, its meandering development, attractive or frustrating? Why?

b. What sorts of values does such a textual form imply? What does it suggest about the nature of truth? What does it suggest about the knowledge? What does it suggest about the value of certainty and uncertainty?

c. How do you think your teachers would respond if your essays followed this kind of exploratory format, beginning not with a thesis that you supported with evidence, but rather with a question to which you provided multiple different answers? Why do you think they would respond this way?

Suggested Writing Assignments

1. Try your hand at Cunningham's approach to writing on questions of human nature. First, generate a list of those questions about human behavior that have always baffled you, but that you really don't know the answer to: Why do people stay with abusive partners? Why do people still become Deadheads? Why do people become addicted to getting tattoos? Then, select one that interests you enough to sustain your efforts over several weeks of research. Next, using interviews, field study, library work, and other kinds of investigation, write an exploratory essay like Cunningham's that attempts to present as many different answers to your question as possible, and attempts to address your question from as many different disciplinary perspectives as possible, melding answers from anthropology, psychology, biology, literary studies, physics, engineering, and so on.

2. Write an essay in which you emulate Cunningham's exploratory fascination with and analytical work on a "small" topic. Her essay does a great deal to demonstrate the significance of something we typically overlook as unworthy of our interest. "Smiles," she writes, "are not the small and innocuous things they appear to be" (paragraph 3). First, insert your own "small" topic into her construction: "Shoelaces [handshakes, guitar strings, hamburgers, etc.] are not the small and innocuous things they appear to be." Then, conduct wide-ranging research and render the evidence necessary to prove that your assertion is valid. Your goal here is to show that your topic is far more complex and interesting than it first appears. In how many different ways is your topic significant and worthy of our time and interest? How many different fields of study can shed light on its hidden complexity and importance?

Roxane Gay

A Tale of Three Coming Out Stories

Full Edition, p. 178; Shorter Edition, p. 77

Roxane Gay first published this essay in the online magazine the *Rumpus* in 2012 and also included it in her essay collection *Bad Feminist,* which was published in 2014. When she wrote this essay, gay marriage was legal in only seventeen states. In June 2015, a decision by the Supreme Court made same-sex marriage legal nationwide. Although some laws have changed since this essay was first published, Gay's reflection on personal privacy and public advocacy remains relevant. She critiques the public's need to know the personal details of the lives of public figures even as she recognizes the importance of public advocacy, especially in terms of civil rights for the LGBT community. She acknowledges, too, that "it is still an unreasonable burden that someone who is marginalized must bear an extra set of responsibilities" (paragraph 30). Her larger argument, though, is not about whether celebrities who are gay have the right to privacy. She argues that *all* people, whether they are public figures or not, need to take responsibility for fighting "great and small" injustices (paragraph 32).

QUESTIONS FROM *THE NORTON READER*

1. Compare the similarities and differences among the "three coming out stories" referred to in the title of Roxane Gay's essay. What do the lives of Sally Ride, Anderson Cooper, and Frank Ocean, as described in this essay, tell us about the process of publicly declaring one's sexual orientation?

2. Throughout the essay, Gay discusses the balance between privacy and the disclosure of personal information for the greater good. She ends her essay with a question for those of us who are not celebrities: "How helpless are *we* willing to be for the greater good?" (paragraph 33). When, if ever, might it serve the greater good to give up some privacy?

3. Research one of the news stories Gay references here (e.g., the hate crimes listed in paragraph 22, or the testimony referred to in paragraph 31). In an essay, compare how several different news outlets treat the same story. What do those differences suggest about how attitudes toward sexual orientation differ based on region or political affiliation?

TEACHING SUGGESTIONS

1. Sally Ride, Anderson Cooper, and Frank Ocean (as well as the other celebrities Roxane Gay writes about) do not have identical "coming out" stories. These differences help complicate what might, at first, seem like a divide between the privileged class of celebrities and the rest of the public. Encourage students to consider the complex ways social class, race, gender, religion, personality, and a number of other factors affect access to privacy.

2. Although Gay often uses "we" to refer to the general public and "they" to refer to celebrities, she also makes the point of saying that celebrities "are flesh and blood" and "sacred to those they love" (paragraph 9). She argues that it's not only prominent figures who are responsible for social change (paragraphs 32–33), and that fighting injustice is a shared responsibility. Although Gay's essay focuses on sexual orientation, you can broaden the discussion about giving up privacy. What other personal information—such as a disability, a health condition, or a past experience—might someone disclose for the public good? (You might want to point to other readings in *The Norton Reader* to

provide examples: Nancy Mairs [FE p. 64]; Scott Russell Sanders [FE p. 87, SE p. 36]; and Brent Staples [FE p. 267, SE p. 141].) Are there ever circumstances in which another person should be "outed"? As you discuss these questions and issues in class, be sensitive to the fact that some of your students may feel vulnerable—especially if there are aspects of their identity, experience, or beliefs that they wish to keep private.

3. If you plan to assign question 3 in *The Norton Reader*—asking students to compare different reports of the same event—bring examples to class. You can use stories about the events Gay mentions or choose a current event and the stories surrounding it. Help students see that headlines, quotations, organization, visuals, information included, and information withheld all affect the message sent.

Suggested Writing Assignments

1. Examine Gay's use of pronouns. To whom is she referring when she uses "we" and "our"? (See, for example, paragraph 9.) Write an essay analyzing Gay's use of pronouns, making a claim about why it is or isn't effective.

2. In paragraph 5, Gay asks a series of rhetorical questions about privacy. Write a response essay reflecting on how you think Gay would answer her own questions (using evidence from the text as support) and whether or not your answers to those questions differ.

3. Gay asks, "How helpless are *we* willing to be for the greater good?" (paragraph 33). Write a personal essay reflecting on this question and your own answer to it.

Gwendolyn Ann Smith
We're All Someone's Freak

Full Edition, p. 184

The first five essays in the "Gender and Human Nature" chapter deal with differences between men and women. Gwendolyn Ann Smith's "We're All Someone's Freak" expands the conversation about gender and human nature by considering the varied social expectations and constraints faced by those who are transgender. She opens with a direct statement: "Being transgender guarantees you will upset someone," and she explains the multiple and conflicting ways people can be upset. By the middle of the essay, she makes a broader argument that "everyone has someone they view as a freak" (paragraph 10), showing that marginalization is a human phenomenon and not something either faced or perpetrated by only one group of people (paragraph 11). She claims that shunning those who are different (or even those who are similar) is a human failing and that "basic human dignity is not a privilege of the lucky superior few, but a right of all or none" (paragraph 20).

Questions from *The Norton Reader*

1. In paragraph 12, Gwendolyn Ann Smith claims that we seek out other "freaks" like us or try to blend in with the mainstream. What examples does she provide throughout her essay to support this claim?

2. Why, according to Smith, do some people get upset by transgender people? How might her ideas relate to Roxane Gay's assertion in "A Tale of Three Coming Out Stories" (FE p. 178, SE p. 77) that we like "taxonomy, classification, [and] definition" (paragraph 2)?

3. Smith argues that everyone is someone else's freak (paragraph 11), and conversely that everyone makes a freak out of someone else. Write an essay in which you discuss this reciprocal relationship in a social setting you know well.

Teaching Suggestions

1. Ask students to list reasons individuals sometimes push others—especially those who are similar—away. Smith provides one reason: to fit in better. Are there other reasons (self-hatred? to feel special?)? Conversely, why do we seek out others like us? Smith mentions comfort and company (paragraph 12). What are some other reasons (to take political action? to avoid being challenged? to feel safe?)? Such an exercise further shows the complexity of human motives and actions related to both affiliation and detachment.

2. Ask students to read both Smith's essay and Roxane Gay's "A Tale of Three Coming Out Stories" (FE p. 178, SE p. 77). How might issues related to privacy and advocacy be even more complex for those who are transgender?

3. Smith writes of "endless, often circular" taxonomies of difference used to exclude others—even others with shared beliefs, practices, or identity (paragraph 11). Ask students to consider a particular group they know well and to make a visual representation (a chart, a list with categories and subcategories, a diagram, etc.) that shows differences among the group.

Suggested Writing Assignments

1. Write an essay that begins with a variation on Smith's first line: "Being _____ guarantees you will upset someone."

2. Smith writes that it should be irrelevant to her "what any other transgender person opts to do," that another person's action does not change who she is (paragraph 15). Do you agree? Why or why not? Write an essay in which you explore some element of identity alongside these questions.

3. Smith claims that "we are all somebody's freak" (paragraph 20). In "Falling Down Is Part of Growing Up" (FE p. 187, SE p. 83), Henry Petroski writes, "We are all engineers of sorts" (paragraph 1). Is there something you believe is true for all humans? Write an essay in which you make and support a claim about some element of human nature.

Henry Petroski

Falling Down Is Part of Growing Up

Full Edition, p. 187; Shorter Edition, p. 83

In "Falling Down Is Part of Growing Up," Henry Petroski uses nursery rhymes and fairy tales as well as an extended metaphor to explain the ways that "structural failure is part of the human condition" (paragraph 17). Petroski uses his knowledge of engineering to reflect on a broader issue. As you discuss this essay with students, encourage them to analyze Petroski's use of metaphor and the ways in which he incorporates children's literature into his argument. You might also ask students to use their specialized knowledge to explain something they believe to be part of the human condition.

Questions from *The Norton Reader*

1. Henry Petroski begins his essay with a metaphor: "We are all engineers of sorts, for we all have the principles of machines and structures in our bones." Does he convince you of his point by the end of the essay? How are we like and not like engineers and the structures they build?

2. Petroski intersperses his prose with excerpts from nursery rhymes, riddles, and fairy tales. Do you find this technique effective? Why or why not? In what ways do the different texts reinforce each other?

3. Describe a time when you or someone you know overstressed his or her body or a piece of furniture. Incorporate excerpts of your favorite rhymes, fairy tales, poems, or songs in your essay.

Teaching Suggestions

1. Ask students to analyze Petroski's use of metaphor. For example, he compares doctors and nurses to cranes and forklifts (paragraph 2), arms to bridges (paragraph 3), and arms and cribs to beams, girders, and columns (paragraph 3). What is the purpose of this use of metaphor? Do students find it effective?

2. Discuss the ways Petroski incorporates nursery rhymes into his essay. Analyze the ways they illustrate his larger point about structural failure. Why do students think he uses nursery rhymes to illustrate his point?

3. Ask students whether Petroski's description of childhood matches their experience. Do the generalizations hold?

Suggested Writing Assignments

1. Petroski begins with the claim, "We are all engineers of sorts" and then explains why (paragraph 1). Write an essay in which you begin with a broad claim—"We are all . . ."—and explain why.

2. Write a reflective essay in which you consider what you learned from childhood nursery rhymes and fairy tales.

ELISABETH KÜBLER-ROSS
On the Fear of Death
Full Edition, p. 194; Shorter Edition, p. 90

Dr. Elisabeth Kübler-Ross, a Swiss psychologist, was a pioneer in examining attitudes toward dying and death; her book *On Death and Dying*, from which this essay comes, was published in 1969. In it Kübler-Ross announces as her intended audience professionals who work with the dying, like chaplains and social workers (paragraph 2), and her excursus on the communications of the dying may be of particular interest to them. The book, however, was a best seller that clearly transcended the particular audience she had in mind. In the selection reprinted here, Kübler-Ross presents and analyzes various kinds of material—experience, observation, and reading—to make a series of related points about patients and their needs and the often competing needs of those who take care of them and the families who arrange for their care. Her psychiatric orientation—what she claims as the unconscious motives that impel the behavior of the dying and the living—may need careful scrutiny. Do students understand the claims she makes and the Freudian psychology that warrants them, which she takes for granted?

Since the publication of *On Death and Dying*, medical technology has made it possible to prolong life almost indefinitely, and court cases have complicated what Kübler-Ross regards as patients' rights. Students will probably have some familiarity with these issues; they may need prompting to discuss them with reference to the rights that Kübler-Ross articulates.

QUESTIONS FROM *The Norton Reader*

1. Elisabeth Kübler-Ross incorporates various kinds of evidence—experience, observation, and reading—in this essay. Mark these kinds of evidence and describe how she integrates them into her text.

2. Kübler-Ross attends to the needs of the living and the rights of the dying. Describe where and how she addresses each and how she presents the conflicts, actual and potential, between them.

3. In paragraphs 24–27 Kübler-Ross describes the experience of being in an ambulance, emergency room, and hospital from a patient's point of view. What does this shift in point of view contribute to the essay?

4. Imagine a situation in which a child or children are not isolated from death. What might be the consequences? Using this situation and its possible consequences, write an essay in which you agree, disagree, or both with Kübler-Ross's views.

TEACHING SUGGESTIONS

1. You may ask students to reread paragraphs 15 to 17 and consider what Kübler-Ross's vignette—her personal account, so to speak—enables her to say and to imply about dying and death. The implication may be of two sorts: the

texture and emotional resonance of the episode she recollects and its modern obverse. How would this farmer die today?

2. Consider what Kübler-Ross has to say about the mechanical prolongation of life. Ask students to gather other material—newspaper or magazine articles, scientific studies, etc.—about this issue and try to articulate the various views that exist today.

3. Look at Kübler-Ross's discussion of avoidance techniques (paragraph 22). You may wish to ask students to discuss these and other techniques for avoiding unpleasant truths. What would be the consequences of speaking plainly and acting openly?

SUGGESTED WRITING ASSIGNMENTS

1. Write an essay in which you focus on your own experience of the death of someone you love. Frame it by considering Kübler-Ross's point that our treatment of the dying ordinarily reflects the needs of the living.

2. Do library research on one court case involving the mechanical prolongation of life. Look in particular at who is on each side and what arguments their lawyers make. Write an essay in which you describe and analyze the arguments of each side with respect to the rights of the dying and the needs of the living as Kübler-Ross conceives of them and as you conceive of them.

3. Kübler-Ross's attention to death and dying is repeated now in college courses on death and dying. If your institution offers one, get a copy of its syllabus, interview a couple of students who are taking or have taken it, and write an essay in which you describe the course and analyze what you understand to be Kübler-Ross's influence on it.

Cultural Analysis

ANNIE LEONARD

The Story of Bottled Water:
A Footnoted and Annotated Script

Full Edition, p. 200; Shorter Edition, p. 96

Annie Leonard is best known as the creator of *The Story of Stuff* (2007), an online documentary exploring the environmental and social impact of excessive consumerism. In 2008, inspired by this documentary's success, Leonard founded The Story of Stuff Project, a community of "changemakers" dedicated to fostering "a more healthy and just planet." Among other resources, *The Story of Stuff Project* website, storyofstuff.org, offers additional videos, including *The Story of Bottled Water*, along with annotated scripts and FAQ pages. In 2014, Leonard was named executive director of Greenpeace USA.

Although *The Norton Reader* presents "The Story of Bottled Water: A Footnoted and Annotated Script" as a printed text, the piece is best interpreted within the context of *The Story of Stuff Project* website, where it contributes to broader arguments for responsible consumption and social and economic justice. The argument of "The Story of Bottled Water" itself hinges on the concept of "manufactured demand," that is, demand for consumer goods driven by the companies that make them. "The Story of Bottled Water" counters the manufactured demand for bottled water by refuting claims that bottled water is healthier and better tasting than tap water and by illuminating the many ways in which bottled water has a detrimental impact on the environment. The piece concludes by directly exhorting its audience not only to change its consumption habits but also to work actively to ban bottled water itself. Considered as an argument, "The Story of Bottled Water" thus raises challenging questions about the consequences of persuasion: if we find Leonard's argument convincing, are we impelled to take action?

QUESTIONS FROM *THE NORTON READER*

1. Why, Annie Leonard wonders, do consumers buy so much bottled water when it is far more expensive, and arguably less tasty and healthy, than ordinary tap water? How does Leonard answer this question? What assumptions about consumers does her answer imply? Can you imagine other possible answers to her question?

2. The footnotes to Leonard's piece are much longer than the main text itself. Why do you think Leonard and her staff at The Story of Stuff Project

decided to document the text so heavily, filling it with references to websites, books, and articles? Compare the style in which the footnotes are written to the style of the main text. Is there a style you prefer? Why or why not?

3. Leonard wants to persuade her audience to change a deep-seated habit, to give up bottled water and "[take] back the tap" (paragraph 26). To this end, she develops her argument in stages. Trace the stages of her argument. Is her approach effective? Why or why not?

4. This piece is a "footnoted and annotated script" of Leonard's short animated documentary *The Story of Bottled Water*, available at http://storyofstuff .org/movies/story-of-bottled-water. Watch the movie and then re-read the printed text. How would you characterize its style? How is its style related to its origin as a movie? Did watching the movie change your response to Leonard's argument? If so, how?

5. Write a script for a short movie of your own, modeled on Leonard's, addressing an issue you care about deeply. Consider including footnotes to provide additional information for your readers.

TEACHING SUGGESTIONS

1. "The Story of Bottled Water: A Footnoted and Annotated Script" provides an opportunity for students to consider questions of multimodality, genre, and rhetorical context. To explore ideas of genre, you can try the following: Have students identify the different kinds of rhetorical work Leonard's script is intended to perform; compare the script as printed in *The Norton Reader* to the video on *The Story of Stuff Project* website; and consider the ways in which Leonard's script appropriates features of different genres, such as the academic footnote or the style of the op-ed piece. You might check out other videos on the site as you think about how the script's appearance in an anthology changes its genre.

2. "The Story of Bottled Water" is a brief argument supported by copious research, and you can use it as both an impetus and model for students' own research projects. Have students research social or economic issues they care about and then use what they learn to write advocacy pieces or to create videos modeled on Leonard's.

SUGGESTED WRITING ASSIGNMENTS

1. Write an argument of your own urging your readers to address some social, political, or economic issue you care about. Document your argument with carefully researched and detailed notes as modeled by Leonard.

2. Leonard directs her argument to bottled water's consumers. Write a parallel argument addressing the problem of bottled water that is directed to another constituency: your college or university administration, elected officials, or bottled water's producers and distributors. You might model your argument on the open letters published in the op-ed pages of newspapers.

TOM BISSELL

Extra Lives: Why Video Games Matter

Full Edition, p. 214; Shorter Edition, p. 110

Journalist, essayist, critic, and fiction writer Tom Bissell is the author of seven books, including *Extra Lives: Why Video Games Matter* (2010), from which this selection was taken. He is himself a gamer and has written scripts for a number of video games. This essay is, most simply, an extended review of the video game *Fallout* 3. But Bissell also uses review to understand "open-world" video games as a new kind of storytelling, a narrative form. The essay invites its practitioners to explore their subjects from multiple perspectives, and as an essayist, Bissell accepts this invitation. Although he is clearly captivated by video games, he offers us not a simple celebration of them but a rich reflection that probes their limits and possibilities.

The essay begins autobiographically, as Bissell recounts how he missed Barack Obama's 2008 presidential acceptance speech because he had gone on a seven-hour binge playing *Fallout* 3. Bissell uses this anecdote to frame his reflection on the appeal of video games in utterly personal terms: "And was I really missing a cardinal event in American history to keep playing it? I had, and I was, and I could not really explain why" (paragraph 15). Bissell's essay is an attempt at this explanation. While he is interested in situating open-world video games in relation to other kinds of storytelling, such as novels and films, he is ultimately concerned with registering his own complex and ambivalent responses to video games. His tentative answer is that unlike other forms of storytelling, video games do not obligate their reader or viewer to a single narrative line; rather, they allow gamers to immerse themselves in possibility.

QUESTIONS FROM *The Norton Reader*

1. A common objection to video games is that they encourage violence. How do you think Tom Bissell would respond to this objection? How does he treat violence in his essay?

2. Bissell asserts, "The pleasures of the open-world game are ample, complicated, and intensely private; their potency is difficult to explain" (paragraph 4). What sorts of pleasures does Bissell find in games? How are these pleasures connected or in tension with each other? How, in his prose style and manner of arguing, does Bissell wrestle with the difficulty of explaining these pleasures?

3. In sharing his responses to *Fallout* 3 and *Oblivion*, Bissell is also teaching us how to experience, interpret, and appreciate video games ourselves. Scott McCloud in "Understanding Comics" (FE p. 921, SE p. 537), Susan Sontag in "A Century of Cinema" (FE p. 927), and Aaron Copland in "How We Listen" (FE p. 938) endeavor to do the same for art forms they care about: comics, cinema, and music. Choose one of these essays to compare and contrast with Bissell's essay. How are they similar? How are they different?

4. Bissell concludes his essay with a series of questions. What is the effect of this gesture? Write an essay that responds to these questions. If you are a

gamer, consider relating your own experiences to Bissell's. If not, consider interviewing a gamer or writing about an activity that is important to you.

Teaching Suggestions

1. You may find that your students have much more experience with video games than you do. When you teach this essay, let your students be the experts. Allow them to teach you about video games and their appeal and to guide discussion and interpretation of the essay.

2. Throughout his essay, as throughout much of his work, Bissell is concerned with politics and particularly with the legacy of the Cold War. Have students consider Bissell's essay from this perspective. In what ways is his essay not only personal but also political?

3. Over the past two decades, many researchers have examined the psychological and social effects of video games. Have your students consider Bissell's account of his personal experiences with video games in light of this research.

Suggested Writing Assignments

1. Bissell notes that video games are a new medium. Create a multimodal composition of your own that annotates and responds to Bissell's essay. You might, for example, create a website annotating the essay with information, images, video clips, and your own commentary.

2. In the final sentence Bissell asks, "To what part of me do games speak?" Write an essay in which you ask this question about another art form.

Bill McKibben
The Case for Single-Child Families

Full Edition, p. 223; Shorter Edition, p. 118

American environmentalist Bill McKibben is the author of many books, including *The End of Nature* (1989), *Deep Economy* (2007), and most recently *Eaarth* (2010). This essay is an excerpt from *Maybe One* (1998). In this short essay McKibben makes a short and cogent argument for family planning. Specifically, he argues for the environmental necessity of small, even one-child, families. The essay begins quite personally indeed, with an account of McKibben's vasectomy, and then moves outward to his family's decision to stop at one child. He quickly goes from this very personal decision to global environmental issues, especially overpopulation and America's massive use of resources.

This essay is very much about maturity and living for others. All of McKibben's reasoning flows out of a sense of the importance of becoming an adult. Throughout the essay, McKibben contrasts his decision to have only one child with two poles: those who choose not to use birth control and those who choose to have no children at all. For McKibben, who is active in the Methodist church and frequently a spiritual writer, there is appeal in the attitude of those who use no birth control within their marriages, claiming to be letting God set the number of children they have. Nonetheless, he concludes that in this historical moment, such an attitude is environmentally reckless. By contrast, he is skeptical of the selfishness he hears in the attitudes of those who choose to remain childless. Most students probably will not have thought about either family planning or environmentalism in this context. McKibben brings these ideas together skillfully through the account of a personal decision combined with references to several other texts.

Questions from *The Norton Reader*

1. Bill McKibben tells of how his five-year-old daughter Sophie "has already used more stuff and added more waste to the environment than many of the world's residents do in a lifetime" (paragraph 13). Make an inventory of how much "stuff" you use in an average week, and then discuss whether your inventory proves McKibben's point.

2. McKibben's essay was originally published in the *Christian Century*, a magazine that addresses political and cultural topics from a Christian perspective. Consider the role of faith and religion in McKibben's argument. How might his argument differ if it were written from a purely secular perspective?

3. McKibben ends his essay by stating, "This is a special time, and that turns everything on its head." How does he demonstrate that this is "a special time"? Do you agree with him? In what sense does his argument depend on this being "a special time"?

4. Like McKibben, Chief Seattle (FE p. 543, SE p. 315) and Wallace Stegner (FE p. 544) also argue that we have a responsibility to care for the earth. But Chief Seattle was writing in 1855 and Stegner in 1960. Write an essay comparing and contrasting McKibben's essay to one or both of these older pieces.

Teaching Suggestions

1. The essay uses personal evidence throughout. Discuss several instances of McKibben's turning and returning to the personal. Why, for example, does he want us to have so much information about what the vasectomy felt like? How does he make his experience relevant to the argument?

2. Ask students to consider the contrast between childless families and families with many children. How are the people presented? How does that presentation affect our attitude toward each choice? What does this reveal about McKibben's sympathies and prejudices?

3. Ask students to list the childless people McKibben profiles in the essay: which are mature, which immature, according to his perspective? Do you agree?

4. Note that McKibben's essay was written almost twenty years ago, and have students research population trends over the past two decades. In what ways is McKibben's argument still relevant today?

5. McKibben quotes Pope John Paul II's comments prior to the 1994 Cairo Conference on population (paragraph 28). Invite students to consider McKibben's argument in light of statements on development and the environment by some

of today's religious leaders, such as Pope Francis I's 2015 encyclical *Laudato Si'* (*Be Praised*). How do you think McKibben would respond?

Suggested Writing Assignments

1. Write a paper in which you defend what for you is the ideal family size not on grounds of personal preference but in terms of some larger social good.
2. McKibben refers to Alice Walker's essay "One Child of One's Own." Find that essay (collected in the 1984 volume *In Search of Our Mothers' Gardens*). Write an essay comparing Walker's justification for limiting her family size to one on feminist and artistic grounds with McKibben's. How does their reasoning differ? Which do you find most persuasive and why?

Malcolm Gladwell
Java Man

Full Edition, p. 232

Malcolm Gladwell has been a staff writer with the *New Yorker* magazine since 1996. He is the author of five books, *The Tipping Point: How Little Things Can Make a Big Difference* (2000), *Blink: The Power of Thinking without Thinking* (2005), *Outliers* (2008), *What the Dog Saw* (2009), and *David and Goliath* (2013), all of which had their origin in the *New Yorker*.

In this essay Gladwell writes about caffeine as a drug, offering a history of its many uses across cultures and over time. You might begin with some definitions of what counts as a drug, the appropriateness of that term to caffeine, and the effect of that word on the piece overall. You might fill in some more of the history of coffee shops in democracy for your students. (The central section of Jürgen Habermas's *The Structural Transformation of the Public Sphere* [1962] offers a standard account of the link.) Gladwell is flippant about the 1960s, making a quick reference to Joan Baez, a folksinger who will likely be unknown to most traditional-age students: you might want to pause and fill in the history (and the pharmacological joke). Gladwell teases us for putting so much stock in what is ultimately a silly distinction: coffee or tea, but he thrives on such distinctions, setting them up only to shatter them as falsehoods. Reading a good Gladwell piece is like watching an exciting debate. Showing students this master rhetorician at play can give them a sense of the fun of a good argument.

This essay was originally a review of a couple of books on drugs and caffeine from the *New Yorker*. The Norton editors have omitted the telling bibliographic details, but both books are mentioned in the second paragraph. Students almost certainly will not see this. After informing students of the occasion for the piece, discuss the difference between a review and a review essay. Go back through the essay, looking for signs of its origins. Ask your students to discern Gladwell's opinion of each book.

QUESTIONS FROM *The Norton Reader*

1. How serious do you think Malcolm Gladwell is when he says that we're all drugged on caffeine? How can you tell?

2. Gladwell creates a binary between coffee and tea. Describe another binary between two closely similar forms—such as seashore vs. mountains; Coke vs. Pepsi; skis vs. snowboards. How do binaries work? What limitations do you see in the binary you created or in Gladwell's?

3. Gladwell offers several hypotheses for caffeine's success as the drug of choice for the modern world. Which one do you find most persuasive, and why?

4. Write a description of some of the rituals that you or someone you know indulges in with coffee or tea.

TEACHING SUGGESTIONS

1. Break the essay into sections and then have students identify each section's focus: history, medicine, or political science. How does the perspective shift? Are there other shifts, such as of tone or style? Then, turn to paragraph 9, where biology and political science combine in Gladwell's discussion of the salutary effects on conversation of a combination of cigarettes and coffee.

2. Pick a seemingly trivial distinction (Apple or PC, Honda or Chevy, basketball or baseball, straight leg or boot cut) and tease out the implications of preferring one to the other.

SUGGESTED WRITING ASSIGNMENTS

1. Research the coffee culture in your town. Find a coffee shop with a history of talk—artistic, political, or both. Interview the manager or owner, some employees, and some regulars. Hang out there, too, so that you can judge the place's atmosphere for yourself. Write a paper in which you discuss the role of this place in the cultural history of your town.

2. Read another essay that takes an in-depth look at a common thing (such as Annie Leonard's "The Story of Bottled Water: A Footnoted and Annotated Script" [FE p. 200, SE p. 96] or David Foster Wallace's "Consider the Lobster" [FE p. 697]). Write an essay analyzing the methods of both Gladwell and the other author. Discuss which techniques for getting us to look at the familiar anew seem most effective and exciting to you and why.

3. Research a familiar food or beverage as Gladwell has done and write an essay in which you show it to us from many angles. What can be learned from further research into something so common?

JESSICA MITFORD

Behind the Formaldehyde Curtain

Full Edition, p. 238; Shorter Edition, p. 128

Jessica Mitford's essay is drawn from her brilliant book, *The American Way of Death* (1963), a biting analysis of American funeral practices. Mitford revised and updated her book for a new edition just before her own death in 1996; it was published in 1998.

The masterful opening warrants attention. The metaphor of stage presentation governs the entire essay (as the title suggests), so the *Hamlet* quote is apposite. The object of the behind-the-scenes drama is to prepare the body for "public display," the ultimate objective a "Beautiful Memory Picture" (paragraph 2). Contrasted with this use of metaphor is her litany of verbs: "sprayed, sliced, pierced, pickled, trussed, trimmed, creamed, waxed, painted, rouged. . . ." (paragraph 2). (Otto von Bismarck's remark that it is better not to see sausages and laws being made might usefully be extended to "memory pictures.")

Mitford's British background gives her the distance that is needed to survey American funeral practices with a traveler's eye; what seems normal to us seems quite odd to her. Interestingly, this was not the only British send-up of America's funeral industry. Evelyn Waugh's *The Loved One* (1948) focused on pet cemeteries and extravagances such as Los Angeles's famous Forest Lawn Memorial Park. (It was made into a movie starring Robert Morse and Jonathan Winters.)

QUESTIONS FROM *The Norton Reader*

1. Jessica Mitford's description might be called a "process essay"—that is, it describes the process by which a corpse becomes a "Beautiful Memory Picture." What are the stages of the process? Mark them in the margins of the essay, and think about how Mitford treats each one.

2. Mitford objects to the American funeral industry and its manipulation of death, yet she never directly says so. How do we as readers know her attitude? Cite words, phrases, or sentences that reveal her position.

3. Describe a process that you object to, letting your choice of words reveal your attitude.

TEACHING SUGGESTIONS

1. As a follow-up to question 2 above, you might look closely at paragraph 4 as a typical expression of Mitford's attitude. Some students might find it disagreeably superior; others, appropriately sarcastic. Students can look closely at how her word choice denigrates the people who pay so much money for embalming. One might usefully ask why she omits any mention of the survivors' state of mind at the time they decide such matters.

2. A close look at names reveals Mitford's scornful delight in incongruities. The "Vari-Pose Head Rest" (paragraph 8), the Eckels College of Mortuary Science (paragraph 9), Flextone (paragraph 11), and "Lyf-Lyk tint" (paragraph 11) are only

a few of the odd names Mitford mentions in her deadpan style. Ask students to list more from the essay. The next step would be to come up with some odd-sounding names for commonly used products and ask about the source of amusement in them. With Mitford's sardonic eye for incongruity, such slightly odd names turn up everywhere.

Suggested Writing Assignments

1. Take a common social practice and describe it from the perspective of someone from a distant country who doesn't automatically get it. Suggestions: engagement rings, football pep rallies, cheerleading, hanging out in malls, school newspapers.

2. Write an account of a procedure in the Mitford style, going step by step and providing both the main actions as well as suggesting alternatives.

Henry Louis Gates Jr.

In the Kitchen

Full Edition, p. 245; Shorter Edition, p. 135

Henry Louis Gates Jr., a literary critic and professor of African American studies at Harvard University, published his memories of growing up in *Colored People* (1994); this section of that memoir appeared in the *New Yorker*, not usually an outlet for university professors but one appropriate for this personal reminiscence.

Gates's subject is hair in the African American community during the 1950s and 1960s. Students should note that he does not discuss the well-known reactions to these hairstyles, the Afros of the late 1960s and 1970s, as worn by such cultural icons as Jimi Hendrix and the young Michael Jackson. Instead, his essay can be seen as an act of recovery. The cultural practices he celebrates have mostly fallen into disuse. During the 1970s they were vigorously opposed by activists who denounced the "process" as too imitative of white styles. Gates's essay is not a refutation of such denunciations but an attempt to pin down exactly what styles existed, set in the context of his family life in West Virginia of the 1950s, and why they were popular. Interestingly, though he starts out with an extensive portrait of his mother's hair preparation, his real subject is men's hair, especially his own relation to the figures he admired.

Questions from *The Norton Reader*

1. "Kitchen" has two meanings here; write a brief explanation of the significance of both uses of the word in Henry Louis Gates Jr.'s essay.

2. Why do you think Gates alludes to so many celebrities (mostly from the 1950s and 1960s) and brand-name products? Note his preferences and progression. What is the significance of the allusions and brand names?

3. Gates observes, "If there was ever a part of our African past that resisted assimilation, it was the kitchen" (paragraph 5). What does *assimilation* mean

in the context of this sentence? What do you think it means generally? What does the essay imply about Gates's stance on African American assimilation?

4. Write an essay in which you use memories from childhood—including sensory details, popular allusions, and brand-name products—to describe some element of your culture or identity.

Teaching Suggestions

1. Note the colloquial air to paragraph 2, the back-and-forth movement of "I liked that smell. Not the smell so much, I guess, as what the smell meant for the shape of my day." Ask students what reactions they have to this movement. What kind of mental operation is suggested by it? What kind of relationship to the reader does Gates assume by writing this way?

2. Students might consider whether Gates's obvious admiration for hair like Nat King Cole's "magnificent sleek black tiara" (last paragraph) indicates that he favors such hair for himself today or, on the contrary, that he regards it as an impressive achievement for the 1950s but not to be imitated.

3. Analyze the elements that make the concluding paragraph so effective. Include Nat King Cole, the African setting (Zanzibar is off the east coast of Tanzania), the hair itself. (Some students will not know what Cole looked like; they might need to see a photo.)

4. Ask students to use Gates's essay as an occasion for identifying and analyzing instances of assimilation in their community or campus. They might, for example, consider the ways in which their college or university integrates international students into the campus community.

Suggested Writing Assignments

1. How were hair and hairstyles regarded in your family? Write about hair-care incidents, pleasant or unpleasant, you remember from growing up. Connect them to the kind of family you had or the type of person you were then.

2. Report on hairstyles and practices among identifiable communities and/or subgroups. Suggestions: nursing homes, military bases, punk rockers, farmers, teenage girls from particular cultures, sports figures. (Just make sure the group you pick is well defined.)

JAMES BALDWIN
Stranger in the Village

Full Edition, p. 251

This classic essay is a product of James Baldwin's stay in a Swiss village, where he went to live in a friend's family chalet to get some writing done. Baldwin's experiences with the Swiss villagers' reaction to a black man in their midst causes him to see a paradox. In the normal course of things, the relationship of Europeans to Americans is straightforward: Europeans came first; Americans are of the New World; therefore, Europeans are more worldly, more sophisticated, more complex. But in matters of race, Baldwin argues, it is the Europeans who are naive, simple, and somewhat foolish. They have a few unsophisticated attitudes toward a black visitor in their village: fear and wonder, or at most a grudging acceptance. In fact, it turns out that these Swiss are much like the stereotypical Africans who first encountered white-skinned Europeans (though Baldwin knows there is a difference between an American black in Europe and whites in nineteenth-century Africa).

For Baldwin, America, more than anyplace else, is where black and white citizens have had the most interaction, the most to do with one another. Difficult as that relationship has been, Baldwin sees America as the only place where racial interactions are likely to continue to make progress.

Questions from *The Norton Reader*

1. James Baldwin was an American, but he lived for many years in France. Consider the role of geography in this essay. How does Baldwin use his experience in the Swiss village to comment on America?

2. Trace the use of the word "stranger" over the course of the essay. How does Baldwin's use of the word evolve as the essay develops?

3. Baldwin relates the white man's language and legends about black men to the "laws" of the white man's personality. What conviction about the source and the nature of language does this essay suggest?

4. Describe some particular experience that raises a large social question or shows the workings of large social forces. How might Baldwin help in the problem of connecting the particular and the general?

5. Baldwin writes, "There is a dreadful abyss between the streets of this village and the streets of the city in which I was born, between the children who shout *Neger!* today and those who shouted *Nigger!* yesterday—the abyss is experience, the American experience" (paragraph 14). There is no word in contemporary American public discourse that is more fraught than the "N-word." Write an essay that explores the contemporary news media's handling of this word. Focus your essay by analyzing one or more specific examples.

Teaching Suggestions

1. Baldwin's picture of Africa is drawn from what he knew in the 1950s, over half a century ago. Recent developments in recapturing the past might have given him a somewhat different attitude toward African history, though without altering his main point. What knowledge about the African past is missing from Baldwin's picture?

2. Like Baldwin, some of your students might regard themselves as strangers. For example, your class might include international students or first-generation college students. Invite students to discuss the ways in which the experience of being a stranger has affected them or changed their perspectives toward their home communities.

3. Use Baldwin's essay to broach a conversation on race and ethnicity in the twenty-first century. What might Baldwin contribute to that conversation?

Suggested Writing Assignments

1. Describe the experience of being an outsider in a community.

2. In an essay, show whether or to what extent American attitudes have changed since 1955, when Baldwin published his essay. Is his basic point still valid, or have conditions altered so much that this essay has more value as history and literature than as contemporary commentary?

Patricia Williams

The Death of the Profane: The Rhetoric of Race and Rights

Full Edition, p. 261

Patricia J. Williams, James L. Dohr Professor of Law at Columbia University, is the author of several books, including *The Alchemy of Race and Rights* from which "The Death of the Profane" is taken. Her areas of interest include race, gender, and the law. These areas of interest and concern can be seen in this essay included in *The Norton Reader* as well as in Williams's monthly columns ("Diary of a Mad Law Professor"), which she writes for the *Nation*. Nearly all of her writing includes a mix of personal narrative and a call for social and legal justice.

Students will recognize that mix in "The Death of the Profane," which is more about Williams's *telling* of the story of being barred from Benetton than it is about actually being barred. As you discuss the essay in class, encourage students to consider what Williams's different tellings of the same story (in different forms, in different contexts, and with different responses) say about rhetorical efficacy. In analyzing the organization of the essay and considering purpose and audience, students will gain a greater appreciation for the multiple ways personal narratives can also be shaped into arguments.

Questions from *The Norton Reader*

1. Patricia Williams's essay is about how the "objective," "neutral" forms writing often takes can drain away the significance of a particular person's story. Can you find examples of this phenomenon in other writing you read? Or can you find examples of it on TV or radio talk shows, for instance?

2. How does Williams move from the Benetton story to her larger point?

3. How would you characterize the tone of Williams's essay? Does any of her original rage remain?

4. What do you think of Williams's posting her reaction on the Benetton window? Write your opinion of the function and effectiveness of this action.

Teaching Suggestions

1. Ask students to outline the organization of Williams's essay: paragraphs 1–8 deal with the first telling of the story of being barred from Benetton's;

paragraphs 9–12 deal with the second telling—this one in a law journal; paragraphs 13–21 deal with the third telling of the story—this version at a conference on Equality and Difference; the remaining paragraphs recount questions Williams has been asked after telling the story. Ask students to consider why Williams organizes the essay in this way.

2. After students have outlined the organization of the essay, ask them to consider the purpose of each "telling" of the story. Although the purpose of the first "telling" seems to be to express rage, the other two detailed accounts not only express the author's feelings but also make specific arguments. In the second telling, for example, Williams analyzes "how the rhetoric of increased privatization, in response to racial issues, functions as the rationalizing agent of public unaccountability and, ultimately, irresponsibility" (paragraph 9). The essay itself might even be considered a fourth telling of the story. What is Williams's purpose in this fourth telling?

3. After students have analyzed organization and purpose, ask them to think about audience. Who was the audience for each telling of the story? How did Williams's various audiences respond? In what ways did Williams anticipate audience response (in paragraph 12, for example, she considers the ways readers might respond if the information about her race is not included in her story)?

Suggested Writing Assignments

1. Think about something significant that has happened to you. Write three versions of that experience with three different audiences in mind (perhaps your English teacher, a class of fourth-grade students, and another person who was involved in the experience but might have a different memory of it).

2. Rewrite a personal anecdote in order to emphasize a particular point or to make an argument. For example, if you have written a journal entry about something that happened, try to use that story in a different context—perhaps as the opening anecdote for a longer argument paper. After writing your new piece, consider what you changed in your story. Were there details you added or took out? What other changes did you make? Write a two-page reflection about the process of using a personal anecdote as support for an argument.

BRENT STAPLES
Black Men and Public Space

Full Edition, p. 267; Shorter Edition, p. 141

In this essay Brent Staples writes about himself as an individual and as a universal—that is, as a well-educated and nonviolent black man who, by virtue of his gender and race, is perceived as belonging to a class: violent black men. He is not unsympathetic to women who avoid him on the streets at night: "the danger they perceive is not a hallucination" (paragraph 5). The essay provides an account of his initiation into awareness and his attempts to distinguish himself from other members of his putative class.

"Black Men and Public Space" is an episodic narrative with commentary. You might call students' attention to the four times and places of the essay—childhood in Pennsylvania, graduate school in Chicago, Chicago of the late 1970s and early 1980s, and New York City now—and how Staples manipulates chronology. You can also have them note how the particularized narrative of the opening (his first encounter with a "victim" as a graduate student in Chicago) reverberates against his more generalized narrative of other times and places.

QUESTIONS FROM *The Norton Reader*

1. Brent Staples writes of situations rightly perceived as threatening and of situations misperceived as threatening. Give specific instances of each and tell how they are related.

2. Staples's essay contains a mixture of rage and humor. Does this mix distract from or contribute to the seriousness of the matter? Explain your answer.

3. Staples, like Patricia Williams in "The Death of the Profane" (FE p. 261), writes about his "rage" at being misperceived because of his race. Compare their reactions and responses: what do they have in common and where do they differ?

4. Write an essay reflecting on a time you were wrongly perceived because someone associated you with a certain class or group of people.

TEACHING SUGGESTIONS

1. Ask students to distinguish between narrative and commentary in this essay—and to notice how Staples combines them. It is more than a personal report; it calls attention to larger problems.

2. The pressure of the unspoken in this essay generates irony. Students might consider verbal irony, such as Staples's describing the woman he encountered in Chicago as his "victim," and dramatic irony, such as his whistling Vivaldi and Beethoven when he walks the streets late at night. Another irony would be Staples's "solution": his precautions against being taken for a mugger and a rapist. Are they a solution? How does the unspoken exert pressure? What are the advantages and disadvantages of irony in this essay?

SUGGESTED WRITING ASSIGNMENTS

1. Analyze Staples's essay as an unironic indictment of America as a racist society.

2. Write a personal essay about your experience of reading (and discussing) "Black Men and Public Space."

3. A longer version of this essay appeared in the September 1986 issue of *Ms.* magazine as "Just Walk on By." Find it in the library, read it, and write an analysis in which you focus on two things: the relation of "Black Men and Public Space" (excerpted for *Harper's Magazine*) to the longer "Just Walk on By" (published in *Ms.*) and the question of audience in both essays. Why might *Harper's Magazine* have printed the shorter version? What is omitted, and what is the effect?

DEBRA DICKERSON

Who Shot Johnny?

Full Edition, p. 270

This essay launched Debra Dickerson's career as a writer, commentator, and activist. Dickerson defines herself in the opening paragraph: she is black, single, middle-class, feminist, Harvard-educated, and well-read in contemporary American politics. What happens to her nephew is not what she (or we) would expect: he is shot and paralyzed in a random and still unexplained attack by another black man.

In the first two-thirds of her essay, she gives us a careful narrative of the episode and her frustrated attempt to make sense of it. Yet the final four paragraphs startle the reader. Dickerson shifts to the language of the streets, a language of rage and a style of derisory parody. Students will inevitably want to discuss the shift; it will be important for them to see the relation of both styles, the effectiveness of the shift, and the use of the "colloquial" in the face of the limitations of the "academic."

QUESTIONS FROM *THE NORTON READER*

1. What purpose does the first paragraph of this essay serve? Do you think Debra Dickerson's essay would be more or less effective if it began simply with the sentence "On July 27, 1995, my 16-year-old nephew was shot and paralyzed"?

2. Dickerson feels—and expresses—anger throughout this essay. How? Against what or whom?

3. Why does Dickerson use the term "brother" in the final paragraphs? How does this composite characterization work? How does it answer the question "Who shot Johnny?"

4. Both Brent Staples (FE p. 267, SE p. 141) and Dickerson write about stereotypes of African American men. Staples writes as an African American man judged according to these stereotypes, and Dickerson writes as an African American woman and feminist coming to terms with her nephew's shooting. Write an essay about the different ways the authors describe these stereotypes, or choose another point of comparison to write about.

TEACHING SUGGESTIONS

1. Why is it important for Dickerson to describe her immediate reaction to the shooting as well as the routine in its aftermath? That is, how does she gain pathos and establish ethos?

2. Dickerson does not conclude with a sociological analysis, with a discussion of the economic, social, or historical sources of violent crime. Yet her enraged commentary shows that she is aware of such sources. Ask students to discuss sentences that show her awareness.

3. In recent years, the violent deaths of a number of mostly young African American men have received significant attention in the media, prompting renewed discussions of race, civil rights, crime, and policing. Use Dickerson's essay, with its complex positions on race, gender, crime, and violence, to open a discussion of these issues. You might have students investigate specific cases and the discussions they provoked, analyze the rhetoric of the Black Lives Matter movement, or read some of Dickerson's commentary on these issues, much of which is available online.

SUGGESTED WRITING ASSIGNMENTS

1. Who shot Johnny? Write a sociological analysis of the causes of the crime that Dickerson describes.

2. Read Molly Ivins's "Get a Knife, Get a Dog, but Get Rid of Guns" (FE p. 384, SE p. 214). Write a brief essay in which you explain how the proposal might have prevented the crime Dickerson describes—or why it might not.

Food

MARION NESTLE
Utopian Dream: A New Farm Bill

Full Edition, p. 274; Shorter Edition, p. 144

In this essay, food and nutrition advocate Marion Nestle (rhymes with *wrestle*) offers something distinct from the more personal essays that follow in this chapter: a nutritionist's perspective on the politics of food. Nestle has a Ph.D. in microbiology and is the author of many books on food and nutrition. Her research focuses on the role food marketing plays in food choice, food safety, and obesity. Students may comprehend her authoritative tone more fully if they learn more about her respected position in the nutrition field. She has appeared in many food documentaries (including *Super Size Me* [2004] and *A Place at the Table* [2012]) and many short documentary clips on a wide range of food topics, which are on *YouTube*.

The essay offers an example of a problem/solution format, opening with ideas about what the farm bill could and should be from Nestle's students, a description of the problem of the current bill (including historical context on why it's so problematic), and then a clear alternative. As students sometimes struggle to write papers that ask genuine questions, Nestle offers a clear example for them. In her essay she models how an experienced researcher with an informed opinion still lets seemingly simple questions drive her inquiry: What makes the farm bill so problematic, and what can be done to improve it?

QUESTIONS FROM *THE NORTON READER*

1. According to Marion Nestle, what are the main problems with the farm bill? What specific sentences and paragraphs illustrate her objections?

2. What are some of the causes of obesity that Nestle identifies? What evidence does she provide that links obesity to the farm bill?

3. What effect does Nestle's use of headings and subheadings have on your understanding of the text?

4. Write your own "Utopian Dream," an essay in which you address the problems with a specific piece of legislation (current legislation is available at congress.gov) and a plan for fixing that bill or act.

TEACHING SUGGESTIONS

1. If you're discussing question 3 from the book, you might use the subheadings to help students see the essay's structure. You might also note that

Nestle asks, "what's wrong with the current farm bill?" rather than "is the farm bill helpful or harmful?" This is one way that Nestle signals to her readers how problemetic she finds the bill to be.

2. Nestle's piece offers insight into the oftentimes messy workings of the legislative process, far from the utopian ideals of basic civics. Discuss this gap between aspiration and reality with students and Nestle's use of the word "utopian" to describe her reformist aspirations. Ask students to identify Nestle's stance toward the government's role in food policy. (Is it cynical? Hopeful? Skeptical?) Then, have them assess the effectiveness of that stance as a rhetorical technique.

3. The House of Representatives has the full text of the farm bill (agriculture .house.gov/farmbill). Look at the document with students to get a sense of its size and scope. Then, choose a portion of the bill for students to analyze, assessing its provisions in light of Nestle's criticisms. Alternatively, the USDA website includes a two-page summary of the bill, as well as many other resources. Select—or have students select—several of these resources and compare how the government depicts what it has done with Nestle's indictment of the bill.

SUGGESTED WRITING ASSIGNMENTS

1. Choose one of Nestle's suggestions and find a few other sources on the same topic. Write a short op-ed in which you agree, disagree, or both, with Nestle based on the research you've done.

2. Read a brief essay or editorial written by a supporter of the farm bill. Write a short paper explaining the difference of opinion between that author and Nestle. Offer a solution (or a direction toward a solution) between the two sides in your conclusion.

3. Research an issue of food policy that affects your community—a crop grown in your county, the availability of healthy snacks on campus—and, following Nestle's model, write a paper that explains the problem and the obstacles to solving it, and offers practical solutions.

JJ GOODE
Single-Handed Cooking

Full Edition, p. 280; Shorter Edition, p. 150

JJ Goode writes books and articles about food and cooking, restaurant reviews for magazines, and cookbooks for publishers. This highly personal piece reveals how he has surmounted the difficulty of having only one true arm. It's hard to cook one-handed, and particularly difficult to do the prep work involved in many cuisines. Think of chopping carrots and onions for a Chinese dish, for instance. Goode details some of the difficulties he has faced and, more often than not, overcome. Though most of his readers have full use of their arms, they will be fascinated with the details of how he has overcome his handicap and triumphed in the kitchen.

Questions from *The Norton Reader*

1. How would you characterize JJ Goode's attitude toward his disability? What parts of the essay reveal his attitude?

2. Goode presents cooking as an adventure, writing, for example, that when he adds wine to a dish he springs into action and wedges the wine bottle between his thighs (paragraph 11). Two strategies he uses to heighten this sense of adventure are present tense and strong verbs. Which verb choices do you find especially effective? Why?

3. Good writes, "turn a spotlight on any accomplishment, however minor, and it seems like a triumph" (paragraph 12). Write an essay about a minor accomplishment you've had. Use present tense, strong verbs, and detail to make that accomplishment seem like a triumph.

Teaching Suggestions

1. Ask students to describe a meal they've eaten recently, thinking of themselves as restaurant reviewers. Though students are quite interested in food, they will face difficult problems if they don't have a template for a review. They can easily find models to imitate on the web: roadfood.com for down-home cooking, bonappetit.com for somewhat more upscale food writing, and jjgoode.com for our author's own restaurant reviews.

2. Compare Goode's writing to M. F. K. Fisher's writing about food in "Young Hunger" (FE p. 283, SE p. 153). These two writers demonstrate how wide a range of attitudes is possible on this topic.

3. Have students make a list of things they would have trouble doing if they had only one hand available for the tasks. Compare lists in class and then ask students what surprised them about the lists. Did the process of sharing the lists make them understand Goode's accomplishment better?

Suggested Writing Assignments

1. Describe a meal you've cooked (or observed being cooked), giving plenty of detail about the different steps and then the actual eating.

2. Compare Goode's essay with Nancy Mairs's "On Being a Cripple" (FE p. 64) and Alice Walker's "Beauty: When the Other Dancer Is the Self" (FE p. 74, SE p. 22) in terms of tone and attitude toward their disabilities.

3. Write an essay about one of your own failings (e.g., chronic messiness, inability to follow directions, overeating), revealing what difficulties your problem has led to. If you have developed ways to cope successfully, explain how you did so.

M. F. K. Fisher

Young Hunger

Full Edition, p. 283; Shorter Edition, p. 153

In "Young Hunger," M. F. K. Fisher recalls the hunger experienced by adolescents and she details the intensity of her own "young hunger" in writing about an experience of visiting her godparents when she was eighteen. Although Fisher reminisces about this experience from an adult perspective, the level of detail she uses demonstrates her clear memory of hunger's "ferocious demands" (paragraph 2). This essay provides a model not only for writing about food (Fisher is known as one of the most impressive American food writers) but also for writing about past experiences with the kinds of sensory details that allow readers to imagine those experiences and get a sense of the accompanying emotions.

Questions from *The Norton Reader*

1. M. F. K. Fisher's world is highly class-stratified. What markers of the upper class did you notice in her essay? Did they interfere with your enjoyment of it, or add to your pleasure as a reader? Why?

2. Describe a time when you have been truly hungry. Was your experience like Fisher's—or different?

3. Narrate an episode when you or someone you know went on an eating binge. Was it truly enjoyable? Use Fisher as a model to describe your experience.

Teaching Suggestions

1. Ask students to consider Fisher's use of comparison and contrast in this essay. For example, she contrasts youth and old age. What other comparisons and contrasts does she make? Do students agree with the distinctions Fisher makes?

2. Both Fisher and Henry Petroski in "Falling Down Is Part of Growing Up" (FE p. 187, SE p. 83) write about youth. Ask students to compare and contrast these two authors' descriptions of youth. What do they have in common? How do they differ?

3. Fisher writes about a past experience. She includes enough detail that the essay could be rendered in the present tense from the perspective of Fisher's eighteen-year-old self, yet she chooses to write in the past tense. Why might she have made this choice? What does her use of the past tense allow her to do that using the present tense would not allow?

Suggested Writing Assignments

1. Of eating a stash of chocolate bars, Fisher writes, "I unwrapped their rich brown covers and their tinfoil as silently as any prisoner chipping his way through a granite wall" (paragraph 21). Write about a memorable moment of secret eating.

2. Write an essay in which you compare and contrast some element of youth with one of old age.

LAD TOBIN
Here Everything Is Possible

Full Edition, p. 286; Shorter Edition, p. 156

Lad Tobin opens this essay with a self-parodying account of pestering a waiter for precise information about the food he is about to order, and uses it to segue into a different context entirely: memories of his mother's enthusiastic but complex relationship to food. As the essay returns to the restaurant for its conclusion, Tobin introduces yet another context: his daughter's gift of the family leftovers to a woman begging on the street. For Tobin and his mother, the emotions surrounding food—the relationships it can build, the ways it can be used to express joy and love—are as important as the food itself. His mother's life was shortened by her obesity: she chose to overeat even when her health was compromised. Tobin's daughter, by contrast, seems (in this essay) to see food in the context of social justice, hunger, and poverty. The relationship among food, weight, and health is a complex but familiar one. Students will almost certainly have a lot to say on these topics, but it may help to steer them away from what they already believe and know to examining the nuances Tobin brings to the story: his genuine love and admiration for his mother's generosity and his ambivalence about the more damaging elements of that generosity, which he has inherited.

QUESTIONS FROM *The Norton Reader*

1. Lad Tobin explores his own relationship to food by reflecting on his mother's food-related habits and behaviors. How do their relationships to food differ? How are they similar? Use examples from the essay to support your claims.

2. Throughout his essay Tobin uses lists, usually lists of specific foods, dishes, or activities related to preparing or serving food (e.g., paragraph 14). Where do these lists appear? What do you notice about them? Why are they important to the essay?

3. Tobin tells family stories and offers his own and sometimes someone else's interpretation (e.g., paragraphs 16–18). In a short essay, tell one of your own family stories, offering at least two perspectives on what that story illustrates or means.

TEACHING SUGGESTIONS

1. Tobin's essay includes multiple perspectives: his mother's, his own, his daughter's, and even his grandmother's. Especially if you're assigning question 3 from the book, discuss with students how the other figures in the essay might

perceive the events Tobin describes. How and where does his writing encourage us to see another's point of view? Which points of view are highlighted and which are minimized or even excluded?

2. Discuss the meaning of the title, "Here Everything Is Possible." What does it seem to mean to the waiter who speaks the phrase, and how does that meaning shift over the course of the essay? Is "everything is possible" a good or a bad thing?

3. This essay develops through episodes, each separated by a line break. Have students list these episodes and discuss how each relates to the others, their order in the story, and their relationship to the main themes of the essay.

Suggested Writing Assignments

1. Read another essay on the relationship between food and family (e.g., M. F. K. Fisher [FE p. 283, SE p. 153], Chang-rae Lee [FE p. 3], or Teresa Lust [FE p. 310]) and write a short paper comparing how different authors approach the theme.

2. Read Marion Nestle's "Utopian Dream: A New Farm Bill" (FE p. 274, SE p. 144). Focus on her discussion of obesity from a food-policy point of view. Write an essay discussing the challenges of reducing obesity, taking both the global perspective (as represented by Nestle) and the personal (as represented by Tobin) into account.

3. Write a food memoir in episodes. Be sure to include a range of times, characters, and situations. Consider how the sequence of your memories will affect your overall theme.

JULIA CHILD
Le Cordon Bleu

Full Edition, p. 296

Although she was once the most famous American chef and a regular on TV, Julia Child and the classical French cooking techniques she strove so hard to master—and then to introduce to American home cooks—may be unfamiliar to today's students. Some background on Child's role in laying the foundation for our current infatuation with food may help; equally helpful may be some discussion of classical French cuisine as a distinct art with specific rules and techniques. In this excerpt from her memoir, Child describes her apprenticeship at Le Cordon Bleu cooking school in post–World War II Paris. She combines enthusiasm for French food with profound respect for the techniques, two qualities that became the hallmarks of her cookbooks as well as her TV shows. Showing students *YouTube* clips of Child cooking may help them picture her personality as well as her cooking style; the classic *Saturday Night Live* parody, in which Dan Ackroyd plays Child and cooks in spite of a badly bleeding finger, brings home the point on an even sillier note. Also significant to this piece is Child's struggle for the respect of both her colleagues and her teachers. For a long time, neither took her seriously and she fought against both groups' stereotypes of American women. As Child herself indicates, this class was an exercise in her learning to take herself seriously as well: even after graduating from college and working in intelligence during World War II, Child had not found her life's work. In throwing herself into the serious study of the art and craft of cooking, Child found joy. Discuss with your students the interconnectedness of finding a purpose, experiencing joy, and engaging in hard work. What might Child's essay have to offer them?

Questions from *The Norton Reader*

1. Based on her description, do you think Julia Child's learning experience at Le Cordon Bleu was positive, negative, or both? Point to specific passages to support your interpretation.

2. Child mentions many French dishes, sometimes explaining what they are, other times just mentioning a name. Do an online search for the dishes that were unfamiliar to you. Look for photos, recipes, or descriptions. How might such research improve your understanding and appreciation of Child's writing?

3. What words would you use to characterize the tone of Child's writing? What is her attitude toward herself? others? learning?

4. Child shows how her teacher, Chef Bugnard, taught her to make scrambled eggs. Write an essay in which you show how someone taught you a different way of doing something you had done before.

Teaching Suggestions

1. Many of the essays in this chapter focus on striving for mastery of cooking techniques. Have students read another such essay (JJ Goode [FE p. 280, SE p. 150], Chris Wiewiora [FE p. 316, SE p. 169], or Chang-rae Lee [FE p. 3]) and compare Child's efforts to theirs.

2. Especially if you plan to teach question 4, bring in copies of Child's recipe for scrambled eggs from *Mastering the Art of French Cooking* and compare her explanation of the recipe to the one she gives here (paragraphs 15–22). Discuss Child's delight in her teacher's care in making perfect scrambled eggs. Ask students to share seemingly simple tasks that they also take care to do the right way (whatever "right" means to them).

3. Discuss with students the difference between learning to cook without a recipe and the kind of cooking class in the tradition of a national cuisine that Child took. Analogies to other arts (music, dance) and sports may help students grasp how Child's effort differs from the effort to become a competent home cook.

4. In spite of all her study, Child did not pass the test the first time. Discuss with students the frustrations of test-taking and study strategy. What lesson does Child's particular way of failing—and her reaction to it—have for college students?

SUGGESTED WRITING ASSIGNMENTS

1. Write a short paper analyzing why Child found both joy and purpose in her cooking classes. What confirmed her sense that she should continue to pursue this path in spite of its challenges? What does that tell you about Child and her attitude to education?

2. Read Chris Wiewiora's "This Is Tossing" (FE p. 316, SE p. 169) and write an essay comparing the way Child had to master the skills of French cooking with the way Wiewiora worked to learn to toss pizza dough.

3. Write a recipe for something simple but that benefits from a precise technique (toast, a hamburger). Then write a short essay justifying the reasons for taking extra care in making this dish.

4. Write an essay about a test that you took, especially one with a practical component (such as a swimming or driving test). How did you study and how did you perform?

DAN BARRY

Back When a Chocolate Puck Tasted, Guiltily, Like America

Full Edition, p. 307; Shorter Edition, p. 166

This short, humorous essay celebrates the pleasure of eating a favorite processed snack cake, elevating it to a national symbol. Its author Dan Barry is an award-winning journalist for the *New York Times*, who has visited all fifty states for his "This Land" column. Barry's recent investigative work has focused on youth sports and concussions. His range of interests suggests that we are meant to take the phrase "like America" seriously, and exploring some of Barry's other pieces may help deepen the conversation surrounding this essay. In addition to sparking a discussion about what it might mean for a food to represent a nation or a place, Barry offers a chance to talk about food as a guilty pleasure.

QUESTIONS FROM *The Norton Reader*

1. What do you think Dan Barry means when he claims that Ring Dings taste like America?

2. Barry makes comparisons between Hostess snack cakes and inedible objects such as "the heel of a shoe" (paragraph 3) and "a loofah sponge" (paragraph 8). Locate other examples. Why do you think he makes such comparisons even as he claims to enjoy eating the snack cakes?

3. Barry quotes a food-industry researcher who says that consumers want less processed food and to know "'the story behind their food'" (paragraph 16). Write an op-ed about what information you believe consumers should be provided about food—and why.

Teaching Suggestions

1. From 2007 to 2010 Dan Barry wrote the "This Land" column at the *New York Times,* visiting all fifty states and writing about what he found there. The paper's archive includes short videos of some of the souvenirs he brought back from his travels (nytimes.com). Watch a few of these with your students and discuss how objects can operate as symbols for places. Is there a specific food or object associated with your college's state or region? the students' state or region? How do students feel about the association?

2. Ask students to discuss their own "guilty pleasures" in eating and snacking. As they share, ask them to elaborate on what cultural significance, if any, they ascribe to the food they love.

3. Barry's humor relies on hyperbole. Have students identify his exaggerations and discuss hyperbole as a rhetorical strategy. You might refer students to Jonathan Swift, "A Modest Proposal" (FE p. 756, SE p. 442), or Garrison Keillor, "How to Write a Letter" (FE p. 505), for other examples of humor and satire in *The Reader.* If they are writing a humorous essay of their own, brainstorm strategies, such as hyperbole or understatement, that might be useful in humorous prose.

Suggested Writing Assignments

1. Write a humorous essay about a food that "tastes like America"—or your state, region, or town.

2. Write an essay defending something (a food, a habit, an activity) that you know to be unhealthy.

3. Read Teresa Lust's "The Same Old Stuffing" (FE p. 310) or Chang-rae Lee's "Coming Home Again" (FE p. 3) and compare how those writers define American food with Barry's humorous ode to snack cakes. Which writer's definition is most persuasive? How would you define America through food?

Teresa Lust
The Same Old Stuffing

Full Edition, p. 310

Teresa Lust's Thanksgiving story is a personal essay that makes a definite claim: tradition should be honored, especially at Thanksgiving. For all the essay's lightness and range, Lust begins and concludes her essay by affirming her respect for tradition. Lust's clear point contrasts with Lad Tobin's (FE p. 286, SE p. 156) more ambivalent account of his mother, whose love of food is both a source of pride and sorrow. Whether or not you teach Tobin with Lust, this essay offers an excellent occasion to show students how personal essays can express a clear and direct point of view. Lust tells the story of three Thanksgiving stuffings: the one her mother grew up with, the one her husband grew up with, and a third stuffing that her mother invents. Interwoven throughout this narrative are details about the history of Thanksgiving as well as Lust's own family history. Central to this essay is the idea of tradition, especially the ways in which family and national traditions connect and diverge. Direct students to paragraph 7, where Lust hypothesizes that her husband's family's stuffing was more traditional, and discuss with them the ways that she complicates and challenges that assumption as the essay develops.

Questions from *The Norton Reader*

1. Teresa Lust includes both family anecdotes and historical research in her essay. Was there anything about her description of the development of Thanksgiving as a holiday that surprised you?

2. In different ways, both Lust and Dan Barry (FE p. 307, SE p. 166) describe the ways in which people appreciate foods more once they are gone (even temporarily). What similarities and differences do you see between their essays?

3. Write an essay about a holiday tradition in your family. Use both family anecdotes and historical research. If your essay includes a recipe, consider incorporating it—as Lust does—in narrative form.

Teaching Suggestions

1. To discuss how Lust integrates her research into the essay, have students comb through the essay to identify what information the author knows, what she likely learned from talking to (or interviewing) family members, and what she learned from a book. Then, discuss how she integrates her sources into a single essay.

2. Call students' attention to the opening and closing lines of the essay and their focus on the importance of tradition. Discuss with them the process through which Lust and her mother come to the conclusion that it is best, at Thanksgiving, to stay traditional. Ask them to consider the extent to which they agree or disagree.

3. Have students read Lad Tobin's "Here Everything Is Possible" (FE p. 286, SE p. 156) and compare the authors' attitudes toward their mothers' cooking. Use this as an occasion to discuss the connections between food and family.

Suggested Writing Assignments

1. How important is it to honor tradition when celebrating Thanksgiving? Write an essay in response to Lust, in which you argue for what you deem the best balance between tradition and experimentation in a Thanksgiving menu.

2. Write an essay about the recipes that are essential on your Thanksgiving table, including their origins. Interview family members for your sources. Be sure to discuss any differences of opinion about what is essential or where certain recipes came from.

3. Research a holiday that your family celebrates and write an essay discussing the differences between its origin and what it means to you now.

4. Take a dish that is traditional for your family and write up a recipe for it clearly enough that a stranger could cook it. Then, write a short essay describing that dish's importance, incorporating the recipe into your narrative as Lust does here.

CHRIS WIEWIORA
This Is Tossing

Full Edition, p. 316; Shorter Edition, p. 169

Chris Wiewiora is one of the younger writers anthologized in *The Norton Reader* and students may take an interest in his biography and other work, available on his website (chriswiewiora.com). His essay celebrates an old-fashioned skill—tossing pizza to stretch the dough—in a setting that will be familiar to many students. Show students how the essay derives energy and tension from the time pressure of the job, so that the careful explanations of the process are made more urgent by the sense of time passing. Since students often have to describe a process, it is worth pausing over how Wiewiora describes what he does (paragraph 9 and on). Ask students if they can picture each step of the process, and see if they can determine which descriptions are most vivid and effective, and why. You might compare the description to a video tutorial. (There are many on *YouTube*.) Wiewiora's tribute to the dignity of this solitary labor offers an opportunity to have a wider discussion about work, labor, class, and education. What skills do your students possess that, like tossing, do not come from books? How do they value those skills in comparison to the ones they are working to acquire in the classroom?

QUESTIONS FROM *THE NORTON READER*

1. Chris Wiewiora uses sensory language—specifically sight, sound, touch, and visual cues—to help readers imaginatively experience the process of tossing a pizza crust. Locate places in the essay where his use of sensory language helps you imagine this process clearly.

2. Wiewiora uses the second-person point of view ("you") and present tense. Why do you think he uses that perspective and verb tense? How do these choices affect your reading of the essay?

3. Write an essay in which you guide readers through a process, teaching them to do something that may be unfamiliar to them. Like Wiewiora, use sensory language, the second-person point of view, and present tense.

TEACHING SUGGESTIONS

1. Wiewiora's essay celebrates taking on a challenge. Have students read another such essay (JJ Goode [FE p. 280, SE p. 150], Julia Child [FE p. 296]) and

compare the challenges the writers face, their motives for taking them on, and their attitudes toward their performance.

2. Assign Mike Rose's "Blue-Collar Brilliance" (FE p. 449, SE p. 262) and discuss how both Wiewiora and Rose assign dignity to the jobs of waiting tables and tossing pizza. You might use this occasion to open a student discussion about types of intelligence: how might the intelligence necessary to become good at tossing compare to other intelligences (athletic prowess, mathematical skill, creativity, etc.)?

3. To discuss Wiewiora's use of the second person here, have students rewrite a paragraph or two of this essay in the imperative voice (common for recipes), or first or third person. Ask them what is gained and lost in the change.

4. Especially if students have answered question 1 from the book, have them go through the essay and highlight the sensory language in the essay, noting which sense Wiewiora uses in each case. Discuss which sensory images are the most and least effective.

SUGGESTED WRITING ASSIGNMENTS

1. Make or buy pizza dough and toss it, following Wiewiora's directions. Try again, following the instructions from an online video. Write a brief essay comparing your experience tossing with the different types of instructions.

2. Read Julia Child's "Le Cordon Bleu" (FE p. 296) and write an essay comparing the way that Child and Wiewiora hone their craft as cooks.

3. Write an essay describing in detail the challenges of a job you have had. Work to persuade a skeptical audience that it is harder than they could have imagined.

Sports

ROGER ANGELL

The Interior Stadium

Full Edition, p. 320; Shorter Edition, p. 174

Roger Angell is perhaps America's most revered writer on baseball; he is now over ninety and has an impeccable literary pedigree: stepson of E. B. White, fiction editor for the *New Yorker* for many years, and author of a renowned baseball book, *The Summer Game*. Like most of the essays in this chapter, Angell's piece addresses sports from the perspective of a spectator, not a player. And Angell's spectator role covers many years, from his father's reminiscences of Cleveland baseball in 1904 to the time he wrote this piece in 1971, close to the 1968 World Series he describes in paragraphs 12–17. (Students of the class of 2020—many of whom were born in 2002—will have their own recollections of a memorable series they have witnessed in their own lifetimes. You can ask them if their recollections can match the detail of Angell's, a longtime professional observer.)

The essay mixes personal reminiscence with an extended argument about what Angell regards as one of the greatest pleasures of baseball, the "inner game" (paragraph 2). It is worth asking students if they agree with Angell's statement: "I have watched many other sports, and I have followed some—football, hockey, tennis—with eagerness, but none of them yields these permanent interior pictures, these ancient and precise excitements" (paragraph 4). It may well be that students can supply "interior" pictures from sports besides baseball that they have observed.

The last two paragraphs provide an extended riff on baseball as physics and mathematics, which makes the game somehow more abstract, and which contrasts with the very precise images Angell described in earlier pages of the essay. In those concluding paragraphs, Angell notes, "mathematicians that we are" (paragraph 18) can appreciate the mystery of the game. Students should recognize that Angell's vision depends on our being privileged enough to actually be present, "in the upper stand" (paragraph 18), so that the game's abstractions become clear to us, rather than watching on television, which "cannot bring us the essential distances of the game" (paragraph 5).

QUESTIONS FROM *THE NORTON READER*

1. Roger Angell wrote, "Sports are too much with us" (paragraph 1) in the early 1970s. Think about sports today: the endless speculation about signings

and contracts, gossip about players' salaries and behavior, and twenty-four-hour sports channels. Are sports even more "with us" today? What does "too much with us" mean to you?

2. Gerald Graff writes of his youthful obsession with baseball with its "challenging arguments, debates, problems for analysis, and intricate statistics" (paragraph 11) in "Hidden Intellectualism" (FE p. 418, SE p. 237). What signs do you see of a not-so-hidden intellectualism in Angell's essay?

3. In paragraph 1, Angell writes "More and more, each sport resembles all sports; the flavor, the special joys of place and season, the unique displays of courage and strength and style that once isolated each game and fixed it in our affections have disappeared somewhere in the noise and crush." But his essay refutes this statement, singling out baseball as an example of a sport that retains its distinctiveness. Pick a different sport you know well and in an essay (as a spectator, like Angell, or as a participant), describe that sport, showing how it does or does not resemble "all sports."

TEACHING SUGGESTIONS

1. In many uncanny ways, Angell's essay recalls his stepfather E. B. White's "Once More to the Lake" (FE p. 158, SE p. 66): the father-son relationship, the ability to recall the distant past in precise detail, and extended riffs (that seem like digressions but serve to reinforce the writer's command of his subject matter). Students will enjoy picking out further connections between two quintessential American topics about summertime events that we enjoy in the present and that also link us to the past.

2. Invite students to take up Angell's claim that televised baseball isn't nearly as good as the real thing. Does he mean to claim that most Americans have to settle for a pale imitation? Can students argue that the close-up focus on television gives us some advantages that the more distant perspective of the stadium deprives us of?

3. Angell's recollections are all visual. Ask students whether they have listened to a game on the radio. What kind of recollections does a radio broadcast of a game produce? What's similar? What's different?

4. Students who have played a sport might have a very different perspective from Angell's. Ask the class to point out either how playing a sport allows one to understand the things a spectator might miss or how the experience of playing a sport makes one a different kind of spectator.

SUGGESTED WRITING ASSIGNMENTS

1. Angell opens his essay by alluding to the poem "The World Is Too Much with Us" by the Romantic poet William Wordsworth. The poem begins,

The world is too much with us, late and soon.
Getting and spending we lay waste our powers.

Do you agree that "Sports are too much with us," that as a nation we are obsessed with sports to an unhealthy extent? If so, why? If you don't agree, show why the amount of sports we now have is a useful or valuable part of our society.

2. In the preface to his most famous book of poems, *The Lyrical Ballads* (1800), William Wordsworth wrote:

> I have said that poetry is the spontaneous overflow of powerful feelings: it takes its origin from emotion recollected in tranquility: the emotion is contemplated till, by a species of reaction, the tranquility gradually disappears, and an emotion, kindred to that which was before the subject of contemplation, is gradually produced, and does itself actually exist in the mind.

Write an essay about how Angell's attitude toward baseball is like the way Wordsworth believed poetry was created, focusing on the way both writers value the recollection over the immediate experience. Is this the way you think sports should be experienced? Did Angell persuade you to view sports in a different way? Why or why not?

3. Compare the way Angell describes the 1968 World Series between the Detroit Tigers and St. Louis Cardinals with the way David Halberstam (FE p. 361, SE p. 191) describes the 1998 NBA finals between the Chicago Bulls and Utah Jazz.

Joe Posnanski
Mariano Rivera's a True Yankee

Full Edition, p. 329

Underlying this piece is the sense of what a "true Yankee" is, and Joe Posnanski wants to put forward Mariano Rivera as the most appropriate candidate. To do so he makes an extended comparison to Ernest Hemingway's novel, *The Old Man and the Sea*. (Those familiar with the book can explain the simple plot to the rest of the class.) The hero of the novel is the old fisherman, of course; what helps keep him going is the thought of Joe DiMaggio, the Yankee "legend" who played from 1936–51. Is it time for a new hero? And time for a Latino—finally— to stand at the apex of Yankee "mythology"? Students ought to realize that it's a very bold move on Posnanski's part, and that the essay's title is meant seriously. (Nobody is arguing against Rivera's place in the Yankee pantheon; Posnanski, however, seems to want to place Rivera near the very top.)

Questions from *The Norton Reader*

1. What do you think Joe Posnanski means by the phrase "Yankee mythology" (paragraph 1)? What does this mythology consist of? What other sports teams have a mythology of their own?

2. Posnanski includes allusions to and quotations from an Ernest Hemingway novel. Why do you think he does this? What effect does it have on your understanding of Mariano Rivera and the Yankees?

3. Posnanski's essay provides an example of epideictic rhetoric, a piece that either praises or blames someone or something. Can you think of another figure in sports who is comparable to Rivera, either in longevity or success over time? Write an essay that praises or blames that figure, showing that person's accomplishments, blunders, or both.

Teaching Suggestions

1. One issue worth raising with the class is our need to mythologize sports figures. How is the way we treat them the same or different from the way we treat politicians and statesmen? actors? authors? military heroes? saints? other public celebrities?

2. You might also compare the way Roger Angell (FE p. 320, SE p. 174) and Posnanski describe events in baseball. Posnanski's perspective differs greatly from Angell's; one collects statistics to further support his argument, while the other visualizes events in his mind's eye and describes them to his readers, arguing that such visualizations represent the true essence of appreciation.

3. All three baseball pieces in this section are highly literary. Angell begins with Wordsworth, Posnanski invokes Hemingway, and A. Bartlett Giamatti (FE p. 358)—a literature scholar—invokes the Renaissance poet Edmund Spenser. It's worth pointing out how different these three uses of literature actually are. Angell and Giamatti frame their whole pieces with literary analogies, while Posnanski invokes the thoughts of a literary character about his own hero, a Yankee outfielder.

Suggested Writing Assignments

1. In an essay, compare Posnanski's approach to heroism to the way Tom Wolfe describes another, very different kind of hero, Chuck Yeager (FE p. 114). What differences do you detect in the way the comparisons work? Posnanski, for instance, employs statistics with Rivera, while Wolfe shares stories with Yeager. Which piece gives you the better view of the figure? Which seems most convincing? Which did you enjoy reading more?

2. Write about people's impressions of the New York Yankees, keeping in mind that even people who don't like baseball will have an opinion. You don't have to rely on statistics the way Posnanski does, since you'll be describing attitudes rather than actual events.

DeNeen Brown
Six-Pack Abs at Age 74

Full Edition, p. 334

DeNeen Brown's profile of Ernestine Shepherd treats her as a prime example of a senior citizen who has used bodybuilding to overcome the perceived limitations of age to become a model of fitness for all people. Brown shows her amusement with Shepherd, certainly, but she's also impressed—encourage students to think about this interesting mixture of amusement and admiration.

It's worth stressing that the portrait of Shepherd is incomplete, since we don't get any glimpse of her fuller life: her religious beliefs, her attitudes toward politics, or her views on poverty, for instance. (In paragraph 17 we're told that Shepherd arises at 3 A.M. every day to meditate, but we're not told what kind of meditation regime she follows.) We simply see the outside of Shepherd, which is attractive enough, but throughout we know that the main point here is her age. It's worth asking students whether Brown would have written about Shepherd if she had been forty-four or fifty-four or even sixty-four.

It's also useful to ask whether students would wish for the kind of life Shepherd seems to have achieved for herself (always acknowledging that we don't have a full picture of it). Ask students whether they want to pay the price for such physical prowess and invite them to consider some of the costs. What kinds of benefits does Shepherd get out of her success? Are they the kinds of achievements college students would like to have?

Questions from *The Norton Reader*

1. In paragraph 13, DeNeen Brown quotes her subject, Ernestine Shepherd: "'We can do it! Why?' Shepherd asks. 'Because we are determined, dedicated and disciplined to be fit. You can. You can do it.'" Do you believe anyone can be fit, no matter what age? Why or why not? What factors besides determination, dedication, and discipline affect a person's level of fitness?

2. In response to people saying, "You will die soon," Shepherd replies, "We are all going to die. But it's the quality of life while I'm living" (paragraphs 103–105). What do you think Shepherd means by this statement? Cite details from the text that help reveal Shepherd's attitude toward life.

3. Write a profile of someone who has turned his or her life around by getting fit, stopping a bad habit, or making some other significant change. Be as detailed as you can, and use quotations from the person you are profiling.

Teaching Suggestions

1. A focus on Brown's use of quotations can reveal how this piece is put together. Ask students to analyze their function. Are Shepherd's statements

lengthy or short? Are they pithy and to the point or are they complex and convoluted? Is there any pattern to where Brown usually inserts them?

2. Shepherd tells of undergoing two separate conversion experiences, one when she was fifty-six (paragraphs 20–23) and one after her sister Mildred died (paragraphs 74–85). Ask students if they believe this is the way most lives are punctuated, with sudden flashes of insight leading to change, or if change comes as a long, slow process. Or perhaps a bit of both?

3. Look at the way Brown uses the present tense, sentence fragments (as in paragraphs 2, 7, 10, and 11), and short paragraphs. How do these elements contribute to the flavor of the piece?

Suggested Writing Assignments

1. Some people might think that Shepherd's quest for fitness is somewhat excessive. Write an essay in which you agree, disagree, or both, with that position. How would it be if everyone followed Shepherd's example? Or is it not an example we should follow?

2. After her sister's death, Shepherd endures a long period of depression and then comes out of it with what some would call a conversion experience (paragraphs 74–85). Recount exactly how this conversion happened and explain what you found either missing or convincing in Brown's account.

3. Compare Brown's account of Shepherd's unusual case with Joe Posnanski's account (FE p. 329) of Mariano Rivera's unusual achievements. In what ways are the profiles similar? In what ways are they different?

Michael Lewis
From *The Blind Side*

Full Edition, p. 342; Shorter Edition, p. 183

Michael Lewis is one of America's premier nonfiction writers, notable for his books and essays on Wall Street, baseball, and football. He has the ability to recount actions that fit within the seemingly narrow boundaries of his subject—a deal in the stock market, a play in baseball—and yet create a larger meaning relevant to society as a whole. Here he deals with a significant change in football—the arrival of linebacker Lawrence Taylor and his unique style—and places it in the larger cultural context of violence in American life.

The portrayal of the actual hit on quarterback Joe Theismann is handled in a complex manner. Lewis builds up to it through a mix of background (recounted in the past tense), with a switch to the present (beginning at paragraph 13) for the injury. It's a style that students will be able to appreciate, along with an artful inclusion of what seems like the perfect quotations from players and coaches.

Questions from *The Norton Reader*

1. Examine the way Michael Lewis tells the story of Joe Theismann's career-ending leg injury, interspersing narrative with analysis. What effect

does such a manner of writing have on your reading experience? Does his approach have anything in common with other writers in this chapter on sports?

2. Football-related injuries are frequently covered in the news, and the implications of these injuries are often discussed. Has your attitude toward the game been affected by reports of injuries? Why or why not? Brainstorm a list of ways such injuries might be prevented.

3. Lewis describes a significant change in football tactics in response to the threat of Lawrence Taylor. Do some research on the invention of a new tactic in a sport and then describe it in an essay (for example, the T formation in football, the zone defense in basketball, the designated hitter in baseball, improved safety in race cars, or the invention of free climbing). If you wish, tie the change to the presence of a single player or a distinct group of players.

TEACHING SUGGESTIONS

1. Discuss the institutionalized violence of football, asking students how they respond to it. Is that part of their rationale in following the sport? Or would they rather see less violence in football? (An underlying question is, would football with less violence be the same sport?) Obviously other sports have violence associated with them (boxing, hockey, auto racing, wrestling are prime candidates), but few have the reputation of football.

2. Recent years have seen a noticeable increase in reports of concussion-related football injuries, resulting in serious brain damage. Ask students whether they would be willing to make the tradeoff between a chance for fame and fortune at the cost of possible incapacity later on in life. It's not a choice many of us are called upon to make, but students will find it interesting to contemplate, for themselves or for their children.

SUGGESTED WRITING ASSIGNMENTS

1. Describe an event in the way Lewis does, giving background in the past tense and switching to the present tense when you come to the details of the action itself. Use quotations where appropriate. The event doesn't have to be connected to sports.

2. Argue why violence in football does or does not need to be addressed. You might need to do some online research on the prevalence of violence in the sport in order to make your case. Think of specific ways to curb violence (e.g., better helmets or padding, different rules about tackling or about protecting players) as you support your position.

3. Write an essay exploring whether there is something in our national culture that prizes the violence of football, keeping in mind that the sport has always needed limits on violent behavior. (For instance, in 1905 President Theodore Roosevelt held a White House conference to reduce the high death rate in college football.)

FRANKLIN FOER

How Soccer Explains the American Culture Wars

Full Edition, p. 350

With this not quite tongue-in-cheek title, Franklin Foer's piece characterizes soccer lovers as fans of globalization and soccer haters as foes. He goes on from that stark dichotomy to distinguish between residents of red states (soccer haters) and blue states (soccer lovers), using the sport, as his title would have it, to "explain the American Culture Wars." In this sense, Foer's piece is one of many attempts to characterize the split that many believe has come to exist in the nation.

It's useful to think of Foer's essay as dealing with very large generalities, and students can easily think of counterexamples. (For instance, within the very red state of Texas is Austin, the state capital, a very blue area.) One question is, how useful are red and blue for examining the complexities of American political and cultural attitudes?

Foer argues from his personal experience about the attraction to soccer: his yuppie parents sought to have him play a sport that was less violent and more egalitarian, one in which every player received a "participation" trophy (paragraph 7). Students will all have some opinions about such awards; they might have received some themselves. Is soccer an apt symbol for the tension between "American exceptionalism" (paragraph 21) and a more global perspective?

QUESTIONS FROM *The Norton Reader*

1. How does Franklin Foer characterize soccer as a sport? Do you agree or disagree with his characterization, and why? How much of a role does social class play in soccer?

2. Did you play a sport in elementary school or high school? If so, describe your parents' attitude toward your participation. Were you encouraged? Compare or contrast your experience with Foer's as he describes it in paragraphs 1–5.

3. Foer analyzes soccer through the cultural attitudes people bring to it. What reasons for following soccer does he leave out? List some other reasons people like soccer.

4. Write about attending a sporting event as a fully committed fan. For models you might use Maya Angelou's essay on Joe Louis (FE p. 371, SE p. 201) or A. Bartlett Giamatti's essay (FE p. 358).

TEACHING SUGGESTIONS

1. Have students divide some commonly played sports into categories according to social class: golf, tennis, sailing, power boating, bowling, basketball, skiing, skateboarding, baseball, football, auto racing, and mountain climbing are just a few. Then ask students to make a distinction between spec-

tators and participants. Are there any differences? Within those sports there are significant distinctions: Consider NASCAR vs. Formula One, for instance; NBA vs. college, high school, or urban playground leagues; college and professional football. Is there any sport that's *totally* upper class? *totally* working class?

2. Ask if anyone has changed allegiance to a particular sport. Has someone gone from avidly following football to avidly following baseball, for instance? (Many baseball followers must have made a switch away, if we are to believe reports of the sharp decline in the sport.)

Suggested Writing Assignments

1. Describe the strongly held attitudes of a pundit you have seen or read about. (Sometimes discovering them will require a bit of digging, but you should be able to find them.) Use quotations to illustrate the attitudes you find.

2. Test Foer's claims by contrasting the behavior of fans reacting to two different sporting events, one representing the so-called blue state attitudes and the other representing the more red state attitudes. How deep do the differences go?

3. Some think that an attractive sport should have plenty of action, including many scores. Write about soccer with that criterion in mind. Is there enough action? (There certainly aren't many scores.)

A. Bartlett Giamatti
The Green Fields of the Mind
Full Edition, p. 358

A. Bartlett Giamatti, the former president of Yale University, explains what baseball means to him. Like many New Englanders, he's a fan of the Boston Red Sox, a team which, until 2004, had a long history of letting its fans down. Giamatti writes like a true pre-2004 Red Sox fan, as if being disappointed is a given, built in from the beginning of each season. He recounts—in the present tense—the last game of the 1977 season, with the Sox needing a win to tie the league-leading Yankees, yet falling one run short. Like Roger Angell (FE p. 320, SE p. 174), Giamatti frames his essay with literature, in this case Dame Mutability as created by Renaissance poet Edmund Spenser. (Before becoming a college administrator, Giamatti had been a scholar of English Renaissance literature.) Baseball has always attracted intellectuals and fine writers; Angell and Giamatti are two examples.

Questions from *The Norton Reader*

1. A. Bartlett Giamatti transitions from present tense to past tense throughout the essay even though he is describing a game that took place the previous day. Why do you think he made this choice? How would the essay be different if he had chosen to write only in the past tense?

2. Both Giamatti and Maya Angelou (in "Champion of the World," FE p. 371, SE p. 201) describe a particular game or match. How are their essays similar? How are they different?

3. In framing his essay, Giamatti reflects on "Mutability" (paragraph 2), how the only thing that is certain is change. How does he connect the themes of baseball, seasons, and change? How does his description of a particular game support or illustrate those themes?

4. Using present and past tense, write about a particular moment from a sports event that you have witnessed, using Giamatti's narrative as your model.

TEACHING SUGGESTIONS

1. This piece takes the form of an argumentative essay, starting with its claim that "It [baseball] is designed to break your heart" (paragraph 1). But of course Giamatti is only half-serious; indeed, many of his readers are like the people Giamatti alludes to in paragraph 8, those "who were born with the wisdom to know that nothing lasts. These are the truly tough among us, the ones who can live without illusion, or without even the hope of illusion." He admits that he is "a simpler creature, tied to more primitive patterns and cycles" (paragraph 8). Ask your students what their attitude toward a favorite team (or politician) is. Are class members full of hope, or wary enough to live without illusion? How did they get that way?

2. Examine the way Giamatti transitions from present to past in paragraphs 2–3. Also focus on the way he employs deliberate sentence fragments at key moments of his narration.

3. Compare Giamatti's paragraphs with Michael Lewis's (FE p. 342, SE p. 183) or Roger Angell's (FE p. 320, SE p. 174). Giamatti's are by far the longest. Can students speculate on any connections with him being an English professor?

4. Reflect on Franklin Foer's idea (FE p. 350) about baseball being prone to "nostalgia-drenched celebration" (paragraph 18). Do students see any signs of that tendency in Angell's or Giamatti's essays?

SUGGESTED WRITING ASSIGNMENTS

1. Describe a time when you were let down by a team or a politician or something else you had high expectations about. Is it comparable in any way to Giamatti's description of his feelings? (Notice that Giamatti doesn't give us details of his letdown, just of the game itself.)

2. In DeNeen Brown's essay (FE p. 334), part of Ernestine Shepherd's motivation in getting fit is to stop time, the same motive Giamatti admits to. Compare the two rationales behind their very different devotion to sports, asking which writer seems to have a more realistic attitude toward life.

3. Write an answer to Giamatti, showing him how he's made a serious mistake by putting his hopes into the fortunes of a baseball team (or especially the Red Sox).

DAVID HALBERSTAM

Jordan's Moment

Full Edition, p. 361; Shorter Edition, p. 191

Like many other essays in this chapter, "Jordan's Moment" is a profile, though it differs from many in that it concentrates on a single moment (really a series of games) to demonstrate Michael Jordan's greatness. Like many sportswriters, David Halberstam is fascinated with the very highest level of athletic prowess, trying to account for the achievements of Michael Jordan, universally acknowledged as one of the best basketball players ever. He provides an extended comparison between Jordan and another great player, Karl Malone, both to establish how high the level of competition was and to demonstrate just how far Jordan's skills exceeded those of his excellent contemporary and rival.

Since Halberstam and his readers knew what happened in the winning game of the Utah-Chicago series—that Chicago won—Halberstam had to make his topic something other than the outcome of the series. He settled on describing Jordan's particular qualities as a competitor. He also needed to collect and then provide plenty of background material that would have been unavailable to most fans watching in the arena or on television. Thus he slowly sets the scene, reveals Jordan's illness, and during the action, breaks for carefully chosen asides and quotations that he collected from other key spectators.

QUESTIONS FROM *THE NORTON READER*

1. Michael Jordan retired from basketball in 2003. Do you agree with David Halberstam's final claim in the essay, that Jordan should be remembered as the greatest player in basketball's history? Why or why not?

2. At the heart of Halberstam's essay is an extended comparison of the Utah Jazz and the Chicago Bulls, with individual comparisons of different players, notably Karl Malone and Michael Jordan. Examine how Halberstam makes these comparisons. What does he emphasize the most? What has he left out? What other comparisons does he make?

3. Does Halberstam make clear Jordan's greatness? Write an essay in which you describe the qualities you believe a great athlete ought to have. Use examples that you know about from experience or do some research.

TEACHING SUGGESTIONS

1. Discuss how Halberstam uses the first five paragraphs as a kind of introduction, then follows with more background information before getting to Jordan's "moment." Ask students if the "moment" is the last game of the playoffs or the whole Utah-Chicago playoff series.

2. Point to the way Halberstam interrupts his narrative at crucial places (paragraphs 23–24, 28, 37), moving away from the action on the court to focus on spectators (Armstrong, Ebersol, and Williams). Though these interruptions

break the stream of the narrative, they enable Halberstam to insert crucial background comments while the action is taking place.

3. Michael Jordan has been retired for over a decade, yet he is still a potent symbol of athletic prowess, as the renown of Nike's Air Jordan sneakers testifies. Have students name other famous celebrities linked with consumer products. Ask what is the precise nature of the attraction behind such celebrity endorsements.

SUGGESTED WRITING ASSIGNMENTS

1. Joe Posnanski (FE p. 329) and Halberstam both deal with older athletes, great players well past the days of their youth but still operating superbly. In an essay, discuss what kinds of skills an athlete loses when youth goes away and the advantages that come with age, such as experience and perspective.

2. Paragraphs 38–39 describe the disappointment of the Utah fans as Jordan sinks the winning basket. A. Bartlett Giamatti's essay (FE p. 358) also describes how a fan on the losing side feels. It's more than simple disappointment for Giamatti, and though we're not sure about the Utah fans' anguish, we can easily imagine how they felt. In an essay, describe how you felt at a particularly disappointing sports moment you have experienced. You can take a philosophical approach, as Giamatti does, or go in the direction of description of your feelings.

MAYA ANGELOU
Champion of the World

Full Edition, p. 371; Shorter Edition, p. 201

Maya Angelou depicts a scene from her youth, in 1935, when Joe Louis, "The Brown Bomber," defeated Primo Carnera in a heavyweight championship fight. The setting is a rural Southern store ("the Store," paragraph 1) with an all-black cast of Louis supporters. Angelou makes absolutely no pretence of neutrality. She intersperses quotations from the radio announcers with accounts of the crowd's wildly partisan intensity, which she shared. For our narrator, the fight is more than an athletic bout—Joe Louis carries the hopes of all the African Americans in the Store and beyond, so this piece is about much more than boxing. In fact, there is very little here about boxing itself, with a small amount from the radio announcers but practically nothing except reaction from the spectators. In another sense, Angelou's is a portrait of local mores, a depiction of southern blacks at a particular time in American history.

Angelou was by no means the only prominent African American writer to depict Joe Louis as the champion of his race. Richard Wright depicted the way Harlem residents responded to Louis's victory over the German boxer Max Schmeling: "With their faces to the night sky, they filled their lungs with air and let out a scream of joy that it seemed would never end, and a scream that seemed to come from untold reserves of strength." This essay gives students the opportunity to reflect on other symbolic sporting events they may have experienced in their lifetime.

Questions from *The Norton Reader*

1. Some athletic contests have larger things at stake than just the win of one opponent against another, like the racial pride in the fight Maya Angelou recounts. Can you recall a match you witnessed in which the stakes were greater than the contest itself?

2. Angelou uses hyperbole, or deliberate overstatement, in her writing. For example, Angelou writes, "It was another lynching" (paragraph 16) and "women greedily clutched the babes on their laps" (paragraph 17). Pick out some other examples in the text. How do these overstatements work to make Angelou's point about the fight and the position of blacks in America in the 1930s?

3. Look closely at Angelou's use of dialogue, as she tries to capture the exact sounds and grammar of her fellow listeners as well as the voices on the radio. How does she manage it? How would her piece read if she didn't use dialogue?

4. Note that much more than half of Angelou's account is about the spectators, not the fight. Using Angelou's essay as a model, write about a crowd's appearance and reaction during an athletic contest. Give plenty of detail about the action both on and off the field.

Teaching Suggestions

1. Angelou composes the frame to this essay in Standard Written English. But within that framework she depicts the rural southern black dialect of the 1930s. It's possible to use Angelou's piece in order to contrast two different but equally effective registers of English.

2. Invite students to consider the different reasons one might have for following an athletic contest: rooting for one's country, city, or school; interest in following a particular player (see David Halberstam's essay on Michael Jordan [FE p. 361, SE p. 191]); appreciation of the intricacies of the game itself (Roger Angell [FE p. 320, SE p. 174]); the pure joy of being present at a spectacle. (Students can no doubt think of more reasons.) Is pure racial pride (or fear of racial shaming) still a factor?

3. A close look at the paragraph structure reveals Angelou's narrative strategy. She devotes a single paragraph to every sentence from an announcer, interspersing each one with descriptions of the crowd. Have students discuss the resulting effect of two different narrative voices.

Suggested Writing Assignments

1. Use Angelou as a model to describe a game you see on TV or hear on the radio, interspersing the words one hears from the broadcast with the reactions you have while watching at home.

2. Roger Angell's essay disparages TV, A. Bartlett Giamatti (FE p. 358) alludes to following the Red Sox on the radio, and of course Angelou had only radio back in 1935. In an essay, make an argument about following sports on the radio. What's missing? What does radio allow the listener to do that TV might not? Could it be that radio is closer to Roger Angell's ideal of "The Interior Stadium" (FE p. 320, SE p. 174)?

JOYCE CAROL OATES
Rape and the Boxing Ring
Full Edition, p. 374; Shorter Edition, p. 204

Joyce Carol Oates is a prominent and prolific novelist, a renowned literary figure who has managed the difficult task of impressing the literary establishment while achieving commercial success with a more general audience. In addition to composing fiction, Oates has written extensively on boxing, including *On Boxing* (1987), in keeping with the long tradition of literary figures (Ernest Hemingway, A. J. Liebling, George Plimpton, Jack London, David Remnick, and Norman Mailer prominent among them) following the sport. A serious writer following boxing is not unusual; what is different is Oates's perspective. She sees boxing from a perspective that bridges feminism and journalism.

QUESTIONS FROM *The Norton Reader*

1. Think about your impressions of Mike Tyson and boxing before and after reading Joyce Carol Oates's essay. Did your impressions change, stay the same, or both? How so?

2. What can you tell from Oates's essay about her own relationship to boxing? She offers examples of her revulsion, but are there also signs that she understands why some people are attracted to watching fights? Cite examples from the text.

3. Write a comparison of Oates's and Maya Angelou's (FE p. 371, SE p. 201) essays on boxing, concentrating on each writer's portrayal of the boxers Mike Tyson and Joe Louis, respectively.

TEACHING SUGGESTIONS

1. A close examination of paragraph 3 can be rewarding. Oates covers a great deal of territory as she examines the "deep play" motivations behind boxing and other "dangerous" sports. It's worth going over Oates's list with students to see if the dangerous sports she lists are all commensurate. (For instance, in what ways is dueling a sport? Is fencing truly "dangerous"?) To what extent does the danger of these sports serve as part of their attraction? Or, to put it another way, how much of the attraction of these sports lies in their danger? Is the attraction for participants, spectators, or both?

2. Ask students if they have ever witnessed a boxing match, either on TV or in person. How much of boxing appears to be the kind of aggression Oates describes, and how much of it is formalized and controlled by the referee, the timekeeper, and the rules of the game? (Oates calls it "a highly organized ritual" in paragraph 5.) In other words, the brutal violence takes place within very strict constraints. What is the relationship between the rules and the aggression? Does the ritual make the violence more or less attractive or repellent?

SUGGESTED WRITING ASSIGNMENTS

1. After reading Maya Angelou and Oates, write an essay contrasting their very different approaches. Angelou depicts the fight she describes as possessing cultural roots, a test of skill between an African American hero and his Italian opponent. Oates does not focus as much on the cultural component (though she certainly alludes to it); instead she speaks of deeper roots, specifically male-female relationships that transcend race and are infused with sexuality.

2. Oates, A. Bartlett Giamatti (FE p. 358), Franklin Foer (FE p. 350), and Roger Angell (FE p. 320, SE p. 174) illustrate how a discussion of sports can shed light on culture. Argue whether or not a description of any sporting event necessarily involves giving the readers a sense of how the sport fits into the larger cultural world.

Op-Eds

Sharp disagreements over public policy, over what the government or a group or individual citizens should do, once took place orally, in law courts and parliaments, in the Greek or Roman forum, or on famous occasions such as the Lincoln-Douglas debates. When newspapers and magazines grew popular in the 1700s, they helped carry these arguments into print. The *Federalist Papers*, by Alexander Hamilton, James Madison, and John Jay, were public policy arguments carried out in the pages of periodicals. Today we still have our political debates at election time, but they are very far removed from Lincoln and Douglas's. The quick-paced format dictated by TV, the internet, and social media does not lend itself to thoughtful explorations or even to sharply argued attacks of any complexity. It's hard to argue a complicated point in sound bites, so most public policy arguments are written out and made available in print and online.

Open any newspaper or news website and, in addition to the news, you'll find a diversity of arguments and opinions. Personal opinion appears in columns, critical opinion appears in reviews. Additionally, newspapers traditionally reserve a special place, the editorial page, for the owners' official stance on matters of politics, culture, and current events. On the editorial page the paper's editors endorse particular political candidates and take stands on current public controversies.

In the 1970s, in an effort to reach more readers, many newspapers expanded the space given to editorials and expressions of opinion. The term used for this section, "op-ed," emerged when the *New York Times* appointed one of its most thoughtful editors, Charlotte Curtis, to oversee an enlargement of its editorial page. She doubled the size of the editorial content of the paper, reserving the page opposite the editorials for opinion (thus the name Op-Ed page), commissioning opinion pieces from a whole range of writers and encouraging readers to write their own arguments.

Nowadays, almost every paper has followed suit. Most have an editorial page, letters from readers, and 500- to 800-word op-ed pieces by professional columnists or members of the public. Maureen Dowd; Charles Blow, and Paul Krugman are some prominent current examples; most are "syndicated," that is, their work is bought and reprinted by many papers.

Op-eds have some clear ground rules. Length is strictly limited: 500 to 800 words for newspapers; magazine opinion pieces can be considerably longer. Styles range from the sharply argued, without a great deal of respect for the opponents, to mild, neutral-sounding inquiries into the logic of the issue. Tone ranges from thoughtful to smart-alecky and name-calling is permitted only discreetly; strongly argued pieces predominate, with nuances of argument tending to get lost in the shorter pieces. These pieces are timely; whether written for a newspaper or a magazine, all open with a hook, a clear reference to the issue at hand.

It is tempting to connect op-eds to high school and college debates, which feature starkly opposed viewpoints on an important issue. But many op-eds are a good deal more complex. They are not at all like many school or college debate contests, which have only two possible sides to an issue, pro and con. Sometimes, for instance, the issue is not whether to allow or ban guns but which kinds of guns to regulate and how much regulation is reasonable. That's a more subtle issue, though people can get just as heated over it. Issues are usually not presented as starkly in print; in fact, one reason one writes such an essay is to lay out the issues or to show people what the real issues truly are.

Furthermore, unlike debaters, who each have an equal chance of being the winner, given an impartial audience simply judging the performance (on logical as well as technical grounds), op-ed writers often do not realistically expect to emerge winners. Thoughtful writers know that their pieces will never change everyone's mind. Instead, they are often content to force their readers to face unpleasant truths or think in ways they might not have wanted to. Then, too, sometimes it's just important for a new perspective to be heard, to give its best arguments, not to be left out, to show the flag. Sometimes writers don't care about a victory; they would be content to shape the public debate, to point out what the key issues really are.

Anna Quindlen
Stuff Is Not Salvation

Full Edition, p. 378; Shorter Edition, p. 208

Anna Quindlen, a columnist and novelist, writes in this op-ed about Americans' neurotic addiction to consumption, an addiction fueled by credit cards and desire that's not necessarily linked to need. One way into this op-ed is to ask students to analyze the relationship between their own desire for and need for "stuff." What is the difference between desire and need? What things have meaning?

Quindlen also writes of happiness, claiming that the happiest families she knows are neither the ones with the biggest houses nor those in true need. She lists some things people need (paragraph 9). What do students believe is the relationship between happiness and consumption? What do they need to be happy?

Questions from *The Norton Reader*

1. What does Anna Quindlen gain from tying her essay so closely to the recession that began in 2008, the year her column appeared? What in it might soon appear dated, and what will be enduring?

2. Does Quindlen talk enough about the "stuff" in her own life? How is she like the "us" she analyzes, and how might she be different?

3. Write an essay about the "stuff" in your life. You may take Quindlen's approach, condemning Americans as a nation of shallow "collectors," or make a completely different argument.

Teaching Suggestions

1. Ask students whether they agree with Quindlen's main point, that many Americans are addicted to consumption. Do students believe they are addicted? Do they know people who are? What are the roots of such an addiction?

2. Quindlen points to a question her friend asked herself: "'. . . why did I buy all this stuff?'" (paragraph 7). Discuss with students what drives people to purchase things beyond what they need and for which they have the ability to pay.

3. Ask students to consider the objects that have meaning for them and what gives those objects meaning.

Suggested Writing Assignments

1. Write a three-page essay about an object that has meaning for you and why. Tell the story of how you acquired that object. Be sure to use vivid detail to describe the object.

2. Write about a time when you purchased something you did not need. Try to analyze what created the desire for that item. What influenced your purchase?

Tim Kreider
The "Busy" Trap

Full Edition, p. 380; Shorter Edition, p. 210

In "The 'Busy' Trap," cartoonist and essayist Tim Kreider challenges our conventional notion of "busyness." Far from being an unavoidable condition of twenty-first-century life, he holds, busyness is in fact a choice that provides "a kind of existential reassurance" (paragraph 6) that our lives, work, and commitments are in fact significant and meaningful. Kreider offers himself as a contrarian example, portraying himself as consciously eschewing the trap of busyness to find meaning in a "resolute idleness" that allows for genuine human relationships: "Life," he offers in a closing paradox, "is too short to be busy" (paragraph 12).

Although Kreider critiques a contemporary piety—busyness is a virtue— he participates in a tradition of reflection that runs back at least to Montaigne, who similarly wrote on such abstract topics as idleness, friendship, cruelty, and repentance. In this vein, Kreider juxtaposes *busyness* with a range of affiliated and contrasting concepts, including *tiredness, laziness, idleness,* and *indolence.* Kreider thus relies on a careful defining of terms to which you might draw your students' attention. Unlike Montaigne's essays, however, Kreider's piece is less open-ended reflection than an argument with a definite thesis, which Kreider delivers in his final paragraph. When teaching this essay, therefore, you might ask students to consider the various argumentative strategies Kreider employs and whether or not he is persuasive.

Questions from *The Norton Reader*

1. Tim Kreider writes against the American penchant for "busyness" and in favor of idleness. What reasons does he give for being against "busyness"?

2. In paragraph 7, Kreider claims, "I am the laziest ambitious person I know." What details of the essay reveal his ambition? What anecdotes of other writers and inventors support his case?

3. Kreider admits in paragraph 2 that being busy is not the same as being tired. What kind of people fall into the category of "tired"? Does this op-ed address their situation, or is it written for another kind of reader? How can you tell?

4. Take a position against Kreider's and argue for the value of keeping busy. You might include examples from your own life or the lives of friends and family.

Teaching Suggestions

1. Kreider positions himself as a contrarian who consciously chooses idleness over busyness. Invite students to take a similarly contrarian approach to Kreider's argument. Why might he find his stance attractive? What does he leave unsaid? What aspects of modern life does he downplay or even ignore?

2. Kreider relies repeatedly on paradox, asserting for example, "I am the laziest ambitious person I know" (paragraph 7) and concluding, "Life is too short to be busy" (paragraph 12). Define *paradox* for your students. Have them discuss these paradoxes and others they might find in Kreider's piece. Why does Kreider rely so heavily on this device?

3. Many of Kreider's cartoons are archived on his website, www.thepaincomics .com, where they are accompanied by Kreider's own commentary. Invite students to explore this website and to compare the "arguments" of his cartoons to that of his essay. How is the worldview he expresses in his cartoons related to that which informs his essay?

Suggested Writing Assignments

1. Write an essay that, like Kreider's, challenges some piety of contemporary life.

2. Draw a cartoon that responds to Kreider's critique of busyness. Accompany your cartoon with an analysis and explanation of its connection to Kreider's essay.

MOLLY IVINS
Get a Knife, Get a Dog, but Get Rid of Guns

Full Edition, p. 384; Shorter Edition, p. 214

If op-eds range from dull and earnest to witty and smart-alecky, Molly Ivins is firmly in the latter camp. Agree or disagree with her, everyone is pretty clear about exactly where she stands. Here her title says it all. You don't need to read on to find out what she thinks of guns. But when you do read on, you find out why.

For many readers, Ivins provides a short, sharply argued "take" on a subject. Here she sets out to skewer Second Amendment traditionalists by quoting them the entire amendment and telling exactly what she thinks it means by glossing it with statements such as "Fourteen-year-old boys are not part of a well-regulated militia" (paragraph 5).

This is not subtle writing. It's not meant to be. Ivins is certainly simplifying a difficult and complex subject. Courts almost always rule that the government can regulate firearm possession and use. But they also affirm the rights of individuals to possess guns. For Ivins, however, there is no gray area: "Ban them all" (paragraph 15). You might ask students to consider Ivins's position in relation to the constraints of the op-ed: would Ivins adopt a different or more nuanced position if she had more space to write?

QUESTIONS FROM *The Norton Reader*

1. What do you think of Molly Ivins's examination of the Second Amendment? What kind of evidence would convince you even more of her argument? Why doesn't Ivins provide more evidence?

2. Characterize Ivins's language. What words, phrases, or structures seem typical of her style?

3. Write a response in which you examine the analogy between guns and cars. How well does it hold up? Where does it break down?

TEACHING SUGGESTIONS

1. Ask students to examine the Second Amendment, which Ivins quotes (paragraph 5). Does the second clause depend on the first? What is the link between "militia" and "the people"? How do we decide precisely what the amendment means? Whose interpretation gets to "count"?

2. Ivins says that the Second Amendment is clear. Many disagree with her. What arguments do her opponents give? Many students in the class, no matter what their beliefs, should be able to lay out the two sides of the argument.

3. Examine Ivins's diction to pick out the words that make her writing seem sharp and down-to-earth.

4. Ivins lived in Texas, where guns have historically been highly popular and readily available. Are there any signs of her Texas roots in this essay?

SUGGESTED WRITING ASSIGNMENTS

1. Answer Ivins in a piece of your own, trying for a similarly brisk, no-nonsense style.

2. Research some of the material supplied by pro-gun and gun-control advocacy groups and explain how their approaches are different from or similar to the way Ivins argues.

JO-ANN PILARDI
Immigration Problem Is about Us, Not Them

Full Edition, p. 386

Jo-Ann Pilardi is a professor of philosophy and Women's Studies at Towson State University. She is not a regular writer of op-eds. This op-ed is a citizen's contribution to the Op-Ed page, a fact that may inspire your students to send their own op-eds to the local paper. Pilardi opens her editorial with a radical suggestion: that we treat the employers of illegal immigrants as criminals; she then lists all the ways that we currently criminalize undocumented workers. She does not seriously advocate such a policy change, however, but concedes that "these suggestions make us squirm" (paragraph 7). This is a wise and moderate rhetorical move worth discussing with your students. On the one hand, she loses her most radical followers, but that may permit her to reach across to opponents.

One of the strengths of this op-ed is its attentiveness to the language of the immigration debate. In shifting the debate, Pilardi chooses provocative terms, and relocates our attention from "small brown bodies" (paragraph 1) to "INEs" or "illegal native employers" (paragraph 2). Pilardi is adamantly opposed to guest worker programs, an opposition rooted in her knowledge of the problems such programs have given rise to in Europe. Her op-ed only glosses these matters, so it may be worthwhile to provide some background for your students and to discuss with them how a tiered system of citizenship might lead to greater racism.

QUESTIONS FROM *The Norton Reader*

1. Consider Jo-Ann Pilardi's first three paragraphs. Do you think she is being serious or sarcastic? What do you think the reaction would be if people did as Pilardi says and started hounding employers, the ones she terms INEs?

2. According to Pilardi, who benefits from illegal immigration? Who loses?

3. What does Pilardi have against the idea of "guest workers"? Why doesn't she think that solution would work? What do you think?

4. In paragraph 13, Pilardi states, "We need to create a fair immigration program for those who want to stay." Write an op-ed in which you make a case for a fair immigration program. What would be its main features?

Teaching Suggestions

1. Since 2006, the issue of unauthorized immigration has figured promi-
nently in the news. Find a few current op-eds and share them with your students. How has the debate evolved or shifted?

2. Discuss with students the power of naming and developing key terms.
Is the phrase "small brown bodies" (paragraph 1) a slur? What is the difference
between "illegal immigrant" and "undocumented worker" (paragraph 7)? Can
students think of a neutral vocabulary to adopt? (The nonpartisan Pew
Research Center, for example, uses the term "unauthorized immigrant.")

3. Arguments about unauthorized immigration are often supported by
appeals to values rather than actual evidence. Ask students to locate and review
some of the research on the economic effects of unauthorized immigration.
What does it tell us? Does it challenge their assumptions or beliefs? Is there a
consensus among researchers?

Suggested Writing Assignments

1. Pilardi ends her op-ed by expressing the hope that the United States will
be able to solve the problem of unauthorized immigration "humanely" (paragraph 15). Write a paper elaborating on this statement. What specifically would
qualify a solution as humane?

2. Rewrite Pilardi's op-ed as a serious political satire, along the lines of
Jonathan Swift's "A Modest Proposal" (FE p. 756, SE p. 442). What would a
proposal to criminalize INEs (illegal native employers) look like?

BRENT STAPLES

Why Colleges Shower Their Students with A's

Full Edition, p. 388

With its strong opinions about the deterioration of American colleges, Staples's
op-ed can provoke some sharp reaction among students, who will not always
see things the way he does. A teacher can turn that student reaction into valuable writing assignments.

The first issue is getting to Staples's real point: that the rules of economics
force colleges to keep the customers satisfied by raising grades. The experience
of a class of first-year students might not extend to grade inflation, but they can
do some research on their own. It is not difficult to find out which departments
and programs on campus are hard and which are easy. It's the kind of research
students will be doing on their own anyway, so it's relatively simple to channel
it into composition assignments.

Staples's op-ed also lets students examine some of the rhetorical strategies
good writers employ. One is the generalization. Staples employs the terms "colleges," "departments," "students," and "teachers" but is rather short on specific examples, on individual cases. Is that permissible? Don't generalizations

need support? What constitutes sufficient support? (Short op-ed pieces often don't supply much support, as Staples and the *New York Times* demonstrate here, and as Molly Ivins does in her op-ed column on gun control [FE p. 384, SE p. 214].)

Another useful term is "analogy." For Staples, the college is a "product" and the students are the "customers." Class members can trace this commodity analogy throughout the essay and then decide how accurate it is. Do they think of themselves as customers? Just what happens when we think of college as a product? Is the market analogy a sign of the rising prominence of business in American life?

Questions from *The Norton Reader*

1. Have you or your friends ever experienced grade inflation like the kind Brent Staples describes? What do you think were the causes for it taking place?

2. Staples writes, "An Ivy League professor said recently that if tenure disappeared, universities would be 'free to sell diplomas outright'" (paragraph 4). Analyze this statement. What are its implications? Why does the professor think tenured faculty serve as protection against the "selling" of diplomas?

3. Staples notes that a Duke University statistics professor proposed "recalculating the grade point average to give rigorously graded courses greater weight" (paragraph 10). He was opposed by humanities professors. What might have been the source of their opposition? What is the situation on your campus: do math professors grade more "rigorously" than English professors? Who are the hardest graders?

4. How broad is Staples's range of examples? Would he need to adjust his position if he considered other colleges? Write an analysis of the situation at your college either to confirm or to contest Staples's argument.

Teaching Suggestions

1. Staples's market analogy does not include the notion of college as a brand name. Do some students regard colleges like designer labels? Are these students making an informed judgment about the value of different colleges? What can go wrong in such thinking? This train of thought can lead to excellent discussion, since students are likely to have their own college searches fresh in their minds.

2. Are there any traces of elitism in Staples's op-ed? The University of Phoenix, a for-profit school with a job-focused, "superficial" curriculum, is his first example of a "less rigorous" college. On what evidence does he brand Phoenix as watered down? Does Staples supply any evidence that Phoenix gives higher grades? His other examples are strictly Ivy League, which often but inaccurately serves as a convenient stand-in for "college." (For instance, Staples's op-ed doesn't reflect the fact that many first-year students begin at a community college, and that the large majority of students attend public universities.)

3. As a class, conduct a survey of the grading practices among some departments in your college. Which have the highest percentages of A and B grades? Which mark on curves? Which have the highest dropout rates?

Suggested Writing Assignments

1. Write about the college searches conducted by people you know, including yourself if you wish. What kind of information did prospective students find or receive? How did they make up their minds?

2. Describe a campus tour you took while considering a particular college. Was that tour helpful in making up your mind? In light of Staples's op-ed, what information could you have used in making your decision?

3. Write a response to Staples's depiction of college as product and student as customer based on your own experience.

David Brooks
The Gender Gap at School

Full Edition, p. 390

David Brooks is a journalist and a regular columnist for the *New York Times* Op-Ed page. Previously, he was on staff at the *Weekly Standard*, *Newsweek* and the *Atlantic*. He is also a regular news commentator on TV and radio. He is a conservative with a special interest in social issues and education. Although this op-ed's title signals the focus on schools, it takes Brooks a few paragraphs to get there. He moves from a discussion of reading taste to mounting evidence of the differences between male and female brains to the problem of the essay: boys are falling behind in school because they do not read enough. Brooks's hypothesis, that boys might read more if they encountered books with more masculine appeal, is provocative and should prove interesting to discuss.

Brooks's account is factual: boys and men read less than girls and women. Students may not know, however, that this has been true for centuries. Ask students to consider Brooks's argument in light of this fact. Does it support or subvert his biological argument for why boys need to be taught differently? Does it challenge his implication that education is unfair to boys? After all, the fact that women read more books (especially fiction) has hardly led to the fall of patriarchy. This discussion can help students see ways to write back to an op-ed without challenging its central premise: that it would be good if boys read more. Whether or not students agree with Brooks, his op-ed piece provides an opportunity to discuss the difficulties of responding to this kind of broad and general argument, since any individual example that seems to contradict him (the male who reads avidly, the female who reads books from the "male" section of the store) can be dismissed as simply an individual aberrant case. Discuss with your students what kind of evidence, what kind of rhetoric, might best counter Brooks's argument.

1. Does your experience support David Brooks's claim that boys and girls read differently? Use some examples from people you know.

2. According to Brooks, what is at stake if we don't recognize the differences between boys and girls?

3. Examine the evidence that Brooks uses to support his claim that girls' and boys' brains are different. Do you think Brooks produces enough evidence to support his claim? What evidence might he be omitting?

4. Do a brief survey of favorite books of males and females, and see if it supports Brooks's claim. Write up your findings in an essay in which you agree, disagree, or both with Brooks's argument.

Teaching Suggestions

1. Break the op-ed piece into sections: bookstores, biological research, and education. Then, having identified the sections, discuss the transitions (or lack thereof) and the implicit logic connecting these three topics. Why is the essay organized the way it is? How does Brooks create a sense of a whole in a short space with such widely varying contexts?

2. How segregated are bookstores? How segregated are our reading tastes? Poll the class and discuss the results. Discuss the extent to which their favorite books are written by writers of their gender or have protagonists of their gender. Where would they categorize the Harry Potter books: written by a woman but featuring a male lead? What conclusions can you draw from this informal survey and what do those conclusions tell us about Brooks?

Suggested Writing Assignments

1. Write a proposal for a new high school or middle school English course that will inspire male students to read.

2. Identify another gender gap and write an editorial that explores how society encourages it and how it might be redressed.

David Epstein
Sports Should Be Child's Play

Full Edition, p. 393; Shorter Edition, p. 216

Upon reading sportswriter David Epstein's op-ed on childhood sports, your students will likely have much to say about their own experiences with sports. Some of them will likely be athletes, and some may have suffered sports-related injuries. You might encourage students to approach Epstein's argument in light of these personal experiences.

You might also ask students to consider Epstein's audience. Who do they think he is writing for? Note that this op-ed originally appeared in the *New York*

Times. Note also his specific appeals. Because good arguments are designed to persuade specific audiences, the lines of argument writers choose to pursue tell us much about who they are writing for. This is certainly true in Epstein's case. He argues that premature specialization in a single sport not only renders children more vulnerable to injury but also may keep them from achieving their full potential as athletes. These arguments are not exactly what one would expect. Epstein acknowledges the "national furor over concussions" (paragraph 1) only to turn his attention to other ways in which premature specialization in a sport increases a child's risk of injury. Similarly, to support his contention, he appeals not to nostalgia for the pickup games of yore but to academic research suggesting that these practices may be the best way to foster athletic skills. What types of readers would find this op-ed persuasive? Who wouldn't find if persuasive? What values do they hold?

QUESTIONS FROM *THE NORTON READER*

1. David Epstein makes two arguments against early specialization in a sport—what he calls "hyperspecialization" in paragraph 2. Identify these two arguments. Do you find one more convincing than the other? Why?

2. Consider Epstein's use of evidence. What types of evidence does he use to support his arguments? Where is that support most effective? Where is it least effective? Why?

3. Among Epstein's solutions to the problem of children specializing too early is "futsalization," based on the game of futsal played in Brazil. What features of futsal does Epstein praise and believe should be modeled in other children's sports?

4. Interview three or four campus athletes who play a sport, asking them when they started their sport, what other sports they played, and what their goals might be in participating in collegiate sports. Write an essay in which you agree, disagree, or both with Epstein's position, incorporating the testimony of the athletes you interviewed.

TEACHING SUGGESTIONS

1. Epstein describes several characteristics of sports suitable for children. Ask students to identify them and to discuss them in light of their own experiences playing sports.

2. Epstein calls for the "futsalization of youth sports" (paragraph 18). Ask students to explain what he means by this phrase. Then invite them to imagine futsalized versions of other sports: baseball, football, tennis, and so on.

3. Epstein asserts that the norm for elite athletes is to specialize only as teenagers. *The Norton Reader* includes profiles of several elite athletes: Joe Posnanski's "Mariano Rivera's a True Yankee" (FE p. 329), Michael Lewis's "The Blind Side" (FE p. 342, SE p. 183), David Halberstam's "Jordan's Moment" (FE p. 361, SE p. 191), and Maya Angelou's "Champion of the World" (FE p. 371,

SE p. 201). Ask students if these profiles bear out Epstein's assertion; some additional research may be required to learn about these athletes' upbringing.

Suggested Writing Assignments

1. Write a response to Epstein's argument defending organized youth sports and early specialization.

2. Write a personal essay reflecting on your own childhood experience with sports.

Jane McGonigal
Be a Gamer, Save the World

Full Edition, p. 396; Shorter Edition, p. 220

Op-eds often offer strenuous arguments for positions in which their writers passionately believe. This piece by writer and video-game designer Jane McGonigal is a case in point. She doesn't merely defend video games from the common charge that they are a waste of time and a negative influence; instead, she argues passionately and enthusiastically that video games "consistently fulfill genuine human needs that the real world fails to satisfy" and that they "may prove to be a key resource for solving some of our most pressing real-world problems" (paragraph 1). In other words, reality is the problem and video games are the solution.

McGonigal's op-ed has a structure typical of much argumentative writing: it begins by acknowledging a generally accepted position and then offers a thesis that counters that stance. The body of the piece elaborates on and supports the thesis. The conclusion doesn't just summarize what has come before but gestures toward additional implications of the argument. Because McGonigal relies so explicitly on this structure, her piece could serve as a good model for students learning to write arguments. Of course, you could also encourage students to consider the limitations of this structure: how does it shape or constrain what McGonigal says?

McGonigal's claim about the real-world value of video games is perhaps her most intriguing and provocative. Invite students to ponder and question it: do they too see the potential of video games to address real-world problems? Why or why not?

Questions from *The Norton Reader*

1. In the opening paragraph, Jane McGonigal admits that video games are usually dismissed as "escapist" and "a mind-numbing waste of time." She presents a more positive case for gaming, arguing that it provides "four ingredients that make for a happy and meaningful life" (paragraph 5). What are those ingredients? What evidence does McGonigal provide for each?

2. In the final paragraphs, McGonigal gives examples of games that allow gamers to make positive contributions to global problems. What evidence does McGonigal provide that these games "make us better and change the world" (paragraph 15)?

3. Given the word limitations, op-ed writers often have little space to acknowledge counterarguments. What negative aspects of gaming does McGonigal not acknowledge? How could including other viewpoints have strengthened her own argument?

4. Play or research one of the games McGonigal mentions in her op-ed. Write an essay evaluating the positive and negative aspects of the game.

TEACHING SUGGESTIONS

1. Use McGonigal's op-ed to teach patterns and moves typical of argumentative writing. Have students analyze the structure of her essay, and ask them to look for similar patterns and moves in other genres of prose writing.

2. Note that McGonigal makes two distinct claims: that gaming is psychologically fulfilling and that gaming is socially beneficial. Ask students to consider the relationship between these claims. How are they connected? Does one have priority over the other?

3. Have students read McGonigal's op-ed in conjunction with Tom Bissell's essay "Extra Lives: Why Video Games Matter" (FE p. 214, SE p. 110). Like McGonigal, Bissell also discusses the appeal of video games and argues for their value. Your students will notice similarities between their positions; encourage them also to note subtle differences.

SUGGESTED WRITING ASSIGNMENTS

1. McGonigal defends video games from the charge that they are a waste of time or even a bad influence. Write a defense of another activity you value but that others might disparage.

2. McGonigal describes two video games that have helped to solve real-world problems: *Foldit,* which contributed to cancer research, and *EVOKE,* which helped to prepare its players to found new socially responsible companies. Write a proposal for a new video game that would similarly address some real-world problem. Describe the game and how it would achieve its impact.

DAN BARBER
What Farm-to-Table Got Wrong

Full Edition, p. 400; Shorter Edition, p. 224

In this op-ed, food writer and chef Dan Barber turns a critical eye on the farm-to-table movement, aiming to dispel its naïve assumptions about how sustainable farming actually works. By the end, in fact, he calls into question the name of the movement itself, noting that it implies a passive, "grocery-aisle mentality" (paragraph 22) toward the processes by which food is produced, distributed, and consumed. Yet Barber writes not as an opponent of the farm-to-table movement but as a supporter of it whose perspective has evolved as his knowledge of the economics of sustainable farming has deepened. His op-ed describes that evolution.

Barber's piece is a fine example of an inquiry-driven argument. He begins not with a thesis but with a conundrum—despite overwhelming public support for sustainable agriculture, industrial farming is stronger than ever—and a question: "How do we make sense of this odd duality: a food revolution on one hand, an entrenched status quo on the other?" (paragraph 4). In pondering this question, he arrives at a number of surprising insights, including that the farm-to-table movement must work within, and indeed embrace, the mechanisms of a market economy: "As heretical as this may sound," Barber writes, "farm-to-table needs to embrace a few more middlemen" (paragraph 21).

In his willingness to unsettle accepted orthodoxies, Barber resembles Michael Pollan, and his essay may be fruitfully compared to Pollan's "An Animal's Place" (FE p. 681, SE p. 398). Students will notice both affinities and differences. You might also pair Barber's piece with Marion Nestle's "Utopian Dream: A New Farm Bill" (FE p. 274, SE p. 144), which also concerns the infrastructure through which the food we eat is produced and distributed.

Questions from *The Norton Reader*

1. The phrase "farm-to-table" suggests a simple process of transferring locally grown produce to nearby homes and restaurants. How does Dan Barber complicate our understanding of this process? Why is this complication important to his argument?

2. Barber suggests ways that he, as a chef, can aid local organic farmers by utilizing grains and vegetables essential to crop rotation—as in paragraph 18 where he describes "Rotation Risotto." Can you infer from his argument how consumers who read his op-ed might also aid the cause?

3. Visit a farmers' market, restaurant, or organic grocery store that sells locally grown produce. Choose a grain or vegetable you haven't eaten or don't know well, research it, and write a short account of its cultivation and uses.

Teaching Suggestions

1. Barber writes as both an authority and an inquirer. Guide students to consider the relationship between these two stances. Have them identify passages in which Barber establishes his authority. What techniques does he use? Similarly, have them identify passages in which Barber raises questions, admits surprise, or changes his mind.

2. Invite students to consider Barber's chief example, his visit to Lakeview Organic farm, operated by Klaas and Mary-Howell Martens. Barber uses this example in at least two ways: to educate his readers about sustainable farming and to dramatize his own deepening understanding of the economic

infrastructures needed to support it. How does Barber's example achieve these ends?

3. Barber's purpose is not simply to offer a friendly critique of the farm-to-table movement. Like Annie Leonard in "The Story of Bottled Water" (FE p. 200, SE p. 96), he wants to change consumers' behaviors, writing: "It's one thing for chefs to advocate cooking with the whole farm; it's another thing to make these uncelebrated crops staples in ordinary kitchens" (paragraph 19). Ask students to consider why this turn in Barber's argument is important. Then use the essay to prompt a discussion of students' own eating habits, the economic structures that support them, and possibilities for change—both personal and systemic.

Suggested Writing Assignments

1. Write an essay in which you recount a change in your own mind on some question or issue. As Barber does, explain this change by developing a single concrete example.

2. Write a letter to your institution's dining services or a nearby restaurant advocating the use of sustainably produced foods.

Education

FREDERICK DOUGLASS

Learning to Read

Full Edition, p. 404; Shorter Edition, p. 228

This essay is chapter 7 of the *Narrative of the Life of Frederick Douglass, An American Slave, Written by Himself,* published in 1845. "Written by Himself" is important: as Douglass tells us, it was "almost an unpardonable offence to teach slaves to read in this Christian country" (paragraph 4). He was taught by Sophia Auld, until her husband put a stop to lessons. There were obvious practical reasons for keeping slaves illiterate: reading and writing made information accessible to them and multiplied their opportunities to escape. But there were also symbolic reasons: the ability to read and write was evidence of their rationality and humanity. Douglass escaped to the North when he was eighteen. His powerful *Narrative of the Life of Frederick Douglass* gave powerful support to the Abolitionists in their campaign to end slavery. He wrote two additional autobiographies, one, *My Bondage and My Freedom*, before the Civil War, and another, *The Life and Times of Frederick Douglass*, after.

In this selection Douglass tells how, after his introduction to literacy, he virtually taught himself to read and write. His account, dignified in presentation, has moments of high drama, sharply rendered. It also contains passages of impressively subtle analysis that students should be asked to look at with some care.

QUESTIONS FROM *THE NORTON READER*

1. Frederick Douglass's story might today be called a "literacy narrative"—an account of how someone learns to read and write. What are the key features of this narrative? What obstacles did Douglass face? How did he overcome them?

2. Many literacy narratives include an enabling figure, someone who helps the young learner along his or her way. Is there such a figure in Douglass's narrative? Why or why not?

3. At the end of this narrative, Douglass mentions that he wrote "in the spaces left in Master Thomas's copy-book, copying what he had written" (paragraph 8). To what extent is imitation (copying) part of learning? To what extent does this narrative show originality?

4. Write your own literacy narrative—an account of how you learned to read and write.

Teaching Suggestions

1. Slavery, according to Douglass, gave his mistress Sophia Auld "irresponsible power" (paragraph 1). Ask students to look carefully at Douglass's analysis of the corruption that accompanies such power.

2. Look at the selections from *The Columbian Orator* Douglass names (paragraphs 5–6). Why were they important to him?

3. Ask students to look carefully at Douglass's analysis of why learning to read "had been a curse rather than a blessing" (paragraph 6).

4. Douglass's essay is a classic literacy narrative. Have students identify the features and functions of this genre, using Douglass's essay as their main exemplar. Then have students apply these descriptions to other essays in this chapter: how, for example, do Eudora Welty (FE p. 409), Gerald Graff (FE p. 418, SE p. 237), or Adrienne Rich (FE p. 443) employ, adapt, or depart from the conventions of the classic literacy narrative?

5. Have students research contemporary references to Douglass. How is he used or invoked in contemporary discussions of social and political issues?

Suggested Writing Assignments

1. A number of people helped Douglass in his attempts to read and write. Who were they? Why do you think they helped him? Locate all the evidence that appears in Douglass's narrative and write an essay in which you answer this question.

2. Look in either *My Bondage and My Freedom* or *The Life and Times of Frederick Douglass* to see what Douglass says about learning to read. Write an essay in which you consider how and why these accounts differ from the account in the *Narrative of the Life of Frederick Douglass, An American Slave, Written by Himself.*

3. Write a literacy narrative, an account of how someone else learned to read. If suitable, include details about the specific book or books remembered as important.

EUDORA WELTY
Clamorous to Learn

Full Edition, p. 409

"Clamorous to Learn" and "One Writer's Beginnings" (FE p. 877, SE p. 509) both come from Eudora Welty's best-selling memoir *One Writer's Beginnings* (1985). Taken together, they comprise an account of her curricular and extra-curricular education and may well be read together. Welty was fortunate to grow up in a family of readers, in a house rich with books and music. While her formal schooling was rich in books as well, she was not dependent on it for her acquisition of literacy. Rather, she was permitted to enroll in school at age five (when, today, a child would be enrolled in kindergarten) because she already knew how to read.

"Clamorous to Learn" is memorable for its portrait of Welty's elementary school principal, Miss Duling. The other adults Welty talks about are minor characters: Mrs. McWillie, the stern fourth-grade teacher; other teachers; and her parents. Miss Louella Varnado, her own fourth-grade teacher, gets short shrift. Welty depicts Miss Duling from a significant distance. She remembers her as a figure of power and authority, much larger than life. Miss Duling tells the governor how his daughter will be named, and she calls on old grads when she wants to right some obvious wrong. It's clear that Welty admires Miss Duling's exercise of authority in a good cause, educating the children of Jackson. In retrospect, she sees Miss Duling's life as one of denial; as a child, "this possibility was the last that could have occurred to us" (paragraph 4). From the perspective of a child, authority figures are all-powerful and complete in themselves.

Questions from *The Norton Reader*

1. Eudora Welty describes a number of strong women in the essay: her teachers, her mother, and a younger version of herself. What does this essay state or imply about their motives and ambitions? What kinds of power or opportunities do they have? What kinds of power or opportunities are they denied?

2. Analyze Welty's descriptions: what rhetorical or literary techniques does she use to evoke her teachers so vividly? Locate a few examples in the text.

3. In the final paragraph, Welty recalls her disappointment at missing Mrs. McWillie's reading of the English author John Ruskin's "The King of the Golden River." Welty then concludes, "When in time I found the story in a book and read it to myself, it didn't seem to live up to my longings for a story with that name; as indeed, how could it?" Why do you think she was disappointed? (If you can, read Ruskin's story for yourself.)

4. Write a profile of a teacher who was important to you. Use techniques you learned from Welty to capture that teacher's motivations and ambitions, distinguishing quirks or characteristics, and personality.

Teaching Suggestions

1. Welty does not mention that the schools in Jackson were segregated, that the Jefferson Davis School was for whites only. The black school had, no doubt, considerably less resources; see Maya Angelou's "Graduation" (FE p. 45, SE p. 4) for a description of a black school in a small southern town. Ask students what effect this omission has on their understanding of Welty's account.

2. Why does Welty describe Miss Duling's physical characteristics and clothing so thoroughly?

3. According to Welty, "I did nothing but fear her [Miss Duling's] bearing-down authority, and did not connect this (as of course we were meant to) with our own need or desire to learn, perhaps because I already had this wish, and did not need to be driven" (paragraph 7). This complex statement needs

unpacking: Welty makes some connections between fear and learning and implies others. Ask students what they believe about the relation between fear and learning, what they think most people believe, and what beliefs were embedded in their own educations.

4. Welty's left-handedness was "broken" when she entered the Jefferson Davis School, though her parents were not in agreement (paragraphs 14–15). Why are children no longer forced to write right-handed? What does it signify about schooling that they once were?

5. Welty mentions "deportment" (paragraph 16). Ask students if the word has any resonance for them. Some will never have heard it, while others are likely to have had it engraved on their consciousness. Ask them if they know the word "conduct." Then ask them if they see any significance in different schools naming concepts differently.

SUGGESTED WRITING ASSIGNMENTS

1. Write a Welty-like piece on memorable teachers, coaches, or authority figures you have known, keeping an eye out for the telling detail or quotation.

2. Write an essay in which you compare Welty's description of her teachers with Adrienne Rich's description of hers in "Taking Women Students Seriously" (FE p. 443). Pay particular attention to questions of gender stereotyping.

3. According to Welty, the people of Jackson, Mississippi, believed in "the value of doing well in school"; see paragraph 16 for details. Write an essay in which you consider how much emphasis your own community puts on doing well or, alternatively, compare your own community and Jackson, Mississippi, in this respect.

4. Write an essay in which you analyze the role of fear in one or more particular episodes in your own education; see teaching suggestion 3 (above).

LYNDA BARRY
The Sanctuary of School

Full Edition, p. 414; Shorter Edition, p. 233

Lynda Barry is a cartoonist, writer, and teacher best known for her comic strip *Ernie Pook's Comeek*. She has also published several acclaimed graphic novels, a play that was performed off-Broadway, and most recently, *Syllabus: Notes from an Accidental Professor* (2014), a collection of lesson plans from her creative writing workshop Writing the Unthinkable. Barry's blog, *The Near-Sighted Monkey*, which is associated with her workshop, is available at thenearsighted monkey.tumblr.com and may be interesting for students to explore.

"The Sanctuary of School" originally appeared in the *New York Times* on January 5, 1992. In this short essay, Barry offers an argument for the importance of public schools based on a recollection from her childhood. Barry organizes the essay around a series of contrasts, the main one being the contrast between what she calls her "unhappy home" (paragraph 10) and the safe haven, or sanctuary, of school. But there are others: between the noise of her parents' arguments and the quietness of the outdoors, between the glow of late-night television and the darkness of early morning, between the neglect she experienced at home and the personal attention she receives from the staff and teachers at her school, between the narcotizing power of watching television and the healing power of creating art. The essay mixes genres as well: it begins in the register of a memoir, with Barry recalling a deeply personal moment from her childhood, and concludes almost as an op-ed. The essay thus pays attention not just to its argument but to the way that argument unfolds.

Questions from *The Norton Reader*

1. How does Lynda Barry's school experience contrast with her home life? What specifically makes school a "sanctuary"?

2. In paragraphs 19–21, Barry calls for better funding for public schools. Imagine that Barry has received an unrestricted $100,000 grant to improve her elementary school. How do you think she would spend it?

3. Compare Barry's view of school to Jonathan Kozol's (FE p. 423, SE p. 242) or Gerald Graff's (FE p. 418, SE p. 237). What aspects of school does each author emphasize? Where do they agree? Where might they disagree?

4. Drawing on your own experience, write an argument about how we might improve our schools.

Teaching Suggestions

1. Have students discuss the essay's different registers. Why does Barry begin so personally? Why does she choose to end with a public appeal? Use this essay to broach a more general discussion of how writers' personal histories and experiences shape or influence their arguments and positions.

2. A turn occurs in paragraph 15, when the essay shifts from narration to reflection and analysis: "It's only thinking about it now, 28 years later," Barry writes, "that I realize I was crying from relief." Have students discuss this sentence and its importance to the essay as a whole. Why does Barry experience "relief"? How does her realization support her conviction about the importance of public schools?

3. Have students read the essay closely, paying attention to the details of Barry's descriptions: the thin ice cracking under her shoes (paragraph 6), Mr. Gunderson's jingling keys (paragraph 11), the 11×17 sheets of paper on Mrs. LeSane's art table (paragraph 17). How do these details contribute to the mood and tone of the essay? How do they support or enrich its argument?

4. Invite students to consider how their own childhood experiences have shaped their attitudes toward school and education, either publicly through class discussion or privately in writing.

5. Barry is a teacher, and some of her teaching materials are available free online through her blog, *The Near-Sighted Monkey*. Invite students to explore these materials and to connect them to Barry's essay. How is the stance toward school that she expresses in her essay exemplified in her lesson plans and the kinds of work she asks her own students to do?

Suggested Writing Assignments

1. Write an essay of your own modeled on Barry's: begin by narrating an important experience or event from your personal history, then reflect on its significance and connect it to some larger public issue.

2. Write a dialogue between Barry and one or more of the other writers in this chapter of *The Norton Reader*. Then write yourself into the dialogue by including your own ideas.

3. Barry is best known as a cartoonist. Create a multimodal composition of your own addressing one or more of Barry's themes.

Gerald Graff
Hidden Intellectualism

Full Edition, p. 418; Shorter Edition, p. 237

An esteemed scholar, teacher, and academic administrator, Gerald Graff has written and lectured widely on educational issues. He is especially known for his view that educators should emphasize rather than hide the intellectual "conflicts" that subtend academic disciplines and, more generally, for his conviction that argument and argumentation belong at the center of a liberal arts curriculum.

"Hidden Intellectualism" is adapted from Graff's 2003 book *Clueless in Academe*, which asks why so many students seem mystified or alienated by the academy. In this essay, Graff troubles the common tendency to equate the academic and the intellectual, arguing both that intellectual activity is not limited to the academy and, conversely, that conventional schooling is in fact anti-intellectual. He then proposes a solution: introduce students to the challenges and joys of real intellectual work by allowing them to study and argue about topics they actually care about, whether or not these topics are typically "academic."

Some students may find this essay challenging because it is addressed to teachers: Graff writes *about* students but not *to* them. On the other hand, students may relate to the autobiographical strain in the essay and find Graff's irreverent stance toward conventional schooling appealing. Graff is known for his agonistic approach to argumentation—he is, with Cathy Birkenstein, co-author of the argument textbook "*They Say / I Say*"—and a fine way to approach this essay is to invite students to be in a conversation with Graff, to counter or complicate the argument he advances.

Questions from *The Norton Reader*

1. Gerald Graff observes that through sports, he "experienced what it felt like to propose a generalization, restate and respond to a counterargument, and perform other intellectualizing operations" (paragraph 10). Where and how does Graff offer generalizations in this essay? Where and how does he restate and respond to the arguments of others or develop counterarguments? What other kinds of "intellectualizing operations" does he perform?

2. Graff and Roger Angell (FE p. 320, SE p. 174) both write about baseball. How are their perspectives similar? How are they different?

3. Frederick Douglass's "Learning to Read" (FE p. 404, SE p. 228) is also a literacy narrative: an account of how someone learned to read and write. Compare Graff's essay to this essay. Would you characterize Graff's essay as a literacy narrative? Why or why not?

4. In an essay of your own, summarize and respond to Graff's argument about intellectualism and what he calls "school culture" (paragraph 11). Consider writing about an activity or experience that fits the definition of what Graff might call "hidden intellectualism."

Teaching Suggestions

1. Initially, Graff presents sports simply as a topic that happened to interest him, as something to write about. But he then goes further, using sport as a metaphor for intellectual activity. Invite students to interrogate this metaphor. Notice how Graff introduces it (paragraph 9): What do Graff's words illuminate about the nature of intellectual activity? What do they obscure? You might suggest that in characterizing intellectual activity in terms of sport, Graff is offering an alternative to Western culture's dominant metaphor for argument: that argument is war. Graff hints at this substitution when, alluding to Carl von Clausewitz's famous assertion about war and policy, he describes his love of sports rather than schoolwork as "not anti-intellectualism so much as intellectualism by other means" (paragraph 5). Is sports a better metaphor for argument than war?

2. Direct students' attention to Graff's style and mode of address. Note, for example, that he opens with a commonplace about "everyone" and slides easily into writing in the first-person plural: "What a waste, we think . . ." (paragraph 1). Who is this "we"? Look also at how Graff uses the story of his own "adolescent experience" (paragraph 5) both as evidence for his argument about the nature of intellectualism and to establish *ethos*. You can also use Graff's story to broach issues of social class.

3. Invite students to view Graff's ideas about intellectualism and education skeptically: what does he overlook, distort, or get wrong? Encourage students to develop their own views by talking back to Graff. (Then, perhaps, note that such talking-back is exactly what Graff advocates.)

4. Like Graff, William Zinsser (FE p. 437, SE p. 256) and Adrienne Rich (FE p. 443) also write about the experience of academic work. Have students stage a dialogue among these three writers. Encourage students to look for

surprising points of agreement rather than simply emphasizing these writers' more obvious disagreements.

Suggested Writing Assignments

1. Take up the implicit challenge at the end of Graff's essay: write a "sharply argued" essay or research paper on a non-academic topic you care about.

2. Graff's essay relies on an extended metaphor: intellectual activity is a sport. Write an essay in which you explore the implications of Graff's metaphor and then offer an alternative metaphor of your own.

3. In his final paragraphs, Graff offers a proposal: students should be able to write about subjects of their own choosing, so long as they approach these subjects through "academic eyes" (paragraph 17). Write a response to this proposal.

Jonathan Kozol
Fremont High School

Full Edition, p. 423; Shorter Edition, p. 242

Jonathan Kozol is a noted education researcher and an outspoken advocate on behalf of impoverished children. In this essay taken from his 2005 book *The Shame of the Nation*, Kozol offers a profile of an overcrowded Los Angeles high school. It's a heartbreaking account of students whose eagerness to learn is every day challenged by a series of humiliations and setbacks, from a lack of bathrooms to a lack of AP classes. Students will undoubtedly be eager to share their own stories of how high school failed them. What may be more challenging is to turn the discussion from anecdote toward a profile (of student, school, or teacher) or even an argument. Focusing their attention on the range of evidence Kozol brings to bear on his profile is one way to show them how first-person accounts, reporting, and research come together to create a richly detailed portrait of a failing school. There is not much argumentative language here, but Kozol's sympathy with the students (and their teachers) is clear. For this reason, it might make sense to show students the words and phrases Kozol uses to signal his opinion.

A crucial turn in the piece comes when Mireya begins crying in frustration at the lack of academic challenge in her schedule. Through the young man called Fortino, Kozol introduces the larger issues of social injustice, so that a bad high school becomes a symptom of a society that needs to produce more seamstresses and thus offers sewing classes to poor children. This hint that the problem goes beyond one school or one school district returns in the essay's conclusion.

Questions from *The Norton Reader*

1. Jonathan Kozol draws on various sorts of evidence in his portrait of Fremont High School: numerical data, court documents, comparisons to other

schools, and testimony from teachers and students. How does he arrange his evidence? Which sort of evidence does he emphasize? Why?

2. Kozol adopts a journalistic style, but he also puts himself into the story. How does Kozol use the first person ("I")?

3. Kozol identifies many problems with Fremont High School, but he does not offer any solutions explicitly. Why? Of the problems he identifies, which are the most significant? What solutions do you think Kozol would support?

4. Using Kozol's essay as a model, write a portrait of a school that you know well.

Teaching Suggestions

1. Go through the essay and underline everywhere Kozol makes clear that his sympathies lie with the students. How does he show it without saying it outright? Discuss the reasons he might have for being more subtle than explicit.

2. Read Mike Rose's celebration of blue-collar intelligence ("Blue-Collar Brilliance," FE p. 449, SE p. 262) and compare that celebration to the Fremont High students' frustration at not wanting to be hairdressers and seamstresses.

3. Have students read one of the first-person accounts in this chapter about a passion for learning (from Frederick Douglass [FE p. 404, SE p. 228], Eudora Welty [FE p. 409], or Gerald Graff [FE p. 418, SE p. 237]) and then discuss how a bad school can affect that passion.

4. Discuss Kozol's choice to end the essay as he does, with the sense that neither he nor Mireya has an answer to the problems of her school. Does such an ending invite action or despair?

5. Have students research national efforts over the past decade to improve public schools. They might, for example, investigate the Common Core, the increasing importance of high-stakes testing, or alternatives to traditional public schools such as magnet schools. Can such reforms address the kinds of problems Kozol identifies?

Suggested Writing Assignments

1. In the final four paragraphs of "Taking Women Students Seriously" (FE p. 443) Adrienne Rich offers a series of suggestions for college teachers. Read her suggestions, and following her model, write a conclusion for Kozol's piece that suggests what individual students, teachers, or administrators should do to improve a school like Fremont High.

2. Write a fictional account of what it would be like to teach at Fremont High.

3. Write a research paper that explains and evaluates one approach to improving the state of public education. You might, for example, write about the Common Core, about high-stakes testing, or about alternatives to traditional public schools such as magnet schools. Can this approach improve conditions in schools like Fremont High? Why or why not?

CAROLINE BIRD

College Is a Waste of Time and Money

Full Edition, p. 428; Shorter Edition, p. 247

In *The Case against College* (1975), Caroline Bird argues that the college experience, good though it may be for many young people, is not good for all of them. In this chapter, also published as an essay, Bird argues that while providing a college education to all high school graduates is "a noble American ideal" (paragraph 3), many students don't want to be there, and college itself is a bad investment for them and their parents. Her evidence? Plenty of anecdotes from faculty and students.

Your students may share her bleak outlook; asking them what they think of Bird's essay may lead to lively discussion. Although it was written some forty years ago, Bird's arguments are still relevant. Indeed, today there seems to be a kind of disenchantment with college—and certainly resistance on the part of parents and taxpayers to assume its costs.

QUESTIONS FROM *THE NORTON READER*

1. Caroline Bird published this article four decades ago. How are today's college students similar to or different from the ones Bird writes about?

2. Much of Bird's article focuses on the dubious economic value of a college education. Are there reasons beyond (or in addition to) economics why you or your classmates are attending college? To what extent does Bird consider or ignore these other reasons?

3. In paragraphs 48–50, Bird compares liberal arts education to religion. Why does she make this comparison? What do you think her attitude is toward the liberal arts? Is it similar to or different from yours?

4. In paragraph 6, Bird discusses the hard-sell advertising techniques of many academic institutions. Look into your own school's "advertising techniques" (view books, pamphlets, information sent to homes and high schools, websites, and so on). How do these sources present the school to parents and potential students? Write an analysis of one of these sources.

TEACHING SUGGESTIONS

1. Ask students to list Bird's bad reasons for attending college. How many of them do they take seriously? This exercise may well be done in groups.

2. Bird frankly admits that she addresses the issue as a journalist, not as a scholar or policy analyst. Ask students to point to examples of what Bird calls "the journalistic tools of my trade" (paragraph 11).

3. Bird relies on different kinds of evidence to support her arguments, including anecdotes, quotations from authorities like the Carnegie Commission and college administrators, and somewhat rough financial calculations. Ask students to evaluate her evidence. Do they have anecdotes of their own

that confirm or contradict Bird's? Do her financial arguments still hold up? Can they find more recent statements from authorities that support or challenge her positions?

4. Bird observes that "the liberal arts are a religion in every sense of that term" (paragraph 49). Invite students to discuss and evaluate this analogy. In what senses are the liberal arts like a religion? What positive and negative aspects of a liberal arts education does the analogy illuminate?

Suggested Writing Assignments

1. Interview students, teachers, and college officials you know and write an essay that updates Bird's. Are conditions the same as they were thirty years ago? Is the outlook for someone without a college degree still the same?

2. Some regard a college degree as a necessary kind of license, a union card, a piece of paper they have to have. Write about people who believe this, showing how such a belief colors their attitude toward learning, classes, and interaction with other students.

3. According to Bird, in 1970 colleges were spending more than thirty billion dollars annually to educate half of America's high school graduates. Do research to ascertain the comparable figures today, or figures for as recent a time as they are available. Write an essay in which you consider how economists justify such an expenditure. Are there other economists who regard it as a bad investment?

William Zinsser
College Pressures

Full Edition, p. 437; Shorter Edition, p. 256

William Zinsser, a writer and journalist, taught at Yale University from 1971 to 1979. For most of this time, he served as the master or head of Branford College, one of Yale's twelve residential colleges. "College Pressures" was published in 1979; students will probably notice that room, board, and tuition in most private colleges then cost as much as $7,000 and that students might leave college with a debt of as much as $5,000. What are room, board, and tuition now?

Zinsser introduces "College Pressures" with notes from students and then, in an odd maneuver, first generalizes and then limits their relevance: "students like the ones who wrote those notes can also be found on campuses from coast to coast—especially in New England and at many other private colleges across the country that have high academic standards and highly motivated students" (paragraph 2). Does Zinsser restrict the relevance of this essay to elite colleges? Are most/many/some students still harried, driven by the same external and internal pressures he describes? Which students, and where are they to be found? Among the pressures Zinsser does not mention are work and family. How do these exert pressure on students, and on which students?

"College Pressures" appeared in a little-known magazine, *Blair and Ket-chum's Country Journal*. Who does Zinsser think his audience is? What evidence is there in the essay? Is it written to students, to professors, to parents, to outsiders? Which elements of it seem directed to each of these groups?

Zinsser uses a four-part classificatory scheme in characterizing the pressures on students as economic, parental, peer, and self-induced. His scheme does not provide structure for his entire essay. It is, however, elaborately framed, and the divisions according to kinds of pressure are not only weighted with illustrations but also cross-referenced (see, for example, paragraphs 15–19 and 24). Zinsser apparently sees his classificatory scheme as rhetorically useful in ordering his material but distorting in compartmentalizing it. You may want to discuss the value of using classification within an essay rather than as the framework for an entire essay.

Questions from *The Norton Reader*

1. What are the four kinds of pressure William Zinsser describes for the 1970s? Are they the same kinds of pressure that trouble students today, or have new ones taken their place?

2. Compare Zinsser's attitude toward college to Caroline Bird's (FE p. 428, SE p. 247). In what ways do they agree? In what ways do they disagree?

3. Write an essay in which you explain how you have experienced and handled the pressures of college.

Teaching Suggestions

1. Zinsser combines personal experience with description, analysis, and both explicit and implied prescription. Ask students to locate personal passages and discuss their contribution to the essay. What is Zinsser's authority to describe, analyze, and advise, and how does he claim it in this essay?

2. Ask students to imagine Zinsser's four-part classificatory scheme as organizing this entire essay. What parts of "College Pressures" would remain, what parts would go? What would be the effect of these omissions?

3. "Where's the payoff on the humanities?" Zinsser inquires (paragraph 20). Ask students to define the payoff Zinsser illustrates.

Suggested Writing Assignments

1. What are the pressures on college students today? Write an essay in which you describe and analyze them, perhaps using evidence from Zinsser's essay to suggest that some pressures remain the same.

2. "Where's the payoff on the humanities?" Zinsser asks (paragraph 20). Write your own answer to this question, drawing on experience, observation, and reading.

3. Zinsser writes of trying to show students that their futures don't need to be entirely mapped out for them by bringing to campus men and women

who have succeeded in all walks of life. Interview at least three adults that you admire and ask them, as Zinsser did with his guests, "to say a few words about how they got started" (paragraph 40). Write a paper that reports and reflects on your findings. Did you notice any patterns in your subjects' responses? Did anything surprise you? Did the interviews change your own views of college? If so, how?

Adrienne Rich
Taking Women Students Seriously
Full Edition, p. 443

Adrienne Rich was a poet as well as an essayist. Born in 1929, she graduated from Radcliffe College in 1951, the year her first book of poems was published; her early poetry antedates the women's movement. In "Taking Women Students Seriously," an address given to teachers of women, Rich professes her intention not to lecture but to "create a context, delineate a background" for discussion (paragraph 1). She begins with her own education and her experience teaching minority students as well as her own women students. "The personal is political"—this is a maxim of the women's movement and an enabling principle of consciousness raising. It is also a strategy of feminist writing.

Rich sets in parallel form the questions discussed by instructors of minority students and the questions she came to ask about teaching women. Both minorities and women are disadvantaged, she believes, and the pedagogy appropriate to one has parallels with the pedagogy appropriate to the other. Note Rich's emphasis on activity versus passivity, questioning rather than accepting. Her discussion of women as students leads to a discussion of women in society: the academy mirrors society at large in putting women down or not taking them seriously.

Even though it was written in 1978, this essay has an abiding resonance. When teaching it, you might note the date of its publication and invite students to reflect on how the experiences of women at college have and haven't changed over the past four decades.

Questions from *The Norton Reader*

1. Adrienne Rich discusses the importance of listening to silences and of paying attention to absences. In one of your classes, listen and observe; take note of who speaks and who doesn't; and watch for responses from the instructor. What sense can you make of these silences and absences? Do your conclusions correspond to Rich's, or do they differ?

2. Rich and David Brooks in "The Gender Gap at School" (FE p. 390) come to very different conclusions. What do you think accounts for their differences?

3. In paragraph 10, Rich discusses the relationship between intellectual independence and physical safety. Do some research on the public safety policies on your own campus (escorts, lighting, etc.) or in your neighborhood, and also consider your own experiences. Do you feel safe walking alone? To what extent does your sense of physical safety affect your intellectual work? Write a journal entry or article on these issues.

TEACHING SUGGESTIONS

1. Rich discusses what she calls "the precariously budgeted, much-condescended-to area of women's studies" (paragraphs 8–9). What does women's studies teach, and why, according to Rich, do women need to learn these things?

2. Rich speaks of women (and men) as if gender unites them more than other circumstances—large circumstances of social and economic class, of race and ethnicity, or small circumstances of infinite variety—divide them. She creates universals that may well be false. Consider the following: "Men in general think badly: in disjuncture from their personal lives, claiming objectivity where the most irrational passions seethe" (paragraph 16). Does Rich's generalization suggest a counter-generalization about how women think? Are there familiar generalizations about how women think?

3. "Feminists are depicted in the media," Rich says, "as 'shrill,' 'strident,' 'puritanical,' or 'humorless,' and the lesbian choice—the choice of the woman-identified woman—as pathological or sinister" (paragraph 12). Might some of Rich's readers think that she conforms to any of these labels through the course of her lecture? Would she care?

SUGGESTED WRITING ASSIGNMENTS

1. From your experience and observation (of high school or college or both), are women students taken seriously? Do teachers and faculty members treat them the same way as male students? Do male students regard them as equals? Write an essay addressing these questions. You might also consider differences between male and female teachers and between fields of study, for example, between education and engineering, or English and physics.

2. He: "Women take everything personally." She: "The personal is political." Write an essay in which you make a case for or against the personal.

3. Write an essay on a larger issue in which you focus on your own experience as evidence and illustration.

4. If you have a women's studies or gender studies program at your institution, find out more about it. What are its aims, what courses does it teach, and who teaches them? Interview some students, some faculty, or both who are active in women's or gender studies. Write an essay in which you discuss women's or gender studies at your institution. Enunciate your own position with respect to women's or gender studies as part of your discussion.

Mike Rose
Blue-Collar Brilliance

Full Edition, p. 449; Shorter Edition, p. 262

Mike Rose's classic text *Lives on the Boundary* (1989) combines memoir, reporting, and research to paint a sympathetic portrait of the struggles faced by first-generation college students. At the heart of his story is the fact, alluded to here, that he spent the first half of high school on the vocational track (due, in part, to his high school's having two students named Mike Rose). Thanks to *Lives on the Boundary* and his many other books, Rose has become one of our foremost experts on the centrality of compassionate class consciousness in the writing classroom. In this essay, Rose depicts his blue-collar roots in a new way: instead of documenting his struggle to become educated, he celebrates the intelligence, apparent but unappreciated, in his mother and, by extension, all blue-collar workers.

The son of Italian immigrants, Mike Rose was born in Altoona, Pennsylvania, and raised in Los Angeles, California. On his blog, he writes, "If I had to sum up the philosophical thread that runs through my work, it would be this: A deep belief in the ability of the common person, a commitment to educational, occupational, and cultural opportunity to develop that ability, and an affirmation of public institutions and the public sphere as vehicles for nurturing and expressing that ability."

Questions from *The Norton Reader*

1. In his closing paragraph, Mike Rose asserts that the expanded understanding of intelligence for which he is arguing suggests "a model of the mind that is worthy of a democratic society." What are the social or political implications of this connection between mind and democracy?

2. Rose's essay was originally subtitled "Questioning assumptions about intelligence, work, and social class." What assumptions is Rose questioning, either directly or indirectly?

3. Rose introduces his general argument with detailed accounts of the work-lives of two family members: his mother and his uncle. Why do you think he makes this choice?

4. Rose describes himself as writing "'cognitive biographies' of blue-collar workers" (paragraph 15). Drawing as Rose does on interviews and careful observation, write a cognitive biography of your own.

Teaching Suggestions

1. Invite students to re-read the opening description of Rose's mother's restaurant, asking them to pick out the detail that is most vivid to them. Discuss their choices and the role of these specific details in the larger essay.

2. In the final paragraph, Rose asserts that acknowledging "diverse intelligence" is not "softhearted." Ask students to debate this claim. Should the

kinds of skills that he describes here be called "intelligence" or something else? What other kinds of intelligence might we want to value?

3. Bring in a few pages from Rose's *Lives on the Boundary* and discuss how he navigates his respect for his mother against his own desire for a different kind of education. What is the role of Rose's personal voice and experience in both instances?

4. Some of your students will almost certainly have done blue-collar work at some point in their lives. Invite them to talk about the intellectual complexities of the kinds of work they have done. Then ask them to relate the challenges of that work to the kinds of academic work they are doing in college.

Suggested Writing Assignments

1. Write a paper celebrating another, underappreciated form of intelligence (e.g., emotional, spiritual, or athletic). Following Rose's example, incorporate detailed observations of people who possess this quality into your argument for its importance.

2. Rose delights in the lingo of his mother's workplace. Interview people at your workplace—or one near where you live—and create a glossary of the special lingo there. Write an essay about what this lingo tells us about the job, its challenges, and the relationships among workers.

3. Read "College Is a Waste of Time and Money" (FE p. 428, SE p. 247) and, combining Caroline Bird's arguments with Rose's celebration of blue-collar work, write a paper arguing who should and should not go to college and why.

4. Rose is best known as a scholar on how to teach writing; he is a scholar of composition theory. Research his work in this field and write an essay that puts this essay into the larger context of his career.

Language and Communication

LESLIE JAMISON

Mark My Words. Maybe.

Full Edition, p. 458

Leslie Jamison's essay explores the ways bodies, symbols, and words communicate, often in ways that are unintended. Although Jamison is thoughtful about her reasons for getting a tattoo (to mark the end of a relationship and to assert her independence) and the personal meaning to her ("empathy and camaraderie," paragraph 7), those who see the tattoo do not always respond in the way she hopes. Jamison even comes to doubt her tattoo's meaning and effect, writing, "The tattoo was supposed to represent a new freedom but in that moment it felt like a shackle" (paragraph 19). By the end of this reflective essay, Jamison comes to understand the complexity of her tattoo and its meaning— both to herself and to others. You can use this essay to help students explore the complexity of symbols, communication, and self-representation.

QUESTIONS FROM *THE NORTON READER*

1. Leslie Jamison initially thinks her tattoo will help her get over a breakup, but it comes to mean several different things. What do you think the tattoo ends up meaning to her? Point to passages in the text that support your answer.

2. Jamison titles her essay "Mark My Words. Maybe." Who might she be addressing with this title? Consider the reactions of the drugstore clerk (paragraphs 10–16) and Jamison's father (paragraph 17) as you think about how this title relates to the broader points she makes in her essay.

3. Jamison writes about the power bodies have to communicate messages that would otherwise be expressed through speaking and writing. Write an essay discussing the power and the limitation of tattoos as a mode of communication. If you have a tattoo, consider incorporating your personal experience.

TEACHING SUGGESTIONS

1. By the end of the essay, Jamison doesn't pin down an absolute meaning for her tattoo. She recognizes how it represents opposite meanings and desires: "an idea and its refutation, a man and his absence, a vote of confidence from the world and . . . something more like the opposite" (paragraph 22). Whether or not students have a tattoo, they can probably think of a symbol, quotation, hairstyle, piece of jewelry, or something else that has shifted in meaning for them,

depending on later experiences and on the responses of others. As an in-class writing assignment, ask students to reflect on a symbol or quotation that has changed meaning for them over time.

2. The quotation Jamison chooses for her tattoo is a translation from a line in Terence's play *Heauton Timorumnos*. Bring in a copy (or several translations) of the play and discuss with students the quotation in its original context before discussing how others have interpreted the line. This exercise might lead to a discussion of why certain lines from plays, songs, poems, or other texts come to be quoted out of context.

3. A modification of question 3 in *The Norton Reader* can be used to assign a range of genres: a personal essay, in which a student reflects on the meaning of his or her tattoo; a profile, in which a student focuses on someone else and that person's tattoo; an argument about either the power or limitations of tattoos as a form of communication; or a cultural analysis of a specific symbol frequently chosen as a tattoo.

SUGGESTED WRITING ASSIGNMENTS

1. Interview someone who has a tattoo; ask about its meaning, why the individual chose it, and how others have responded to it. Write a profile of that person and his or her tattoo. Include a photo if you'd like.

2. Research the history of tattoos and write about their place in a specific culture or subculture.

3. Choose a symbol, quotation, hairstyle, piece of jewelry, item of clothing—something you have worn or chosen to make a statement or to represent yourself or your beliefs. What did you hope to communicate? How did others respond? Write an essay reflecting on your experience.

MAXINE HONG KINGSTON
Tongue-Tied

Full Edition, p. 461; Shorter Edition, p. 270

Maxine Hong Kingston's *The Woman Warrior* (1976) combines autobiography with family history, cultural myth, and fictional tale to capture the meaning of growing up female and Chinese American. As in other sections of her autobiography, Kingston here retells a story originally told by her mother to probe the problem of silence and speech. Though painful, even cruel as Kingston retells it, the story prepares for the complexity of Kingston's linguistic responses, a paradoxical combination of refusing speech and speaking out, depending on the context.

If students have read Gloria Anzaldúa's "How to Tame a Wild Tongue" (FE p. 471, SE p. 280), you might ask them whether her position that language is a form of political dominance and social control applies to Kingston's situation: why can't Kingston speak in English school, for example, when she can speak, shout, even scream in Chinese school? If students have read Richard Rodriguez's "Aria" (FE p. 465, SE p. 274), you might compare the essays to explore the complex patterns of gender, ethnicity, and class that affect students' ability to speak. Such discussion will prevent students from assuming that only one factor creates a condition of silence. Both Kingston and Rodriguez, female and male, suffer from an inability to speak in school; yet Kingston can speak at home and in Chinese school, whereas Rodriguez notes the growing silences at the family dinner table. In addition, learning a new language affects family members in different ways: the mothers in these two families learn to speak out in English, whereas Rodriguez's father (Kingston does not mention hers) becomes quiet, almost shy, as his family learns its second language. Anzaldúa speaks different "home tongues" with different members of her dispersed family.

Questions from *The Norton Reader*

1. Like Gloria Anzaldúa in "How to Tame a Wild Tongue" (FE p. 471, SE p. 280), Maxine Hong Kingston uses the tongue as both a physical body part and a metaphor for speech. Locate examples of these uses of "tongue" and explain them.

2. Why does Kingston call non-Asians "ghosts" (paragraph 9)? Are these the only ghosts Kingston confronts? Discuss her usage of this term in the essay and in the subtitle of her autobiography, *Memoirs of a Girlhood among Ghosts*.

3. Have you ever had difficulty speaking up? Think about a time when it was difficult to speak. Write an essay about the experience, incorporating family or social context, as Kingston does.

Teaching Suggestions

1. As Kingston tells it, her mother cut her frenum to loosen her tongue. Nevertheless, her essay includes a Chinese proverb to the effect that "a ready tongue is an evil" (paragraph 2). Gloria Anzaldúa's "How to Tame a Wild Tongue" (FE p. 471, SE p. 280) contains additional proverbs about tongues. As a follow-up to the first question from *The Norton Reader*, ask students if they know of similar proverbs from other cultures. Why is the tongue a universal metaphor for speech? Why are loose tongues attributed to women, and why are women chastised for them?

2. Encourage students to interpret the story that Kingston's mother tells. What meanings do they see? What meanings does Kingston emphasize?

3. How does Kingston convey the differences between being a person, an "I," in English versus being one in Chinese? What other strategies does she use to explain the differences between being Chinese and being American?

4. Compare Kingston's experiences in grade school with Rodriguez's ("Aria" [FE p. 465, SE p. 274]). How and why are they similar or different?

SUGGESTED WRITING ASSIGNMENTS

1. Retell a story that your mother, father, or grandparent told to communicate appropriate (or inappropriate) behavior within your ethnic community. Try to capture the richness of the story, as well as your responses to it.

2. Is silence always a mark of social control? Can it also be a form of resistance? Analyze Kingston's, Rodriguez's, or Anzaldúa's account to suggest ways in which they are both being controlled and resisting control.

RICHARD RODRIGUEZ
Aria

Full Edition, p. 465; Shorter Edition, p. 274

"Aria" comes from the first chapter of an autobiography, *Hunger of Memory: The Education of Richard Rodriguez* (1982). This selection is its opening, in which Richard Rodriguez draws on the memories he has narrated and makes a case, explicitly and forcefully, against bilingual education. When *Hunger of Memory* was first published, it provoked heated controversy among Spanish-speaking Americans. Rodriguez opposes bilingual education not only because he believes that it delays the acquisition of English crucial to American citizenship but also, more important, because he believes that all education requires the assumption of a "public" voice and the loss of "private" language. To avoid the process of loss and gain is, for Rodriguez, to undermine or sentimentalize education.

If you have students whose first, "public" language is not English, this essay provides an occasion for allowing them to speak for—or against—bilingual education. If they agree with Rodriguez, you might ask them to narrate incidents that support his views and the analysis he provides. If they disagree, you might help them find alternate modes of analysis or counter-arguments to define their own positions. Even with classes of students whose only language is English, the issue of the "private" language of home versus the "public" language required at school can provoke an excellent discussion of education.

QUESTIONS FROM *The Norton Reader*

1. What, according to Richard Rodriguez, did he lose because he attended an English-speaking school without a bilingual program? What did he gain?

2. Rodriguez frames this section of his autobiography with an argument against bilingual education. What evidence does he use to support his argument? Do you find it convincing? Why or why not?

3. According to Rodriguez, what are the differences between private and public languages, private and public individuality? Can both exist when the family language and the school language are English? How might a native speaker of English describe the differences?

4. Make a case, in writing, for or against bilingual education using material from Maxine Hong Kingston's "Tongue-Tied" (FE p. 461, SE p. 270), Gloria

Anzaldúa's "How to Tame a Wild Tongue" (FE p. 471, SE p. 280), or Gloria Naylor's "Mommy, What Does 'Nigger' Mean?" (FE p. 481), as well as your own experience, observation, and reading.

TEACHING SUGGESTIONS

1. What is Rodriguez's thesis? How does he use the arguments of opponents to define and support his own view? After the opening paragraphs, at what other points does he introduce the arguments of his opponents in order to refute them?

2. How does this essay incorporate personal narrative within an argumentative structure? To get at this question, try analyzing the opening sentences of paragraphs 1 through 4, in which Rodriguez articulates his position on bilingual education, and the opening sentences of paragraphs 5 through 10, in which he condenses his educational experiences.

3. Rodriguez's account shows both Spanish and English to be "rich" languages. How—and why—does he accomplish this?

4. Have students read Gloria Anzaldúa's "How to Tame a Wild Tongue" (FE p. 471, SE p. 280). Compare the ways in which Rodriguez and Anzaldúa show Spanish and Chicano Spanish, respectively, to be "rich" languages.

5. Rodriguez's autobiographical account of his education might be subtitled "Loss and Gain." What are the gains Rodriguez discusses? What are the losses? Are there some losses or gains that Rodriguez might have avoided mentioning? Why? What are they?

6. What persona does Rodriguez create in this essay—that is, what kind of person do we as readers imagine him to be? In classical rhetoric "persona" involves the issue of "ethos," and argument involves the issue of "logos." How do the two interact in this essay?

SUGGESTED WRITING ASSIGNMENTS

1. Is the transition from the private language of the home to the public language of the school a necessary part of education? Write an essay, based on your experience, observation, and reading, in which you address this question.

2. If your native language is something other than English, recount your own experience(s) of learning English in school, either implicitly or explicitly agreeing or disagreeing with Rodriguez's position on bilingual education.

GLORIA ANZALDÚA
How to Tame a Wild Tongue

Full Edition, p. 471; Shorter Edition, p. 280

Gloria Anzaldúa was a Chicana, that is, an American of Mexican descent, born in south Texas; she was also Latina. She was a writer, a poet, a feminist, and a social activist. This essay, "How to Tame a Wild Tongue," comes from a collection whose title, *Borderlands/La Frontera* (1987), is bilingual, like the essay itself. Anzaldúa mixes English and various forms of Spanish, often without translating the Spanish. Call students' attention to her statement near the end of the essay: "Until I am free to write bilingually and to switch codes without having always to translate, while I still have to speak English or Spanish when I would rather speak Spanglish, and as long as I have to accommodate the English speakers rather than having them accommodate me, my tongue will be illegitimate" (paragraph 27). In this essay she claims that freedom for herself.

Readers who don't know Spanish might be put off and see Anzaldúa's use of untranslated Spanish as an act of linguistic defiance: she compels them to accommodate her. Much of the essay, however, can be understood without translating the Spanish. Anzaldúa defies the convention that, in writing, one translates from a subaltern language to the dominant language, and by doing so, she registers her protest against Anglo dominance. (Indeed, she insists that editors who collect her work leave the Spanish untranslated.)

In this essay Anzaldúa explains—and celebrates—varieties of Chicano Spanish, the five "home" tongues on the list of eight that Chicanos speak (paragraph 14). However, she begins this essay by complaining about the Chicano culture that silences women and even, grammatically, excludes their bonding. The word she didn't know existed, *nosotras*, is the female form of "we"; in Chicano Spanish the masculine form, *nosotros*, is used by women and men alike (paragraph 8). Yet the gendered inflections of Chicano Spanish allow her to make distinctions that English does not: have students note when she uses the masculine singular *Chicano* and *Tejano*, the feminine singular *Chicana* and *Tejana*, and the gendered plurals *Chicanos* and *Chicanas*.

QUESTIONS FROM *The Norton Reader*

1. Gloria Anzaldúa includes many Spanish words and phrases, some of which she explains, others which she leaves untranslated. Why do you think she does this? What different responses might bilingual versus English-only readers have to her writing?

2. The essay begins with an example of Anzaldúa's "untamed tongue." What meanings, many metaphoric, does Anzaldúa give for "tongue" or "wild tongue"? How does the essay develop these meanings?

3. Anzaldúa speaks of Chicano Spanish as a "living language" (paragraph 11). What does she mean? What is her evidence for this point? What other languages do you know that are living, and how do you know they are living?

4. If you speak or write more than one language, or come from a community that uses expressions that you believe to be unique or uncommon, write an essay in which you incorporate that language and/or alternate it with English. Think about the ways that Anzaldúa uses both English and Spanish.

Teaching Suggestions

1. Anzaldúa refers to Chicano Spanish as a "patois" (paragraph 12), a term that can connote a regional dialect considered substandard by those who do not speak it. Why does she use this term? Ask students what "patois"—or, less pointedly, regional or ethnic language varieties—they have encountered or know of.

2. Ask students how many of them think they speak with an accent. What does it mean, in the United States, to speak with an accent? Do some accents have a higher status than others? Have any students been told to get rid of their accents? Have any tried to get rid of their accents? Why?

3. According to Anzaldúa, Chicano Spanish is necessary "for people who live in a country in which English is the reigning tongue but who are not Anglo" (paragraph 12). Why?

4. Richard Rodriguez, in "Aria" (FE p. 465, SE p. 274), apparently agrees with many of Anzaldúa's points about "home" languages. Nevertheless, he argues that children must give them up as soon as possible to learn what he calls the "public language" (paragraph 1). Why? Do you think Anzaldúa would agree?

5. Those who grew up speaking Chicano Spanish "have internalized the belief that we speak poor Spanish" (paragraph 22), Anzaldúa writes. How widespread is mistrust of one's ability to speak "good English"? Ask students how many people feel uncomfortable about their English? What are some of the reasons?

Suggested Writing Assignments

1. Anzaldúa asserts that "language is a male discourse" (paragraph 8). Use her piece to write an essay in which you explore features of speech and the gendered power relations they reflect. Or, alternatively, take issue with Anzaldúa and argue against her statement.

2. Do research on the French language spoken in Canada, particularly its incorporation of anglicisms, and write an essay in which you discuss parallels between the Spanish in the United States as Anzaldúa describes it and French in Canada. Or do research on the "Singlish" spoken in Singapore, and write an essay about the controversy over "Singlish" versus "pure" English.

3. Write a personal essay in which you describe one or more occasions when your "incorrect" speech made you uncomfortable, or one or more occasions when you heard someone else's "incorrect" speech. You may use Anzaldúa's "How to Tame a Wild Tongue" as a model, but you need not.

GLORIA NAYLOR
"Mommy, What Does 'Nigger' Mean?"

Full Edition, p. 481

A graduate of Brooklyn College and Yale University, now a novelist, Gloria Naylor takes up the question of racially charged language in this essay reprinted from the "Hers" column of the *New York Times*. For Naylor the term "nigger" can, when used by whites, be an insulting, destructive epithet; yet, when used within black communities, it can become a term of endearment, even pride. Analyzing the examples Naylor gives from her childhood will help students to draw out the principles by which she makes this distinction and the position against which she argues.

If it seems relevant, you can discuss the problem of racially charged language on campuses today. Many colleges and universities have adopted a "code" that would prohibit insulting language based on race, class, gender, sexual orientation, or ethnicity; others have given them up. If your campus has (or had) such a code, analyze it to determine whether it is consonant with the principles underlying Naylor's argument or whether it takes the oppositional position to which she alludes at the end of her essay (paragraph 14). If your campus has faced any alleged violations of the code, or if students can cite incidents that might violate such a code, ask them to imagine what Naylor's analysis of the incident(s) might be.

QUESTIONS FROM *THE NORTON READER*

1. In her opening paragraph, Gloria Naylor writes that she considers "the written word inferior to the spoken." In what ways does she demonstrate the superiority of the spoken word in this essay?

2. Naylor claims that "[w]ords themselves are innocuous; it is the consensus that gives them true power" (paragraph 2). As a class, brainstorm a list of words that can have different meanings and connotations, depending on who uses the words or in what context they are spoken.

3. Think of a word that has several different meanings in your own family or community. Write a personal essay in which you detail those meanings. Like Naylor, use grammatical terms (as well as age- and gender-specifics, if applicable) to categorize the different meanings.

TEACHING SUGGESTIONS

1. Like other pieces written for the "Hers" column, Naylor's essay uses a combination of personal experience and impersonal generalization. Discuss with students why Naylor chooses to begin with two paragraphs of generalization rather than with her experience in the third grade.

2. What makes Naylor's narrative of her third-grade experience so powerful? Help students analyze the concise, objective style, the effect of words such as "nymphomaniac" and "necrophiliac," as well as the unstated assumptions about black students that Naylor writes against.

3. The bulk of Naylor's essay recounts memories in which "nigger" occurs in nonderogatory contexts. Why does Naylor wish to show the richness of this term within the black community? How does this richness contrast with the starkness of the white third-grader's language?

4. In paragraph 14, Naylor summarizes a position against which she is arguing: "the use of the word nigger at this social stratum of the black community

[is] . . . an internalization of racism." Ask students what evidence they might bring to support the opposing argument—and why Naylor treats it only briefly when and where she does.

5. Naylor never tells us how her mother answered the question, "What does 'nigger' mean?" Instead, she simply concludes: "And since she [her mother] knew that I had to grow up in America, she took me in her lap and explained." Discuss with students why Naylor ends this way.

6. What persona does Naylor create in this essay—and how? What kind of person do we imagine her to be? Why is this persona important to her argument?

Suggested Writing Assignments

1. Write an essay about the use of the term "nigger" in which you disagree with Naylor and take the opposing position that she alludes to: "the use of the word nigger at this social stratum of the black community [is] . . . an internalization of racism" (paragraph 14).

2. Write an analysis of a term that can have negative or positive meaning, depending on the context in which it is used.

3. Write an essay about your own experiences with a word that someone used to insult or denigrate you. As you analyze your experience, try to draw out the various connotations of the word used.

Benjamin Franklin
Learning to Write

Full Edition, p. 484; Shorter Edition, p. 290

Benjamin Franklin was born in 1706. As a child, he loved to read; as young as eleven years old, he was reading Plutarch, Defoe, and Cotton Mather. Franklin's love for reading is also evidenced in the selection from his *Autobiography* included in *The Norton Reader*. In "Learning to Write," he discusses many of the books and other publications that influenced him and helped him develop as a writer. Additionally, Franklin shows the power of books to motivate a different way of living. He chooses to be a vegetarian after reading a book, and with the money he saves from his new diet, he buys additional books and finds more time to study. When you discuss "Learning to Write" in class, encourage students to think of their own relationship to books—what books have informed their writing and other aspects of their lives.

Questions from *The Norton Reader*

1. Benjamin Franklin describes his youthful practice of imitating successful writers' sentences. Have you ever done this? If so, how was it helpful or unhelpful? What might writers likely learn from such a practice?

2. Franklin has been called an autodidact, a self-teacher. Recount what Franklin learned in this manner, and note what he failed to teach himself.

What kinds of knowledge did Franklin seek to acquire? Was his learning broad or narrow? What kinds of endeavors was this knowledge most suited for?

3. When he was sixteen, Franklin read a book about vegetarian diets and immediately was converted. Write about how you or someone you know was converted to following a distinct path, either religious, ethical, or physical. Did the conversion happen suddenly, as it did with Franklin, or did it take place slowly, over time? In your essay you might consider imitating Franklin's style, or that of a writer you admire.

TEACHING SUGGESTIONS

1. Ask students to consider Franklin's allusions to and citations of other texts. If your library provides access to old issues of the *Spectator* or the books Franklin mentions, consider bringing samples to class. (You can access early issues of the *Spectator* online at gutenberg.org) What elements of writing in the *Spectator* pieces are similar to Franklin's writing?

2. Twice in "Learning to Write" (paragraph 2), Franklin writes about finding faults in his writing and correcting them. He does so by referencing writing in the *Spectator*. Ask students to discuss whether they are able to find their own writing faults and correct them. If so, how do they do so? Do they, like Franklin, measure their writing against writing they admire? Do they imitate other writers? Do they use handbooks as references? If they are not able to ascertain the faults in their own writing (and correct them), ask them to brainstorm strategies for doing so.

3. Franklin offers many strategies for learning to write better (imitation, changing genres, wide reading, etc.). After discussing some of the strategies Franklin suggests, ask students to brainstorm a list of their own strategies for becoming a better writer.

SUGGESTED WRITING ASSIGNMENTS

1. Franklin, in teaching himself to write better, chose to imitate passages he admired from the *Spectator*. Find a passage in a text written by an author whose writing you admire. Take note of the elements in that text that are most effective and try to incorporate those elements into your own writing.

2. Another strategy Franklin offers for improving writing is to change genres. In paragraph 2, he writes, "I took some of the Tales and turn'd them into Verse: And after a time, when I had pretty well forgotten the Prose, turn'd them back again." Choose a short story or essay (one of your own or one from a published text) and rewrite it as a poem.

3. Franklin writes about many of the books that influenced his writing and life. In a journal entry or a short autobiographical essay, reflect on the books that have most influenced you and your writing. Be sure to include specific titles and reflections on what you learned from those books.

Joan Didion

On Keeping a Notebook

Full Edition, p. 487

Joan Didion is best known for her nonfiction reportage of contemporary cultural and political trends and for her novels *Play It as It Lays* (1971), *A Book of Common Prayer* (1977), and *Democracy* (1984). "On Keeping a Notebook," one of the most personal of Didion's essays, reflects on the relation of fact and fiction in personal life. "Why did I write it down?" Didion asks in paragraph 4 of the essay—and that question might provoke a discussion about why people keep diaries, journals, and personal notebooks. Perhaps even before students read Didion's essay, you might ask if they have ever kept a journal and what they hoped to gain (or if not, why they did not). Their initial answers might be compared with Didion's, whether to confirm their practices as writers or to offer possibilities for kinds of journal writing they haven't considered before.

If you're asking students to keep a notebook or journal, you might want to discuss some of Didion's detailed reflections on her "facts" to show students how to analyze their own experiences. (Paragraphs 4–5 and 16–17 are useful on this score.) Didion concentrates on the personal and professional values of keeping a notebook: on persons afflicted with a sense of loss who for psychological reasons need to write things down, and on professionals who keep a writer's notebook for future use in constructing stories. She does not consider journals like Dorothy Wordsworth's, written to record facts of natural history, or commonplace books like Henry David Thoreau's, kept to record his own and others' words of wisdom.

Questions from *The Norton Reader*

1. What distinction does Joan Didion make between a diary and a notebook? What uses does a notebook have for Didion?

2. Didion says she uses her notebook to "tell what some would call lies" (paragraph 7). Why does she do this? Would some people call these things truths? Why?

3. Didion says, "*How it felt to me*: that is getting closer to the truth about a notebook" (paragraph 8). What writing strategies does she use to convey "how it felt"?

4. Try keeping a notebook for a week, jotting down the sorts of things that Didion does. At the end of the week, take one or two of your entries and expand on them, as Didion does with the entries on Mrs. Minnie S. Brooks and Mrs. Lou Fox (paragraphs 12–13).

Teaching Suggestions

1. This essay is loosely structured: it begins with an incident once recorded in a notebook now recalled and reflected on, followed by two sections on the

motives for keeping a notebook. Ask students about the purpose of each section and what they think is the "heart" of each.

2. At what point does the reader realize that the woman in the plaid dress is Didion herself? Why does Didion describe herself in the third person? How does this objective form of description, used in her notebook, help Didion understand herself and her situation?

3. Didion is a master of observing and analyzing details. Ask students what details they remember best from the essay, why they remember them, and what purpose these details serve. The discussion might usefully connect with the students' own writing and their use of details.

4. In an essay titled "Why I Write" Joan Didion has noted: "I write entirely to find out what I'm thinking, what I'm looking at, what I see and what it means." In the same essay she reveals that for her "certain images shimmer" and that these images determine the "arrangement of words." Apply these comments to "On Keeping a Notebook" as well as to Didion's "On Going Home" (FE p. 1, SE p. 1).

Suggested Writing Assignments

1. Choose an incident or a detail from a journal you have kept and expand it into a short story or nonfictional narrative. (Alternatively, let someone else read your journal and select the incident.) What extra details does such an expansion require?

2. Keep a notebook for a week or so; carry it with you and record whatever you like. At the end of the week review it, then write an analysis and commentary on your notebook. Do you share the same interests and motives in writing as Didion?

3. Write an essay in response to Didion's observation: "We are well advised to keep on nodding terms with the people we used to be whether we find them attractive company or not" (paragraph 16).

STEPHEN KING
On Writing

Full Edition, p. 493; Shorter Edition, p. 293

Stephen King tells a story about his first encounter with a serious editor. Throughout, he compares what his sports editor did with what his English teachers had done with his writing. One might ask, how did King learn to write those sports stories in their unedited form if not from his English teachers? But he wants to make an unfavorable comparison between the academic criticism he received (which he doesn't give examples of) and the "real-world" editing he gets from John Gould.

Students will likely know of King, and many will have read his fiction. It's worth asking whether his prose still exhibits some of the characteristics he says he learned from this encounter: directness, absence of flourish, connection to readers. It might be interesting to ask if that's the only way to go, if students can imagine another approach to prose. (Tom Wolfe's "Yeager" [FE p. 114] might form a useful comparison here. Wolfe, about the same age as King and someone who worked many years on newspapers, has a highly complex style that draws attention to itself, very unlike King's.)

Questions from *The Norton Reader*

1. Stephen King provides an example of the way his editor marked up his work. What rationale can you provide for the edits? Would you have made different choices if you were the editor? Why?

2. King uses dialogue and description to help characterize his editor. In which parts of the text do you get the best sense of who Gould is? Why are those parts effective?

3. King writes about learning from an editor. In "Learning to Write" (FE p. 484, SE p. 290), Benjamin Franklin writes about learning from his reading, while, in "On Keeping a Notebook" (FE p. 487), Joan Didion writes about her notebook. Which of these techniques, if any, has helped you as a writer? How?

4. Write about a time someone responded to your writing in a way that helped you learn to be a better writer. What kinds of comments and edits did that person make? Why was that response helpful to you?

Teaching Suggestions

1. Have students look at the comments on a paper they've had returned and see if they can discover a common thread in them, as King does in the editorial comments on his sports piece.

2. What is there about certain kinds of sportswriting that encourage direct, uncluttered prose? Could it be the strict focus on the story? Ask students what kinds of sportswriting work best with that kind of focus, and which work best with more evaluative language?

3. With King it's the subject matter itself that gets complex and baroque, while the prose remains simple and straightforward. Ask students whether this has any connection to King's his first experiences of getting edited for the sports section?

Suggested Writing Assignments

1. Watch a sporting event (live or on TV) and write a feature story on it.

2. Write an account of helping someone else with his or her writing. How did you go about it? What did you decide to stress most? Did you successfully avoid hurting the writer's feelings? Do you think your help "stuck," or made a change in the writer's approach?

3. Write about some piece or pieces of writing advice you've received. Did you try to follow this advice? What happened? Did you ignore the advice? What was the result?

JASWINDER BOLINA
Writing Like a White Guy: On Language, Race, and Poetry

Full Edition, p. 496

In this essay, Jaswinder Bolina considers the relationships among race, class, language, and assimilation in America. Rather than making an argument for or against assimilation, he shows that writing and language are shaped by education, profession, class, and other factors—just as a person is shaped by family, experiences, expectations, and his or her own commitments and interests. Bolina contrasts his father's experiences and expectations with his own, and yet shows how his parents supported him and his education. As a child of immigrants, he shows ambivalence about his own assimilation, writing, "Assimilation is pragmatic, but pragmatism calls for concessions that compound and come to feel like a chronic ache" (paragraph 14), and he admits, "The voice in my head is annoyed with the voice in my writing" (paragraph 16).

Bolina works through this ambivalence about language and racial identity in his writing, never settling on an easy answer. He recognizes that race in America cannot be overlooked (paragraphs 6 and 17) and that, although he might sound "white" in his writing, his awareness of racial identity never goes away, whether he writes about it or not. At the end of the essay, he rejects a dichotomous choice, refusing "to choose between being the brown guy writing like a white guy or the brown guy writing about being Othered" (paragraph 22), taking ownership of and responsibility for his own use of language.

QUESTIONS FROM *The Norton Reader*

1. Throughout this essay, Jaswinder Bolina compares the role of race in his life with the role of race in his poetry. List some of his ambivalent feelings, explore their sources, and discuss where he seems to land in the end with regard to the relationship between his poetry and his race.

2. What, according to Bolina, is the relationship between language and race in the United States? How is this relationship different from other countries he discusses?

3. Bolina writes that, as a child, he tried to "out-white" (paragraph 13) other Asian kids on the playground. In "How to Tame a Wild Tongue" (FE p. 471, SE p. 280), Gloria Anzaldúa writes about avoiding speaking Spanish with Chicanas and Latinas she does not know well. Based on these two accounts, what can be difficult about encountering another person who shares the same minority status?

4. Using Bolina's essay as a starting point, write about how an artist should balance artistic ambitions with the need or desire to speak for a group to which she or he belongs (e.g., racial or ethnic minority, religion, sexual orientation, and so on).

Teaching Suggestions

1. As you discuss Bolina's ambivalence about the role of race in his life and the poetry he writes, ask students to consider both the usefulness and limits of categories. What does it mean to write "like a white guy"? You might bring in a range of examples of poetry—poems by Bolina and others (both "white guys" and people of color)—to discuss issues of language and identity.

2. Bolina considers the ways in which race and class are connected (or assumed to be connected) in America. Ask students to trace the ways in which race and class are connected (or not) in Bolina's essay.

3. Minority status can be marked by race, class, sexual orientation, or other factors. Students can discuss these issues in relation to essays in "Language and Communication" (such as Gloria Anzaldúa's "How to Tame a Wild Tongue" [FE p. 471, SE p. 280]) or "Gender and Human Nature" (such as Gwendolyn Ann Smith's "We're All Someone's Freak" [FE p. 184]). In these essays, the writers consider the ways in which those in minority positions sometimes seek power and acceptance through assimilation, but they also reflect on times when assimilation is not the best option either personally, culturally, or politically. Remind students that identity and expressions of self—through language and association—are not fixed or static.

4. For many people, the idea of being a "writer," "artist," or "poet" means approaching language or experience in a particular way. These definitions of self and vocation can be as limiting or as empowering as claiming any other label (racial, ethnic, religious, or otherwise). Question 4 in *The Norton Reader* asks students to write about balancing "artistic ambitions with the need or desire to speak for a group." What does it mean to be a "woman writer," a "black poet," a "Christian artist," or a "gay musician"? Who gets to define these or other categories? What is at stake both personally and politically? To help students further consider these questions, you might ask them to read Roxane Gay's "A Tale of Three Coming Out Stories" (FE p. 178, SE p. 77).

Suggested Writing Assignments

1. Bolina recounts comments others have made to him that might be offensive (paragraphs 5 and 19), but he says he's not offended and presents his critique in an understanding way. Write about a time someone said something to you that might sound offensive, explaining the comment and situation in a way that shows both your critique and understanding.

2. Write an essay called "Writing Like a _____." You fill in the blank. You may choose "college student," "English major," "country girl," "urban guy"— any label that will allow you to explore language use and some element of identity or experience. Even as you use a label, try to move beyond stereotypes in your writing.

3. Bolina compares language to a tool, writing, "Language, like a hammer, belongs to whoever picks it up to build or demolish" (paragraph 22). Write an essay that shows your understanding of language through the use of a simile. Is language a tool like a hammer, capable of building or demolishing? Is it—like water—necessary to sustaining life but also capable of drowning a person? What is language like to you?

GARRISON KEILLOR
How to Write a Letter and *Postcards*

Full Edition, p. 505
Full Edition, p. 508

Garrison Keillor offers sound advice about writing in these two easy, seemingly off-the-cuff essays. He is an accomplished monologuist, as listeners to *A Prairie Home Companion*, his long-running show on National Public Radio, will know. You may want students to listen to a broadcast, online at prairiehome.org. Students should be able to hear Keillor's diffident, breathy voice behind these essays, as in "We shy persons need to write a letter now and then, or else we'll dry up and blow away" (paragraph 1).

Keillor's instructions for writing letters are applicable to writing in general, freewriting and first drafts in particular, and they may make more of an impression coming from the sage of Lake Wobegon than from a writing instructor. You may assign this essay early in the semester so students can get instructions from Keillor first. If you assign it later in the semester, ask them which instructions have been working for them and which haven't; you (or Keillor) may even persuade them to try again instructions that haven't been working. With "Postcards," you may want to ask students to try their hand at writing short, fifty-word, informative descriptions or narrations of what they have done each day within a single week. These short pieces of writing can be valuable on their own or as possible starting points for longer essays.

QUESTIONS FROM *THE NORTON READER*

1. In "How to Write a Letter," Garrison Keillor offers several suggestions. Make a list of the suggestions that seem most helpful. Why might Keillor have included the other, less practical suggestions?

2. Keillor addresses "How to Write a Letter" to shy people (a group in which he includes himself—"We shy persons . . ."). Does his advice also apply to those who are not shy? Why or why not?

3. Analyze the progression of "Postcards." How is the piece organized? Why do you think Keillor chose this organization?

4. Keillor wrote these pieces in the 1980s before people texted or used email. Does any of his advice apply to the way we text or write emails today? Explain your reasoning in an essay.

Teaching Suggestions

1. Have students mark Keillor's self-deprecating statements. What is their effect? What does he gain and what does he lose by making them? Is being self-deprecating in a piece of writing ordinarily risky?

2. Discuss with students Keillor's reasons for writing letters rather than telephoning? How many of these reasons also apply to using email or texting rather than telephoning?

3. "The telephone is to shyness what Hawaii is to February," Keillor observes (paragraph 1). His riddling comparison provokes suspense—until he resolves it, wittily and somewhat enigmatically: "it's a way out of the woods." Ask students to mark Keillor's metaphors in both essays and to look at the ways he handles them. (This exercise can be done in small groups.)

4. Try handing out small, postcard-size pieces of paper at the beginning of the semester and assigning students five other students to whom they will write a postcard in the first two weeks of class. According to Keillor, letters are saved, reread, and "improve with age" (paragraph 15). You can follow up this exercise by asking if the same holds true for postcards.

Suggested Writing Assignments

1. Write an essay explaining the benefits of communicating through a specific form or medium.

2. "Writing is a means of discovery, always," Keillor writes (paragraph 14). Write an essay in which you discuss Keillor's observation in relation to something you have written this semester.

3. Read around in the collected letters of some nineteenth- or twentieth-century figure who interests you. Choose a couple of letters you would have enjoyed receiving and analyze what makes them good letters. Use Keillor's instructions for writing letters if they help your analysis.

George Orwell
Politics and the English Language

Full Edition, p. 510; Shorter Edition, p. 296

This essay on language and meaning from one of the twentieth century's best English prose stylists is justifiably famous. Most of us share a belief that "language is a natural growth and not an instrument which we shape for our own purposes" (paragraph 1). George Orwell, on the other hand, refuses to take a passive stance; rather, he actively seeks to purge the English language of errors, obfuscation, cant, and corruption. He does more than diagnose its illnesses; he offers prescriptions that are practical—though not painless. Implicit in his proposals for the reform of the English language is the need to reform political systems as well, for, as Orwell sees the matter, corruption in the use of language and corruption in politics are interrelated.

QUESTIONS FROM *THE NORTON READER*

1. State George Orwell's main point as precisely as possible.
2. What kinds of prose does Orwell analyze in this essay? Look, in particular, at the passages he quotes in paragraph 3. Where would you find their contemporary equivalents?
3. Apply Orwell's rule iv, "Never use the passive where you can use the active" (paragraph 19), to paragraph 14 of his essay. What happens when you change his passive constructions to active? Has Orwell forgotten rule iv or is he covered by rule vi, "Break any of these rules sooner than say anything outright barbarous"?
4. Orwell wrote this essay in 1946. Choose at least two examples of political discourse from current media and discuss, in an essay, the extent to which Orwell's analysis of the language of politics still applies today. Which features that he singles out for criticism appear most frequently in the examples you chose?

TEACHING SUGGESTIONS

1. Ask students to describe Orwell's goals and methods in "Politics and the English Language." Which methods do they find most effective? Least effective?
2. Orwell turns a passage from Ecclesiastes into "modern English of the worst sort" (paragraphs 9–11). Why does Orwell use the Bible to illustrate his point?
3. Does Orwell seem to lose his way in the first half of this essay, particularly after paragraphs 1 and 2, in which he discusses politics and language? Is his deliberate postponement of his analysis of the five writing samples an effective device?
4. Orwell writes, "In our time, political speech and writing are largely the defence of the indefensible" (paragraph 14): he names as indefensible British rule in India, Russian purges and deportations, and dropping atom bombs on Japan. Did his readers agree? What contemporary equivalents can students name? Do they agree?
5. Ask students to find and evaluate some of Orwell's metaphors. Are they fresh and lively? Are they dated or drawn from a cultural context too far removed from those of the students? Ask students which metaphors they find most and least powerful—and why.
6. Ask each student to summarize Orwell's essay by extracting six statements that best represent the spirit and intention of the writer. Then ask

students to compare their choices of the six statements. What does it mean that we, as readers, make so many of the same choices?

7. Ask students to bring in examples of the problems discussed by Orwell and to rewrite at least one passage for consideration in class.

SUGGESTED WRITING ASSIGNMENTS

1. Revise an essay written for this course by following Orwell's six rules.

2. Locate a speech made by a politician on an issue you consider indefensible; the *New York Times* is a good place to look, since it is a newspaper of record. Write an analysis of the speech based on Orwell's ideas in "Politics and the English Language."

3. Give the speech and your analysis of it (see teaching suggestion 4, above) to a classmate who finds the issue defensible. Have the classmate write his/her own analysis, either taking issue with or not taking issue with yours.

4. Select another essay by Orwell and analyze it according to his principles and standards.

Nature and the Environment

JOHN MCPHEE

Under the Snow

Full Edition, p. 521; Shorter Edition, p. 307

This essay gives a very personal account of John McPhee's encounter with bears in the Pocono Mountains of Pennsylvania. What will strike many readers is the way this group of wild animals is "managed" by an array of wildlife biologists, pilots, journalists, politicians, and assorted spectators, all of whom conspire to keep the bears comfortable and healthy in the midst of civilization. There's something quite paternal about the relationship between humans and the bears, a fact highlighted by McPhee's opening paragraphs about his own daughters. Yet despite its down-to-earth approach, the whole essay is suffused with a sense of wonder, as the conclusion makes clear.

Ask students to point to evidence of the personal in this essay, and then ask them to explain what is gained by making the piece so personal. Is anything lost? It's worth suggesting that McPhee can serve as a useful model for students' own writing.

QUESTIONS FROM *THE NORTON READER*

1. John McPhee opens with a memory of holding his daughter when she was an infant, saying she would stick to his shoulder "like velvet" (paragraph 1). Two paragraphs later, he writes about holding a bear cub that stayed on his shoulder "like a piece of velvet" (paragraph 3). Why do you think McPhee makes this comparison? What purpose does it serve in this essay?

2. Trace McPhee's use of simile throughout the essay. For example, he compares bears to chocolate chips (paragraph 11), likens their movement to "clowns from a compact car" (paragraph 13), and describes a researcher positioning a bear "like a doughnut" (paragraph 17). What is the effect of such comparisons? What other similes are significant in this essay?

3. What is the purpose of the kind of bear trapping and biological study McPhee describes? What is your position on this interaction between humans and wildlife? Write an argument in which you either defend the kind of research McPhee describes or make a case for leaving wildlife alone. Consider using a specific animal (as McPhee uses bears) in making your claim.

TEACHING SUGGESTIONS

1. In paragraph 4 McPhee writes, "In winter, Buck Alt flies the country listening to the radio, crissing and crossing until the bears come on." That phrase

"crissing and crossing" is unusual, a clever take on the usual "criss-cross." Point to other, similarly (or unusually) clever phrases: "The plane he flies is a Super Cub" (paragraph 4), "in the wintertime tropics of their own mammalian heaven" (paragraph 5), "Alt has overcome this problem by stuffing sows' noses with Vicks VapoRub" (paragraph 6), and "He stuffed it with bear and hung it on a scale" (paragraph 8). Ask students whether McPhee is having fun with the language, showing off, or creating a new way of writing about his subject.

2. Ask students to describe the incongruous, "unnatural" positions bears are forced into by the wildlife biologists. Are they ever depicted as "natural"?

3. Brian Doyle (FE p. 526, SE p. 312) moves from relatively impersonal description to a very personal reaction; McPhee sandwiches his descriptive account between highly personal depictions of his daughters and his very powerful memory of the encounter as he's driving home. Discuss these strategies and their effectiveness.

SUGGESTED WRITING ASSIGNMENTS

1. Use "Under the Snow" as evidence to support—or dispute—the argument of William Cronon's "The Trouble with Wilderness" (FE p. 550).

2. Describe an encounter you have had with a wild animal, making it personal as well as factual.

3. Examine the words actually spoken by Alt. How does his everyday language differ from the language McPhee employs to describe the scene? Give an account of this contrast, including possible reasons behind McPhee's choices.

4. Write about what you had thought about bears before you read McPhee's piece and what you think now that you've read it. In other words, tell whether and/or how McPhee's piece changed your attitude to these animals.

BRIAN DOYLE

Joyas Voladoras

Full Edition, p. 526; Shorter Edition, p. 312

In this brief, lyrical essay, Brian Doyle specializes in the oracular, making claims that he doesn't feel the need to back up or justify: "Every creature on earth has approximately two billion heartbeats to spend in a lifetime" (paragraph 3), "There are perhaps ten thousand blue whales in the world" (paragraph 4), and so on. Where other essays in this chapter make arguments often combining politics and science, this essay dwells in wonder. Why no footnotes or references? Probably because what Doyle mentions is common knowledge to the people who study these creatures, just like the distance from the earth to the moon is not worth referencing in such an essay.

After paragraph 3 the hummingbirds are gone, never to return. We move on to hearts, which Doyle has introduced to us in the first three paragraphs. And in paragraph 6 we end with the human heart, not with its beating or its size but with its capability of being moved. Doyle makes a move common in nature writing, going from the animal world to the human. Here it is handled superbly, convincingly.

QUESTIONS FROM *THE NORTON READER*

1. Brian Doyle considers the hearts of hummingbirds (paragraphs 1–3), blue whales (paragraph 4), and humans (paragraph 6) in this lyric essay, which uses poetic features such as metaphor, contrast, and repetition. What is his purpose in doing so? How does he make a transition from a focus on animals to a focus on humans?

2. Doyle incorporates several lists into this essay. Trace his use of lists throughout the essay. Which list do you find most effective? Why?

3. Write a lyric essay in which you closely consider some element of human and animal nature. Consider using some of the poetic features identified in the first question.

TEACHING SUGGESTIONS

1. It's worth asking students why the piece has such a title. First, why is it in Spanish, and second, why is it about hummingbirds? The class will agree that the "subject" of this essay is definitely not hummingbirds. They are certainly what gets the essay started but not at all where it ends up. So is the title misleading? Too indirect? Inappropriate?

2. From the first paragraph it's evident that we are in the presence of someone who is not primarily interested in presenting information. Look at the second, third, and fourth sentences, which seem to go against everything students have heard about linguistic variety. Or in paragraph 2, the second, third, and fourth sentences all begin with the same two words, "they can." Ask students to point to other examples of language that is out of the ordinary. Discuss the effects of these deliberate choices.

3. The "catalogue" of hummingbird names at the end of paragraph two suggests someone in love with the details of the natural world and, at the same time, enthralled with language. Are there any other passages that suggest the same things? Ask students if Doyle's enthusiasm translates to the reader.

SUGGESTED WRITING ASSIGNMENTS

1. Write a piece comparing the way Doyle moves from the world of nature to the world of humans with the very different way Edward Abbey (FE p. 535) does the same thing.

2. Do some research on a different kind of creature and then write a couple of paragraphs describing its seemingly incredible attributes or characteristics (some examples: black widow spiders, ants, peregrine falcons, salmon).

3. Write about the things that can knock down any walls that you might have built up to protect your heart. Be as specific as Doyle is in his final paragraph, where he uses not grand but homely examples.

John Muir
A Wind-Storm in the Forests

Full Edition, p. 529

In this lushly descriptive essay, America's seminal naturalist tells his tale of climbing a hundred-foot spruce "rocking and swirling in wild ecstasy" (paragraph 9) during a winter windstorm in California. John Muir's treatment is archly Romantic: the windstorm is a "grand anthem" (paragraph 8); the trees respond to it with "invincible gladness" (paragraph 13); the sunset at the end of the storm is construed as an explicit communion between the trees and their "Creator."

Students will be challenged by Muir's prose style, which is marked by long, labyrinthine sentence structures and complex accumulations of clauses joined by semicolons. In addition, these lengthy, flowing passages are frequently interrupted by complicating parenthetical remarks set off by dashes. The result is that the reader is forced to keep a great many related ideas or images in suspension while waiting for the final punctuation. A primer on the flora mentioned in the piece would be helpful as well so that students are not caught off-guard by the references to the *librocedrus, manzanita,* and the *madroños* when they appear, for instance.

Questions from *The Norton Reader*

1. What preconceptions might a reader bring to John Muir's title, "A Wind-Storm in the Forests"? Does the opening sentence—indeed, the entire opening paragraph—suggest a different perspective? How so?

2. The central adventure in this essay occurs when Muir climbs a Douglas Spruce (paragraph 9). Why does Muir undertake this climb? What does he wish to experience?

3. Write about an experience you have had in nature, whether dramatic, as in Muir's essay, or more quiet.

Teaching Suggestions

1. Muir's prose style was recognized even in the author's day for its eccentricities: his editors often tried to revise away his "gloriouses." Ask students to locate one of his particularly long and complex sentences (examples end each of his first two paragraphs, for instance) and consider the significance of his style. What might this style reveal about the author himself? What does his style reveal, if anything, about his attitude toward the subject at hand? What is the effect of Muir's style on the reader? Do students like it? Why or why not? What lesson can they draw from their response to Muir's style that might apply to their own writing?

2. Consider Muir's overall treatment of his subject matter in this essay. How would students describe his artistic relationship to nature? How would they characterize his philosophical relationship to nature? Have students locate specific passages in this text in which the artistic or philosophical relationship

they discerned is clearly evident and explain how, exactly, these passages manifest that particular artistic or philosophical stance.

3. Ask students if they like Muir's artistic/philosophical treatment of nature in this essay. Why or why not? What about his treatment speaks to them, personally? What about it does not ring true? If they were to write an essay on nature, would they adopt Muir's general stance toward the subject? Why or why not?

Suggested Writing Assignments

1. Muir twice acknowledges a close cause-and-effect relationship between violent forces and beauty. Early in the essay he writes, "we are compelled to believe that [these forests] are the most beautiful on the face of the earth, however we may regard the agents [hurricanes, avalanches, etc.] that have made them so" (paragraph 4). Likewise, in his conclusion, he notes that as he "gazed on the impressive scene, all the so-called ruin of the storm was forgotten, and never before did these noble woods appear so fresh, so joyous, so immortal." Shifting the context away from the effects of weather on the natural landscape, write an essay in which you argue for or against Muir's position that violence can lead to beauty. Consider the possible relationships between violence and beauty in art, sports, physics, or contemporary fashion, for instance. Be sure to make your argument within a singular, narrowly defined context and to address the ethics of your position at some point in your essay.

2. Muir describes the trees' "strong and comfortable" enjoyment of the storm, their response to its "most enthusiastic greetings" (paragraph 13):

> We hear much nowadays concerning the universal struggle for existence, but no struggle in the common meaning of the word was manifest here; no recognition of danger . . . ; no deprecation; but rather an invincible gladness as remote from exultation as from fear. (paragraph 13)

In human terms, another, simpler way to describe this state might be "contentment." Have you ever had the good fortune to experience such "an invincible gladness as remote from exultation as from fear"? If so, write an essay in which you tell the story of one particular time in your life when you felt content. Be sure to explore and explain both the causes of your contentment and its effects on you and those around you. What conclusions can you draw from your experience about the nature of contentment?

Edward Abbey
The Great American Desert

Full Edition, p. 535

In this humorous essay from *The Journey Home* (1977), Edward Abbey gives all the reasons for not venturing into the desert as, ultimately, a means of explaining his great love of the desert. Abbey's machismo and brash sense of humor emerge as he lists all the negative qualities of a place he clearly loves. In an era of extreme sports, students may not have encountered a defense of more old-fashioned, less managed risk. As such, this essay offers an opportunity to talk about risk, danger, and adventure as they relate to our relationship with nature and the environment. Abbey served for fifteen years as a fire lookout and park ranger in the American Southwest, much of the time at Arches National Monument. He is the author of many books, both fiction and nonfiction, including *Desert Solitaire* (1968). Abbey's later novel, *The Monkey Wrench Gang* (1975), which portrays a group of environmental guerrillas, became so well-known that it inspired the formation of the radical environmental group *Earth First!*.

Questions from *The Norton Reader*

1. Edward Abbey loves the desert, as he states in the first sentence. Why, then, does he enumerate all of its negative features? What is his strategy?

2. Many paragraphs in this essay use lists. Choose one list, analyze its structure (if there is one), and explain what the arrangement of details achieves.

3. How do you explain the ending of this essay—both what Abbey discovers and how he uses it to convey his point?

4. Write an essay about a place you love, detailing its negative features as Abbey does.

Teaching Suggestions

1. Discuss the relationship between nature and danger with your students, comparing the relative dangers of various activities they may enjoy, including hiking, skiing, fishing, and ziplining.

2. Choose one or more of Abbey's lists (such as the one in paragraph 5, 6, or 13) and contrast it to Brian Doyle's list in paragraph 2 of "Joyas Voladoras" (FE 526, SE p. 312). Discuss how these catalogues are organized, the internal logic of the lists, and their importance to the purpose of the essay overall. Compare the use of a list in a satirical essay with that in a lyrical one.

3. Abbey offers two classifications of the Great American Desert: the standard one and his own. Have your students work with a map of a familiar place (campus or your town or county) and perform a similar exercise of classification. What do street, place, or building names convey? How does their connotation change depending on how well one knows the place? This can be a preliminary exercise before the second writing assignment on the next page.

4. Have students bring in some background information on *Earth First!* and Abbey's life to put the essay into a broader context. Discuss how this lighter essay might fit into Abbey's career. In what ways does "The Great American Desert" make an implicit argument for preservation? What role can and should humor and satire play in environmental arguments?

Suggested Writing Assignments

1. Write an essay about something that others might consider dangerous but which you enjoy doing. Following Abbey's example, use your careful inventory of all the potential hazards to reveal, gradually, your love of the activity.

2. Study a map of a place you know and love well and write a description of that place. Use categories—perhaps contrasting your own private categories with more official ones—and lists in your description.

3. Read Wallace Stegner's "Wilderness Letter" (FE p. 544) and write an essay comparing Stegner's general idea of wilderness to Abbey's specific account of the desert.

Chief Seattle
Letter to President Pierce, 1855

Full Edition, p. 543; Shorter Edition, p. 315

Chief Seattle's "Letter," like the essay "The Trouble with Wilderness" by William Cronon (FE p. 550), argues for the interdependence of man and the natural world—in Seattle's words, that "All things are connected" (paragraph 3). Yet these writers argue their case in quite different ways, using different styles and rhetorical strategies. Seattle's "Letter," for example, abounds in maxims: "Continue to contaminate your bed, and you will one night suffocate in your own waste" (paragraph 5) or "Whatever befalls the earth befalls the sons of earth" (paragraph 3).

You might also use Seattle's "Letter," and the essays that follow, to discuss how a writer gains authority to speak out on an issue of public importance. Today, we might assume that Seattle, chief of the Dwamish, Suquamish, and allied Indian tribes, would be respected for the wisdom about the natural world he and his people had accumulated; but, speaking in 1855, Seattle knew that many Americans considered the Indian to be only "a savage." Seattle takes this common view and recasts it ironically—repeating the phrase "the red man is a savage and does not understand" in somewhat different variations at moments when the white man's behavior seems most foolish and destructive. His speech, transcribed and edited by a white man, shows the way that a minority point of view can become an effective and necessary counterpoint to majority opinion.

Questions from *The Norton Reader*

1. Chief Seattle repeatedly refers to the red man as "a savage" who "does not understand," yet he gives evidence of a great deal of understanding. What is the purpose of such ironic comments and apparently self-disparaging remarks?

2. Scholars have suggested that Chief Seattle's "Letter" is in fact the creation of a white man, based on Seattle's public oratory. If so, what rhetorical techniques does the white editor associate with Indian speech? Why might he have done so?

3. Chief Seattle demonstrates an awareness of ecology—the study of relationships among organisms, and between organisms and their environment—when he says, "whatever happens to the beasts also happens to man. All things are connected" (paragraph 3). Locate two or three similar observations, and explain their effectiveness.

4. Chief Seattle says that the red man might understand the white man better "if we knew what it was that the white man dreams, what he describes to his children on the long winter nights, what visions he burns into their minds, so they will wish for tomorrow" (paragraph 5). Write a short essay explaining—using irony if you'd like—how "the white man" might reply. If you prefer, write the reply itself.

Teaching Suggestions

1. Listeners who heard Chief Seattle speak said that he was an impressive public orator. What elements of his style would contribute to this effect?

2. Ask students to compare/contrast Chief Seattle's ironic style with Wallace Stegner's straightforward appeal in "Wilderness Letter" (FE p. 544).

Suggested Writing Assignments

1. Choose a maxim from Chief Seattle's "Letter" as the thesis for an argument you wish to make about a topic of environmental importance. Examples: "Continue to contaminate your bed, and you will one night suffocate in your own waste" (paragraph 5) or "[A]ll things share the same breath—the beasts, the trees, the man" (paragraph 2). Add your own evidence and experience to support the argument.

2. Write a letter to the president on an environmental issue of relevance today, or recast the material from another essay in this chapter into the form of a letter to the president.

3. In many essays on environmental topics, a member of a minority group (or a person holding a minority opinion) must persuade the majority to alter its course. Write an argument on an environmental topic that concerns you deeply, using your position as a minority writer as part of your strategy for persuading the majority to change its view.

WALLACE STEGNER
Wilderness Letter

Full Edition, p. 544

This essay presents an argument for preserving American wilderness. Novelist, historian, and environmentalist Wallace Stegner served as special assistant to Secretary of the Interior Stewart Udall under Presidents Kennedy and Johnson and wrote this defense of wilderness in that capacity. Stegner argues that a large part of the American character is formed by the wilderness experience.

Moreover, it's necessary to preserve the wilderness for the sake of the body and soul. Stegner's position remains highly relevant today, in spite of critiques, such as the one by William Cronon in "The Trouble with Wilderness" (FE p. 550). Stegner, known as the "Dean of Western American Writers," was a novelist and nonfiction writer. He served as director of the Stanford Writing Program for many years and was a major influence on American writers from Edward Abbey (FE p. 535) and Wendell Berry to Ken Kesey and Larry McMurtry.

Questions from *The Norton Reader*

1. Wallace Stegner wrote his letter with a purpose: to influence Congress to pass the Wilderness Bill, which would set aside large tracts of undeveloped land in a National Wilderness Preservation System. As he argues his case, what are the primary values he associates with wilderness?

2. "We are a wild species," Stegner writes (paragraph 4), claiming Charles Darwin as his source. What connections does Stegner make between humans as "wild" and the need for protected wilderness areas?

3. What kinds of land does Stegner recommend preserving as wilderness? Why does he include more than "virgin country" (paragraph 10)?

4. Read William Cronon's "The Trouble with Wilderness" (FE p. 550). Compare and contrast his views about wilderness with Stegner's, evaluating the strengths and weaknesses of both authors' claims.

Teaching Suggestions

1. Stegner's essay participates in a longstanding, distinctly American relationship to land in general and wilderness in particular. Explore the National Park Service website's presentation of wilderness with your students (http:// wilderness.nps.gov/default.cfm) and contrast it with Stegner's essay as well as other presentations of wilderness in literature and pop culture.

2. The Wilderness Act of 1964 celebrated its fiftieth anniversary in 2014. Have students research the Wilderness Area (or Areas) nearest your school (you can find lists at (www.wilderness.net). What aspects of wilderness, as Stegner defines it, does this specific place have? How has our need for wilderness changed in the past fifty years, if at all?

3. This essay inspired William Cronon's rebuttal, "The Trouble with Wilderness" (FE p. 550). Stegner and Cronon's disagreement is deep but also subtle in ways that are worth delving into with students: both writers would find themselves firmly on the side of environmental preservation in many political arguments. Have students read both and stage a debate between Stegner and Cronon's ideas.

4. You can find an account of more recent political threats to wilderness at wilderness.org. Have students research one or more such recent issues and discuss the extent to which Stegner's arguments might be brought to bear in these contemporary contexts.

Suggested Writing Assignments

1. Research the history of a wilderness area that matters to you. Write a short paper about its specific value, describing the land in detail while building on Stegner's ideas.

2. Write an essay arguing for the preservation of a piece of land that matters to you. Be sure to consider what type of use—if any—you think appropriate for this piece of land (e.g., hiking, snowmobiling, foraging, hunting, or as wilderness). Consider both moral appeals (such as the one Stegner makes here) and others (scientific, aesthetic, economic, etc.).

3. Read William Cronon's "The Trouble with Wilderness" (FE p. 550) and write an essay in which you lay out your sense of the role wilderness should play in our national imagination and politics. Be sure to make reference to both Cronon and Stegner, establishing the extent you agree and disagree with each.

WILLIAM CRONON
The Trouble with Wilderness

Full Edition, p. 550

This essay, particularly the first part, will seem oddly contrarian to many students; William Cronon himself says his argument seems at first glance to be "perverse." He argues that we should understand the concept of "wilderness" as a human creation, and as soon as he makes this claim, some readers will get it while others will scratch their heads in puzzlement. This is not to say that Cronon in any way disparages or denounces wilderness, only the quick assumptions that allow humans to easily demarcate such a concept from their everyday lives. As he reminds us, those who helped create the concept were often city folks with little or no understanding of what it is like to work the land.

If your class contains a good mix of rural, suburban, and urban students, have them compare their own notions of wilderness with both the strict definition and the looser one Cronon seems to be employing throughout, a definition that encompasses Great Plains ranches as well as trackless forests in the Sierras. Alternatively, have students read Wallace Stegner's "Wilderness Letter" (FE p. 544), a key document in the mythology as well as in the establishment of designated "wilderness areas" within state parks. Discuss why Cronon might feel the need to offer a corrective.

The last three paragraphs witness a turn toward a lesson. This is where Cronon tells us what we ought to do about wilderness and how we ought to react. Some will find the tone a bit preachy, but a careful reading will demonstrate that this tone has been carefully prepared for earlier on. In fact, the entire essay has the form of a classic sermon, one that examines a single word, in this case "wilderness," and derives a moral lesson from its conclusions.

Questions from *The Norton Reader*

1. In paragraph 12 William Cronon writes, "We live in an urban-industrial civilization, but too often pretend to ourselves that our real home is in the wilderness." Cronon gives no examples. What examples might back up Cronon's statement? Can you think of counterexamples as well?

2. Who is Cronon's "we" throughout his essay? Why does he use "we" so frequently?

3. Paragraph 2 raises the issue of whether wilderness provides us with a "mirror." Look through the essay for similar visual imagery; then explain the role that such imagery plays.

4. If you found significant counterexamples in response to Question 1, write an essay in which you question or object to one or more aspect of Cronon's argument.

Teaching Suggestions

1. This essay is taken from a book entitled *Uncommon Ground: Toward Reinventing Nature*. Ask students to show how this essay's subject matter and approach are appropriate for a book with such a title.

2. Cronon talks of "a natural landscape that is also cultural" (paragraph 14). Have students explain what he means.

3. Does Cronon show much awareness that his readers might have a very different view of the word "wilderness"? How does he meet his readers' expectations?

4. If wilderness is a construct, mainly mental, ask students to identify the rules for deciding what is wilderness and what is not. Who gets to decide?

Suggested Writing Assignments

1. Write about a place that would fit Cronon's notion of wilderness so your readers can decide if his main point is accurate.

2. There are many specifically designated "wilderness areas" in national parks and national forests. Is it contrary to the spirit of the term "wilderness" to have foot trails through these areas? Bicycle trails? Horse trails? Snowmobile trails?

3. Interview people about what the term "wilderness" means to them. Write up your findings.

Sandra Steingraber
Tune of the Tuna Fish

Full Edition, p. 554

Between her sophomore and junior years of college, Sandra Steingraber—a scientist, poet, and nonfiction writer—was diagnosed with bladder cancer. It runs in her family—her *adopted* family. In *Living Downstream*, Steingraber traces connections between cancer and the environment. In *Having Faith*, a book that recounts her pregnancy and the early childhood of her daughter Faith, she considers environmental hazards to fetuses as well as the contamination of breast milk. Given Steingraber's experiences and research, her focus in "Tune of the Tuna Fish" is not surprising. She understands the real connections between environmental concerns and human bodies.

One way of teaching this essay is to use it as a model for ways of communicating scientific information to various audiences. In the narrative included, Steingraber tries to find appropriate ways of explaining the dangers of mercury poisoning to her six-year-old daughter. The essay itself, however, is written for adults—presumably those who vote on various issues affecting the environment and who make conscious choices about what they buy, eat, and feed to others.

Questions from *The Norton Reader*

1. Sandra Steingraber's essay informs readers of the high levels of mercury in fish and the dangers of eating a tuna fish sandwich. Why, then, does she begin with her daughter's piano playing? What roles do her daughter, Faith, and later her son, Elijah, play in this essay?

2. What facts about industrial pollutants, including methylmercury, does Steingraber provide? Where do they appear in the essay? How do they relate—structurally and conceptually—to the episodes with her daughter?

3. Does Steingraber suggest a solution to the problem of industrial pollutants? In terms of the environment, does the essay end on a hopeful or despairing note?

4. Write an essay about another kind of environmental problem, ideally one with personal or local significance. Interweave facts with examples or short narratives.

Teaching Suggestions

1. Aristotle writes about three artistic appeals that aid in persuasion: logos (appeals to reason and logic), ethos (the writer or speaker's character and reputation), and pathos (appeals to emotion). After explaining these terms to your students, ask them to locate sections in Steingraber's essay in which they see each of these appeals at play. For example, paragraphs 4 and 5 rely heavily on scientific studies, support for logical appeals. The rhetorical questions in paragraph 9 are meant to provoke emotion from the reader. And the mix of reason and appeals to emotion—both the author's scientifically based studies and her care as a parent—evidence her ethos. Which parts of the essay do students find most persuasive?

2. Ask students to consider purpose. In her essay, Steingraber mixes narrative and argument. What is her purpose in doing so? Is she trying to provide a model for how to discuss difficult issues with children? Is she trying to educate

her readers on the dangers of mercury poisoning? Or does she have another purpose?

3. Like Steingraber, Terry Tempest Williams, in "The Clan of One-Breasted Women" (FE p. 557, SE p. 316), uses a mix of research data and personal experience. Ask students to compare and contrast the ways this strategy works in both essays. Do they find it more effective in one than in the other?

4. What is the tone of Steingraber's essay? Do students find it hopeful? Why or why not?

SUGGESTED WRITING ASSIGNMENTS

1. Choose an issue (perhaps an environmental issue, though it need not be) that is important to you. Think of an audience you would like to inform and perhaps persuade to take some sort of action. Consider the appeals you will use. Will you, like Steingraber, mix logos, ethos, and pathos, or will your article be more heavily weighted toward one appeal? Will you use narrative, a straightforward argument, or some mix of both? Write a piece that you think will be persuasive to the audience you've chosen.

2. Steingraber explains a difficult issue—mercury poisoning—to her six-year-old daughter. Write about a time when you talked with someone younger than you about a difficult issue. Use dialogue and setting to dramatize the conversation.

TERRY TEMPEST WILLIAMS
The Clan of One-Breasted Women

Full Edition, p. 557; Shorter Edition, p. 316

Terry Tempest Williams explains the literal meaning of her title in the first paragraph: the women in her family suffer from breast cancer, and mastectomies are a frequent, devastating result. Students may also want to know about the mythological tribe of women warriors, the Amazons, who according to some legends cut off their right breasts in order to wield their bows and arrows more freely. This allusion prepares for Williams's discussion, later in the essay, of her dilemma about whether or not she, as a Mormon woman, should fight governmental authorities and risk imprisonment. Should she, like other Mormons, passively accept the risks that threaten her, or should she, like the Amazons, actively fight against them?

Williams served as naturalist-in-residence at the Utah Museum of Natural History and published several books of nature writing: *Pieces of White Shell: A Journey to Navajoland* (1984), *Coyote's Canyon* (1989), *Refuge* (1991), *An Unspoken Hunger* (1994), *Leap* (2000), and *Red* (2001). This essay combines powerful personal experiences with research into historical and environmental issues to argue against nuclear testing in the desert. Students may find the combination of personal experience and research data rhetorically useful if they choose to write essays that take a stand on environmental issues. You might suggest that they use Williams's essay as a model for structure and for argument.

QUESTIONS FROM *The Norton Reader*

1. Terry Tempest Williams uses a variety of evidence in this essay, including personal memory, family history, government documents, and other sources. List the evidence and the order in which she uses it. Why might Williams present her material in this order?

2. The essay begins with a description of what Williams later calls a "family nightmare" (paragraph 35) and ends with a dream vision. What is the rhetorical effect of this interactive opening and closing?

3. What do you think Williams means by the statement "I must question everything" (paragraph 36)?

4. Conduct some research on an environmental issue that affects you, your friends, or your family, and, using Williams as a model, write an essay that combines both your personal experience and research.

TEACHING SUGGESTIONS

1. The first section of Williams's essay narrates family history and personal memory. How does Williams shape her narration to build to a startling revelation?

2. How—and why—does a writer incorporate factual evidence into what is essentially a personal essay? In the second section (paragraphs 20–29), Williams condenses facts from several historical and governmental studies (see footnotes 1–10). You might ask students to look up these sources and explain how Williams uses evidence from her research, especially the quoted phrases. You might also discuss why Williams does not quote her research materials in certain places, whether because she can assume knowledge on the part of her readers or because her personal rendition of the material is more compelling.

3. What influence does Mormon culture and religion have on Williams's personal behavior? How does she convey her attitude toward her religious background, especially in the third section?

4. Williams's rhetorical strategies include many that might be called "feminist": naming her mother and grandmothers (paragraph 34), recounting her "dream" and the song of the Shoshoni women (paragraphs 38–39), metaphorically comparing the pangs of women giving birth with the death pangs of the desert (paragraph 42), referring to her memory of the Joshua trees (paragraph 57), and, more generally, as in her title, alluding to women's history and myth. Instructors interested in the possibilities of feminist rhetoric might want to consider the use of women's history and myth as an alternative to more traditionally "masculine" modes of argument in pieces of environmental writing, such as Edward Abbey's (FE p. 535).

Suggested Writing Assignments

1. Choose an environmental issue for which you have personal experience and factual data to draw on. (If you don't have factual data when you start, do research to collect the relevant evidence.) Write an essay about that issue in which you, like Williams, combine personal experience and objective facts.

2. Use an incident or story in your family's history as the starting point for an essay that makes an argument (explicit or implicit) about some important public issue.

3. Consult one of the sources Williams cites in her footnotes to learn more about nuclear testing in Utah and other western states. Instead of a personal essay, write a historical summary of the events that lie behind Williams's family experience. What purpose might your version of the events have that Williams's does not?

MICHELLE NIJHUIS

Which Species Will Live?

Full Edition, p. 564

In this essay, award-winning science journalist Michelle Nijhuis asks a gut-wrenching question: in this era of widespread extinctions, which species should we try to save and why? Specifically, the essay examines the concept of "conservation triage" (paragraph 6), or the idea that we have a responsibility to direct conservation efforts so that they provide "maximum benefit for nature as a whole" (paragraph 12). Since some species will inevitably be favored over others, the argument goes, it is better to acknowledge that fact and to proceed systematically and transparently.

Nijhuis acknowledges that the concept is controversial and notes that the 1973 Endangered Species Act was motivated by the very different imperative that she, following Charles C. Mann and Mark L. Plummer, terms the "Noah Principle." This principle holds that "all species are fundamentally equal, and everything can and should be saved, regardless of its importance to humans" (paragraph 7). After staking out this basic opposition, Nijhuis describes several different approaches to conservation triage. She concludes her essay by affirming the Noah Principle as an ideal, even as she acknowledges the practical necessity of conservation triage.

You will almost certainly provoke a vigorous discussion by posing a version of Nijhuis's title question to your students: Which species should live? Which should we work to preserve? But the essay has other merits as well. Nijhuis dispassionately summarizes the different approaches to conservation triage, and she also recognizes not just the intellectual but also the affective dimensions of her subject. The essay is thus a fine example of balanced argument, in at least two senses.

QUESTIONS FROM *THE NORTON READER*

1. Michelle Nijhuis explains several ways scientists and policy makers "triage" species threatened with extinction. What are these ways? Which do you find most effective and why?

2. Compare the attitudes toward nature that inform the debate over "conservation triage" (paragraph 6) to those expressed by Chief Seattle (FE p. 543, SE p. 315), Wallace Stegner (FE p. 544), or William Cronon (FE p. 550). Would these writers embrace or reject conservation triage? Why?

3. Although Nijhuis acknowledges the need for conservation triage, she also holds up the "Noah Principle" (paragraph 7) as an ideal. What is this principle, and why does Nijhuis consider it so important?

4. Write a paper explaining a difficult decision you've made. How did you balance competing goals, values, and principles?

TEACHING SUGGESTIONS

1. Ask students to offer their own answers to Nijhuis's title question: "Which species will live?" Use the discussion as an occasion to cultivate good arguments. Encourage students to support their positions with good reasons and to acknowledge alternative views.

2. Lead students to consider the essay's introduction. Why does Nijhuis open with the anecdote about the Wildlife Conservation Society's decision to ignore the plight of the ashy storm-petrel? How does this beginning frame the rest of the essay?

3. Nijhuis explains conservation triage through an analogy to battlefield triage. Have students identify places in the essay where she uses this analogy and ask them to analyze its effect. What aspects of the struggle to preserve endangered species does it illuminate? What aspects does it obscure?

4. Discuss the essay from an emotional perspective. How does Nijhuis address or acknowledge the emotional challenges conservation triage involves? What kinds of emotional reactions do your students have to the essay? How does Nijhuis evoke and manage those responses?

SUGGESTED WRITING ASSIGNMENTS

1. Write an essay explaining the criteria you would use to triage species for preservation. In your essay, be sure to consider and respond to potential objections to your approach.

2. Write an essay analyzing the ethical issues involved in conservation triage. Do human beings have the right or responsibility to choose which species will live? Why or why not?

3. Research one endangered species. Imagine that you are a scientist who has been asked by the Wildlife Conservation Society whether it should be preserved. Write a *white paper*—a brief explanation of an issue with a policy recommendation—supporting your position.

Media and Technology

NICHOLAS CARR

Is Google Making Us Stupid?

Full Edition, p. 572; Shorter Edition, p. 324

Nicholas Carr is an American writer who focuses on technology and its impact on business, education, and general culture. His books and articles arouse controversy—as in the heated rebuttals from executives of Microsoft, Intel, and Hewlett-Packard after the publication of *Does IT Matter? Information Technology and the Corrosion of Competitive Advantage* (2004), which argued that American companies spend billions of dollars on information technology (IT) that fails, in the end, to produce any real competitive advantage. "Is Google Making Us Stupid?," published in the *Atlantic* in 2008 and then expanded in *The Shallows: What the Internet Is Doing to Our Brains* (2010), has similarly generated sharp debate. Michael Agger in *Slate* calls it "a *Silent Spring* for the literary mind," whereas Todd Gitlin in the *New Republic* argues that it suffers from "exaggeration and overkill," as the title of his review suggests: "The Uses of Half-True Alarms." Classroom discussions are likely to generate similarly sharp debate, with students pointing out pros and cons of Carr's position and (most likely) bringing up examples he hasn't considered.

QUESTIONS FROM *THE NORTON READER*

1. Nicholas Carr poses a question with the title of this essay. How would you answer it? What main examples does he offer to illustrate how Google is making us stupid? What counterexamples does he offer? What examples, on either side, would you add?

2. What are the most important advantages of "Taylorism" (paragraphs 21–24), or the application of scientific methods to human behavior? Are there aspects of human behavior that cannot be improved by such methods?

3. Carr is ambivalent about our reliance on technology, but Thomas Goetz (FE p. 587) is more enthusiastic. Compare Carr's attitude about a new technology with Goetz's. What is your stance on these authors' relationships to technology, and why?

4. Interview a few people, including some who grew up using the internet and some who remember doing research mainly using books. Write your own analysis of the impact of the internet on our ability to think, reason, and research, building on Carr's essay and the anecdotes you collect.

TEACHING SUGGESTIONS

1. Since Carr's title is so broad, you might want to focus on specific arguments he makes—for example, about our ability to read long books like *War and Peace* (paragraph 6) or about the effect of technology on writing (paragraphs 12–14). Are the anecdotes Carr gives actually evidence for becoming more "stupid"—or are they about changes with good and bad aspects?

2. Ask students to figure out the relationship between anecdote (stories Carr tells about himself or people he knows) and research (citations of scientific or historical studies). Does the anecdote generate the citation of research, or vice versa? If you want to pursue further the issue of Carr's use of research, ask students to look up one of the books, articles, or scientific studies he cites.

SUGGESTED WRITING ASSIGNMENTS

1. Look up one of the scientific studies or historical cases Carr cites and describe how he uses his source: what he selects, what he omits, what he emphasizes or possibly distorts.

2. Two essays in the "Media and Technology" chapter are phrased as questions: "Is Google Making Us Stupid?" and Tasneem Raja's "Is Coding the New Literacy?" (FE p. 600, SE p. 339). Compare and contrast the rhetorical techniques of these two essays, including the authors' use of anecdotes, scholarly or scientific evidence, comparisons, allusions, and rhetorical questions.

3. What question related to media or technology interests you? Use that question to guide your research, and use it as your title. Write an essay in which you seek to answer that question. Use both anecdotes and research to support your answer.

EULA BISS
Time and Distance Overcome

Full Edition, p. 581; Shorter Edition, p. 333

Eula Biss is a nonfiction writer known for her lyric essays—associational meditations that combine research and personal narrative. "Time and Distance Overcome" was published in *Notes from No Man's Land: American Essays*; many of the essays in that collection focus on race in America. In this essay, Biss considers the history of the telephone, a technology meant to connect people. She presents early resistance to the "urban blight" of telephone poles (paragraph 10) and then moves to a troubling historical use for the poles: lynching, another "American invention" (paragraph 17). She writes that it "was only coincidence that they became convenient as gallows" (paragraph 21), but as Biss lists the violent, racially motivated killings and the number of black men hanged, the telephone pole begins to lose its symbolic association as a means of connection to take on negative and violent associations. The end of the essay takes a more hopeful turn when Biss writes that "some green telephone poles grew small leafy branches" (paragraph 37), perhaps symbolizing life and change, but the disturbing associations remain.

QUESTIONS FROM *THE NORTON READER*

1. Eula Biss focuses on the historical coincidence of the installation of telephone poles with lynching. List the ways Biss connects the topics and discuss the merits of the juxtaposition. How does she make the coincidence into something meaningful?

2. How does paragraph 18, on "the children's game of telephone," connect to the themes of the rest of the essay?

3. Following Biss's model (paragraphs 38–40), write an author's note for an old research paper in which you describe how the paper changed as you did your research.

4. Every new technology brings benefits and problems, as Biss explores. Choose a different medium or technology (e.g., TV, smartphones, texting) and write an essay discussing its benefits and problems, using Biss's essay as a model.

TEACHING SUGGESTIONS

1. Ask students to examine Biss's use of passive voice and the ways her choice of verbs and sentence structure contribute to the overall effect of the essay. For example, Biss writes "a black man was hanged from a telephone pole" (paragraph 26), a construction that emphasizes who was killed and provides an associational link to telephone poles, but does not say who did the killing. Humans were responsible for the killing, but Biss's use of passive voice shifts people's attention away from who or what was to blame.

2. Rather than using explicit transitions between paragraphs, Biss makes associational leaps. Students might need help making connections between different parts of the essay and understanding the purpose of Biss's juxtapositions. Ask students to look for irony—how something associated with connection can also be a symbol of division.

3. Biss includes a research note that explains how her purpose and topic shifted because of her research. After students have written an essay that requires outside research, ask them to reflect on their own process and to explain how they refined a topic or discovered a new approach because of their research. Also encourage students to use research notes—or footnotes or endnotes—to explain information that they chose not to include in the body of the text.

SUGGESTED WRITING ASSIGNMENTS

1. Write an essay about the emergence of a particular medium or technology. How did the public respond?

2. Write a lyric essay using short paragraphs linked by association rather than explicit transitions.

3. As Biss states, the telephone poles were not to blame for the way people used them (paragraph 21). Write an essay in which you reflect on an object that has been used (for good or ill) in surprising ways.

Thomas Goetz
Harnessing the Power of Feedback Loops
Full Edition, p. 587

Thomas Goetz has an M.A. in public health and is the author of books such as *The Decision Tree: Taking Control of Your Health in the New Era of Personalized Medicine* (2010) and *The Remedy* (2014). He also co-founded a health technology company, which was inspired by his research on medical data and the need he identified to make that data easier for individuals to read and use. His TED talk "It's Time to Redesign Medical Data" (2010) is available online at ted.com. Goetz's interest in public health is also evident in "Harnessing the Power of Feedback Loops," which describes ways of providing individuals with information that they can use to change their own actions and develop better habits. He also outlines the stages of an effective feedback loop. Although some of the specific technologies and products Goetz describes have changed or been supplanted by others, his explanation of feedback loops and human behavior remains relevant, and students will likely recognize the role feedback loops play in their everyday lives.

Questions from *The Norton Reader*

1. In paragraph 9, Thomas Goetz describes the four stages of the feedback loop. Look again at his definition and then find how those stages work in several of the inventions he describes here. How does the repetition of the loop several times across the essay affect your understanding of the process?

2. Goetz is careful to distinguish between monitors that send information to the consumer from those that send information to the government or to a company. Are there any instances in which it might be appropriate for the government or a private company to monitor individual consumption (e.g., of water during a drought, of unhealthy food after surgery)? Why or why not?

3. Think of a behavior or habit that you would like to change and write an essay in which you describe an invention to encourage that change based on the principle of the feedback loop.

Teaching Suggestions

1. Question 2 in *The Norton Reader* asks students to consider times when it might be appropriate or beneficial for information to go not just to an individual but to a governmental agency or a private company. This question moves beyond Goetz's focus on individuals changing their own behavior through feedback loops and helps students consider both the possible benefits and potential

abuses of tracking information through sensors and monitors. Who should have access to tracked information? For what purposes? Who benefits—and in what ways? Who might be harmed—and in what ways?

2. Once students understand the stages of the feedback loops Goetz describes and how different inventions use those stages to provide information to users, ask students to think of other inventions or devices that use feedback loops (beyond the ones Goetz writes about). Now that students have an understanding of them and their potential, ask them what other problems might be addressed through feedback loops. Can they imagine a device, app, or online platform that would solve a current problem?

3. Some students have experience wearing pedometers or fitness trackers. Many students carry a smartphone that tracks steps and distance walked. There are apps and devices meant to help users increase productivity, get more sleep, lose weight, and so on. If you ask students to write about the benefits and challenges of changing behavior based on feedback, be sure that they incorporate these kinds of examples.

SUGGESTED WRITING ASSIGNMENTS

1. Goetz provides a list of goals and associated products that use feedback loops. Research other products that use feedback loops and make your own list of goals and products.

2. Write an analysis of the images included in Goetz's essay. Are they effective? Why or why not?

3. Goetz suggests using feedback loops to help create positive change. Write a narrative about a time you made a change in your own behavior. How did you do it? What helped you make that change?

TASNEEM RAJA

Is Coding the New Literacy?

Full Edition, p. 600; Shorter Edition, p. 339

Tasneem Raja—a journalist who writes about the intersection of race, gender, and technology—argues not just for the importance of coding but for teaching a way of thinking: computational thinking. She compares the importance of computational literacy to the importance of reading and writing, arguing that an understanding of computational thinking will help people learn to ask the kinds of questions that allow for solutions to real-world problems. Education in computational literacy, Raja argues, is taking place in other countries and should be more central to education in the United States. And it should be practical, helping students "make use of various algorithms" in different situations (paragraph 56). Raja argues further that "diverse teams produce better products" (paragraph 67), so computer science education for both girls and boys and students of all races and ethnicities is also essential.

QUESTIONS FROM *THE NORTON READER*

1. Tasneem Raja covers many topics—the difference between coding and computational literacy, the history of learning to write, and the importance of encouraging women to remain in STEM fields. Make a list of the broad topics she covers and discuss how they are related to each other.

2. The online version of this essay (at MotherJones.com) included dozens of hyperlinks, but only four footnotes. Go to the online version and follow a few of Raja's links. What is the difference between the information she chose to footnote and the information she linked to?

3. According to Raja, what are some of the main obstacles to teaching coding and computational literacy? Do you think coding should be an academic requirement? Why or why not?

4. Write an essay about your experience learning to code. (If you have never tried, spend a few hours on a beginner's site.) How is learning to code like learning to write? How is it different?

5. Research one of the pioneering women in computer science and computer education whom Raja mentions (paragraphs 56, 60, 65) and write a paper on that woman's contribution to the field.

TEACHING SUGGESTIONS

1. Raja discusses reading, writing, and computational literacy. Her original online publication implicitly shows how all these forms of literacy are connected. That is, choosing what to footnote and what to link to requires a range of literate competencies. Encourage students to see connections among writing, reading, and programming.

2. Ask students to consider what subjects should be academic requirements and why.

3. If students have never learned coding, they can try out different sites. They can put "best free sites for learning how to code" into an internet search engine and come up with lists of reviewed sites to try.

SUGGESTED WRITING ASSIGNMENTS

1. Raja uses an extended metaphor comparing computational thinking to cooking and recipe-making (paragraphs 11–17). Write an essay in which you argue for a way of thinking. Use an extended metaphor to help readers understand that way of thinking.

2. Revise something you've written to be published online. Use hyperlinks in addition to footnotes to support and illustrate your claims and to make connections to other sources.

3. Raja focuses not just on the importance of learning coding but also on learning to ask certain kinds of questions and to imagine different ways of solving problems. She opens with an example of coders developing a website that allows residents to "adopt" a hydrant that they will dig out after a snowstorm,

which will save firefighters time if there's a fire. Make a list of other websites that could help solve real-world problems.

FRED VOGELSTEIN
And Then Steve Said, "Let There Be an iPhone"
Full Edition, p. 617

Both the title of and images in Fred Vogelstein's "And Then Steve Said, 'Let There Be an iPhone'" suggest Steve Jobs was a god-like figure able to speak an invention into existence. In the essay, however, Vogelstein details the work, stress, and multiple people involved in the success of the iPhone. He shows the importance of leadership and risk but also suggests that success comes with a cost; the stress and secrecy clearly took a toll on many workers at Apple. Still, Vogelstein—with his focus on Jobs and Grignon—emphasizes the success of the iPhone unveiling. This essay can be used to discuss issues ranging from leadership style to the place of competition in technological innovation.

QUESTIONS FROM *The Norton Reader*

1. This essay focuses on the contributions of both Steve Jobs and the less-famous Andy Grignon to the development of the iPhone. What did each contribute to the project overall? How would you assess their relative importance?

2. Fred Vogelstein tells several anecdotes about Steve Jobs as a leader. Look at them and identify some of Jobs's personality traits. What do you see as the relationship between these traits and his success?

3. Does knowing this story behind this invention add to your appreciation of the iPhone in particular and smartphones in general? Why or why not?

4. Vogelstein offers many details about both internal rivalries at Apple and Apple's rivalry with Google. Write an essay about the role of competition in technological innovation. You may want to do some additional reading or research.

TEACHING SUGGESTIONS

1. Steve Jobs's personality traits and leadership style have been the subject of many books, articles, and films, so students will likely have some familiarity with Jobs even before reading Vogelstein's essay. As students discuss the relationship between Jobs's personality traits and success, you might also provide examples of other kinds of leadership styles. (Articles comparing and contrasting, for example, Steve Jobs and Bill Gates are available online.) You might also want to point out that "success" can be measured in different ways.

2. Major accomplishments often take the work of more than one person. Ask students to analyze the title, images, and narrative in Vogelstein's essay. Do these different aspects of the piece send a clear message? Does the narrative

undermine the message sent by the title and images? Who is the focus of the essay?

3. As students consider the role of competition in technological innovation, ask them also to consider other factors (education, collaboration, different ways of approaching and solving problems, different kinds of expertise, and so on). How might Tasneem Raja, author of "Is Coding the New Literacy?" (FE p. 600, SE p. 339), approach the question of the relationship between competition and technological innovation? Would she and Vogelstein have similar or different points of view?

SUGGESTED WRITING ASSIGNMENTS

1. Research a technological innovation or product that interests you. How was it created and introduced to the public? Write an essay that shows the different roles of major contributors to that innovation or product.

2. Write an essay outlining three qualities of a good leader. Provide an example of someone who embodies those qualities.

3. Vogelstein writes, "Smartphones . . . have become extensions of our brains. They have fundamentally changed the way people receive and process information" (paragraph 9). Research the effect of smartphones on how people process information. Write an essay arguing whether the effect has been positive, negative, or a mix of both.

JUDITH NEWMAN

To Siri, with Love: How One Boy with Autism Became BFF with Apple's Siri

Full Edition, p. 628; Shorter Edition, p. 356

Judith Newman calls her personal essay "a love letter to a machine" (paragraph 11), and although the essay is not actually addressed to Siri—Apple's computerized "personal assistant"—it does explain and show Newman's appreciation for the role Siri plays in communicating with her autistic son, Gus. She writes, "My son's practice conversation with Siri is translating into more facility with actual humans" (paragraph 25). In addition to presenting anecdotal evidence of the value of Siri "to those with speech and communication problems" (paragraph 26), Newman interviewed William Mark, vice president at the research and development company that helped develop Siri, and learned that the company is seeking to develop technologies that would help those with communication problems in other ways, too. Despite her initial concerns about being a bad mother for allowing her son to communicate with Siri, Newman concentrates on the positive effects of a particular technology, showing not only the role Siri plays in helping her son learn communication skills but also how the "intelligent personal assistant" (paragraph 1) is helping her avoid frustration and learn more about her son.

Questions from *The Norton Reader*

1. Judith Newman describes how her autistic son learns about communication and etiquette from Siri, Apple's "intelligent personal assistant." What examples does Newman offer to support this observation?

2. Often inventions end up being useful for reasons other than their original intent. What did programmers originally think Siri would be used for? How do people use it? Find other examples of technology that has a surprising application.

3. In "Harnessing the Power of Feedback Loops" (FE p. 587), Thomas Goetz defines "enchanted objects" as types of inventions that "don't register as gadgets or even as technology at all, but rather as friendly tools that beguile us into action. In short they're magical" (paragraph 35). Using this definition, write an essay exploring the extent to which Siri (or another invention that helps people overcome challenges) is "enchanted."

Teaching Suggestions

1. Computers can help people communicate—software can help teach reading, writing, new languages, and more. Social media, email, and texts can help people stay in touch, but some researchers claim these modes of communication can also cause social isolation and inhibit the development of relationships. Ask students to offer examples of both positive and negative effects of technology on communication—from the positive effects of speaking to a loved one on the phone to the negative effect of being ignored by someone who is constantly texting rather than engaging in conversation with those physically present.

2. Some inventions have unexpected benefits (some medications, for example, have been found to treat conditions they were not intended to treat); others have unanticipated drawbacks (for example, airbags in vehicles are meant to save lives but have caused injuries to children riding in the passenger-side front seat). Invite students to offer their own examples.

3. Despite the fact that some technologies and inventions have unexpected benefits for people and populations they were not meant to serve directly, diversity in the experience, identity, and concerns of those who develop technologies can help increase benefits for a range of people. Individuals with different experiences and concerns will see different problems and different possibilities for solutions. Ask students to consider the similarities and differences among the authors and subjects included in the chapter "Media and Technology."

Suggested Writing Assignments

1. Write a "love letter" to a device, app, or technology that has helped you or someone important to you.

2. Newman uses dialogue to show how her son and Siri communicate. The types of questions Gus asks help reveal something about him and his concerns. Write an essay in which you use dialogue to show something about yourself or another person.

3. If you use a "personal assistant" on your phone or another device, write an essay describing the benefits or challenges of using it.

DENNIS BARON

Facebook Multiplies Genders but Offers Users the Same Three Tired Pronouns

Full Edition, p. 634; Shorter Edition, p. 362

On his blog *The Web of Language*, Dennis Baron writes about language and technology. His blog posts—like op-eds—are often linked to current events. When Baron posted "Facebook Multiplies Genders but Offers Users the Same Three Tired Pronouns" in February 2014, Facebook offered a list of choices for users to signify gender. Since then, the company has changed its site, allowing users to choose "female," "male," or "custom." If the user chooses "custom," a blank box appears, allowing the user to self-define. Still, three pronouns are offered: her, him, them.

Although students might see options for gender and pronoun usage as a contemporary issue, Baron provides historical context for discussions of pronoun options, drawing from grammarian James Anderson's eighteenth-century work, which offered 234 pronouns (paragraph 7). Baron writes that since 1850, "eighty common-gender pronouns have been coined" (paragraph 9). Students can learn more about the history of gendered language in Baron's book *Grammar and Gender* (1986). Baron's essay can also be used in chapters on "Gender and Human Nature" and "Language and Communication."

QUESTIONS FROM *The Norton Reader*

1. Faced with the complexities of referring to people by pronouns, Dennis Baron details two approaches taken by linguists: a proliferation of pronouns and the invention of a single common pronoun. Which approach do you prefer, if any, and why? If you could invent your own language, what kinds of pronouns would you create?

2. Read Gwendolyn Ann Smith's "We're All Someone's Freak" (FE p. 184). What do you think Smith would have to say about Facebook's policy on gender terms?

3. Look at a long, personal form (such as a census form, college or job application, medical history, or online profile setup). Which questions need more options? Which are unnecessary or intrusive? Write a letter to the author of the form suggesting revisions and reasons supporting them.

Teaching Suggestions

1. Baron announces in his first paragraph that gender can be complicated. Some students might disagree, preferring to recognize just two options: male and female. Before discussing additional options for gendered pronoun use, you may need to have a broader discussion of when—and for whom—pronoun use is more complicated.

2. Facebook may limit pronoun options to three, but that's not the case everywhere. For example, in 2015, Scripps College began allowing students to self-identify—to choose from ten sets of pronouns in an online portal. In a section on pronouns, nonbinary.org shows numerous examples of different pronouns and explains their origin. This site also shows options for constructing sentences without pronouns. You can show students these examples and encourage them to bring in their own examples.

3. Baron's essay pairs well with Gwendolyn Ann Smith's "We're All Someone's Freak" (FE p. 184) not only because both essays consider gender and categories, but also because Smith's use of gendered pronouns does not always fit traditional grammatical categories. Show students, for example, where Smith writes that it should be irrelevant "what any other transgender person opts to do" (paragraph 15) and follows this statement by using the plural pronoun: "Their action does not change who I am."

Suggested Writing Assignments

1. Consult several different grammar or style handbooks to see what the authors recommend for avoiding sexist language. Report on the options offered, making a case for which options are best—and why.

2. Baron lists the custom gender options Facebook once offered (paragraph 4). Research and write definitions for the different terms listed, suggesting a pronoun to match each term.

3. Choose a paragraph or section from an essay either in *The Norton Reader* or one you have written that includes gendered pronouns. Rewrite that paragraph or section in two ways: with no pronouns and with some form of gender-neutral pronouns (see the pronouns page of nonbinary.org for examples). Then write a reflection on what is lost and gained in these revisions.

Ethics

MARK TWAIN
Advice to Youth

Full Edition, p. 637; Shorter Edition, p. 365

Mark Twain—or Samuel L. Clemens—is nineteenth-century America's best (and best-known) comic author and satirist. "Advice to Youth," a lecture Twain gave in 1882, was not published until 1923; we do not know the circumstances under which he gave it or who was in the audience. He says he was asked for something "suitable to youth. . . . didactic, instructive, or . . . good advice" (paragraph 1). He then proceeds to mimic a conventional form of precepts for behavior delivered by age to youth. Those in the audience who expected comedy from him would probably have taken his "serious" beginning ironically—that is, as saying one thing and meaning another. Those who did not would have been startled by—or perhaps even missed—the comic turn he gives his first precept, "Always obey your parents" by adding "when they are present" (paragraph 2). The pattern of precept subverted by irony persists throughout the lecture. Eventually, we imagine, most of the audience would have apprehended Twain's mode of speaking as ironic. Students should be able to identify his two modes, the ironic and the comic.

Irony is an unstable mode whose success presupposes ideal auditors (and readers)—in this instance, adults who would be amused by Twain's satirizing the pompous advice age delivers to youth. Ironists contribute to its success by evoking an ideal audience. But irony can go wrong. Have students imagine a range of responses from the adults in Twain's audience, from enjoyment to indignation. Then raise the question of children in the audience who, in the nineteenth century, attended lectures. How might they have responded? How might their presence have complicated the adults' responses?

Satire can be for as well as against. However, in "Advice to Youth" we can identify what Twain is satirizing (what he is against) more surely than we can identify what he is commending (what he is for). Students who have read Jonathan Swift's "A Modest Proposal" (FE p. 756, SE p. 442), in "History and Politics," should look again at paragraphs 30 to 31, where Swift lists "other expedients," that is, what he is for. Is it possible to make a similar list of what Twain is for?

QUESTIONS FROM *THE NORTON READER*

1. Underline the various pieces of "serious" advice that Mark Twain offers and notice where and how he begins to turn each one upside down.

2. Twain was already known as a comic author when he delivered "Advice to Youth" as a lecture in 1882; it was not published until 1923. We do not know the circumstances under which he delivered it or to whom. Using evidence from the text, imagine both the circumstances and the audience.

3. Rewrite "Advice to Youth" for a modern audience, perhaps as a lecture for a school assembly or a commencement address.

TEACHING SUGGESTIONS

1. Have students, as a class or in groups, imagine a range of responses from adults in Twain's audience. What evidence in the text would have triggered these responses?

2. What is Twain for? Ask students, as a class or in groups, to list or describe the values implicit in his lecture.

SUGGESTED WRITING ASSIGNMENTS

1. Imagine yourself an auditor offended by Twain's talk and write a letter to its sponsors berating them for inviting him to give it. Or imagine yourself an adult amused by Twain's talk and write a letter to its sponsors commending them for inviting him to give it. Or write both letters.

2. Take Polonius's precept-filled speech to his son Laertes (*Hamlet* 1.3) and use it as the skeleton of a talk in which you alternate irony and comedy in the manner of Twain.

3. Invent a series of precepts for youth to deliver to age, and write a talk in which you alternate irony and comedy in the manner of Twain.

4. Write a letter of advice to an adult invited to give a high school commencement address about what kind of serious advice to give and how to give it without sounding pompous.

PETER SINGER

What Should a Billionaire Give—and What Should You?

Full Edition, p. 640; Shorter Edition, p. 368

In this essay, first published in the *New York Times Magazine* (2006) and later in *Best American Essays* (2007), philosopher Peter Singer challenges us collectively to end global poverty, an issue with which he has been concerned throughout his career. As a philosopher, Singer adheres to a position known as *preference utilitarianism*, which identifies the good with the optimal satisfaction of the informed preferences of all parties involved in a given situation. In teaching this essay, you might emphasize its double argument. Singer begins with a question that has no practical consequences for the vast majority of his readers—what should a billionaire give?—but he also issues a moral exhortation to all of his readers: and what should you? Have students consider the way in which Singer integrates these two strands into a coherent argument. Singer's argument carries significant moral force; indeed, it may seem to students to be unassailable. For this reason, students may require extra encouragement to engage the argument critically and to imagine possible objections, qualifications, or alternatives.

QUESTIONS FROM *The Norton Reader*

1. Peter Singer's title poses a two-part question: What should a billionaire give—and what should you? At the end of his essay, he gives an answer. Discuss the pros and cons of his proposal, including the effects it would have on the givers and the receivers.

2. What ethical arguments does Singer make before presenting his proposal? What facts and principles underlie his position that all Americans in the top ten percent income bracket should give a specific percentage to alleviate the plight of the poor?

3. Singer's essay depends on anecdotes as well as facts. Choose one anecdote you consider highly effective, and suggest the reasons it succeeds rhetorically.

4. It is possible to read online statements by many of the philanthropists Singer interviews or cites. Choose one whose ideas interest you, read more about his or her philanthropy, and write a brief account of what he or she has contributed and why.

TEACHING SUGGESTIONS

1. In paragraph 8, Singer lists a number of questions around which he structures the essay. Ask students to consider the essay's organization, how Singer progresses from one part of his argument to the next. Ultimately, Singer challenges all his readers to do more than their fair share to end global poverty. How does Singer's essay build to this climax?

2. As a professional philosopher, Singer is certainly capable of offering abstract, technical arguments for his positions. Yet in this essay, he advances his argument largely through stories. Some of these stories are anecdotes about real people, such as Bill and Melinda Gates or the cabdriver who brings Singer to the Inter-American Developmental Bank in Washington, D.C. Others, such as the scenarios about drowning children, implicitly insert Singer's readers into the story. Ask students why they think Singer might have adopted this mode of argumentation. What is it about story that suits Singer's purpose?

3. In his second paragraph, Singer asks us to consider whether our beliefs "square with our actions." He continues throughout the essay to raise this question in different ways. What, for Singer, is the relationship between moral belief and moral action? Ask students what they think it should be.

4. There is an apparent tension in the essay between Singer's idealism and his pragmatism. He notes, for example, that it is better to praise people like Warren Buffett for giving so much than to criticize them for not giving even more (paragraph 31). He similarly observes that "it may be best to refrain from criticizing those who achieve the fair-share level" of giving, when so many fail to do even that (paragraph 43). Ask students to think about why Singer

introduces this pragmatic thread into his argument. Is it merely a concession to his readers, or is it something more? Perhaps consider this question in relation to the anecdote about Zell Kravinsky (paragraphs 28–31).

SUGGESTED WRITING ASSIGNMENTS

1. Singer's essay is specifically about the issue of global poverty. Write an essay modeled on Singer's about another global issue with moral dimensions, such as terrorism, climate change, or immigration.

2. Singer concludes his essay with a bracing exhortation: "The target we should be setting for ourselves is not halving the proportion of people living in extreme poverty, and without enough to eat, but ensuring that no one, or virtually no one, needs to live in such degrading conditions. That is a worthy goal, and it is well within our reach." Write a personal essay in which you reflect on and respond to this challenge.

ATUL GAWANDE
When Doctors Make Mistakes

Full Edition, p. 652; Shorter Edition, p. 380

Atul Gawande is a Harvard Medical School graduate who served as President Bill Clinton's health-care lieutenant during the 1992 campaign and then as a senior advisor in the Department of Health and Human Services during the Clinton administration; he is currently a general and endocrine surgeon at Brigham and Women's Hospital in Boston, Massachusetts. Gawande began writing about medical issues for *Slate* magazine while doing his medical residency in the mid-1990s; soon after, the *New Yorker* solicited his work and appointed him as a staff writer. This essay was published in the "Annals of Medicine" section of the *New Yorker* (February 1, 1999) and was included in Gawande's first book, *Complications: A Surgeon's Notes on an Imperfect Science* (2002). He has continued the theme of medical error in *Better: A Surgeon's Notes on Performance* (2007) and *The Checklist Manifesto: How to Get Things Right* (2009), the latter stressing the importance of careful pre-planning in medicine and the world at large. His latest book is *Being Mortal* (2014). Although "When Doctors Make Mistakes" is included in "Ethics," it could also be taught as a personal narrative, given that Gawande begins with an emergency he faced in the operating room and ends with a gallbladder operation in which he nearly made a disastrous error. Gawande's larger concern is not to chastise doctors for errors but to analyze how and why errors occur.

QUESTIONS FROM *THE NORTON READER*

1. Atul Gawande states flatly: "*All* doctors make terrible mistakes" (paragraph 50), and then proceeds to analyze why. What are the main reasons he offers?

2. In section IV, "Nearly Perfect," Gawande discusses attempts by different medical groups to eliminate or reduce error. What approaches have been effective? What are the limits of these approaches?

3. Although it incorporates significant research, this essay fits the genre of the personal narrative. At the beginning and end, Gawande narrates two of his experiences in the operating room. Are these examples similar or different? Does the rhetorical purpose of the anecdote stay the same, or does it change as Gawande moves through his discussion of medical error? Explain.

4. Narrate a personal experience in which you made a serious error. Try, like Gawande, to incorporate the research or advice of others who might help you understand the reasons for your error.

Teaching Suggestions

1. This essay is long—five sections, totaling approximately 8,000 words. Use the section divisions—"I–Crash Victim," "II–The Banality of Error," "III–Show and Tell," "IV–Nearly Perfect," "V–Getting It Right"—to help students understand the organization of the piece and what Gawande accomplishes in each.

2. Many students will have viewed medical TV shows, including reruns of the popular *Grey's Anatomy* series. Ask students how Gawande's account of the operating room is like/unlike those portrayed on TV, and then ask them to account for the differences, based on Gawande's purpose in this essay.

3. Gawande is a practicing surgeon, whose personal experience is recounted in the first and last sections. Ask students to reflect on his persona—his self-presentation as a doctor. How does this persona add to his authority as a writer on medical issues?

Suggested Writing Assignments

1. Write about the differences between a TV portrayal of an emergency room or operating theater and Gawande's depiction in this essay.

2. As a research project, look up the 1991 papers in the *New England Journal of Medicine*, known as the Harvard Medical Practice Study (available as a pdf by searching *harvard medical practice study 1991*). Write about what facts and conclusions Gawande uses in part II and what data he omits.

Tom Regan
The Case for Animal Rights

Full Edition, p. 670

Tom Regan is a philosopher who writes about theoretical and applied ethics; this essay, contributed to a collection of essays edited by Peter Singer, *In Defense of Animals* (1985), is an abridgment of his book by the same name, *The Case for*

Animal Rights (1983). Regan's contribution to the defense of animals, he believes, is "asking and answering deep, foundational moral questions about what morality is, how it should be understood and what is the best moral theory, all considered" (paragraph 6). He has strong feelings about animals, he claims, and he concludes this essay with some expression of them.

The circumstances of publication may account for his emphasis on both argument and argumentative procedures, which he enunciates along with his case. They may also account for the density of his argument as he lays out four positions—indirect duty, contractarianism, cruelty-kindness, and utilitarianism—and argues against them before advancing his own rights case.

According to Regan, his rights case is rationally the soundest. It also eliminates complexity: the human use of animals as a resource is either right or wrong and, if wrong, no compromises (such as he describes in paragraphs 1–4 and paragraphs 35–36) are possible. But what if Regan had been unable to make a rationally sound case for animal rights? Would a flawed case have altered his experience of what he regards as the abuse of animals? (You will want to call attention to what he says in paragraph 37.) Regan's essay deserves reading in conjunction with experiential essays such as Sallie Tisdale's "We Do Abortions Here: A Nurse's Story" (FE p. 709, SE p. 414). His emphasis on argument and argumentative procedures and Tisdale's emphasis on context raise important questions about the relation of principle to experience in ethics.

QUESTIONS FROM *THE NORTON READER*

1. Tom Regan argues against four views that deny rights to animals: indirect duty, contractarianism, cruelty-kindness, and utilitarianism. Locate his account of each and explain his objections to it.

2. Regan then argues for what he calls a "rights view," which is, he claims, "rationally the most satisfactory moral theory" (paragraph 28). Explain both his view and his claim.

3. What are the advantages of arguing for views that conflict with one's own before arguing for one's own? What are the disadvantages?

4. Regan includes among his goals "the total dissolution of commercial animal agriculture" and "the total elimination of commercial and sport hunting and trapping" (paragraph 1). Do these goals include vegetarianism? If so, why does he not use the word "vegetarian"?

5. Write an essay in which you take a position on an issue about which you have strong feelings. Following Regan's example, focus on your argument even as you acknowledge your personal feelings on the issue.

TEACHING SUGGESTIONS

1. You may want to divide questions 1 and 2 (above) into five parts and have students work in groups on one part each. You may also want to identify students who have encountered these views in philosophy or ethics courses

and assign them to different groups. At the end of this exercise, try asking the various groups to describe their experiences of following and comprehending a philosophical argument.

2. What assertions does Regan make about political and social change? Do your students accept them? How important are they to his argument?

3. Two other essays in this chapter take up questions of animal rights: Michael Pollan's "An Animal's Place" (FE p. 681, SE p. 398) and David Foster Wallace's "Consider the Lobster" (FE p. 697). You might ask students about similar and different concerns, as well as similar and different techniques. Regan, for example, addresses three broad concerns (use of animals in scientific experiments, commercial animal agriculture, and commercial and sport hunting and trapping), whereas Pollan addresses primarily commercial animal agriculture and Wallace, the issue of an animal's pain. Regan argues logically, avoiding personal emotion, whereas Pollan and Wallace introduce their personal experiences with animals they eat.

Suggested Writing Assignments

1. Of the relation of this essay to his book *The Case for Animal Rights* (1983), Regan writes: "Most of the details of the supporting argument are missing. They are to be found in the book to which I alluded earlier" (paragraph 33). Follow, in his book, one of the four views he argues against in his essay or the view he argues for, with attention to its detail. Then write an essay in which you describe the detail he includes and evaluate the difference it makes to his argument.

2. Write an essay in which you imagine and describe, for your own life, the consequences of assenting to and acting on Regan's argument.

3. Look at the collection of essays edited by Peter Singer, *In Defense of Animals* (1985), and survey the other approaches to animal rights. Write an essay in which you choose one approach, describe it, and evaluate it in comparison with Regan's approach.

4. Read Sallie Tisdale's "We Do Abortions Here: A Nurse's Story" (FE p. 709, SE p. 414). Regan alludes to "the terribly difficult question of the morality of abortion" (paragraph 16) and speaks of settling it. What does he mean by "settle"? Does Tisdale attempt to "settle" the question? Write an essay in which you discuss the relative merits and problems of their two approaches to difficult ethical questions.

Michael Pollan
An Animal's Place

Full Edition, p. 681; Shorter Edition, p. 398

This is an overview of animal rights, and as such, makes a good companion to "Consider the Lobster" by David Foster Wallace (FE p. 697). Michael Pollan's book *The Omnivore's Dilemma* has been widely discussed. The author has a Ph.D. in English but has received awards for his science writing and environmental journalism, and he is best known as an advocate for agricultural reform. Trivia buffs may care that his sister and brother-in-law are the actors Tracy Pollan and Michael J. Fox, respectively.

One core premise of Pollan's argument here is that we are divorced from the origins of food—where it comes from and *how* it comes. What are factory farms like? In contrast, what does it mean to grow and kill things humanely? Most Americans have little specific information about where their dinner comes from or how it is processed. This essay changes that. As the author admits, "reading [the classic book *Animal Liberation*] is not something I'd recommend if you're determined to continue eating meat." That is because that book (and arguments from it summarized here) "demand that you either defend the way you live or change it" (paragraph 11).

This essay is long and evenly reasoned; some readers will be impatient with its refusal to pass out the pitchforks and torches to storm the nearest butcher shop. A central point here—raised late in the essay and one not often made elsewhere—has to do with the rights of a species (e.g., an endangered sparrow) versus rights of individuals (a particular pig on a particular farm).

Questions from *The Norton Reader*

1. Precisely how much of the Animal Liberation approach has Michael Pollan accepted? How can you tell?

2. Things change when Pollan visits Polyface Farm, the humane operation run by Joel Salatin. What about the farm convinces Pollan that it represents an alternative to Peter Singer's approach?

3. Describe the structure of Pollan's essay. How does he introduce Animal Liberation and how does he argue against it?

4. Write your own argument concerning some aspect of what "an animal's place" should be. It can be about animal cruelty, whether (and how) animals should be used in experiments or product testing, under what (if any) circumstances humans should eat animals, or some other issue related to animals and ethics.

Teaching Suggestions

1. Depending on where you teach, you may have one or more vegetarians or vegans enrolled, and this essay will allow them a chance to share their convictions. Ask them why they converted (if it was a decision of theirs and not their parents) and how people generally react.

2. The book and movie *Fast Food Nation* raise the related philosophical issue of workers' rights. Raise the topic of workers' rights and discuss the challenges of ethical eating with your students. How do they negotiate these dilemmas? Do they consider them at all?

3. If this essay makes students uncomfortable, allow the class to explore the idea that such discomfort is (or is not) appropriate for college, and indeed may be the most essential part of an education. Discuss with your class the

nature of the controversy here: is Pollan revealing a truth we prefer to ignore or a rift that divides us from each other?

Suggested Writing Assignments

1. "Don't eat things with faces" is one slogan used by vegetarian activists. While there is a weird sort of smile-o-centrism at work here (one presumes a kitten or veal calf has a "face" while a spider does not), this does make a certain kind of intuitive sense. Write a two-part essay, one that is personal and yet contemplative. In the first part, talk about the idea that animals do indeed have personalities, using your own dog or cat as an example. Then extrapolate from that to present your case for or against the personality of those animals we eat and, by extension, the ethics of eating them. If a dog has an individual personality, does that imply as well a sense of self, a sense of awareness, a unique biological value? Would not a horse or cow or sheep have a personality too, and if so, what does that admission do to our perceptions that it's okay for one thing to be food and another not?

2. Imagine you are a public relations officer of McFriendly's, an imaginary fast-food chain, and you are about to launch a campaign promoting your new Triple Whammy, a product with three times as much meat as the usual hamburger. Write an editorial piece refuting Pollan's positions.

3. Ideals serve as moral guideposts but daily life often requires compromises. Even environmentalists need to ride in a car occasionally, or a committed Buddhist may accidentally inhale an insect. Write about a time when your own core personal beliefs (whether religious or otherwise) were challenged when you were faced with a situation in which you were going to have to sacrifice an ideal to make a practical decision. What was the situation, what did you do, and how do you feel about it now?

David Foster Wallace
Consider the Lobster

Full Edition, p. 697

David Foster Wallace was a smart, quick, and postmodern author. His nonfiction finds as much worth in studying the awards ceremonies of the adult movie industry as in the parables of Kafka. Erudition for him meant inhabiting not just T. S. Eliot's wasteland, but also The Who's.

That combination of erudition and pop culture makes Wallace's meditation on the ethics of eating meat initially off-putting for some students. Don't let his self-reflexive prose style fool them, however; his style is not mere narcissism, but rather a complicated response to a contradictory set of moral problems. Some things taste good (he reasons) and the creatures involved may not have a brain (a popular misconception about lobsters, as he points out), so is it okay to boil them alive and eat them at a festival in Maine? Those questions take on additional urgency with two other lines of tension present in this essay.

The first of those has to do with venue and audience. Written for *Gourmet* magazine (and republished in the 2005 edition of *Best American Essays*), this text not only talks about the ethics of eating but does so in a forum that is notoriously oblivious to such discussions. Indeed, this was easily the most controversial piece that *Gourmet* had ever run. Tempers flared; subscriptions were canceled; talk shows buzzed. Ask the class if Wallace was right to break with the "don't ask, don't tell" editorial policy of *Gourmet*, or if he was being inappropriate, perhaps even unfair. The readers did not buy that magazine to be confronted with topics like this; Wallace ambushed them on a sensitive subject.

Another line of tension is Wallace's prose style, with its voluminous list of footnotes. Many love it, some hate it, but few are indifferent. The author's loops and side trips may seem indulgent, even gratuitous, but replicate many of our own thought processes, so are especially appropriate to an overtly first-person narrative.

QUESTIONS FROM *The Norton Reader*

1. David Foster Wallace finally admits to being "confused" (paragraph 31) about the morality of eating lobsters. After reading his essay, what are your feelings? Are they changed from what they were before you read his essay?

2. Comment on Wallace's footnotes, which sometimes add information but at other times seem to carry on another argument on the bottom of the page. Why do you think he includes both kinds?

3. Compare the way Wallace employs footnotes with the footnotes in Annie Leonard's "The Story of Bottled Water" (FE p. 200, SE p. 96). One similarity, for example, is the absolute richness of the notes. What similarities and differences do you notice?

4. Write about a festival or event you have attended, using description and research if appropriate, especially if there is an ethical dimension to your topic.

TEACHING SUGGESTIONS

1. Explore the ways this essay imitates and yet subverts the conventions of the travel narrative. You may need to remind students of those conventions, brainstorming a list of what such narratives include be they Lewis and Clark or "what I did on my summer vacation."

2. Most Americans eat meat, including seafood, readily. (See Michael Pollan's "An Animal's Place" [FE p. 681, SE p. 398]). To help students step outside their assumptions, push them a step further: the Mayans raised puppies as food. What is wrong with that?

3. If the class likes Wallace's approach, you might bring in his longer, funnier essay on cruise ships, "A Supposedly Fun Thing I Will Never Do Again,"

which was published in a book of the same title. If they hate it, give them a chance to write a parody (number 3, below).

SUGGESTED WRITING ASSIGNMENTS

1. Many small communities have a regional celebration such as Oktoberfest, Spring Fling, or Donkey Days. Attend yours (or recall it vividly), linking a social concern about animal rights or land-use patterns to your attendance at the event. What ethical questions *could* have been asked about local practices, that were *not*?

2. As Wallace's essay reminds us, lobster fishing—and fishing in America in general—has a long history. Yet in many areas fish stocks have declined precipitously, and conservationists blame the fishermen, who in turn complain about meddlesome agencies and unfair rules. Pick either a region or a specific fishery and trace its decline and (in some cases) resurrection, researching cause and effect to explain just what should be done next to provide the largest possible social benefit.

3. Write about going to Taco Bell or Dairy Queen but in doing so, parody Wallace's style, using even more footnotes, more hesitancies, more abstruse allusions and links. Have fun; be over the top.

SALLIE TISDALE
We Do Abortions Here: A Nurse's Story

Full Edition, p. 709; Shorter Edition, p. 414

This essay reflects the intimacy and particularity of caring, as well as, of course, the gendering of the nursing profession. Sallie Tisdale is experiential in her approach, and draws on her working experience as she considers the difficult ethical issue of abortion. As she explores it, she moves back and forth in time and also in scale: "I can sweep the horizon with both eyes, survey the scene in all its distance and size. Or I can put my eye to the lens [of a telescope] and focus on the small details, suddenly so close" (paragraph 4).

Although Tisdale does not use the term "situation ethics," this essay may exemplify them. Tisdale plainly subscribes to their first principle: contextuality. She judges acts—insofar as she judges them—in context. She may or may not subscribe to their second principle, love, as a standard for judging her own and others' acts. Is it possible to read Tisdale's "We Do Abortions Here" as exemplifying both principles? The first can be demonstrated explicitly as well as implicitly; the second is problematic.

The five sections of the essay are separated by typographical space rather than connected by prose transitions; within each section Tisdale moves back and forth in both time and space. Note how the structure of the essay does not follow the conventions of "academic" or "college" writing. What are the benefits and/or limitations to such an approach to this topic?

1. Sallie Tisdale speaks of taking both broad views—"as if I am standing on a cliff with a telescope"—and narrow views—"I can put my eye to the lens and focus on the small details" (paragraph 4). Choose one section of this essay and mark the passages you would describe as taking broad views and the passages you would describe as taking narrow views. What is the effect of Tisdale's going back and forth between them? How does she manage transitions?

2. "We are too busy to chew over ethics" (paragraph 21), Tisdale observes. What does she mean by ethics? Does she engage with what you consider ethical issues in this essay? Explain.

3. Although Tisdale takes a pro-choice position, a pro-lifer could use parts of her essay against her. What parts? What are the advantages and disadvantages of including material that could be used in support of the opposition?

4. Write an essay about an ethical issue with which you have some experience. As Tisdale does, use description and dialogue.

TEACHING SUGGESTIONS

1. Some people criticize situation ethics because they are relative rather than absolute. Do students think ethical principles must be absolute?

2. How might situation ethics have provided Tisdale with a framework for a different kind of essay, an analysis or an argument, instead of the associative and accumulative narrative that she wrote?

3. "I don't say 'pain' any more than I would say 'baby'" (paragraph 16), Tisdale observes. Where else in the essay are you aware of her using, as she puts it, "care with my language"? Why is language so important in discussing abortion?

SUGGESTED WRITING ASSIGNMENTS

1. In "The Case for Animal Rights" (FE p. 670), Tom Regan makes a rights case for animals. Can the same case be made for fetuses? Write an essay answering this question.

2. Write an essay in which you have recourse to situation ethics implicitly, like Tisdale, or explicitly. Alternatively, write an essay critical of situation ethics.

3. Tisdale speaks of crisis pregnancy centers advertised in the *Yellow Pages* (paragraph 24). Can you locate one in your town or a nearby city? You might also do an online search. Call them to see what they tell you. Write an account of the experience.

4. Tisdale also wrote *Talk Dirty to Me* (1994). Read parts of it and write an essay in which you discuss her recourse to situation ethics with respect to dirty talk.

NORA EPHRON

The Boston Photographs

Full Edition, p. 716

Many students will know (or know of) Nora Ephron as the novelist, screenwriter, and director who wrote *When Harry Met Sally* and *Heartburn*, both turned into popular movies. But Ephron began her writing career as a serious essayist. As she told a group of aspiring writers, "In college all I could think about was going off to New York and becoming a journalist. If you want to go into screenwriting, become a journalist first, especially if you're like me, and have no area of expertise."

This essay, which explores the ethics of photojournalism, comes from a collection of Ephron's serious journalism, *Scribble, Scribble* (1978). It documents and analyzes the controversy that erupted when the *Boston Herald American* published three dramatic photos by Stanley Forman: a series taken on July 22, 1975, in which a firefighter attempts to rescue a mother and child from a burning apartment building, only to watch them fall from an unstable fire escape. Forman won the Pulitzer Prize in 1976 for these photographs, but for well over a year the controversy raged.

There are several ways to approach this essay and the accompanying photographs. You might ask students to describe what they see in the photographs and to respond to the images before discussing Ephron's essay. Or you might ask students to recall the responses of newspaper readers in 1975 to the photos and ask students why they think viewers responded so vehemently. Or, if you have a local newspaper that prints photographs of fires or other such sensational events, you might ask students to compare these images with Forman's photos and then consider why Forman's caused such a controversy. Ultimately, students should compare their conclusions with Ephron's that the photos "deserve to be printed because they are great pictures, breathtaking pictures of something that happened."

QUESTIONS FROM *THE NORTON READER*

1. Why does Nora Ephron begin with the words of the photographer Stanley Forman? What information—as well as perspective—does her opening paragraph convey?

2. What was public reaction to the publication of the Boston photographs? What reasons did newspeople give for printing them? How does Ephron arrange these responses?

3. Does Ephron suggest any limits to what can be published in print or online? Do you think there should be limits? How would you go about deciding what those limits should be?

4. Find a startling photographic image that recently appeared in print or online, and write an argument for or against its publication.

TEACHING SUGGESTIONS

1. Throughout this essay, Ephron quotes extensively, both the negative viewers' reactions and the defending editor's responses. Ask students to mark these quotations and discuss why Ephron uses them.

2. How much of Ephron's essay is recounting the facts? recounting the viewers' reactions and the editor's defense? giving her own analysis? Ask students to note these parts of the essay and discuss the balance among them.

SUGGESTED WRITING ASSIGNMENTS

1. Choose one of the three Boston photographs and describe, in detail, what you see and what response the image elicits.

2. Find a photograph in your local newspaper of a fire or other human disaster. Compare this image—what it shows, what response it elicits—with Forman's photographs.

3. Imagine yourself to be the editor-in-chief of a newspaper. Write a "code of ethics" for what visual images your newspaper will—and will not—print. Present your policy in a letter to the newspaper staff.

PAUL FUSSELL
Thank God for the Atom Bomb

Full Edition, p. 722

"Thank God for the Atom Bomb" was originally published in the *New Republic* in August 1981. It became the title essay in Paul Fussell's *Thank God for the Atom Bomb and Other Essays*, published in 1988, forty-three years after the bombings of Hiroshima and Nagasaki. Writing on their forty-second anniversary, Fussell says, was prompted "by the long debate about the ethics, if any, of that ghastly affair" (paragraph 1).

Fussell takes on a number of the debaters, mostly those questioning the necessity and the morality of the bombings. You will want students to look at his argumentative strategies, notably his ad hominem arguments (that is, "to the man"). He uses them two ways: in making his own case and in arguing against the cases of others.

In making his own case, Fussell begins by discussing the value of experience, "sheer, vulgar experience" (paragraph 1). He nevertheless embeds his experience in an argument and argues against the cases of others. Fussell sharply and disparagingly contrasts their experience with his—even as he acknowledges the "offensive implications" of what he does (paragraph 9). Those wishing to read what his adversaries have to say will have to search beyond Fussell's essay; sometimes it contains the titles of books and periodicals, but never dates. (Depending on your interests, you might use this essay to consider the advantages and disadvantages of scholarly and popular conventions of annotation.)

QUESTIONS FROM *The Norton Reader*

1. Note the places where Paul Fussell includes personal experience in this essay. How much is his own, how much belongs to others? Why does he include both kinds?

2. Fussell dismisses with contempt those who disagree with him. Locate some examples. How do you respond to them? Would you use Fussell's strategies to dismiss those who disagree with you? Explain.

3. Mark some instances of Fussell's "voice." What kind of voice does he adopt? What kind of person does he present himself as?

4. Write an argumentative essay about a topic that personally affects you. Deliberately take a very strong position, using Fussell and Tom Regan (FE p. 670) as your models.

TEACHING SUGGESTIONS

1. You may want to focus a discussion of Fussell's use of sources by bringing to class photocopies of the debate between Joseph Alsop and David Joravsky in the *New York Review of Books*. This debate, "reduced to a collision between experience and theory, was conducted with a certain civilized respect for evidence," according to Fussell (paragraph 16). Does Fussell fairly summarize the debate? Why does he speak of it as "reduced to a collision between experience and theory"?

2. Fussell ends his essay with "The past, which as always did not know the future, acted in ways that ask to be imagined before they are condemned. Or even simplified" (paragraph 32). Ask students to explain what he means. Is his generalization true with respect to "Thank God for the Atom Bomb"?

SUGGESTED WRITING ASSIGNMENTS

1. August 1995 was the fiftieth anniversary of the bombing of Hiroshima and Nagasaki. As the Smithsonian Institution prepared to commemorate it with an exhibit at the National Air and Space Museum, controversy over the bombing was renewed. Write a narrative account of the controversy using the *New York Times* and the *Washington Post* as sources. (There are various ways of doing this project collaboratively.) The controversy also is detailed in the book *Hiroshima's Shadow*, edited by Kai Bird and Lawrence Lifschultz (1998).

2. After completing the research in suggested writing assignment 1 (above), write an analysis of the issues involved in the controversy.

3. Write an essay in which you consider whether the issues surrounding the debate over the bombing have changed since the 1980s, when Fussell wrote "Thank God for the Atom Bomb."

DAVID EAGLEMAN

The Brain on Trial

Full Edition, p. 735; Shorter Edition, p. 421

David Eagleman is developing a national reputation as an expert on the brain. His book *Incognito: The Secret Lives of the Brain* (2011) was a well-received best-seller, and he served as the writer and host of the PBS series *The Brain*. He majored in English literature at Rice University and then went on to earn a Ph.D. in neuroscience. Eagleman's essay directly challenges traditional views of free will and culpability, claiming that behavior is much more biologically motivated than it is typically thought to be. If what we do is the result of our biology, then it becomes hard to hold us fully responsible for our actions. Consequently, Eagleman argues, the criminal justice system needs to change; courts should take motivation into account and prisons should do more to rehabilitate its prisoners. Of course, judges and wardens claim that they already examine motivation and work to rehabilitate, but some (especially Eagleman) argue that such practice is far from routine.

QUESTIONS FROM *THE NORTON READER*

1. David Eagleman writes that "*we* are not the ones steering the boat of our behavior, at least not nearly as much as we believe" (paragraph 21). What factors does Eagleman point to as affecting behavior? To what extent do you think you are responsible for your own behavior?

2. Look closely at Eagleman's prose and the claims he makes throughout his essay. Does he make unequivocal assertions, or does he use language that hedges his claims? Point to specific examples in the text.

3. Eagleman's essay is a lengthy plea for what lawyers call "diminished responsibility." Look up this concept in law. If we followed Eagleman's suggestions, would we have fewer people in prison? Why or why not?

4. Eagleman's solution for the rehabilitation of criminals is "the prefrontal workout" (paragraph 61). Write an essay in which you evaluate this solution. Consider both its potential strengths and weaknesses.

TEACHING SUGGESTIONS

1. Having students outline Eagleman's essay can show them how it is structured. It covers a lot of territory. Ask students whether or not they think the essay makes a single coherent argument or many smaller arguments within a larger one.

2. At first it seems as if Eagleman wants to understand every criminal's motivation and "cure" each lawbreaker, but that is not the case. He's willing to see many people incarcerated, but he wants prisons to do much more rehabilitation. Ask students exactly which kinds of criminals Eagleman is willing to jail and whether or not they agree.

3. Eagleman proposes a "scientific" approach to crime, putting much more emphasis on new developments in our understanding of the brain in order to understand criminal behavior. This approach conflicts directly with our current system, which depends on juries determining free will and culpability, as a result of a courtroom contest. Ask students to explain whether Eagleman works out the conflict between the two opposing views, and whether they prefer a "jury of their peers" or a behavioral scientist to determine their guilt or innocence and punishment.

Suggested Writing Assignments

1. Write about how our current means of judging criminals would have to change if Eagleman's approach were to be adopted.

2. Imagine a world in which Eagleman's approach to criminal responsibility was the law of the land. Write a description of that world in as much detail as you can.

History and Politics

George Orwell

Shooting an Elephant

Full Edition, p. 750; Shorter Edition, p. 436

"Shooting an Elephant" is a classic example of an author using a personal experience to illuminate a political institution and its social implications: here, the experience of shooting an elephant and the British Raj (the imperial government of India and Burma), as well as colonialism itself. George Orwell carefully and precisely renders setting, action, and character (himself) by developing his responses, feelings, and thoughts with novelistic density. He braids into his narrative the personal responses to the experience: "I often wondered whether any of the others grasped that I had done it solely to avoid looking a fool" (paragraph 14). Orwell, whom students are likely to know as the author of *Animal Farm* and *1984*, served in the British police force in Burma after leaving school. The experience heightened his political consciousness.

You may need to show students that "Shooting an Elephant" is also an essay about how the expectations of others force us to play roles, to behave in ways that we do not choose, and to behave as selves other than the selves we think we are—worse selves, as in this essay, and sometimes better selves as well. Orwell, though he does not use the term, is conscious of what we now refer to as the "social construction of reality." Yet, in "Shooting an Elephant," he both affirms and denies it: that is, he presents role-playing as educative. "I perceived in this moment," he writes, "that when the white man turns tyrant it is his own freedom that he destroys" (paragraph 7).

Questions from *The Norton Reader*

1. Why did George Orwell shoot the elephant? Account for the motives that led him to shoot, and then categorize them as personal motives, circumstantial motives, social motives, or political motives. Is it easy to assign his motives to categories? Why or why not?

2. In this essay the proportion of narrative to analysis is high. Mark each paragraph as narrative or analytic, and note, in particular, how much analysis Orwell places in the middle of the essay. What are the advantages and disadvantages of having it there rather than at the beginning or the end of the essay?

3. Facts ordinarily do not speak for themselves. How does Orwell present his facts to make them speak in support of his analytic points? Look, for example, at the death of the elephant (paragraphs 11 to 13).

4. Write an essay in which you present a personal experience that illuminates a larger issue: schooling, affirmative action, homelessness, law enforcement, taxes, or some other local or national issue.

TEACHING SUGGESTIONS

1. Pose question 1 (above) to demonstrate the dense rendering of Orwell's narrative and how he constructs it, but also to show that Orwell's realization of his motives comes not precisely at the moment he pulls the trigger, but years later as he writes his essay.

2. Ask students to analyze the opening paragraphs in terms of shifts from narration to commentary. As they will soon see, a personal-experience essay moves frequently back and forth from one to the other. It does not, as students sometimes assume, give all narrative first, all commentary last.

3. How does Orwell reconcile social construction and individual freedom?

SUGGESTED WRITING ASSIGNMENTS

1. Rewrite Orwell's "Shooting an Elephant" from the point of view of one of the Burmese.

2. Write an essay in which you consider at least two instances of your own serious (rather than trivial) role-playing, both of worse and of better selves. Is role-playing always educative?

JONATHAN SWIFT
A Modest Proposal

Full Edition, p. 756; Shorter Edition, p. 442

Jonathan Swift's "A Modest Proposal" is often anthologized as a brilliant example of sustained irony. It is also shocking: you may want to ask students to read Mark Twain's "Advice to Youth" (FE p. 637, SE p. 365), in the "Ethics" chapter, to contrast the tameness of his irony with the savagery of Swift's. Swift violates one of our strongest and most universally held prohibitions, the prohibition against eating human flesh; Twain merely upsets a prohibition against dishonoring fathers and mothers, a prohibition most of us upset frequently. Moreover, Swift disquietingly juxtaposes the reasonable voice of his putative author (or invented persona) and his horrifying proposals, horrifying to us as readers but apparently not horrifying to the proposer. The author's "modest proposal" can perhaps be entertained as logically consistent, but in moral terms, it is indefensible. Students need to see that Swift's juxtaposition of reasonableness and horror is ironic: while the putative author of "A Modest Proposal" says one thing, Swift means another.

Understanding irony from another era can be difficult. You might provide information about Irish poverty in 1729, when Swift published "A Modest Proposal," and its historical causes. You will want to have students look at paragraphs 29 and 30, Swift's "other expedients," which will suggest some of the things Swift's audience knew that we no longer know. You may also want to remind them that, had Swift been anxious to prevent a literal reading of "A Modest Proposal," he could have included these expedients earlier; they are, after all, the remedies that a "reasonable" Swift himself proposed. But even three centuries after Swift's pamphlet was published, most students will quickly recognize that this satirical essay was not meant to be taken at face value but represents a deeply and bitterly ironic commentary on the state of things in Ireland.

QUESTIONS FROM *THE NORTON READER*

1. Identify examples of the reasonable voice of Jonathan Swift's authorial persona, such as the title of the essay itself.

2. Look, in particular, at instances in which Swift's authorial persona proposes shocking things. How does the style of "A Modest Proposal" affect its content?

3. Verbal irony consists of saying one thing and meaning another. At what point in this essay do you begin to suspect that Swift is using irony? What additional evidence of irony can you find?

4. Write a modest proposal of your own in the manner of Swift to remedy a real problem; that is, propose an outrageous remedy in a reasonable voice.

TEACHING SUGGESTIONS

1. Ask students to describe how Swift's putative author characterizes himself by his style. If style is the man, what kind of man are we listening to?

2. Although Swift's primary concerns are economic, issues of population control also run through "A Modest Proposal." What do the author's proposals indicate about his views of sexuality and reproduction? Can we infer Swift's proposals and his views of sexuality and reproduction from them? You may want to suggest ways in which time (and changing sexual and reproductive practices) destabilize Swift's irony with respect to population control more than with respect to economic policy.

SUGGESTED WRITING ASSIGNMENTS

1. Write an essay in which you consider your responses to "A Modest Proposal." Some readers have found Swift's irony too shocking, so strong as to detract from his really quite sensible proposals for reform. Does his literary form, for you, subvert his purposes or serve them? How and why?

2. Look up a brief proposal written by a contemporary of Swift, Daniel Defoe, in 1702, "The Shortest Way with the Dissenters," and also an account of its reception in a biography of Defoe. Write a brief essay on the risks of irony using this information.

NICCOLÒ MACHIAVELLI
The Morals of the Prince

Full Edition, p. 763; Shorter Edition, p. 449

Niccolò Machiavelli, the Florentine whose political treatise *The Prince* was distributed in 1513 and published in 1532, acquired in his time a scandalous reputation: he was "Old Nick" (or Satan), who held the diabolical doctrine that the end justifies the means. His reputation was largely established by the chapters on "The Morals of the Prince" reprinted here. Students should notice that Machiavelli is aware of making a controversial case, of writing about the *is*— "the way we really live"—rather than the *ought*—"the way we ought to live" (paragraph 1). Political treatises of Machiavelli's time were ordinarily Utopian. Machiavelli's is not, and consequently, as he announces, he has something new to say. Today we might speak of his politics as "realpolitik," a word derived from German that means a politics based on practical and material, rather than theoretical and ethical, considerations.

You may want to use "The Morals of the Prince" to exemplify shifting boundaries between idealism and realism, realism and cynicism; we can pretty much agree on their definitions, but when we come to apply them, what one person takes to be realistic, another person takes to be cynical. Nevertheless, Machiavelli appears to present his "realistic" argument with the intention of shocking readers. While it may be realistic to discuss the dangers of virtue in a world in which people are "a sad lot, and keep no faith with you" (paragraph 14), it is surely cynical to argue that the appearance of virtue is better than virtue itself. You can call attention to the antitheses in Machiavelli's argument: the qualities in a prince that elicit praise or blame (paragraph 2) and the section headings in which he opposes liberality to stinginess, cruelty to clemency, and love to fear. Part of his shock technique depends upon setting up binary oppositions and arguing for the conventionally pejorative term.

QUESTIONS FROM *THE NORTON READER*

1. This selection contains four sections of *The Prince*: "On the Reasons Why Men Are Praised or Blamed—Especially Princes"; "On Liberality and Stinginess"; "On Cruelty and Clemency: Whether It Is Better to Be Loved or Feared"; and "The Way Princes Should Keep Their Word." How, in each section, does Niccolò Machiavelli contrast the real and the ideal, what he calls "the way we really live and the way we ought to live" (paragraph 1)? Mark some of the sentences in which he expresses these contrasts.

2. Rewrite some of Machiavelli's advice to princes less forcibly and shockingly, and more palatably. For example, "Any man who tries to be good all the time is bound to come to ruin among the great number who are not good" (paragraph 1) might be rewritten as "Good men are often taken advantage of and harmed by men who are not good."

3. Describe Machiavelli's view of human nature. How do his views of government follow from it?

4. Machiavelli might be described as a sixteenth-century spin doctor teaching a ruler how to package himself. Adapt his advice to a current figure in national, state, or local politics, and write about that figure in a brief essay.

TEACHING SUGGESTIONS

1. One feature of Machiavelli's style is his use of aphorisms, that is, terse formulations of truths and beliefs. You might ask students to gather a number of them and describe how Machiavelli uses them and to what effect or effects.

2. What are Machiavelli's customary sources of examples? How frequently does he use them? How extensively does he explain them? What do they indicate about his audience?

3. Man, in the Renaissance chain of being, stands between beasts and angels. You may want to have students look at paragraphs 14 and 15, in which Machiavelli proposes as models for imitation the fox and the lion. What do these metaphors contribute to his argument?

SUGGESTED WRITING ASSIGNMENTS

1. Conduct library research on the politics of Florence during Machiavelli's life (the way Florentines really lived) and write an essay in which you consider *The Prince* as a response to local conditions.

2. Write an essay defining "Machiavellian" by applying it to and illustrating it with examples from contemporary politics.

3. See Suggested Writing Assignments 3 and 4 for "The Declaration of Independence."

HENRY DAVID THOREAU
The Battle of the Ants

Full Edition, p. 770; Shorter Edition, p. 456

Taken from the chapter in *Walden* titled "Brute Neighbors," "The Battle of the Ants" is not so much history as natural history. Yet, because Henry David Thoreau alludes to historical battles and imitates the conventions of history writing, this brief account provides an opportunity for discussing what constitutes a historical event and how a historical style of writing gives status to some events, and not to others. The battle Thoreau describes would not normally be considered historical: it is, after all, only a struggle between two species of ants. But Thoreau's account leads us to ponder how the human struggles called "wars" become history—is it because historians record their maneuvers in detail, praise their leaders and soldiers, and treat their outcomes as decisive? Thoreau potentially subverts this traditional approach to history by suggesting that "history" is created by historians and that the events they present as "historical" attain this status in large part because we accept the conventions of their style.

Questions from *The Norton Reader*

1. Henry David Thoreau uses the Latin word *bellum* to describe the battle of the ants and follows it with a reference to the Myrmidons, the soldiers of Achilles in Homer's *Iliad*. Locate additional examples of this kind of allusion. How does it work? Why does Thoreau compare the ants to Greek soldiers?

2. Ordinarily we speak of accounts of natural events as "natural history" and accounts of human events as "history." How does Thoreau, in this selection, blur the distinction? For what purpose?

3. Look up a description of the behavior of ants in a book by one of the entomologists Thoreau refers to or in another scientific text. Compare the scientist's style with Thoreau's. Take another event in nature and describe it twice, once in scientific and once in allusive language. Or write an essay in which you describe and analyze the differences between the scientist's style and Thoreau's.

Teaching Suggestions

1. In the long first paragraph Thoreau alludes to two well-known wars: the battles recorded in Homer's *Iliad* and the American Revolution, particularly the battles of Lexington and Concord (where the "shot heard around the world" was fired). What effect does Thoreau achieve? By comparing the battle of the ants to classical Greek and American wars, he writes a form of mock heroic that both elevates the actions of the ants and paradoxically deflates the warlike actions of men.

2. This passage comes from a chapter in Thoreau's *Walden* titled "Brute Neighbors." How does the comparison alluded to in the first paragraph, between the fighting ants and human warriors, amplify the meaning of that title?

3. Why does Thoreau describe the wounds of the ants in such detail? You might think of his description as an example of natural history as well as an imitation of historical writing.

4. In the final paragraph Thoreau alludes to American and European entomologists, also called "natural historians." Thoreau's style in this paragraph, however, is not that of a scientist but is a parody of the historian's. Why?

5. What significance might there be in that Thoreau, at the end of this selection, dates the battle of the ants as occurring five years before the passage of Webster's Fugitive-Slave Bill? In Thoreau's mind, what kind of historical event seems to be genuinely significant?

Suggested Writing Assignments

1. Read an account of the battles of Lexington and Concord (where Thoreau lived), then write an essay analyzing the section of Thoreau's account that alludes to these battles, with attention to how Thoreau's fellow citizens might have responded to his allusions.

2. Look up a description of the behavior of ants in a book by one of the entomologists Thoreau refers to or in another scientific textbook. What are the

conventions of scientific description? Why do you think scientists adopt them? Write an essay comparing the style of the scientist with Thoreau's.

THOMAS JEFFERSON AND OTHERS
The Declaration of Independence
Full Edition, p. 773; Shorter Edition, p. 459

These two drafts of the Declaration of Independence—the final draft as printed and Thomas Jefferson's original draft—may provoke students into a fresh reading of a text whose familiarity dulls attention. The original draft is a transcription of a copy in Jefferson's hand (in the Library of Congress), with illegible passages taken from a transcription made by John Adams, and missing passages, presumably added later, taken from a copy Jefferson made for George Wythe (in the New York Public Library). We do not know how many drafts and revisions preceded it; we do know that Jefferson consulted with several people, among them Benjamin Franklin and John Adams. This original draft was edited by members of the Second Continental Congress and probably, in large measure, by Jefferson himself.

Students should notice that the three-part structure of the original and final drafts is the same: Jefferson enunciates a series of principles concerning human nature and the function of government, rehearses the offenses against them by George III, and proclaims the political connection between the American colonies and the king of Great Britain dissolved. The structure is derived from the syllogism: a major premise, a minor premise, and a conclusion. The logic is deductive: given the principles—which Jefferson calls "sacred and undeniable" in the original draft, "self-evident" in the final draft—and given the facts, the conclusion follows ineluctably.

These two versions of the Declaration of Independence illustrate the final revision procedures of an experienced writer. With his argumentative structure and his particulars in place, Jefferson revises at the paragraph and sentence level. Chiefly he prunes and tightens: he recognizes that he has been somewhat overinclusive in his exemplification, somewhat clumsy in his sentences, and long-winded in using more words than he needs to say what he needs to say. While his language in the final draft is simpler and more direct, his sentence structure, especially with respect to repetition and balance, is more artful. In addition, the inconsistent spelling and punctuation of the original draft have been regularized.

QUESTIONS FROM *The Norton Reader*

1. The Declaration of Independence is an example of deductive argument: Thomas Jefferson sets up general principles, details particular instances, and then draws conclusions. In both the original and final drafts, locate the three sections of the Declaration that use deduction. Explain how they work as arguments.

2. Locate the general principles (or "truths") that Jefferson sets up in the first section of both the original and final drafts. Mark the language he uses to describe them: for example, he calls them "sacred & undeniable" in the original draft and "self-evident" (paragraph 2) in the final draft. What kinds of authority does his language appeal to in each draft? Why might he or others have revised the language?

3. Note the stylistic differences (including choices of grammar and punctuation) between the original and final drafts of the Declaration of Independence. What effect do those differences have?

4. In an essay, choose one or two significant revisions that Thomas Jefferson made between the original draft and the final draft of the Declaration, and explain why they are significant.

TEACHING SUGGESTIONS

1. You may want to ask students to work on the first or second sections of the Declaration of Independence in the original and final drafts, noting what has been pruned and conjecturing about the reasons for the omissions. This analysis can profitably be done in groups.

2. You may also want to ask them to "modernize" sentences in the final draft with pronounced repetition and balance by loosening both.

SUGGESTED WRITING ASSIGNMENTS

1. Jefferson died on July 4, 1826, exactly fifty years after the promulgation of the Declaration of Independence. In ill health, declining an invitation to travel to Washington to participate in the fiftieth-anniversary celebrations, he wrote of the declaration:

> May it [the "Declaration"] be to the world what I believe it will be (to some parts sooner, to others later, but finally to all), the signal of arousing men to burst the chains under which monkish ignorance and superstition had persuaded them to bind themselves, and to assume the blessings and security of self-government. . . . All eyes are opened, or opening, to the rights of man. The general spread of the light of science has already laid open to every view the palpable truth, that the mass of mankind has not been born with saddles on their backs, nor a favored few booted and spurred, ready to ride them legitimately, by the grace of God.

Write an essay in which you trace the appearance of the ideas Jefferson singles out as important in this letter in the Declaration of Independence. Does he give them due prominence there?

2. Write a letter to Jefferson from the perspective of today in which you assess the optimism of his letter of 1826. Or do the same in essay form.

3. Write a comparison of Jefferson's positions (in the Declaration of Independence) and Niccolò Machiavelli's positions (in "The Morals of the Prince" [FE p. 763, SE p. 449]) concerning the nature of man, the function of government, and the relationship between morality and political life. What assumptions led them to diverge?

4. Are you a Jeffersonian or a Machiavellian? Explain.

5. Write an argument on a topic of your choice in which you use the three-part structure of a syllogism. Is it possible, for example, to recast the arguments of other essays in this chapter, such as Martin Luther King Jr.'s "Letter from Birmingham Jail" (FE p. 806), in this mode?

Edwidge Danticat

Another Country

Full Edition, p. 780

A natural disaster can call forth a wide variety of comments from concerned citizens and writers. Some view disasters as opportunities to describe acts of either courage or human depravity; others use them as opportunities to picture human helplessness in the face of stronger forces. Edwidge Danticat, a native of Haiti living in the United States, uses the 2005 Hurricane Katrina to depict the United States behaving like a third-world country toward some of its most impoverished citizens, many of them people of color. She's writing before an enormous earthquake struck Haiti in 2010, killing many more than died in Katrina.

Questions from *The Norton Reader*

1. Throughout this essay Edwidge Danticat draws parallels between New Orleans, where Hurricane Katrina hit in 2005, and countries such as Thailand and Haiti, where similar disasters have struck. What is the point of these comparisons? What argument does Danticat make from them?

2. In paragraph 5 Danticat criticizes then U.S. president George W. Bush for initially offering "sixty thousand dollars in aid" to Haitian victims of Hurricane Jeanne. Using online resources, find out how much aid was eventually sent to Haiti and how that amount compares with aid to American victims of Hurricane Katrina.

3. Why do you think Danticat named this essay "Another Country"? Consider paragraph 11 as you formulate your answer.

4. Write an essay in which you present principles for how the federal government should respond to natural disasters. Give examples, positive and negative, from the past decade.

Teaching Suggestions

1. It's worth asking if Danticat's essay can be reduced to a single point, or even a complex sentence. She ranges freely from natural disasters to 9/11, so any summary of her essay must extend beyond nature to include Americans' awareness—or lack of awareness—of their own vulnerability.

2. Ask students how Danticat's characterization of herself as an immigrant helps them understand her essay. Does it give her more or less credibility?

3. Ask students how the epigraph from Zora Neale Hurston's *Their Eyes Were Watching God* helps give resonance and additional context to the essay.

Suggested Writing Assignments

1. Write an essay explaining how you'd imagine Danticat would treat the 2010 Haitian earthquake and the rich nations' response to it. (Do some research online to find out the extent to which America helped Haiti rebuild.)

2. Danticat describes the responses of an Afghan man and the Chilean-born novelist Isabel Allende to the events of 9/11; both felt much more sympathetic toward America as a result. Write about why Danticat herself seems reticent about the effect of 9/11 on her own attitudes toward her adopted country.

3. In an essay, explain how our sympathies are being stretched thin by having to confront again and again natural and human-caused disasters—as well as their incessant media coverage.

Elizabeth Cady Stanton
Declaration of Sentiments and Resolutions
Full Edition, p. 784; Shorter Edition, p. 466

The first women's rights convention was held at Seneca Falls, New York, July 19–20, 1848. It was called by Elizabeth Cady Stanton, Mary Ann McClintock, Lucretia Mott, and Martha C. Wright. The "Declaration of Sentiments and Resolutions"—or the "Seneca Falls Declaration," as it is often referred to—is usually attributed to Stanton; she read it at the convention, where, after some emendations, it was adopted. But, according to the *History of Woman Suffrage*, vol. 1, edited by Stanton, Susan B. Anthony, and Matilda Joslyn Gage (1881, reprinted 1969), the genesis of the "Declaration"—and perhaps its writing—was collective: Stanton, McClintock, Mott, and Wright decided "to adopt the historic document [i.e., "The Declaration of Independence"] with some slight changes, such as substituting 'all men' for 'King George.'"

Students will see how the "Declaration of Sentiments and Resolutions" recapitulates the three-part syllogistic structure of "The Declaration of Independence." They will also see how the language of the first and third sections of the "Declaration of Sentiments" is a paraphrase of the language of the first and third sections of "The Declaration of Independence." They will need to split three paragraphs of the second section of the "Declaration of Sentiments" to come up with the same number of offenses as appear in the second section of "The Declaration of Independence"—eighteen. The collaborators were determined to enumerate at least as many offenses in their declaration as the members of the Second Continental Congress had enumerated in theirs. As George III had been guilty of "absolute Tyranny," so were all men.

QUESTIONS FROM *THE NORTON READER*

1. Elizabeth Cady Stanton imitates both the argument and the style of the Declaration of Independence. Where does her declaration diverge from Thomas Jefferson's? For what purpose?

2. Stanton's declaration was presented at the first conference on women's rights in Seneca Falls, New York, in 1848. Using books or web resources, do research on this conference; then use your research to explain the political aims of one of the resolutions.

3. Write your own "declaration" of political, educational, or social rights, using the declarations of Jefferson and Stanton as models.

TEACHING SUGGESTIONS

1. As a supplement to question 1 (above), ask students to mark examples of how the "Declaration of Sentiments and Resolutions" imitates "The Declaration of Independence" through quotation and paraphrase—that is, by both repeating and changing its words.

2. To what ends do Stanton and her co-authors quote and paraphrase the "Declaration of Independence"? Ask students to consider both the political goal and rhetorical means of achieving it.

3. How is the imitation found in the "Declaration of Sentiments and Resolutions" different from parody—that is, quotation and paraphrase for comedy or ridicule? (Lewis Carroll's parodies are surefire examples; they are reprinted with originals in *Parodies* [1960].)

SUGGESTED WRITING ASSIGNMENTS

1. The "Declaration of Sentiments and Resolutions" concludes with the authors (and signatories) anticipating "no small amount of misconception, misrepresentation, and ridicule" (paragraph 20). Consult the appendix to volume 4 of the *History of Woman Suffrage* (1902, reprinted 1969), which reprints some contemporary responses to the Seneca Falls Convention. Why was the Convention seen as ridiculous in the nineteenth century? Is it seen as ridiculous today? Explain.

2. Frederick Douglass, author of an early slave narrative (1845), participated in the Seneca Falls Convention. Do library research on the role he played and write an essay discussing both how he participated and why he felt betrayed afterward by the women he supported.

3. Do library research on one of the women who organized the Seneca Falls Convention: Mary Ann McClintock, Lucretia Mott, Stanton, or Martha C. Wright. According to the *History of Woman Suffrage*, vol. 1 (1881, reprinted 1969):

> While they had felt the insults incident to sex, in many ways, as every proud, thinking woman must, in the laws, religion, and literature of the

world, and in the invidious and degrading sentiments and customs of all nations, yet they had not in their own experience endured the coarser forms of tyranny resulting from unjust laws or association with immoral and unscrupulous men, but they had souls large enough to feel the wrongs of others, without being scarified in their own flesh.

Write an essay in which you particularize these generalities with reference to the life of one of the organizers.

FRANCES FITZGERALD
Rewriting American History

Full Edition, p. 786

Frances FitzGerald is a talented journalist, popularly known for *Fire in the Lake*, an account of the Vietnam War. This essay, "Rewriting American History," is one of three parts of a long essay that appeared serially in the *New Yorker* in the winter of 1979 and was later included in her book *America Revised*. In this part, primarily, she compares American history textbooks of the 1950s and the 1970s. You will want to ask students if American history textbooks changed again in the 2000s; see question 2, below. If the students in your class vary in age, the discussion will be enriched by their recollections across decades.

Interesting in its own right, FitzGerald's comparison leads to something even more interesting: a general consideration of the nature of history as a discipline, which accounts for changes in history—in the sense of history as a text—and in our understanding of history—in the sense of history as historical events.

QUESTIONS FROM *THE NORTON READER*

1. What differences does Frances FitzGerald find between the American history textbooks of the 1950s and those of the 1970s? In what ways—according to what she states or implies—have they been improved? Does she see any changes for the worse?

2. FitzGerald's *America Revised* was published in 1979, and textbooks, she argues, change rapidly (paragraph 15). Have American history textbooks changed since the late 1970s and, if so, in what ways? What do you remember of the American history textbooks you used in school—and when did you use them? What kind of American history textbooks are being used today? On your own or in a group, write a brief essay updating FitzGerald.

3. By "rewriting," FitzGerald does not mean changing the facts of American history. What is the relationship between the facts of history and history textbooks?

4. FitzGerald says that in the new texts "the word 'progress' has been replaced by the word 'change'" (paragraph 8). Write an essay in which you con-

sider the difference between these two words and the changes that the replacement of one by the other reflects.

TEACHING SUGGESTIONS

1. Ask students to summarize FitzGerald's essay in a sentence or two; then ask several students to read their summaries aloud. From the similarities and differences, begin a discussion about the points most easily grasped, those less easily grasped, and why.

2. What is FitzGerald's understanding of "history"? Why does she think human beings need to create history?

3. FitzGerald relies mainly on the mode of comparison (and contrast) to show how American history has been "rewritten." By focusing on two paragraphs in her essay, perhaps the one beginning "Poor Columbus!" (paragraph 4) and the one beginning "The political diversity" (paragraph 10), ask students to discuss how comparison works.

4. Analyze any single section of "Rewriting American History" to show how FitzGerald defines by example. Possibilities include the section on the political diversity of textbooks today and the section on the physical appearance of textbooks today.

5. If we can't know what really happened, then why study history? Does FitzGerald's essay imply that history presents us with relative rather than absolute knowledge? If so, why do we study history?

SUGGESTED WRITING ASSIGNMENTS

1. Choose an event from American history with which you are familiar—either one that FitzGerald mentions or one that you know well. Write an essay in which you compare its presentation in three textbooks, each written during a different decade; be certain to select texts written for the same grade level.

2. To what extent do history textbooks, or any other history books, present "truths"? Use your own ideas as well as ideas from other writers in this chapter to address this question.

3. The process of rewriting American history has taken away some of its romance and myth. Write an essay in which you consider whether that is good, bad, or both.

4. Read FitzGerald's *America Revised* (1979), and write an essay in which you discuss one or more issues she lays out in the rest of her study. Does she take positions on them? On what kind of evidence? According to what principles?

5. Do research about the recent controversy concerning national guidelines for an American history curriculum, and write an essay about it. You may want to consider the extent to which FitzGerald, in 1979, laid out issues that are still debated today.

JEFFREY OWEN JONES

The Man Who Wrote the Pledge of Allegiance

Full Edition, p. 793

This essay, from *Smithsonian Magazine*, attempts to make history come alive by presenting events in terms of personalities. Here Jeffrey Owen Jones, a well-known, widely published magazine writer, describes how Francis Bellamy came to write the Pledge of Allegiance. He also describes its fraught history. Various groups, each with its own special interests, wanted to change certain words or determine where and when the pledge was recited.

Jones provides some historical background, but leaves out a good deal as well. Bellamy, like his cousin Edward Bellamy, author of the popular 1888 science fiction novel *Looking Backward*, was a strong socialist, believing in popular ownership of the means of production. Jones also leaves out the powerful nationalistic strain in late-nineteenth-century American culture, in which Bellamy participated to a great extent, claiming that the right kind of immigrants were good for America, but arguing forcefully against what he considered the wrong kind, writing,

> Where all classes of society merge insensibly into one another every alien immigrant of inferior race may bring corruption to the stock. There are races, more or less akin to our own, whom we may admit freely, and get nothing but advantage by the infusion of their wholesome blood. But there are other races which we cannot assimilate without a lowering of our racial standard, which should be as sacred to us as the sanctity of our homes. (Cited in Martha Nussbaum, *Liberty of Conscience: In Defense of America's Tradition of Religious Equality*, 201.)

It's useful to think of the Pledge of Allegiance as being written by someone who wrote the previous quote. How does knowing this fact inform our appreciation of the Pledge?

QUESTIONS FROM *THE NORTON READER*

1. Did you recite the Pledge of Allegiance in your school? Did you or other class members refrain from reciting it or omit the phrase "under God"? If so, why?

2. In paragraph 4, Jeffrey Owen Jones wonders what Francis Bellamy, the man who wrote the pledge, would think of the controversy today. Based on the quotations in the essay and additional information you find online (if you choose), formulate a possible answer to this question.

3. Since Jones wrote this column, various states have passed legislation or heard lawsuits about mandatory recitation of the pledge. Using evidence from these cases, as well as interviews with family, friends, or classmates, write an

argument in which you take a stand for or against including the phrase "under God" in the pledge.

TEACHING SUGGESTIONS

1. Students will benefit from learning that the Pledge of Allegiance is a relatively new part of American life rather than something enshrined in the Constitution. While some states require it in schools, others don't.

2. Point out to students that the word "indivisible" had special resonance in the late nineteenth century, since the 1860s had witnessed the Civil War, in which one side claimed that the nation was indeed "divisible."

3. Let students know that in 2004 the Supreme Court ruled that "under God" would not be changed when it declared that the person who brought the suit had no standing.

SUGGESTED WRITING ASSIGNMENTS

1. Describe the effects of some similarly "memorized" statements (the Lord's Prayer, the Hail Mary for Roman Catholics, grace before meals). Argue whether the rote recital of such statements reinforces their effect or detracts from it.

2. Write about a phrase or a well-known maxim or statement that you once misunderstood and explain how you learned the correct wording (examples: "Gladly the cross-eyed bear," "it's a doggy dog world," "taken for granite").

3. Students used to be forced to memorize poems and excerpts from speeches. If you were ever required to do so, describe what effect it had on you. Did you come to appreciate the poem or excerpt more, or was it simply rote memorization to be recalled on demand?

MARK BOWDEN
"Idiot," "Yahoo," "Original Gorilla": How Lincoln Was Dissed in His Day

Full Edition, p. 797

Mark Bowden's essay serves as a useful corrective to those who think that the current state of American political discourse is at a low point. By picking a revered figure like Lincoln, Bowden is able to demonstrate that no politician is exempt from scorn or vituperation. Students would benefit from knowing that American political discourse has often been crude and demeaning, full of hatred and name-calling. It doesn't take much research to uncover similar discourse about other political figures in American life: Thomas Jefferson, Andrew Jackson, Martin Luther King Jr., Harry Truman, Barack Obama, Hillary Clinton, or Franklin Roosevelt, to name a few. Thus Bowden's essay is a good example of the rough-and-tumble discourse that has often characterized American politics. Perhaps that's the double-edged sword that is a free press and widely diverse opinions among the citizenry.

Questions from *The Norton Reader*

1. Mark Bowden quotes many critics of Abraham Lincoln. At the end of his essay, Bowden turns to our modern age and the "snap judgments, the slurs and put-downs" that presidents must endure. What is Bowden's larger point?

2. Read Lincoln's "Second Inaugural Address," which follows this selection, and then revisit the various publications' characterization of the speech in paragraph 11. Do you agree, disagree, or both with their assessments? Why?

3. Choose a living politician whom you admire, and, using online sources, gather judgments about his or her work. Compose an essay, perhaps like Bowden's, in which you present these judgments and assess their fairness and accuracy.

Teaching Suggestions

1. You might ask students how to go about finding slurs against a key figure in American life. What terms would they put into *Google*, for instance, to yield a useful result?

2. Point to the ubiquity of social media and ask whether Americans' jibes and complaints are more likely to be quoted nowadays. What does that mean for political discourse?

Suggested Writing Assignments

1. Choose a "revered" figure in American life and do some online research to uncover the range of opinions about him or her. Write about how they compare with the treatment Lincoln endured.

2. Does Bowden have any solution to the name-calling Lincoln received? Write about some possible solutions, or whether solutions are even permissible given our commitment to freedom of speech.

3. Have you or anyone you know engaged in similar vituperation of a major figure in American life? How seriously was the disparagement meant? Describe how the name-caller would feel about being quoted widely.

4. In some countries, it is a crime to disparage the head of state. Write an essay arguing for or against such a practice in America.

Abraham Lincoln
Second Inaugural Address

Full Edition, p. 801; Shorter Edition, p. 468

Abraham Lincoln's "Second Inaugural Address" is a piece of ceremonial discourse formal in tone and diction, as required by the occasion. Like Martin Luther King Jr., Lincoln assumes Christian belief even while pointing out that, although North and South "read the same Bible, and pray to the same God" (paragraph 3), neither has evidence of God's unqualified favor. Lincoln's strategy is to invite reconciliation with, not alienation of, the South while keeping up the resolve of the North in fighting for a just cause.

If you have chosen to teach some of the speeches in the "History and Politics" chapter, you might want to compare John F. Kennedy's "Inaugural Address"
(FE p. 803, SE p. 470)—in style, form, and tone—with Lincoln's. What does
the modern presidential address owe to Lincoln's seminal speech? Ask students
what similarities and what differences they find.

QUESTIONS FROM *THE NORTON READER*

1. Abraham Lincoln's speech includes both allusions to and direct quotations from the Bible. What argument do these references support? Why might
biblical references be important as a persuasive technique for Lincoln's
audience?

2. In paragraphs 1–2, Lincoln reflects on his first inaugural speech in
order to set the stage for his present speech. Find a copy of the first inaugural
speech online or in the library. In what ways does that thirty-five-paragraph
speech help inform this four-paragraph speech? What aspects of the "Second
Inaugural Address" does it clarify?

3. Read the text of a more recent presidential address and compare or
contrast it to Lincoln's address. (John F. Kennedy's inaugural address follows
this selection; others can be found online.) Does the more recent address use
a similar style, language, or set of allusions? How does it differ?

TEACHING SUGGESTIONS

1. You may want to remind students that Lincoln reviews four years of
history in the course of this brief address. What events does he select, and
what pattern does he see in them?

2. Lincoln uses three types of rhetorical appeal in this address: logical,
emotional, and ethical. Ask students to identify examples of each. Which do
they find most effective? Which do they think Lincoln's audience found most
effective?

3. While Lincoln tries to speak to both North and South, students probably will not find him hypocritical or slippery. You may want to try arguing
that he is, that his presentation of himself as honest and his purpose as single-
minded is ethical posturing, in order to force close reading. How, finally, do we
determine sincerity?

SUGGESTED WRITING ASSIGNMENTS

1. Write an essay in which you compare Lincoln's "Second Inaugural
Address" with John F. Kennedy's inaugural address of 1961 (FE p. 803, SE
p. 470) or some other recent inaugural address. Compare rhetoric, content,
and audience.

2. Do research on the events immediately preceding Lincoln's second term
as president and write an essay in which you consider his "Second Inaugural
Address" as a response to them.

JOHN F. KENNEDY
Inaugural Address

Full Edition, p. 803; Shorter Edition, p. 470

In 1961 many Americans associated John F. Kennedy with youth and modernity, and he was happy to go along with this assumption, saying in this speech, "the torch has been passed to a new generation. . . . born in this century" (paragraph 3). He meant that last phrase literally, since Kennedy, born in 1917 and 43 years old in 1961, was the first president born in the twentieth century. In fact, he was the youngest man to be elected president.

Photographs of Kennedy on January 21, 1961, show him wearing formal clothes and a top hat, just like the presidents of the 1890s. Those clothes, very old-fashioned even in 1961, serve to suggest that Kennedy's speech looks in two directions: strong echoes of the past appear both in his formal garb and in his quite elaborate rhetoric, even though part of the actual burden of the speech is an appeal to America's and the world's youth. Kennedy's phrase "the torch has been passed" also looks both ways: the very traditional metaphor is of a torch of liberty, drawn from classical times, yet that metaphorical torch is being handed from one generation to another. It's the kind of metaphor that had been used for thousands of years in formal speeches, and in employing it again Kennedy is in keeping with the high rhetorical mode he and his writers chose for this address.

Students will benefit from some information about the context for Kennedy's speech, since Kennedy's youth was seen as a potential vulnerability. In the Cold War confrontation between the Communist Soviet Union and the United States and its allies, Kennedy claimed special expertise in foreign policy, and thus his address deals with pressing international issues that were at the forefront of everyone's consciousness. Primary among them was nuclear arms control, since the Soviets and Americans were increasing their nuclear arsenals and Kennedy had campaigned successfully against the Republicans by claiming (incorrectly, it turned out) that America was falling behind. Another pressing international issue was the end of colonialism, as most European powers were relinquishing the remnants of their overseas empires, and the newly liberated nations of Asia and Africa were being courted both by the Communists and the Americans and their allies. Finally there was the new issue of Cuba, where a long-standing U.S.-supported dictatorship had been recently overthrown by Fidel Castro, a leftist with Communist leanings and no feelings of friendship for his American neighbor. All three—arms race, colonialism, and Cuba—were addressed in Kennedy's speech in ways that were obvious to his listeners but are no longer so apparent to today's college students.

The large doses of formal rhetoric here deserve attention. Students will benefit from a metaphor hunt, perhaps starting with the notion of a "torch" being "passed" at the beginning and then moving to the last few paragraphs, where they abound. The notion of the "peroration," the rousing conclusion, is a useful one, since Kennedy and his speechwriters were clearly interested in working up to a grandiose climax.

Individual instructors will have to decide how deeply to investigate the tropes Kennedy and his writers employed. It will come as a surprise to many students that these constructions have names and were part of a speechwriter's repertory of stylistic devices. They might not know the word "device" or the term "trope." It seems useful to explain a little bit, but not too much. For instance, all classes will probably concentrate on the hortatory "Let," which begins eight sentences. Other classes will no doubt concentrate some attention on the very obvious rhetorical tropes marking the highly wrought phrases that have become part of our heritage: "Let us never negotiate out of fear. But let us never fear to negotiate" (paragraph 14) and "ask not what your country can do for you— ask what you can do for your country" (paragraph 24) (both examples of "chiasmus").

Questions from *The Norton Reader*

1. Choose a prominent rhetorical device (for example: repetition, allusion, lists, or juxtaposition) that John F. Kennedy uses in his speech and identify where it occurs. For the device you have identified, read it to yourself and then out loud. Why is it effective?

2. On what level of generality is Kennedy operating? When does he get specific?

3. Consider and deepen your answer to question 1 by writing an analysis of Kennedy's speech. Make a claim about the significance of one or more rhetorical devices used in the speech; support your thesis with specific examples from the text.

Teaching Suggestions

1. The headmaster of Kennedy's prep school had coined a ringing phrase: "Ask not what Choate can do for you—ask what you can do for Choate." Does this copying make Kennedy's speech any less valuable or admirable?

2. Examine the role of the word "let" in the speech. How often does it begin sentences? What kind of person uses such a word? On what type of occasion?

3. Some analysts use Kennedy's speech as an example of changing tastes in political addresses, pointing out that it was highly respected in 1961 but now seems overdone. Point to specific passages or to general issues like tone that some might regard as too much. Do you think they are overdone, or do they still work for you?

Suggested Writing Assignments

1. Look at contemporary newspaper and magazine accounts to see how Kennedy's speech was regarded in 1961, then write an essay reacting to what you discovered when reading those contemporary evaluations. What did you find that surprised you?

2. Describe what parts of Kennedy's fifty-five-year-old speech now seem dated and what parts still seem to address vital concerns of the twenty-first century.

3. View the video of this speech and then write about the differences between reading it, on one hand, and seeing and hearing it, on the other.

MARTIN LUTHER KING JR.
Letter from Birmingham Jail

Full Edition, p. 806

Martin Luther King Jr. was arguably the most important figure in the American civil rights movement before his assassination in 1968, at the age of thirty-nine. He participated in the Montgomery, Alabama, bus boycott in 1955–56 (see paragraph 35) and in the Birmingham, Alabama, demonstrations in 1963, where he was arrested along with many other demonstrators. He wrote "Letter from Birmingham Jail" in response to a published statement by eight Birmingham clergymen who supported the goals of the civil rights movement but criticized King for his "unwise and untimely" activism.

King uses Christian doctrine and Christian belief to make common cause with the white clergymen to whom he addresses his letter; see his reference to the Black Muslim movement and its repudiation of Christianity (paragraph 27). You can use his reference to Black Muslim bitterness and hatred to lead into a discussion of his nonviolent activism. Central to his justification of activism—"civil disobedience"—is his distinction between just and unjust laws (paragraphs 15–20). Ask students to summarize his distinction and how he applies it.

QUESTIONS FROM *The Norton Reader*

1. Martin Luther King Jr. addressed "Letter from Birmingham Jail" to eight fellow clergymen who had written a statement criticizing his activities (see note 1). Where and how, in the course of the "Letter," does he attempt to make common cause with them?

2. King was trained in oral composition, that is, in composing and delivering sermons. One device he uses is prediction: he announces, in advance, the organization of what he is about to say. Locate examples of prediction in the "Letter."

3. Summarize the theory of nonviolent resistance that King presents in this essay.

4. Imagine an unjust law that, to you, would justify civil disobedience. In an essay describe the law, the form your resistance would take, and the penalties you would expect to incur.

TEACHING SUGGESTIONS

1. You can ask students to explain the paradox of King's both urging obedience to the law, namely, the 1954 Supreme Court decision outlawing segregation in public schools, and breaking it.

2. What recent instances of civil disobedience other than those associated with the civil rights movement do your students know about? You might discuss the continued struggle for racial equality—the Black Lives Matter movement, for example—or protests that led to political equality for same-sex couples.

3. King, who expresses his disappointment with whites who call themselves moderates, alternatively characterizes himself as a moderate and an extremist. Students can look at instances of both and the kinds of behavior to which he attaches these labels. Which characterization of King do they think was more accurate in 1963, which more accurate today?

Suggested Writing Assignments

1. If you can't see yourself engaging in civil disobedience, as in question 2 (above), imagine an unjust law and the form someone else's resistance to it would take, then write a letter in which you try to convince this person to obey rather than to resist.

2. King calls into question, in the context of events in Birmingham, "the strangely irrational notion that there is something in the very flow of time that will inevitably cure all ills" (paragraph 26). Is this an "irrational notion"? Supply two or three other contexts in which the notion might figure and write an essay in which you agree or disagree with King.

3. Do library research on Mahatma Gandhi and his doctrine of nonviolent resistance. Then, on the basis of King's "Letter from Birmingham Jail," analyze similarities and differences between Gandhi's and King's ideas about and uses of nonviolent resistance.

4. Sort out, consulting King's text and the notes, the biblical figures King cites, the Church Fathers and earlier theologians, and the contemporary theologians and philosophers. Do research on one of the contemporary theologians and philosophers and write a brief essay in which you consider why he was useful to King.

Science

T. H. Huxley

Goethe: Aphorisms on Nature

Full Edition, p. 820

On being invited to contribute the opening article for the first issue of *Nature*, a new scientific journal founded in 1869 by his friend Norman Lockyer, the biologist and educator Thomas Henry Huxley offered not an original piece but his own translation of Goethe's aphorisms. The choice is striking and worth pondering with your students. Why might Huxley have felt that there could be "no more fitting preface" to a journal dedicated to documenting the "progress of science" than these aphorisms, written almost ninety years previously? One answer might be that he wanted to offer a framework, not scientific but not anti-scientific, through which readers could contemplate the scientific enterprise and the nature of scientific truth. Another might be that he wanted to offer readers an historical and aesthetic perspective that would allow them to consider science in relation to other achievements of the intellect and the arts. Finally, he might simply have wished to caution readers not to forget the essential mystery of nature as they perused scientific papers. We have included Huxley's article in *The Norton Reader* for similar reasons. Specifically, we wanted to open the *Reader's* new chapter on science with a selection that would give students of all educational backgrounds a framework for critically considering the essays that follow.

Because of its elevated style and complex form, Huxley's article might at first pose challenges to some students. But it has a proven appeal and may be approached in a variety of ways. The most accessible points of entry are Goethe's aphorisms themselves, any one of which could prompt a whole class discussion. You might also juxtapose Goethe's aphorisms with Huxley's commentary on them. Huxley, for example, claims that these aphorisms had long been a "delight" (paragraph 31) to him, yet he also takes pains to dissociate himself from Goethe's pantheism. He likewise uses Goethe to create a critical distance from the science of his day. You might also notice the different genres the article subsumes: the aphorism, the letter, and Huxley's commentary on it. Goethe's aphorisms and Huxley's musings on scientific progress also resonate with other selections in this chapter of the *Reader,* especially those by Isaac

Asimov, Thomas S. Kuhn, Stephen Hawking and Leonard Mlodinow, and Alan Lightman.

QUESTIONS FROM *THE NORTON READER*

1. What is Goethe's view of "Nature"?

2. In the title of this essay, T. H. Huxley refers to Goethe's reflections as "aphorisms." What is significant about this choice?

3. Consider the final three paragraphs of the essay. What attitude do they convey about the progress of science? Next, consider the final sentence. What is Huxley suggesting about the differences between scientific truth and poetic truth?

4. Huxley writes that he can imagine "no more fitting preface" (paragraph 31) to a scientific journal than Goethe's reflections. In an essay of your own, consider whether Huxley's observation would hold true today: would Goethe's aphorisms still appeal to a present-day scientist? If so, how? If not, why not? Consider conducting research for your essay by sharing Goethe's aphorisms with some scientists or science majors that you know.

TEACHING SUGGESTIONS

1. Ask students to explain one or more of Goethe's aphorisms in their own words. What do they think Goethe is trying to say?

2. Ask students to identify the different meanings of *nature* in the article. How is the "Nature" of Goethe's musings related to the nature scientists investigate?

3. Ask students to imagine being assigned Huxley's article in an introductory science class. How would reading the article in that context affect their interpretation of it? Why might the professor include it on the syllabus? (This scenario is not far-fetched: the article was in fact recommended to us by a colleague in chemistry who assigns it in his first-year classes.)

4. Have students conduct small research projects to place the article in its historical contexts.

SUGGESTED WRITING ASSIGNMENTS

1. Drawing on your own experience of nature, write an extended meditation on one of Goethe's aphorisms.

2. Select two of Goethe's aphorisms that seem to be in tension. Write an essay that explains or resolves that tension.

3. Huxley imagines future readers looking back on his generation as he looks back on Goethe's. Write a response to the essay from your own twenty-first-century perspective.

Isaac Asimov
The Relativity of Wrong

Full Edition, p. 824

Isaac Asimov is one of the twentieth century's most important writers of science fiction, but he was also a scientist (a professor of biochemistry at Boston University) who wrote prolifically in a range of genres, especially popular science. In this essay, he problematizes two concepts that we typically treat as absolutes—*right* and *wrong*—and argues that, as they pertain to scientific knowledge, they are in fact "fuzzy" (paragraph 8). Asimov represents the history of science as a story of continual progress toward an ever-more accurate and complete understanding of the world, and he unabashedly shares his "gladness at living in a century in which we finally got the basis of the universe straight" (paragraph 2). This position may be fruitfully compared to Huxley's reflective humility about the state of scientific knowledge in his day, to Thomas S. Kuhn's anti-foundationalism (FE p. 829, SE p. 474), to Stephen Jay Gould's insistence that science is about inquiry rather than the amassing of facts (FE p. 843, SE p. 488), and to Stephen Hawking and Leonard Mlodinow's more recent acknowledgment that science may never produce a single, complete theory of everything (FE p. 838, SE p. 483).

Asimov's style and manner of exposition are also worth noting. He frames his essay as a response to a letter from a student, a "young specialist in English Lit" (paragraph 5), who had written to challenge Asimov's happy view of scientific progress. Students will likely respond differently to this gambit. Some may appreciate Asimov's accessible and colloquial style, but others may react negatively to his avuncular tone. Is Asimov fair to the student he takes as his foil? The extended example he develops to illustrate his view of science—our progressively more accurate understanding of the shape of the earth—is also subject to question. How representative is it of science in general?

Questions from *The Norton Reader*

1. Isaac Asimov frames his essay as a response to a letter from a "young specialist in English Lit" (paragraph 5) whom he calls "wronger" (paragraph 6) than those people of the past who thought the earth was flat or spherical. What does Asimov mean by "wronger"?

2. How would you characterize the tone of Asimov's essay? Does his tone make you more or less receptive to his argument?

3. Asimov illustrates his point that scientific theories "are not so much wrong as incomplete" (paragraph 37) with a single extended example: the history of humans trying to determine the size and shape of the earth. Why does Asimov select this particular example?

4. Asimov frames his essay as a response to a letter from a "young specialist in English Lit." Continue the exchange by writing a letter of your own to Asimov.

TEACHING SUGGESTIONS

1. Ask students to explain in their own words how one view can be "wronger" than another.

2. Note that Asimov frames his essay as a response to a letter of criticism he received from a student. Why did he choose to present his ideas this way? He characterizes his essay not as an argument but as an "explanation" (paragraph 8). Is there a difference?

3. Note that Asimov describes the student as a "young specialist in English Lit" (paragraph 5). Why does Asimov include this detail? Compare Asimov's stance toward non-scientists to that of Huxley or Hawking and Mlodinow.

4. What, according to Asimov, is a scientific *theory*? How is his understanding of scientific theories similar to or different from that of other authors represented in this section of *The Norton Reader*?

SUGGESTED WRITING ASSIGNMENTS

1. Write an essay in which you extend Asimov's notion that some scientific ideas are "wronger" (paragraph 6) than others to another domain: art, politics, fashion, relationships, or another area of knowledge or life with which you are familiar.

2. Write an essay comparing Asimov's understanding of scientific progress to that of T. H. Huxley, Thomas S. Kuhn, or Stephen Hawking and Leonard Mlodinow.

3. Write an essay modeled on Asimov's in which you correct a misunderstanding about something you know well.

THOMAS S. KUHN
The Route to Normal Science

Full Edition, p. 829; Shorter Edition, p. 474

Thomas S. Kuhn was a Ph.D. in physics turned historian and philosopher of science; "The Route to Normal Science" comes from his best-known work, *The Structure of Scientific Revolutions* (1962). His concept of a "paradigm" (or a research tradition) and a "paradigm shift" (or the end of one research tradition and the beginning of another) has been widely adopted, which is evidence of his influence. For example, we speak of changes in the teaching of writing—from emphasizing product (or the finished essay) to emphasizing process (or its production through multiple drafts)—as a paradigm shift.

You may begin class discussion of "The Route to Normal Science" by directing students to its first two paragraphs, in which Kuhn briefly and magisterially lays out the concepts that he will illustrate: normal science, the reporting of scientific achievements, the nature of a research tradition, and its relation to scientific practice. He naturally illustrates these concepts with examples drawn from science. You may be able to enlist knowledgeable students to explain current paradigms; they will probably not be able to explain discarded ones—which itself will illustrate their disappearance. To illustrate a current paradigm, you can look at Kuhn's distinction between a textbook and a research report. Your students will probably be able to bring in examples of science textbooks; you can download a scientific research report through a database such as JSTOR or from a journal available online. *Nature*, for example, the opening issue of which included Huxley's article on Goethe's aphorisms on nature (FE p. 820), is available at www.nature.com. To illustrate a discarded paradigm (Kuhn features Newton's optics and Franklin's electricity), you might turn to one of the essays in this chapter that treats science historically: Isaac Asimov's "The Relativity of Wrong" (FE p. 824), Stephen Hawking and Leonard Mlodinow's "The (Elusive) Theory of Everything" (FE p. 838, SE p. 483), or Alan Lightman's "Our Place in the Universe" (FE p. 867, SE p. 500).

QUESTIONS FROM *THE NORTON READER*

1. Mark the important terms in this selection from *The Structure of Scientific Revolutions* and Thomas S. Kuhn's definitions of them. How many terms does he illustrate as well as define? Why does he both define and illustrate?

2. What are prevailing paradigms in sciences other than those Kuhn discusses? You might consider biology, chemistry, psychology, and sociology. Are you aware of older paradigms in these sciences, or have they and the work based on them, as Kuhn says (paragraph 15), disappeared?

3. Kuhn asserts, "The study of paradigms . . . is what mainly prepares the student for membership in the particular scientific community with which he will later practice" (paragraph 2). Does this statement about science apply to other areas of study, to other kinds of communities? Consider these questions in an essay of your own, drawing on your own experience as a student.

TEACHING SUGGESTIONS

1. You may want to look at Kuhn's discussion of paradigms in relation to gathering facts and establishing their relevance (paragraphs 10 and 11). Analogies with writing may be useful here: what gets included and excluded from an essay, when, and why?

2. Kuhn speaks of "the unfortunate simplification that tags an extended historical episode with a single and somewhat arbitrarily chosen name" (paragraph 9). Ask students for examples from history and literature and consider the various ways they function. Is simplification always "unfortunate"?

3. Ask students to compare Kuhn's understanding of how science changes to that of Asimov or Hawking and Mlodinow. What do they have in common? How do they differ? Which explanations do your students find more believable or intuitive?

4. Ask students whether they think Kuhn's notion that science changes through a succession of paradigms could be extended to other fields. Does it apply to, say, literary criticism, or styles of music, or even cooking? Use this discussion to prompt students to think about how science resembles or differs from other domains of human endeavor.

SUGGESTED WRITING ASSIGNMENTS

1. If you have encountered the term *paradigm* in another field of study, write an essay in which you describe what it refers to and how it is used and discuss whether it is used in Kuhn's sense.

2. Kuhn, in "The Route to Normal Science," mentions what happens to scientists who cling to discarded paradigms (paragraph 15). Elsewhere in *The Structure of Scientific Revolutions* he discusses several, including Louis Agassiz, who held out against Darwin. Do research on Agassiz or another holdout and write an essay about him or her using Kuhn's concept of a paradigm.

3. Kuhn's *The Structure of Scientific Revolutions*, published in 1962, engendered considerable debate that was essentially about definitions. Read his postscript to the second edition (1970) and describe the issues of definition he raises.

STEPHEN HAWKING AND LEONARD MLODINOW
The (Elusive) Theory of Everything

Full Edition, p. 838; Shorter Edition, p. 483

Stephen Hawking is a British theoretical physicist and popular science author. Leonard Mlodinow, an American physicist, collaborated with Hawking to write two books of popular science, *A Briefer History of Time* (2005) and *The Grand Design* (2010). In this short essay, originally published in *Scientific American*, they explain to a general audience why it is unlikely that science will ever produce a comprehensive "theory of everything." Like T. H. Huxley (FE p. 820), Isaac Asimov (FE p. 824), Thomas S. Kuhn (FE p. 829, SE p. 474), and Stephen Jay Gould (FE p. 843, SE p. 488), they are concerned with the nature of science and scientific truth, and their essay bears close comparison with those of these other writers.

Hawking and Mlodinow open their essay with a curious anecdote: they note that the Italian city of Monza banned curved fishbowls because they "give the fish a distorted view of reality." They then ask, "How do we know that the reality we perceive is true?" Perhaps we, like hapless goldfish, are condemned to view the world through our own "distorting lens" (paragraph 1). Hawking and Mlodinow use this anecdote to introduce their main point: for years, physicists and cosmologists had sought to develop an "ultimate theory of everything," but it turns out that the search for such a theory may yield not a single, comprehensive theory or a "family" of theories, each describing an aspect of the world in its own way (paragraph 2).

Hawking and Mlodinow see the quest for a "theory of everything" as grounded in the commonsensical but naïve belief in a single, objective reality that we can access through our senses, a belief they term "realism" (paragraph 3). They endorse instead a position they term "model-dependent realism" (paragraph 8), which holds that we can't ask whether a model or description of the world captures reality but only whether it is consistent with observation. It is this stance that makes the possibility of multiple, distinct, overlapping scientific theories acceptable.

The idea of "model-dependent realism" is counterintuitive, and your students may struggle to grasp it. But the rhetorical challenge Hawking and Mlodinow face is precisely how to make this idea and its implications for science understandable to general readers. To this end, they deploy a number of metaphors and analogies, the goldfish in the fishbowl being only the most prominent. The essay thus provides not only an occasion for students to wrestle with challenging ideas but also an opportunity to explore ways of making such ideas accessible.

Questions from *The Norton Reader*

1. Stephen Hawking and Leonard Mlodinow comment that in physics, "realism is becoming difficult to defend" (paragraph 5). What do they mean by "realism" and what do they propose as an alternative?

2. This essay was written for general readers. How, in their writing, do Hawking and Mlodinow make complex scientific ideas accessible to non-scientists? For instance, how does the goldfish example that runs through the essay help readers?

3. In his essay "The Relativity of Wrong" (FE p. 824) Isaac Asimov argues that when it comes to science, "right and wrong are fuzzy concepts" (paragraph 8). He concludes his essay by observing that the scientific explanations of the moment are not wrong but instead "incomplete": science progresses when our current theories and explanations are replaced by others that are more complete. How might Hawking and Mlodinow respond to this idea?

4. Write an essay of your own in which you explain a complex idea or process that you know well to someone who is less familiar with it.

Teaching Suggestions

1. Introduce the term *ethos*, which rhetoricians use to describe the character a speaker or writer projects to his or her audience. Ask students to describe Hawking and Mlodinow's ethos and to explain how they establish it. Invite students to compare Hawking and Mlodinow's ethos to that of other authors in this chapter of *The Norton Reader*, especially Huxley, Asimov, or Gould.

2. Hawking and Mlodinow observe that just like ordinary people, working scientists may find it difficult to surrender their naïve realism. Ask students whether this observation is surprising. Why or why not?

3. Ask students to identify the various metaphors and analogies Hawking and Mlodinow use to make the idea of "model-dependent realism" (paragraph 7) accessible. How helpful are these metaphors and analogies? Are they consistent? Can your students think of others Hawking and Mlodinow might have chosen?

4. Ask students to dramatize a discussion among two or more of the writers represented in this chapter of *The Norton Reader* about the nature of scientific progress and scientific truth.

SUGGESTED WRITING ASSIGNMENTS

1. Write an essay that compares Hawking and Mlodinow's understanding of scientific progress or scientific truth to that of one other writer represented in this chapter of *The Norton Reader*.

2. Write an essay, modeled on Hawking and Mlodinow's, in which you use an extended metaphor or analogy to explain a hard-to-grasp concept or idea.

STEPHEN JAY GOULD

Sex, Drugs, Disasters, and the Extinction of Dinosaurs

Full Edition, p. 843; Shorter Edition, p. 488

Evolutionary biologist Stephen Jay Gould was a professor of geology and zoology at Harvard University, an historian of science, and a prolific popular science writer. "Sex, Drugs, Disasters, and the Extinction of Dinosaurs" first appeared in *Discover* magazine in 1984 and was later published in Gould's collection *The Flamingo's Smile: Reflections in Natural History* (1985). Students might note how Gould's "popular science" style in this essay combines the vocabulary of his field with colloquial, everyday, and familiar language.

In this essay, Gould explains the differences between science and mere speculation. "Science," proclaims his opening sentence, "is a fruitful mode of inquiry, not a list of enticing conclusions." Gould then illustrates this contention with the example of three theories proffered to account for the extinction of dinosaurs, only one of which he regards as real science. Gould explains that unlike the other theories, the "disasters" theory (paragraph 5) can be supported and corroborated by different kinds of evidence. It can also be reconciled with other pieces of accepted scientific knowledge and has implications beyond its immediate context. At the end of Gould's essay, he states the ramifications of this disasters theory as it relates to our contemporary world. The effect of a nuclear explosion, he notes, might be very similar to that of an asteroid or comet striking the planet.

Like several other essays in this section, including Thomas S. Kuhn's "The Route to Normal Science" (FE p. 829, SE p. 474), Stephen Hawking and Leonard Mlodinow's "The (Elusive) Theory of Everything" (FE p. 838, SE p. 483), and David H. Freedman's "Lies, Damned Lies, and Medical Science" (FE p. 850), Gould's essay invites students to reflect on the nature of scientific reasoning and argumentation. When teaching this essay, you might talk with students about the choices Gould made when writing it. Why did he choose the extinction of dinosaurs as his subject? Why does he adopt an informal, even colloquial style? What audience is Gould trying to reach, and what effect does he want his essay to have?

Questions from *The Norton Reader*

1. What criteria does Stephen Jay Gould use to distinguish good science from "silly speculation" (paragraph 3)?

2. Gould writes about dinosaurs, but his goal is to make a point about science. How does Gould use his examples to make this point?

3. The first five essays in the "Science" chapter of *The Norton Reader* were written by scientists or historians of science to explain what science is and how it works. Yet these writers approach their common subject from different perspectives and sometimes seem even to disagree. Imagine Goethe and T. H. Huxley (FE p. 820), Isaac Asimov (FE p. 824), Thomas S. Kuhn (FE p. 829, SE p. 474), Stephen Hawking and Leonard Mlodinow (FE p. 838, SE p. 483), and Gould (or some smaller group of them) as characters in a play having a casual conversation that veers into a discussion of science. Write the script for this scene. Annotate your script by linking your lines of dialogue to passages in the essays.

Teaching Suggestions

1. Students who have experienced science mainly through textbooks may regard scientific knowledge as a collection of facts and scientific authority as unassailable. In what ways does Gould's essay challenge this notion? What distinguishes science as a "mode of inquiry" (paragraph 1)?

2. Gould's writing style is simultaneously colloquial and erudite. Ask students to highlight phrases that they find to be unexpected or surprising in a scientific essay (e.g., "hell of a time" [paragraph 10]). What is the effect of such moments? How does Gould's style contribute to his argument?

3. In "The Relativity of Wrong," Isaac Asimov suggests that there can be differing degrees of rightness and wrongness and that the categories that we tend to think of as absolutes are in fact "fuzzy" (paragraph 8). Would Gould agree with Asimov? How do Gould and Asimov treat observable evidence?

4. In class, read Dylan Thomas's poem "Do Not Go Gentle Into That Good Night." Discuss which lines Gould references in his essay. Why does Gould use these particular lines where he does?

Suggested Writing Assignments

1. Write an essay on a topic about which you have a lot of knowledge. Imitate Gould's writing style by alternating between sophisticated, field-specific vocabulary and colloquial, everyday phrases.

2. Imagine a theory that explains something that you do not understand. Discuss what kinds of logical reasoning would be needed to prove your claim. What observable, quantifiable data might you have to collect? What assumptions would be needed to link that evidence to your claims? What logical ideas might disprove the hypothesis?

3. Write an essay that considers our abiding fascination with dinosaurs. Why do fictional stories like *Jurassic Park* (1993; 2015) continue to be so popular? Why are they and their world relevant? What connection do dinosaurs have to our contemporary life?

DAVID H. FREEDMAN

Lies, Damned Lies, and Medical Science

Full Edition, p. 850

Science journalist David H. Freedman is a frequent contributor to the *Atlantic*, where this essay appeared, and author of the book *Wrong: Why Experts Keep Failing Us—And How to Know When Not to Trust Them* (2010). In "Lies, Damned Lies, and Medical Science," Freedman profiles the Greek medical researcher John Ioannidis, who has shown that medical research is, for the most part, wrong. The essay thus invites students, many of whom may have experienced science only through school classes and textbooks, to think critically about the authority of science and how it justifies its claims. Like Rebecca Skloot (FE p. 862, SE p. 495), Freedman raises questions about the ethics of medical research (albeit from a very different perspective). Like Isaac Asimov (FE p. 824), he challenges readers to reflect on the different ways in which scientific findings can be wrong. And like Stephen Jay Gould (FE p. 843, SE p. 488), he raises questions about the nature and boundaries of scientific argument.

QUESTIONS FROM *THE NORTON READER*

1. David H. Freedman frames his article as a profile of medical researcher John Ioannidis. Why might Freedman have taken this approach, rather than writing about the problems with medical research directly?

2. According to Freedman's article, what factors cause medical research to go wrong? Compare Ioannidis's understanding of "wrongness" to Isaac Asimov's (FE p. 824).

3. According to the researchers Freedman interviews, how should medical research influence how doctors treat patients? Compare the views of these researchers to those expressed by Atul Gawande in his essay "When Doctors Make Mistakes" (FE p. 652, SE p. 380).

4. Near the end of his article, Freedman notes, "[T]he question of whether the problems with medical research should be broadcast to the public is a sticky one in the meta-research community" (paragraph 34). Write an essay that explains and justifies your own opinion on this question.

Teaching Suggestions

1. Discuss the structure of Freedman's essay. Note especially the moments when he transitions, sometimes abruptly, from explanatory discussions of Ioannidis's research to narrative accounts of his interactions with Ioannidis in Greece or descriptions of Ioannidis's personal traits. Why does Freedman switch between these registers?

2. Ask students to discuss the import—the "so what?"—of Ioannidis's contention that medical research is often wrong. What are the potential benefits or detriments of such meta-research? What are the practical implications of Ioannidis's findings? Do they change students' thinking about their own health decisions? About "alternative" approaches to medicine?

3. Share with your students a recent article from a newspaper or popular magazine that offers health advice to readers. Using ideas from Freedman's essay, examine the article critically. What kinds of evidence does it rely on? What assumptions or biases could be inflecting the underlying research?

Suggested Writing Assignments

1. Compare Freedman's essay with another essay in this chapter that calls into question the "truth" of science. How do the essays show that the research, hypotheses, and/or conclusions of scientific research cannot be trusted?

2. Write an essay in which you reconsider a belief you once held to be absolutely true. What happened to make you reconsider your initial belief, to the point that you found it was either partially or completely wrong? What led you astray in the first place? Was your information faulty, or did you have biases that needed to be corrected?

3. Research and document the history of one piece of common medical or health advice (e.g., a low-fat diet is good for the heart). When was it developed? On what evidence is it based? How has it been changed or refined? Are there alternative or competing views? Have any non-medical considerations inflected the recommendation? What does your case study lead you to conclude about such advice generally?

Rebecca Skloot

The Woman in the Photograph

Full Edition, p. 862; Shorter Edition, p. 495

Rebecca Skloot is a freelance science writer whose debut book, *The Immortal Life of Henrietta Lacks* (2010), was a *New York Times* best-seller for two years. This selection, from the prologue to that book, raises a basic ethical question: Do medical researchers have a right to remove cells from someone's body without his or her consent or knowledge for the purpose of scientific study? While students can productively debate this question in the abstract, Skloot's essay offers them an opportunity to consider it within the richer context of a particular life. Skloot tells the story of Henrietta Lacks, whose cervical cancer cells have become "immortal" as they have continued to replicate in petri dishes around the world for the past sixty years. These "HeLa" cells, which can be found in almost any laboratory freezer today, have been used in developing treatments for Parkinson's, cancer, herpes, leukemia, and other diseases. HeLa cells have also aided with advancements in cloning, in vitro fertilization, and gene mapping, and they have even traveled into space. By recovering the story of Henrietta Lacks and her family, Skloot humanizes these cells and thus raises challenging social, ethical, political, and even religious questions.

Students can benefit not only from debating the difficult issues Skloot's essay raises but also from considering the form of Skloot's essay itself—the way Skloot presents Henrietta Lacks's story. Skloot frames Lacks's story through her own. She describes her own background, how she first learned of Lacks and HeLa cells, and her reasons for pursuing the story of Lacks and her family. "There's a photo on my wall," Skloot begins, "of a woman I've never met" (paragraph 1). The essay tells not just the story of the woman in the photograph but also of the woman who has taped it to her wall.

Questions from *The Norton Reader*

1. Was the surgeon who first cultivated Henrietta Lacks's cells for research justified in doing so? Why or why not?

2. Rebecca Skloot writes, "As I worked my way through graduate school studying writing, I became fixated on the idea of someday telling Henrietta's story" (paragraph 29). Why does Skloot find Lacks's story so compelling?

3. This essay is the prologue to Skloot's book *The Immortal Life of Henrietta Lacks.* Why does Skloot dwell so extensively on her own story in the essay?

4. Write the story of a research project of your own. What or who motivated you to undertake the project? How did you go about your research? What obstacles did you encounter? What discoveries did you make? Looking back on the process, what did you learn about yourself as a researcher or as a person?

Teaching Suggestions

1. Invite students to discuss the ethical issues surrounding Henrietta Lacks's medical treatments, how her cells were taken as samples without her consent, and how they were then dispensed and circulated without her knowledge. Do the medical benefits of using HeLa cells outweigh ethical concerns about how these cells were made available for medical research? Perhaps stage a debate about this question. What evidence and reasoning might support the use of HeLa cells for scientific research? What evidence and reasoning oppose it?

2. Henrietta's name remains somewhat mysterious. The caption below her photograph identifies her as "Henrietta Lacks, Helen Lane or Helen Larson" (paragraph 1). Skloot tells us that "[S]he's usually identified as Helen Lane, but often she has no name at all. She's simply called HeLa, the code name given to the world's first immortal human cells—*her* cells. . . ." (paragraph 2).

Ask students to consider how the question of Henrietta's name relates to the ethical questions raised by the use of her cells.

3. Skloot reminds us repeatedly that Henrietta Lacks was an African American woman. Locate places in the essay where Skloot notices Henrietta's race or gender. How did issues of race and gender influence the way Henrietta was treated? Conversely, consider the identity of Skloot, who identifies herself as a white, middle-class woman from the northwest. Do Skloot's race, class, and gender complicate her ability to tell the story of Henrietta and her family?

4. Consider the form and style of Skloot's essay. How does she organize her information and her story? What kind of vocabulary does she use? What compels you to keep reading more?

Suggested Writing Assignments

1. Write an argumentative essay in which you affirm or challenge the right of medical researchers to use HeLa cells.

2. Find a photograph of Henrietta Lacks online. In an essay of your own, describe the photograph and reflect on how it enriches or complicates your understanding of Skloot's essay.

3. Write a biographical essay, modeled on Skloot's, in which you tell the story of someone whose contributions are obscure or forgotten. Write yourself into your essay as Skloot writes herself into hers. How do your own identity and interests affect the way you tell your subject's story?

Alan Lightman
Our Place in the Universe: Face to Face with the Infinite

Full Edition, p. 867; Shorter Edition, p. 500

In this lyrical essay, award-winning novelist, essayist, and Massachusetts Institute of Technology professor Alan Lightman ponders the profoundest of topics, "our place in the universe." His essay thus complements the selection with which this chapter begins, T. H. Huxley's translation of Goethe's aphorisms on nature (FE p. 820). Like this earlier piece, Lightman's essay is ultimately humanistic: as it progresses, its focus shifts from universe in itself—"the qualities of this strange world that we find ourselves in" (paragraph 3)—to "the question of our significance" within it (paragraph 26).

Lightman does not directly answer that question. He never states outright what our "place" in the universe might be. Instead, he approaches his topic from a series of related perspectives, inviting us to contemplate it with him. In the body of his essay, he considers our ever-increasing sense of the expansiveness of the space surrounding us, noting that "each new level of distance and scale" challenges us "to contend with a different conception of the world that we live in" (paragraph 3). He then considers the relationship between the "astoundingly large cosmic terrain" we have discovered through the advance of astronomy and our traditional conception of "Mother Nature" (paragraph 21).

Does this "new universe" (paragraph 21), he asks, include nature? Does nature include us? He closes his essay by remarking on the extreme rarity of life in the cosmos and wondering what this fact implies about our significance.

But he doesn't leave us with this abstract, even nihilistic sentiment. Lightman frames the intellectual ruminations that make up the body of his essay with an intimate recollection of a trip sailing with his wife on the Aegean Sea. In his first paragraph, he recalls setting out to sea, leaving all traces of human habitation behind; in his last paragraph, he recalls their return and his first sight of shore, "a place with houses and beds and other human beings" (paragraph 27), juxtaposing the abstract expansiveness of space with a fundamentally human sense of place.

Because it uses scientific findings to broach fundamental questions about what it means to be human, Lightman's essay can be taught in many ways. Like the essays of Isaac Asimov (FE p. 824), Stephen Hawking and Leonard Mlodinow (FE p. 838, SE p. 483) and Thomas S. Kuhn (FE p. 829, SE p. 474), it historicizes science and scientific knowledge. It also positions science as one contribution to a broader human project of inquiry and discovery, inviting students to discuss the relationship between science and other forms of knowledge. Finally, it can be fruitfully paired with essays from other chapters of *The Norton Reader,* especially "Nature and the Environment" and "Philosophy and Religion."

QUESTIONS FROM *The Norton Reader*

1. What, according to Alan Lightman, is "our place in the universe"?

2. Lightman recognizes that the study of nature is not the purview of science alone: "Naturalists, biologists, philosophers, painters, and poets," he writes, "have labored to express the qualities of this strange world that we find ourselves in" (paragraph 3). How does this sensibility inform his essay?

3. What does Lightman do as a writer to get his readers to experience (not just acknowledge) nature's vastness?

4. Lightman begins and ends his essay by recalling his sailing trip on the Aegean, which he describes as his "most vivid encounter with the vastness of nature" (paragraph 1). Write an essay in which you describe and reflect on a transformative experience of your own.

TEACHING SUGGESTIONS

1. Draw students' attention to Lightman's range of reference. While he focuses mainly on how science has expanded our understanding of the size or scale of the universe, he also nods to literature (Ralph Waldo Emerson [paragraph 24]), the arts (George Cooke [paragraph 24]), and philosophy (George Berkeley [paragraph 25]). Why?

2. Lightman writes, "Somewhere in our fathoming of the cosmos, we must keep a mental inventory of plain size and scale, going from atoms to microbes to humans to oceans to planets to stars" (paragraph 3). Invite students to consider

the different ways in which Lightman addresses size and scale in his essay. How does he work to understand these concepts? How does scale serve as a principle of organization in the essay?

3. Lightman refers to *nature* throughout his essay. Ask students to explain what Lightman means by this word. Have them compare his understanding of nature to that of T. H. Huxley or Isaac Asimov, or to that of John McPhee (FE p. 521, SE p. 307), John Muir (FE p. 529), Chief Seattle (FE p. 543, SE p. 315), or Wallace Stegner (FE p. 544).

4. Invite students to consider the final sentence of the essay. Why does Lightman close his essay with an image of "a place with houses and beds and other human beings"?

SUGGESTED WRITING ASSIGNMENTS

1. Write an essay that considers Lightman's title, "Our Place in the Universe." How does Lightman enrich or complicate our sense of *place*?

2. Contemplating scientific measurements of the universe's size, Lightman comments, "Such numbers cannot but bear upon the question of our significance in the universe" (paragraph 26). In an essay of your own, explain how you think Lightman would answer this question, and then offer your own answer.

3. Lightman offers George Cooke's painting *Tallulah Falls* and Ralph Waldo Emerson's essay "Nature" as illustrations of the view that human beings are "somehow separate from the rest of nature" (paragraph 24). Write an essay in which you examine one of these works in light of Lightman's interpretation. Why do you think Lightman interprets the work as he does? What else does the work have to say about humanity's relationship to nature?

Literature and the Arts

EUDORA WELTY

One Writer's Beginnings

Full Edition, p. 877; Shorter Edition, p. 509

Taken from her best-selling memoir by the same title, this essay turns to the world of Eudora Welty's childhood in Jackson, Mississippi, and offers an adult's reflections on formative early experience. "One Writer's Beginnings" is a chapter from the autobiography of an artist, representing what we now call a "literacy narrative." Welty describes the books read to her and the books she read, notes the texts she admired and adored, and talks about reading as she experienced it—and as she hopes her readers will also experience it. Perhaps the most important aspect of "One Writer's Beginnings" comes near the end, when Welty considers "voice." Her five-paragraph treatment of the subject, beginning with her mother's songs and records played on the Victrola, then retracing her own experience of reading and writing, provides a valuable opportunity to define and illustrate this difficult rhetorical concept.

QUESTIONS FROM *THE NORTON READER*

1. In the opening paragraphs Eudora Welty speaks of what she later calls her "sensory education." What does she mean? What examples does she give?

2. Throughout her essay Welty lists the titles of books that she and her mother read. What is the effect of these lists? Have you read any of the books? Or books like them? How important were they to you?

3. Welty concludes her essay by talking of the writer's voice—of "testing it for truth" and "trust[ing] this voice" (paragraphs 24 and 25). What meanings does she give the key words "truth" and "trust"?

4. Welty grew up before television and computers. How might today's technology affect a child's "sensory education"? Write an essay comparing a modern child's sensory education with Welty's.

TEACHING SUGGESTIONS

1. Follow up on question 2 (above) by considering the following: why does Welty devote so much space to describing the books of her childhood? Are they the forces that most powerfully shaped her, or is she, through memory and words, also (re)shaping the self she presents in this autobiography of an artist?

2. Welty obviously loves books and loves to talk about them. Ask students what strategies she uses to communicate her responses to books—not just

adjectives, but metaphors, memories, anecdotes—and what strategies they most respond to.

3. Ask students why this selection has been titled "One Writer's Beginnings." Would they expect different "beginnings" from the autobiography of, say, a painter or politician or businessperson?

4. This selection might have been placed in "Education," alongside Frederick Douglass's "Learning to Read" (FE p. 404, SE p. 228). Assign that essay also, and ask students to pull out features of these two "literacy narratives" that are similar.

5. In what ways is Welty's essay a cultural document reflecting the world of the American South in the early decades of the last century? You might begin discussing this question by asking students to note what is different about Welty's childhood from their own—or, perhaps, what details from Welty's childhood they have encountered in stories told by their parents or grandparents.

6. In paragraph 24 Welty offers a description of "voice" in a story or poem. After discussing it, ask students to characterize the voice they hear in "One Writer's Beginnings."

SUGGESTED WRITING ASSIGNMENTS

1. In describing her reading of classic tales from *Every Child's Story Book*, Welty notes: "I located myself in these pages and could go straight to the stories and pictures I loved" (paragraph 12). If you have had a similar experience with stories or books, write an essay about it. If your experience with books was quite different, that, too, will provide the subject of an essay.

2. Welty lists many of the children's tales she read and loved as she grew up. If you have read any of them, reread one and, in an analytical essay, suggest why it continues to appeal to children.

3. Welty writes, "Learning stamps you with its moments. Childhood's learning is made up of moments. It isn't steady. It's a pulse" (paragraph 16). Reflect on your own educational process, both formal and informal; then write an essay in response to Welty's observation about how learning occurs.

VLADIMIR NABOKOV
Good Readers and Good Writers

Full Edition, p. 883; Shorter Edition, p. 515

Although Vladimir Nabokov is well known to teachers of literature and writing, his work may be unfamiliar to students. In preparation for this essay on reading and writing fiction, you may want them to read a short story by Nabokov, in order to consider connections among his fiction, his theory of fiction, and the writers he prefers.

More generally, you may want to ask students what they expect from fiction: why they read, what pleases them, what satisfies them at a story's end.

Nabokov's views on what "good readers" ought to expect from fiction are likely to prove quite different from theirs; indeed, through the mock "quiz" he gives, Nabokov insists that action, emotional identification, and historical interest are not "good" motives for reading. Eudora Welty (FE p. 877, SE p. 509) offers a less exacting perspective on reading, while Philip Kennicott (FE p. 935) is similarly strict about viewing art.

Questions from *The Norton Reader*

1. Make a list of the qualities that Vladimir Nabokov believes "good readers" should have; then make a list of the qualities he believes "good writers" should have. Do they match? Why or why not?

2. Nabokov, as he points out in the conclusion to his essay (paragraphs 14–16), considers the writer from three points of view: as storyteller, as teacher, and as enchanter. He has not, however, organized his essay by these points of view. Where and how does he discuss each one? Why does he consider the last the most important?

3. How would Eudora Welty (FE p. 877, SE p. 509) do on Nabokov's quiz? Give what you think would be her answers and explain, using information from her essay, what you think her reasons would be.

4. Take Nabokov's quiz (paragraph 5). Write an essay in which you explain your "right" answers (as Nabokov sees "good readers") and defend your "wrong" ones.

Teaching Suggestions

1. Why does Nabokov use a quotation from the French novelist Gustave Flaubert in the opening paragraph of his essay? Ask students what the quotation tells us about the style, tone, and persona of the writer.

2. Nabokov gives a "quiz" about "good readers" (paragraph 5) that he claims he once gave to students and that question 4 (above) asks students to take. Why does he give this quiz rather than present his ideas more directly? Does he, in a sense, coerce readers into choosing the "right" answers and shame them for choosing the "wrong" ones?

3. Nabokov distinguishes between "minor" and "major" authors in paragraph 4. Look at the metaphors he uses to describe the "major" (or "real") author.

4. Nabokov also distinguishes between two varieties of imagination in paragraphs 8 to 9. What are they? How are they related to his "good" and, by implication, his "bad" readers?

5. At the end of this essay Nabokov retells the story of the boy who cried wolf. In the standard version of this story, the boy is devoured when a real wolf finally comes along; it is a homily on the virtues of telling the truth. Why does Nabokov revise it? What new meanings does he want us to grasp?

6. The essay ends with an image of an artist who "build[s] his castle of cards," which turns into "a castle of beautiful steel and glass" (paragraph 16). Ask students to analyze this image, the sense of the artist it conveys, and why Nabokov chose to end his essay with it.

SUGGESTED WRITING ASSIGNMENTS

1. Write an argument for or against Nabokov's suggestion that "the good reader is one who has imagination, memory, a dictionary, and some artistic sense" rather than an inclination toward "emotional identification, action, and the social-economic or historical angle" (paragraph 5).

2. Read a story written by Nabokov and write an essay in which you consider the ways in which his fiction reflects the values expressed in "Good Readers and Good Writers."

3. Write your own essay on the topic "What Makes Good Writers."

NORTHROP FRYE
The Motive for Metaphor

Full Edition, p. 888

This essay, Northrop Frye explains, is part of a series of six talks for students and critics of literature. The title of each comes from a different poem (paragraph 19); "the motive for metaphor" occurs in a poem by Wallace Stevens that Frye quotes near the end of this essay, after he has developed a theory of poetic language and an apologia for literature. You can start with the poem: ask students about the relations between the self (Stevens's "you") and the world that he depicts in it. Or you can come to the poem after working through Frye's theory of poetic language—either way works.

At the beginning of the essay Frye poses a number of resonant questions with respect to the value of literature, the identity of poets, and the differences between art and science. Ask students what uses they think literature has. Frye locates the roots of imagination in human desires and mental capacities. Students will grasp his distinction between the world they live in and the world they want to live in (paragraph 7). But they may not care to reconcile them in Frye's visionary, quasi-religious manner: religions, he observes, also "present us with visions of eternal and infinite heavens or paradises" (paragraph 18).

QUESTIONS FROM *THE NORTON READER*

1. At what point in his essay does Northrop Frye come to explain the meaning of his title? What is his conception of the motive for metaphor? Why does he wait to explain it?

2. Frye describes three kinds of English, or, rather, he describes one English and three uses to which we put it. What are they?

3. Frye describes metaphor, forcibly, as nonsense (paragraph 20). How, then, do we make sense of it?

4. Why, according to Frye, doesn't literature improve the way science does? What happens to old science? Read Thomas S. Kuhn's "The Route to Normal Science" (FE p. 829, SE p. 474), and do additional research if necessary.

Then write an essay in which you compare the fates of old literature and old science.

Teaching Suggestions

1. How does Frye define three levels of the mind? How does each operate? Why does he take such pains to distinguish among them?

2. In paragraphs 5, 12, and 13, Frye presents his understanding of how science works. Compare his view with that of Isaac Asimov in "The Relativity of Wrong" (FE p. 824) or David H. Freedman in "Lies, Damned Lies, and Medical Science" (FE p. 850).

3. How does Frye distinguish between the arts and the sciences? Ask students what limitations they see in his distinctions. Ask them also about their own values. Students who plan to choose a "practical" major such as biology or engineering instead of a major such as art history or English (an "impractical" major?) will provide examples on the spot of how modern society acknowledges the importance of science and questions the value of art.

4. How does Frye distinguish between poetry and religion?

5. Frye poses the question "Is it possible that literature, especially poetry, is something that a scientific civilization like ours will eventually outgrow?" (paragraph 14). What answer does he expect us to give? Why?

6. Plot the design of this essay, accounting for its organization, development, and points of emphasis. The concluding paragraph merits special consideration.

Suggested Writing Assignments

1. Analogy, according to Frye, is "tricky to handle in description, because the differences are as important as the resemblances" (paragraph 20). Write a description of something in which you liken it to one or more other things. Then explain the points of resemblance that make the analogy (or analogies) work and the points of difference that must be ignored.

2. Choose an essay from this chapter in which metaphor is important, and, using what you have learned from Frye, analyze its use of metaphor.

3. Frye observes, "We notice in passing that the creative and the neurotic minds have a lot in common" in dissatisfaction (paragraph 17). Write an essay in which you make something of his observation.

Ngũgĩ wa Thiong'o
Decolonizing the Mind

Full Edition, p. 896

Ngũgĩ wa Thiong'o rails against the mental colonization of African children who as a result of the hegemony of English language education were discouraged and even punished for speaking in their native languages and, worse, made to feel that their language and culture were inferior. The children were fed a continuous diet of English narratives, English characters, and English traditions. The devaluation of African languages and African culture robbed the children of a strong sense of self-worth rooted in the culture of their parents and grandparents.

This essay could be used to spark a discussion about the privileging of English in the educational system in the United States, a policy that deprives many immigrant children of a chance to remain fluent in their native languages while they acquire English and that begins the process of emotionally severing them from the cultural milieus of their communities. Arguments have been made to support competing views: the position of English-only advocates is that immersion in English is the most effective way to ensure an immigrant child's quick adjustment to the expectations and challenges of life in the United States; opponents of this view cite research that proves that when immigrant children are placed in bilingual programs, where they learn English even as they continue to receive instruction in their native language in some subjects, their academic performance is superior to those who receive all instruction in English. The debate is passionate and divisive, with long-term implications for the United States' understanding of multiple cultures and multiple nations. Social commentators like Margaret Talbot write that Americans' ignorance of languages other than English leads to their misunderstanding the nuances of peoples of other nations.

In many other parts of the world, students routinely receive education in at least two, if not three, languages. Skill with a specific language is the surest way to begin to "enter" and learn about the culture based on that language, because, as Ngũgĩ says, "Culture is almost indistinguishable from the language that makes possible its genesis, growth, banking, articulation and indeed its transmission from one generation to the next."

Questions from *The Norton Reader*

1. The last paragraphs of Ngũgĩ wa Thiong'o's essay contain the names of many classic and contemporary European writers. Why do you think he chose to include them? Can you relate their inclusion to the way Ngũgĩ chooses to present himself in this essay?

2. What literary writers did you read in secondary school? What values were your teachers (or school) imparting in selecting those writers in particular?

3. Ngũgĩ experienced a particularly stark contrast between the values contained within the oral stories of his family and the written English of school. Discuss the different value systems. Have you noticed differences between what your extended family values and what your school seemed to want you to value?

4. Imagine an English class for a bilingual or bicultural community. Write a paper justifying the ideal balance between texts from the second language or culture (in translation or not) and English.

Teaching Suggestions

1. What does it mean to be "mentally colonized"? Under what circumstances can an individual become mentally colonized?

2. Ngũgĩ notes that when the system of education in Kenya was taken over by Englishmen, not only did knowledge of English become the primary marker of one's "intelligence" and worth, but also England and Europe became the center of the universe. Might it be possible to implement a system of education in which a language can be privileged without an accompanying privileging of the history, culture, and traditions associated with that language? Could Kenyans have learned English without feeling that their own languages and traditions were unworthy?

3. What languages other than English should students learn in their schools? Why? In several countries, students learn English, the national language, and usually a third language that is commonly spoken in the region. What are the benefits or disadvantages of learning multiple languages?

4. Many of us read about different cultures and study the history of other nations through books written in English. Ask students what we might be missing or gaining by viewing these peoples and nations through the lens of English. For instance, how would reading a memoir in English about being an Iranian woman be different from reading the same memoir in Farsi?

5. Since 1986, Ngũgĩ has been writing almost exclusively in his own native language—Gikuyu—although he still makes presentations to international audiences in English. What does Ngũgĩ's command of English allow him to achieve? What does his "return" to Gikuyu allow him to accomplish? Discuss whether Ngũgĩ, in the essay, advocates an outright rejection of English.

Suggested Writing Assignments

1. If you speak with reasonable skill a language other than English, discuss what your knowledge of that language does for you—intellectually, socially, emotionally, professionally, or academically.

2. Ngũgĩ writes that when he was young, he was forced to read English writers and texts that recorded experiences that were unlike anything to which he could relate. One could argue that the classroom is the place where one goes to learn not only about experiences similar to one's own but also about experiences that are dramatically dissimilar. What has your own education been like? What do you feel about reading histories and literature that have nothing to do with your life? You may base your essay on a particular text or texts that you've encountered in the classroom.

Virginia Woolf
In Search of a Room of One's Own

Full Edition, p. 904; Shorter Edition, p. 520

This essay is from Chapter 3 of Virginia Woolf's *A Room of One's Own*, a central document in twentieth-century feminist criticism. The work began in 1928 as lectures given to undergraduates at two of Cambridge University's women's colleges, Girton and Newnham. Woolf then developed her lectures into a text. "In Search of a Room of One's Own" presents Woolf at her characteristic best: impassioned, witty, learned, and insightful. The essay operates on the historical, imaginative, and personal levels simultaneously, for Woolf writes about the plight of women writers in history—emblematized by the fictitious Judith Shakespeare—and expresses her concern that women who want to write need to find the means and space to work without distractions.

Questions from *The Norton Reader*

1. At the beginning of her essay, Virginia Woolf wonders about the conditions in which women lived that made it difficult, if not impossible, for them to produce literature (paragraph 2). What does she reveal about those conditions in the course of her essay?

2. Throughout her essay Woolf supplies many examples of the obstacles faced by women writers. Choose two or three that you find particularly effective and explain why they are effective.

3. How does the phrase "A Room of One's Own" suggest a solution to the problems Woolf has enumerated for women writers?

4. What obstacles face writers in the twenty-first century? How do those obstacles vary based on the writer's background or identity? Write an essay, based on research and/or interviews, in which you argue the extent to which Woolf's argument is still relevant for a specific twenty-first-century population.

Teaching Suggestions

1. Ask students what they infer from Woolf's title, "In Search of a Room of One's Own." Does the essay confirm their inferences?

2. Explain what Woolf means when she says that "fiction is like a spider's web, attached ever so lightly perhaps, but still attached to life at all four corners" (paragraph 2). What other images might one use for fiction? Would they serve Woolf's purpose as well?

3. Woolf suggests that women, as depicted in the fiction and poetry of men, seem of the highest importance even when, historically, they had little power (paragraph 4). Discuss this observation with your students. You might use it as an occasion to discuss more generally how writers depict the opposite sex. Where do they find subtlety? Where do they see stereotypes?

4. How does Woolf answer the question she poses: "what is the state of mind that is most propitious to the act of creation" (paragraph 10)?

5. Ask students to focus on the last seven sentences of paragraph 6 (about the bishop), and analyze what each sentence does. What is the total effect of the passage? How does Woolf use the bishop again? Does he become a metaphor in this essay?

6. This essay was once a lecture, shaped by the demands and conventions of spoken performance. After looking for textual clues that characterize the piece as a lecture, look at an another essay by Woolf in *The Norton Reader*— "The Death of the Moth" (FE p. 976, SE p. 573)—written for publication, not for oral delivery. Ask students how Woolf adapts her techniques and style to an audience of readers rather than listeners. Perhaps even direct the reading and discussion toward the preparation of an essay on this topic.

7. In what ways is "In Search of a Room of One's Own" a personal statement? In what ways is it a cultural document?

SUGGESTED WRITING ASSIGNMENTS

1. Write an essay in response to Woolf's description of "that very interesting and obscure masculine complex . . . ; that deep-seated desire, not so much that *she* shall be inferior as that *he* shall be superior" (paragraph 14).

2. "Unimpeded" is a key word in Woolf's essay. Discuss what the term represents in political, physical, and psychological terms for the artists—men, women, or both—whom Woolf discusses.

3. Write an essay in response to the question: Do women today have a room of their own?

MICHAEL CHABON
Kids' Stuff

Full Edition, p. 915; Shorter Edition, p. 531

Michael Chabon is a fiction writer, best known for his Pulitzer Prize–winning novel *The Amazing Adventures of Kavalier & Clay* (2000). As the plot and cover design of this novel immediately reveal, Chabon is fascinated with comic books. The title characters, Joe Kavalier and Sam Clay, become major players in the "Golden Age" of comics, roughly 1930 to 1950. Chabon refers to some comic books of the "Golden Age," but his concern in this essay is less historical than critical and prescriptive: he wants comic book writers ("graphic novelists," in today's terminology) to stop writing for adults and focus once again on kids. His essay, which ends with four principles for creating "the best and most successful works of children's literature" (paragraph 13), can provoke lively discussion not only about what makes a good comic book, but more generally, what makes an appealing, engaging book.

QUESTIONS FROM *THE NORTON READER*

1. Michael Chabon's essay contrasts the comic book writer's desire for respect with the diminishing audience for comics. Discuss the relationships

that link artistic sophistication to both public respect and sales. Do you find Chabon's explanation persuasive? Is he missing something?

2. This essay begins with statistics about the readership of comics, moves to narrative about the evolution of the form, and ends with a manifesto on how to get more kids to read comics. Analyze how each section builds on the others. How does Chabon make the transition from one to another?

3. Chabon is clearly passionate about comics. Choose a passage in which he most effectively conveys that passion, and analyze why it works.

4. Write your own list of principles for how to get kids to love something that you loved as a kid. What elements go into making a comic (or a video game, toy, collectible, or cartoon) great?

TEACHING SUGGESTIONS

1. This essay is a natural for engaging students with a kind of reading most have experienced—indeed, for asking them to bring in favorite comic books and describe their appeal. To focus the discussion, you might ask students to frame their comments about favorite comic books in terms of one or more of the principles Chabon lists near the end of the essay (paragraphs 14–17).

2. Alternatively, this essay could lead to an interesting research assignment as background for discussion or a writing assignment. Ask students to find some of the early comics that Chabon mentions, either by going to a library collection or a store that specializes in comics or by surfing the web. Ask them whether these old comics fulfill the principles he lists or whether they no longer appeal to children.

3. Assign Scott McCloud's "Understanding Comics" (FE p. 921, SE p. 537). Ask students to compare McCloud's analytic approach in his graphic essay with Chabon's principles for good comic books. Do these writers have anything in common, or are their views diametrically opposite?

SUGGESTED WRITING ASSIGNMENTS

1. Write about the role of comic books (or a children's book) in your development as a reader.

2. Using the principles for successful comics that Chabon lists in paragraphs 14–17, analyze a comic book that fulfills these principles. If the example falls short in some feature, explain why.

SCOTT MCCLOUD

From *Understanding Comics*

Full Edition, p. 921; Shorter Edition, p. 537

As students flip through *The Norton Reader* for the first time, odds are, this piece is one of the first ones they stop to read all the way through. Comics are almost universally liked and accessible; even many of your brainiest teaching colleagues turn first to the funny pages with their morning coffee.

Scott McCloud's artistic versatility in imitating diverse visual styles helps make this a tour of the genre as a whole. Since his book was published in 1993, several major American art museums have run retrospective shows on the history of comics, so his attention to the form is timely and convincing—after years of neglect, comics now "are" art. Indeed, sad to say, many of our students probably read more graphic novels than they do conventional prose novels.

Although McCloud is a practicing cartoonist and comic book and graphic novelist, *Understanding Comics* (1993) remains ambitious and revelatory. It was followed by *Reinventing Comics* (2000) and *Making Comics* (2006), which has a particular focus on *manga* (Japanese comics) and graphic novels.

McCloud is a traditionalist and he emphasizes page-based texts. His work is closer to *The Far Side* or *Maus* than *The Simpsons*, which is to say, about comics and not animation. Writing and drawing reinforce themselves, as he points out, and a good caption, like a good haiku, models economy and wit. Exploring this tight relationship between image and text in class may involve letting go of certain boundaries, perhaps by asking students which they are more likely to do in a lecture class (not yours of course): write margin notes or doodle cartoons. Ask the doodlers to share whether their doodling takes their attention away, draws them in, or both. Hand out markers and chalk, let the students draw cartoons on the board, or maybe have them bring in graphic novels and champion their picks as being worthy of being called literature.

Questions from *The Norton Reader*

1. Scott McCloud announces in his title that he wants to help the reader "understand comics." What features of comics does McCloud explain? How do the features of the comic strip form itself aid in that explanation?

2. Choose a frame in which you think word and image work well together, and analyze why they do so. Use one or more of McCloud's categories of analysis.

3. Using the categories that McCloud introduces in the second half of this selection, analyze how a comic strip in your local newspaper works. If relevant, suggest how it might work even better.

Teaching Suggestions

1. Ask students to bring in their favorite comics and you bring in yours. Are they art? Why or why not? If not, why do we like them so much?

2. Bring in—or ask students to bring in—a comic or another example of visual culture (an advertisement, for example). Analyze it using McCloud's terms.

3. Ask the class to share their lecture notes from other classes, their actual lab books, and unrevised, written-by-hand lecture notes. Who doodles the most? What purposes do our little cartoons and doodles serve? Is it bad to draw cars or teddy bears on the margins of our physics notes? Is it bad *not* to?

4. The class gets to ask you—and you have to answer truthfully—why you would not (or would?) allow them to turn in a term project or research paper as a series of original comic pages instead of written prose. You might split the

class in half, a pro side and a con side. Comics, after all, can have a thesis and evidence, so they can be a full argument, and certainly, as with Art Spiegelman's *Maus*, can deal with mature subjects and great philosophical problems. Maybe comics are the new novels—let the class decide.

SUGGESTED WRITING ASSIGNMENTS

1. Write a review of an art form (jazz, music, pottery, BMX racing, or whatever you choose) that is underappreciated, being sure that you provide as much history and insight as McCloud's does. Your review should be in prose, not comics, but needs to open up a hidden world for the general reader.

2. Write a defense of a particular *manga*, graphic novel, or comic book as deserving of treatment as serious art. Cite sources or interviews with appropriate authorities to back your argument up, and be willing to refute the other position.

3. Write a short paper considering form versus content: to what extent is the validity of McCloud's thesis enhanced by the proficiency of his pen? Put another way, if he were a cruddy cartoonist, would his argument still hold up?

SUSAN SONTAG
A Century of Cinema
Full Edition, p. 927

Susan Sontag was a cultural and literary critic, a novelist, and a filmmaker: she wrote and directed several films. She was also, obviously, a cinephile. Her essay, originally titled "The Death of Cinema," appeared in the *New York Times Magazine*; this slightly longer version of it, "A Century of Cinema," appeared in the small-circulation journal *Parnassus: Poetry in Review*. Sontag, assuming that readers of *Parnassus* would be better informed about European films than readers of the *Times*, added references that American students are likely to find obscure.

Nevertheless, her account of one hundred years of filmmaking is accessible as well as elegant. Questions included in the text ask students to locate themselves in relation to the one hundred years she surveys. Instructors will want to locate themselves as well. Some students will probably be taking or will have taken a course in the history of film; ask them to talk about it. You may also suggest, as a topic for research, investigating when cinema became a serious subject of academic study.

Ask students, too, what attitudes they think are characteristic of people who use the terms "cinema," "film," and "movies." Usually "cinema" signifies art, "movies" entertainment, and "film" somewhere in between. But, Sontag argues, in its beginnings film was "heralded as *the* art of the twentieth century" (paragraph 1); now it no longer is. Where else do we find similar splits between art and entertainment? In literature, in music, in the visual arts? What is the cultural significance of these splits?

QUESTIONS FROM *The Norton Reader*

1. Susan Sontag summarizes one hundred years of film history, from 1895 to 1995. Diagram her periodization of this history. Locate her moviegoing period (she was born in 1933) and yours on it. Which of the older films Sontag mentions have you seen? If you have seen other films made before you began going to the movies, name some of them. How did you see them—in a film-studies course, for example, or on your own?

2. What is Sontag's definition of a "cinephile"? Are you one? Why or why not?

3. Sontag expresses strong opinions about contemporary films: they are "astonishingly witless," "bloated, derivative," "a brazen combinatory or re-combinatory art" (paragraph 1), and reduced to "assaultive images, and the unprincipled manipulation of images (faster and faster cutting) to be more attention- grabbing" (paragraph 6). At the same time, they are "disincarnated, lightweight," and don't "demand anyone's full attention" (paragraph 6). Using at least three contemporary films that you have seen, write an essay in which you agree, disagree, or both with her charges.

TEACHING SUGGESTIONS

1. What does Sontag mean when she writes that the "conditions of paying attention in a domestic space are radically disrespectful of film" (paragraph 5)? What are the differences between seeing a film in a theater and seeing it on television or video?

2. What, according to Sontag, are the characteristics of "cinema as an industry" (paragraph 10)?

3. Ask students if they have seen any of the great movie houses of the 1930s. What are they like? (Pittsburgh's downtown movie house, for example, now houses the Pittsburgh Symphony Orchestra. You may need some pictures.) Contrast them with today's movie houses. What does each tell us about the place of movies in our culture?

SUGGESTED WRITING ASSIGNMENTS

1. Watch the same film in a theater and at home. Write an essay in which you consider differences in the film itself and in your experience of viewing it.

2. Watch for the first time one of the older films Sontag describes as a masterpiece and write an analysis of it. You need not formally compare it with a contemporary film, but you should allude to some features of contemporary film as a way of defining features of the older film.

3. Identify a new film that brings in a large amount of money in the first week it is shown, view it, and write an essay in which you identify features that you think make it a success at the box office.

4. Do research on when film studies (or cinema studies) became a serious subject of academic study and write a paper on the founding of the discipline.

Philip Kennicott

How to View Art: Be Dead Serious about It,
but Don't Expect Too Much

Full Edition, p. 935

Philip Kennicott guides readers in this "how to" essay and provides strategies for viewing art. The writing is accessible, but his opinions are strong: leave your watch and cell phone behind, avoid the most famous paintings, do some research before you go to the museum. He is as cranky as he is democratic, although it may take students some close reading to see how he advocates for art's accessibility to all. His position, however, provides an opportunity to discuss education more generally, as Kennicott opposes financial barriers to museum-going but strongly favors viewers reading and studying the art. A glance through his other work in the *Washington Post* may help put this piece in context. This is a terrific essay if you assign your students a trip to a museum or any "how to" essay, but even if those assignments are not part of your course, Kennicott offers a model of expressing a strong opinion in an accessible way. His five directives are interesting, too, not for presenting an order of operations, but instead for increasing in complexity and difficulty as they proceed.

Questions from *The Norton Reader*

1. Philip Kennicott claims, "Our response to art is directly proportional to our knowledge of it" (paragraph 7). Do you agree? Why or why not? How important is study to the appreciation of art?

2. Kennicott uses the form of a list to guide readers in how to view art. Which of his five directives do you think is most important? Least important? Is there anything you would add to his list?

3. In paragraph 3, Kennicott cautions art viewers about feeling rushed, about anything that "will reengage you with the sense of busy-ness that defines ordinary life." Tim Kreider in "The 'Busy' Trap" (FE p. 380, SE p. 210) also warns against busy-ness. According to each of these authors, why is busy-ness a problem?

4. Use the form of a list to write a "how to" essay on a subject about which you could be considered an expert.

Teaching Suggestions

1. Kennicott does not hesitate to offer advice. Use his authoritative tone to discuss tone with your students. In addition to discussing their opinion of the tone, ask them to discuss the extent to which it is appropriate in a "how to" essay.

2. In paragraph 10, Kennicott compares art instruction to ski instruction. Discuss the extent to which this comparison is accurate or fair. Are some lessons or skills more dependent on an expert instructor than others?

What is gained and lost approaching art through feeling? through study and knowledge?

3. Obtain visitors' guides from a local museum or art gallery, or look up such guides online, and have students determine how close their theory of visiting museums is to Kennicott's. Is photography and talking encouraged or discouraged? How much historical and aesthetic background do they offer?

Suggested Writing Assignments

1. Visit an art museum or gallery, following several of Kennicott's instructions. Write an essay describing what you learned. Will you continue to adopt his advice when you go to museums in the future?

2. Visit an art museum or gallery. Choose one work of art that you would not ordinarily spend time with. Do some homework on the art itself, and then spend a substantial amount of time (at least twenty minutes) observing the work itself. Write a short paper describing and analyzing the work of art.

3. Choose one or two of Kennicott's directives and write a short essay in which you take a stand on the value of his advice.

4. Read another "how to" essay, such as Chris Wiewiora's "This Is Tossing" (FE p. 316, SE p. 169), and write an essay comparing how each "how to" essay offers instructions and advice. Pay attention to tone, structure, and the level of specificity in the advice. How does the skill being taught affect the type of instruction? Be sure to explain which method you prefer and why.

Aaron Copland
How We Listen

Full Edition, p. 938

Aaron Copland, an American composer, writes an analysis of the listening process in "How We Listen." Because he wishes to inform and instruct, he takes pains to be clear. He first splits listening into its component parts (or "planes") through classification; he characterizes this splitting as mechanical but useful in providing clarity (paragraph 1). He then proceeds to analyze each part, and, finally, he reintegrates the three. The structure of his essay, his use of example and analogy, and the simplicity of his language lead readers to understand that they listen to music in multiple ways at the same time. His essay provides a model of how an expert can communicate ideas in a form accessible to a lay audience.

Questions from *The Norton Reader*

1. List Aaron Copland's "three planes" of listening to music and explain what each entails. Are these three planes comprehensive? Is there another you would add?

2. In paragraphs 21–24, Copland uses the experience of going to the theater to illustrate his three planes of listening. Can you think of other artistic experiences that can be divided up into different "planes"? To what extent would the planes be the same as Copland's?

3. Copland uses classical music as examples in his explanation of the way humans listen to music. Write an essay about the ways you listen to another kind of music: folk, rap, jazz, hip-hop, pop, or rock.

Teaching Suggestions

1. Ask students to mark Copland's categories in "How We Listen." Are they mutually exclusive and clearly explained?

2. Copland's categories—or "planes"—are hierarchical and arranged in ascending progression. Why? How does he assign value to each?

3. Consider Copland's judgments. How, for example, is Beethoven "greater" than Ravel (paragraph 6)? And Tchaikovsky "easier to 'understand' than Beethoven" (paragraph 11)? What criteria does Copland use?

4. How does Copland use analogy? Ask students to mark his analogies and consider how they work and how effective they are. This exercise may be done in groups.

5. Copland extends his categories, by analogy, to theatergoing. Can they also be extended to viewing art, reading literature, and reading essays?

6. How do we take Copland's references to "simple-minded souls," one "timid lady" (paragraph 9), and "the man in the street" (paragraph 18)? Do we identify with or distance ourselves from them? How, then, do these labels function as rhetorical devices?

Suggested Writing Assignments

1. Write a rhetorical analysis of "How We Listen," detailing the means by which Copland succeeds or fails in discussing a difficult topic.

2. Apply the categories of listening discussed in Copland's essay to a piece of his own music. Consider a piece that has a theme.

3. According to Copland, "A subjective and objective attitude is implied in both creating and listening to music"; see his explanation in paragraph 25. Write an essay analyzing subjective and objective elements in his three categories of listening.

MICHAEL HAMAD
Song Schematics

Full Edition, p. 943; Shorter Edition, p. 543

Michael Hamad is a musicologist, but this hybrid piece is not academic. Instead, it combines a short explanatory essay, a visual essay (or song schematic, as he calls it), and a key to some of the elements of the drawing. Changes in musical key are important to his method. If you or some of your students know enough about music to help others identify key changes, this can be a good occasion to bring that expertise into the classroom. Even without technical knowledge, students will be able to comprehend the concepts and may have other musical details to add to the list Hamad explores here. His *Tumblr* (setlistschematics .tumblr.com) includes many other such drawings as well as further explanations of his techniques (including a link to a *New York Times* video interview). Hamad's method offers an occasion to discuss some of the more creative exercises (brainstorming, mind-maps) that many teachers and students find useful as pre-writing. Students whose high school education did not emphasize the arts may find Hamad's playful approach intimidating, but that is all the more reason to have them try their hand at making such a diagram.

Questions from *The Norton Reader*

1. Michael Hamad provides a key to explain his drawing of a Phish song. What categories does he use to analyze the song? Are there categories he does not use that would be helpful to include?

2. Both Hamad and Aaron Copland in "How We Listen" (FE p. 938) describe ways of listening to music. How do their approaches differ? How are they similar?

3. Write an essay in which you describe how you listen to music. Use a specific song to illustrate your way of listening. Feel free to use Copland's or Hamad's terminology if you find it helpful.

Teaching Suggestions

1. Listen to Phish's "Chalk Dust Torture" with your students. Encourage students to follow the schematic as they listen; using the clock to chart their—and Hamad's—progress through the song. Discuss how this experience of listening enhanced their understanding of Hamad's technique. How is this way of listening to music different from how your students ordinarily listen? Having listened to the song, see if you can reverse-engineer the schematic, turning it into a description of the song as it progresses.

2. Play another piece of music and have students try their hand at a song schematic of their own. Discuss the value of looser, more creative writing on its own terms and in the context of an academic course (perhaps as preparation for an essay or research project).

3. Compare the schematic to other kinds of sketching and note-taking, such as brainstorming, idea-maps, etc. Discuss when these non-linear methods are appropriate. What do they help reveal and what are their limitations? If you are discussing question 1 from the book, revise and add terms of your own to the key.

Suggested Writing Assignments

1. Go to Hamad's *Tumblr* (setlistschematics.tumblr.com) and choose one of his schematics. Study the drawing and listen to the song. Using both, write an essay describing the song. Use as much detail as you can.

2. Make a schematic for a song that you love. Following Hamad, include a key and write a brief essay explaining your drawing and what it reveals about the song (and perhaps your experience of listening to it).

Philosophy and Religion

Salvation

Full Edition, p. 947; Shorter Edition, p. 547

"Salvation" reveals in full measure Langston Hughes's gifts as a storyteller: economy and precision of language, a keen ear for dialogue, a sharp eye for descriptive detail, a detached, ironic voice, and a capacity for seriousness with humor. Hughes's re-creation of a revival meeting in rural America around 1914 or 1915 is an engaging cultural document. It is possible to see the revival both as an exposé of the sometimes dishonest theatrics of a manipulative preacher in front of a gullible flock of souls and as an account of the efforts of a community of believers to induce a reluctant inquirer to share their experience. This essay is also an account of an experience with considerable symbolic importance in Hughes's memory; as such, it might be considered a rite-of-passage narrative.

QUESTIONS FROM *THE NORTON READER*

1. Langston Hughes describes how he lost his faith in Jesus at the age of twelve. How did the grown-ups in his life contribute to the experience?

2 Hughes was twelve "going on thirteen" (paragraph 1) when the event he describes in first-person narration took place. How careful is he to restrict himself to the point of view of a twelve-year-old child? How does he ensure that we, as readers, understand things that the narrator does not?

3. Write a first-person narrative in which you describe a failure—yours or someone else's—to live up to the expectations of parents or other authority figures.

TEACHING SUGGESTIONS

1. How do we know that "Salvation" was written by an adult? You will want students to notice the strategies Hughes uses to record the experience of a twelve-year-old and adult reflections on it.

2. The discussion evoked by Teaching Suggestion 1 can be extended to a discussion of autobiography as both a record of and a reflection on personal experience with cultural resonance.

3. A rite of passage is a ritual associated with a crisis or a change of status. Ask students to determine some of the ways the revival meeting changed Langston Hughes.

4. What is the tone of Hughes's first sentence? Of his second sentence? What is the effect of paragraph 12, which consists of one four-word sentence?

5. Ask students to analyze Hughes's techniques as a narrator. Is his narrative effective? Why or why not?

6. Compare Hughes's ability to recapture childhood experience with that of one of the following authors whose narratives appear in the "Personal Accounts" chapter: Maya Angelou in "Graduation" (FE p. 45, SE p. 4) or Alice Walker in "Beauty: When the Other Dancer Is the Self" (FE p. 74, SE p. 22).

SUGGESTED WRITING ASSIGNMENTS

1. Write an essay on the ways in which "Salvation" re-creates a particular time and place. Why, for example, are some characters named but no specific location cited?

2. Write a personal essay in which you recount feeling pressured into doing something you would have preferred to have avoided. Try to convey, as Hughes does, both your feelings at the time and your present attitude toward the experience.

3. Write your own rite-of-passage narrative.

BARACK OBAMA
Eulogy for Clementa Pinckney

Full Edition, p. 949; Shorter Edition, p. 549

This eulogy appears in the "Philosophy and Religion" chapter of *The Norton Reader*, though it could as easily have been placed in "History and Politics." It's found here because, as one speaker at the ceremony said, it was delivered by "the Reverend Obama." Indeed, delivered as part of a church service, Barack Obama's speech sounds at times very much like a sermon. He makes explicit reference to a religious language and sentiment, from the opening's invocation to his rendition of the Christian hymn "Amazing Grace" to his conclusion. The eulogy was part of an extended service to honor the nine church people killed by a white gunman; many ministers and officials had preceded Obama on the platform, just as many speeches and performances preceded Martin Luther King Jr.'s "I Have a Dream" address. It's important to remember that what we get here is a snippet of the entire service.

In his eulogy Obama mixes the highly personal and the explicitly rhetorical, making use of statements delivered with dramatic flourish, often repeated, with many pauses for emphasis. One characteristic of many sermon traditions is concentration on a single unifying word or theme, in this case "grace."

QUESTIONS FROM *THE NORTON READER*

1. Barack Obama notes that despite Reverend Pinckney's achieve-ments, he lived without "high station" (paragraph 15). What do you think he wants to communicate to his audience with this observation, and how does it help you understand what he means by calling Pinckney "a good man" (paragraph 15)?

2. Read Martin Luther King Jr.'s "Letter from Birmingham Jail" (FE p. 806), and compare how King and Obama speak to their audiences about the history of racism in the United States. What factors might account for the similarities and differences?

3. At several points in his eulogy, Obama calls on his audience to take action. What forms of action does he recommend? What forms of action do you think might help fight racism on your campus or in your community?

4. Look up the lyrics and listen to several recordings of one of the hymns referred to in this eulogy ("Sweet Hour of Prayer" or "Amazing Grace"), and write an essay discussing the appropriateness of the reference in this eulogy.

TEACHING SUGGESTIONS

1. The video of this speech is 45 minutes long, but well worth watching, and is available on *YouTube*. It seems especially important for students to note the details of the setting: choir in the background, the seal on the podium, and the responses from the audience.

2. Obama's reference to Marilynne Robinson, author of the Pulitzer Prize–winning *Gilead* (2004), might seem obscure to many students. You can connect them to Robinson's work with a short, helpful essay about her online at http://www.publicbooks.org/fiction/marilynne-robinsons-reservoir-of-goodness.

3. Students can look at other examples of sermon traditions online. Jeremiah Wright, Barack Obama's former pastor in Chicago; James Forbes, a famous New York City preacher; and the Reverend Clay Evans are three indi-viduals who illustrate the enormous range of the sermon tradition.

SUGGESTED WRITING ASSIGNMENTS

1. As Obama states clearly, he met Pinckney only a few times and did not know him well. Sort out how much of the speech is about Pinckney himself and how much is about what his tragic killing meant to America.

2. "Grace" runs like a leitmotif throughout the speech. In an essay, explain exactly what Obama meant by grace in this case, and how the notion of grace was particularly suitable for this occasion.

3. Research John Newton, the writer of "Amazing Grace," and write about how he is a perfect example of what his hymn states. Explain why his hymn is especially suitable for this occasion.

CHRISTOPHER HITCHENS
When the King Saved God

Full Edition, p. 956; Shorter Edition, p. 556

Christopher Hitchens was a forthright commenter on numerous topics of public interest, including religion, politics, literature, and social policy. An avowed atheist, he here reveals his own complex relationship with religion, noting that most of his fascination is with the language of the Bible, which he claims helps unite readers through its common fund of allusions. Students might know a good deal of Bible verses, sometimes well, sometimes only vaguely. You might ask how students learned them. It might turn out that biblical knowledge is stratified in your class, depending on how students were raised: there should be room for surprises with this information.

QUESTIONS FROM *THE NORTON READER*

1. Why do you think Christopher Hitchens opens with two examples of what people might or might not have said? How does Hitchens's first paragraph prepare readers for his argument?

2. Hitchens provides both historical context and examples of translations he claims were made for political reasons. How much of the information Hitchens provides here was new to you? Provide examples.

3. Compare a verse or selection in two or more translated texts. You may use different translations of the Bible or, perhaps, a poem from another language that has been translated into English in different ways. Write an essay in which you compare and contrast the different translations, showing the significance of different word choices.

TEACHING SUGGESTIONS

1. What does Hitchens expect his readers will know about comparing and contrasting language within various texts? He gives quotations without much explanation, assuming his readers will see the difference. Will they?

2. What kind of audience is this written for? Those who really know their Bible? Those who care deeply about language? Those who share a common culture? A combination of all three?

3. Hitchens can be dismissive; note his comments about Mormons, Millerites, and Jehovah's Witnesses (paragraph 20). Are there any other signs of Hitchens's contempt in the essay? Who are his touchstones of good sense and good taste?

SUGGESTED WRITING ASSIGNMENTS

1. You may not agree with Hitchens about some of the claims he makes. Take one that strikes you as arguable and in an essay make an argument in

which you disagree with him. For instance, are any of his claims too sweeping? too narrowly literary? Is he valuing what you believe to be the right things in the Bible?

2. Pick a piece of writing that you think is particularly weak and give it the "Hitchens treatment," showing what's wrong with it and how you think it could be done better.

3. Describe your own encounters with sacred language, like that in a place of worship or in a particular religious text. Give plenty of particulars about how the language attracted or repelled or puzzled you, and how your attitude toward it might have changed over time.

4. Hitchens made no secret of his atheism. But can you tell about his attitude toward religion from the evidence of this essay? Write an account of what you see here about Hitchens's religious beliefs.

LEON WIESELTIER
Ring the Bells

Full Edition, p. 964

The previous selection by Christopher Hitchens gives an atheist's account of the language of the Christian Bible. This selection presents a Jewish person's changing reactions to the bells of a Christian church and later to the Muslim call to prayer that is broadcast in Harvard Yard. Leon Wieseltier writes from a highly privileged position in American life: college at Harvard, graduate work at Oxford, and a position as literary editor at the *New Republic,* one of the nation's most influential and esteemed publications. Yet he still views himself as an outsider because of his Jewish heritage. You can encourage students to ask who counts as an insider and an outsider in their own neighborhood or community.

QUESTIONS FROM *The Norton Reader*

1. Leon Wieseltier takes a commonplace urban occurrence—the ringing of church bells—and turns it into a meditation on diversity. Do you think he succeeds? Why or why not?

2. Wieseltier includes different perspectives on whether religious symbols (both auditory and visual) should be allowed on college campuses. What is Wieseltier's position on this question? What is yours? What factors influence your answer?

3. What should be the place of religious symbols on a college campus? Choose a specific example with which you have experience, and write an editorial for your college newspaper that shows your position.

TEACHING SUGGESTIONS

1. It's worth exploring students' own attitudes toward church bells. Some will not hear them (because there are none nearby), some will hear them but

not really notice them, some will regard them as an annoying intrusion, and some will think of them as a guide for their day. Ask students to listen carefully to church bells and report back what they hear. Is there anything inherently religious in them?

2. Ask students to try to pin down Wieseltier's "academic" status from a reading of this essay. Is he simply name-dropping (Oxford, Harvard)? Or do the academic sites he mentions play an integral role in the story he is telling?

Suggested Writing Assignments

1. Write an essay exploring how your own neighborhood might respond to a Muslim call to prayer being broadcast. Who would object and who would approve? Would the approval be enthusiastic or reluctant?

2. Research the history of church bells and report what you find in an essay. When did churches first start ringing them? Why? How has the ringing changed over the years? What else can you find about bells and their tradition?

3. Keep track of the noises of a place you know well and write about them. Are there church bells? sirens? car horns? trains passing? birds? ice cream trucks? What counts as an acceptable level of noise and what grates on inhabitants?

Henry David Thoreau
Where I Lived, and What I Lived For

Full Edition, p. 967; Shorter Edition, p. 564

This excerpt from *Walden*, which includes many of the best-known quotations from Henry David Thoreau, is a touchstone of American philosophical thought. In each paragraph, one can recognize the origins of ideas that now permeate our popular culture. Instructors should be prepared to gloss Thoreau's frequent allusions, but a lecture on transcendentalism shouldn't be necessary before students can begin to work profitably with the text, since Thoreau's prose and imagery are mostly straightforward, and important concepts are approached repeatedly from a variety of angles. While students won't be challenged to understand Thoreau, they will be challenged *by* him: both his rhetoric and his message are confrontational, if not accusatory. Thoreau goads us to follow his lead, to live thoughtfully, simply, and morally, to cast off the illusory, cleave through the surface of things, and seek the reality of life.

Questions from *The Norton Reader*

1. Henry David Thoreau's title might be rephrased as two questions: "Where did I live?" and "What did I live for?" What answers does Thoreau give to each?

2. Throughout this essay Thoreau poses questions—for example, "Why is it that men give so poor an account of their day if they have not been slumbering?" (paragraph 7) or "Why should we live with such hurry and waste of life?"

ragraph 11). To what extent does he answer these questions? Why might he leave some unanswered or only partially answered?

3. Thoreau is known for his aphorisms (short, witty nuggets of wisdom). Find one you like and explain its relevance for living today.

4. If you have ever chosen to live unconventionally at some point in your life, write about your decision, including the reasons and the consequences.

TEACHING SUGGESTIONS

1. Thoreau asks, "What should we think of the shepherd's life if his flocks always wandered to higher pastures than his thoughts?" (paragraph 6). What, indeed, should we think of a computer scientist, engineer, architect, chemist whose products at work are the most imaginative things he or she creates? In what ways is that laudable? In what ways is that tragic?

2. Thoreau cites an admonishing inscription on a bathtub: "Renew thyself completely each day: do it again, and again, and forever again" (paragraph 7). What does this advice mean to you? Why do you think it is so strongly worded? How do you renew yourself? Do you think it is possible to renew yourself *completely*, as is suggested? Why or why not?

3. What do you think Thoreau means when he talks of "our Genius"? For instance, he writes that "After a partial cessation of his sensuous life, the soul of man, or its organs rather, are reinvigorated each day, and his Genius tries again what noble life it can make" (paragraph 7). Similarly, he says, "Little is to be expected of that day, if it can be called a day, to which we are not awaked by our Genius, but by the mechanical nudgings of some servitor, are not awakened by our own newly-acquired force and aspirations from within, accompanied by the undulations of celestial music, instead of factory bells. . . ." (paragraph 7). What is the nature of our Genius, according to Thoreau? From where does it originate? What is its purpose?

4. "Our life is frittered away by detail" (paragraph 10), Thoreau contends. How is your life frittered away by detail? How many specific examples of such frittering details can you cite from your daily experience?

5. "We do not ride on the railroad," Thoreau argues, "it rides upon us" (paragraph 10). Consider some piece of technology you interact with on a daily basis. Discuss how this thing uses you more than you use it.

SUGGESTED WRITING ASSIGNMENTS

1. Thoreau goes into great detail about what he can see from his house, eventually noting that "Though the view from my door was still more contracted, I did not feel crowded or confined in the least. There was pasture enough for my imagination" (paragraph 5). What do you see out of *your* door? Write an essay in which you detail what you see from where you live. Do not stop with simple description; be sure to address how what you see provides "pasture enough for [your] imagination." How does what you see affect what you think?

2. In perhaps his most famous question, Thoreau asks, "Why should we live with such hurry and waste of life?" (paragraph 11). In perhaps his most famous maxim, he admonishes us to "Simplify, simplify" (paragraph 10). Write an essay in which you develop and explain your plan to simplify your life. Be specific. What concrete actions can you realistically take to simplify your life? How, exactly, will each of these steps work to reduce the hurry and waste in your life?

VIRGINIA WOOLF
The Death of the Moth

Full Edition, p. 976; Shorter Edition, p. 573

This essay, one of Virginia Woolf's best-known works of nonfiction, combines narration and description in the service of definition. Woolf writes with feeling but not sentiment, offering her reader a carefully realized observation before speculating about its meaning.

Woolf plays the role of observer and reporter in this essay. What begins as idle curiosity becomes conscious speculation, but no explicit conclusions are drawn. Although she points to possible meaning immanent in the death throes of the moth, she does not overshadow the event itself with analysis. Her technique here might be contrasted with that of other essayists who draw out their meanings more directly; students might be asked to think about how writers' choices interact with conventions to create a range of possibilities in the essay form.

QUESTIONS FROM *THE NORTON READER*

1. Trace the sequence in which Virginia Woolf comes to identify with the moth. How does she make her identification explicit? How is it implicit in the language she uses to describe the moth?

2. Choose one of the descriptions of a small living creature or creatures in Annie Dillard's "Sight into Insight" (FE p. 978, SE p. 576) and compare it with Woolf's description of the moth. Does a similar identification take place in Dillard's essay? If so, how; if not, why not?

3. Henry David Thoreau, in "The Battle of the Ants" (FE p. 770, SE p. 456), also humanizes small living creatures. How do his strategies differ from Woolf's?

4. Write two descriptions of the same living creature, one using Woolf's strategies, the other using Thoreau's. Or, alternatively, write an essay in which you analyze the differences between them.

TEACHING SUGGESTIONS

1. Ask students what aspects of "The Death of the Moth" they remember best, and why. Imagery will likely be relevant to their responses. If so, have students select several images and describe the primary appeal of each (visual,

.l, tactile). Then ask them to determine how each image functions within the essay.

2. Does Woolf provide an identifiable thesis statement? Does she have a central point she wishes to make? Or is her essay a speculative exercise, more important for the act of reflecting than for making a point?

3. You may want students to describe the persona Woolf creates in this essay and how she creates it. Call attention to her use of the third person ("one") in much of the essay and her shift to the first person in the last paragraphs. What effects do these pronouns and their sequence create?

4. How and to what effect does Woolf use a kind of triple focus—the world "out there," the moth, and the narrator—in this essay?

5. What is the relationship between the life and death of the moth and the life and death of human beings in "The Death of the Moth"? Does Woolf offer any conclusions about death in this piece?

SUGGESTED WRITING ASSIGNMENTS

1. If the death of an animal has moved you to speculate on significant questions concerning life and death, write an essay describing and analyzing the experience.

2. With ironic understatement, Woolf writes: "The insignificant little creature now knew death" (paragraph 5). Yet this little creature was not insignificant. Write an essay explaining why.

3. Observe an insect and describe it from two points of view—one objective and one subjective, as a scientist might describe it and as a poet or a novelist might describe it.

ANNIE DILLARD
Sight into Insight

Full Edition, p. 978; Shorter Edition, p. 576

Annie Dillard is known for personal essays about nature and spiritual experience. "Sight into Insight," which appeared first in 1974 as a magazine essay, was then included in her best-known book, *Pilgrim at Tinker Creek* (1974). Attending to everyday matters at Tinker Creek, she is, without traveling, a pilgrim who awaits illuminations that reveal the timeless and universal.

Dillard accumulates examples and renders them in detail with a showiness and panache that may put students off. You may want to consider a single paragraph or assign single paragraphs to groups of students to consider; paragraphs 3, 4, 5, 6, 11, 12, 19, 27, and 36 will serve the purpose.

Each of this essay's six sections begins with sight. Section 2 ends with insight, section 3 with blindness, section 4 with untutored infant sight, and sections 5 and 6 with insight. All the passages describing insight warrant close reading. Dillard claims that the effort to achieve insight "marks the literature of saints and monks of every order east and west, under every rule and no rule, discalced and shod" (paragraph 34). Evelyn Underhill, in *The Essentials of Mysticism* (1920), schematizes the stages of mystic experience as reported by mystics themselves across religions and cultures: they go from an intense and enlarged perception of the natural world to a perception of realities above and beyond it to union with divine presences. The first two stages are present in this essay. Students are likely to need help in understanding and characterizing Dillard's descriptions of insight; contrasting them with her descriptions of sight will help.

Dillard also describes insight as unedited and unlearned (see section 4), unverbalized (see section 5), and unwilled (see sections 5 and 6). Sight, she implies, is edited and learned, verbalized, and willed. These distinctions afford another way of contrasting her descriptions of sight and insight.

One of Dillard's masters is Henry David Thoreau. She quotes him directly (in paragraph 33), and his doctrines and strategies can be found throughout this essay. Thoreau is represented in *The Norton Reader* in "The Battle of the Ants" (FE p. 770, SE p. 456), and "Where I Lived, and What I Lived For" in this chapter (FE p. 967, SE p. 564).

Questions from *The Norton Reader*

1. Annie Dillard often uses several examples to support a general claim. In paragraph 3, for instance, she writes, "nature is very much a now-you-see-it, now-you-don't affair" and follows with "[a] fish flashes, then dissolves" and "the brightest oriole fades into leaves." Locate other examples of this technique, marking the general statements and examples that accompany them. What purpose does this technique serve? In what kinds of writing is it appropriate, in what kinds inappropriate?

2. How does the kind of seeing Dillard describes at the end of her essay differ from the kind of seeing she describes at the beginning?

3. Take one of Dillard's general statements and come up with supporting examples of your own.

4. Dillard says, "I see what I expect" (paragraph 8). Write a description of something familiar, paying attention to how you "edit" your seeing. Then write a parallel description of it as if you were seeing it "unedited," as Dillard tries to see "color-patches" like the newly sighted do (paragraph 27).

Teaching Suggestions

1. How can Dillard's descriptive prose be justified or criticized? How does she bind a series of descriptive statements together? How does she make us see?

2. Contrast two of Dillard's individual pieces of description, one of sight and one of insight. What are the components of each?

3. Identify doctrines and strategies in a selection by Thoreau that also appear in this essay by Dillard.

Suggested Writing Assignments

1. Dillard takes some ordinary creek water and places it in a white china bowl to look for small creatures. Do the same with some rain, creek, pond, or puddle water and report what you see, first in a plain, factual style and then with elaboration in Dillard's fashion.

2. Dillard opens her essay by describing a childhood practice of surprising others by hiding a penny (paragraph 1). She writes, "There are lots of things to see, unwrapped gifts and free surprises. The world is fairly studded and strewn with pennies cast broadside from a generous hand" (paragraph 2). Write a narrative essay about some "free surprise" you have discovered in nature or in a relationship.

PLATO

The Allegory of the Cave

Full Edition, p. 989; Shorter Edition, p. 586

In "The Allegory of the Cave," Plato uses two important elements of literary form: dialogue and allegory. Both the form of Socratic dialogue and the use of extended metaphor are pedagogical methods. Why does Socrates use dialogue to teach his pupils? How does Socratic dialogue differ from other forms of conversation? (Ask students to analyze how the student answers Socrates' questions.) How does Plato's use of form work to educate readers?

Questions from *The Norton Reader*

1. Plato uses Socratic dialogue, a question-and-answer form in which characters discuss moral and philosophical problems, usually with a philosopher-teacher instructing a student. Locate the key questions the teacher poses, and answer them in your own terms. Are your answers similar to those of Glaucon, the student? Why or why not?

2. Plato begins with an analogy (or allegory) in which he likens human knowledge to visual sight in an underground den. Locate Plato's interpretation of this allegory. What points does he derive from it?

3. Write an allegory in which you characterize some aspect of human existence, and embed your interpretation within your essay.

Teaching Suggestions

1. Ask students whether their teachers use Socratic dialogue as a pedagogical method. Do students find this method effective for teaching? Why or why not?

2. Make sure students understand what allegory is and how it functions. In what situations have students encountered the use of allegory? Sermons? Teaching? Books? How do they respond to this literary device?

3. Plato's allegory brings up the philosophical question of what is real. How does he answer this question? Do students answer that question differently?

SUGGESTED WRITING ASSIGNMENTS

1. What teaching method (dialogue, using visuals, hands-on learning, etc.) have you found most effective in your learning? Write an essay that demonstrates the efficacy of that teaching method.
2. Write a dialogue about the nature of what is "real." Set the dialogue in a contemporary classroom.

JESUS
Parables of the Kingdom

Full Edition, p. 992; Shorter Edition, p. 590

Like allegories, parables function as a form of analogy, often suggesting or explicitly stating a moral or a lesson. How students respond to these parables in particular might depend, to some extent, on the religious education they have had and whether the parables have been interpreted for them through sermons and lessons. What lessons are embedded in these parables? How do students respond to this method of teaching through illustration?

QUESTIONS FROM *THE NORTON READER*

1. Many parables end with a moral explicitly stated. What explicit lessons does Jesus append to his parables?
2. Is it possible to deduce more than one moral from a biblical parable? Think of additional or alternative morals that you might draw from one of Jesus' parables.
3. Write a parable that, while using narrative form, has a moral or lesson embedded within it.

TEACHING SUGGESTIONS

1. Ask students to look closely at the style and form of Jesus' parables. What features do they note? (For example, nearly every verse of the prodigal son parable begins with "and." What other repetitions do students recognize?) What effects do these features have?
2. Ask students what cultural references they don't fully understand. (Perhaps, for instance, they do not know about the wedding rituals referenced in "The Ten Virgins.") Ask them to research the cultural references they do not understand, bringing their research to class for discussion.
3. In both "The Ten Virgins" and "The Ten Talents," a comparison is made to "the kingdom of heaven" (paragraph 1). Ask students to compare and contrast these parables. Does each parable teach the same lesson about the kingdom of

ɔn? If so, why might Jesus tell both stories? If not, what are the significant ....ences?

SUGGESTED WRITING ASSIGNMENTS

1. Find different interpretations of one of the parables included in this chapter. Write a response to these interpretations, making an argument for which interpretation is most sound and why.

2. Write a parable that teaches a lesson. As two of these parables do, make the metaphor you are creating clear in the opening sentence. ("The Ten Virgins" opens, "Then shall the kingdom of heaven be likened unto ten virgins. . . ." [paragraph 1]; "The Ten Talents" begins, "For the kingdom of heaven is as a man travelling into a far country. . . ." [paragraph 1].)

ZEN PARABLES

Muddy Road, A Parable, Learning to Be Silent

Full Edition, p. 996; Shorter Edition, p. 593

Both Zen parables and New Testament parables embed religious teachings in story. The Zen parables differ from the biblical parables in that the moral is less explicit. You may wish to ask students why that might be the case. Which do they prefer, parables that embed an explicit message or those open for interpretation? Why?

QUESTIONS FROM *THE NORTON READER*

1. Although some parables end with an explicitly stated moral, Zen parables often do not. Which parables include an explicit lesson? Which require the reader to deduce a lesson?

2. Is it possible to deduce more than one moral from a Zen parable? Try writing two different lessons that you might draw from one Zen parable.

3. Write a Zen-like parable that uses narrative form, includes two characters, and ends with a surprising lesson.

TEACHING SUGGESTIONS

1. Ask students to compare and contrast the Zen parables and Jesus' parables. What elements are the same? (For example, all are written from the third-person perspective. Also, the parables may contain cultural references unfamiliar to students.) What elements differ? (For example, the lessons are less explicit in the Zen parables.)

2. Ask students to come up with contemporary examples that illustrate the same lessons or principles evident in these parables.

3. Ask students to consider who is the audience for Zen parables.

Suggested Writing Assignments

1. Take one of the parables and write an essay—using your personal experience—that illustrates the same lesson.

2. Analyze the stylistic features of one of the Zen parables (length, use of dialogue, use of imagery, etc.), then use your analysis as evidence for an argument about how such features help reinforce the meaning or effect of the parable.

Index